ABOUT THE AUTHOR

Feroz Ahmad is Emeritus Professor of History at the University of Massachusetts and a Visiting Scholar at the Fares Center for Eastern Mediterranean Studies at Tufts University. He is widely respected as an expert on modern Turkey and Middle East history and, since 2005, has been teaching history and politics at Yeditepe University, Istanbul.

TURKEY

The Quest for Identity

Feroz Ahmad

ONEWORLD

A Oneworld Book

First published by Oneworld Publications 2003
This revised edition published in 2014

Copyright © Feroz Ahmad 2003, 2014

The moral right of Feroz Ahmad to be identified as the Author of this
work has been asserted by him in accordance with the Copyright,
Designs, and Patents Act 1988

ISBN 978-1-78074-301-1
eISBN 978-1-78074-302-8

Printed and bound in Denmark by Nørhaven A/S

Oneworld Publications
10 Bloomsbury Street
London WC1B 3SR
England

Stay up to date with the latest books,
special offers, and exclusive content from
Oneworld with our monthly newsletter

Sign up on our website
www.oneworld-publications.com

Contents

Preface

The Ottomans were a rare imperial people who had no homeland to retreat to as their empire waned in the nineteenth and twentieth centuries. Other imperial peoples had returned to various homelands: the British to their island base when they were forced to decolonize; the French to France, the Spanish to Spain, and so on. By the twentieth century, the Ottomans had no homeland for they had originated as tribal peoples who, for a variety of reasons, had been forced to migrate from the steppes of Central and Inner Asia and went in different directions. Some of these tribal confederations, including the ones who came to be known as Ottoman (*Osmanlı*) adopting the name of their leader, Osman (d.1324), migrated into the Islamic world and adopted Islam.

These peoples came to be described as 'Turks' by the people they intermingled with. But they themselves were called by the name of the head of their tribal confederation: thus the Seljuks, the Danişmend, the Menteşe and the Osmanlı or Ottomans. The Ottomans reserved the name 'Turk' for the nomadic tribesmen and peasants who continued to live under their rule but were as yet untamed or 'uncivilized'. The merchants from the Italian city states of Venice and Genoa who came in contact with the Ottomans nevertheless called them Turks or Turque, as did the English and the French respectively. The Greek Orthodox described the rule of the Ottomans as 'Tuorkokratia', the rule of the Turks. For Europeans and Christians, the term 'Turk' was synonymous with Muslim; thus when Christians converted to Islam, they were often said to have 'turned Turk'. Turkey was also the English-language synonym for the Ottoman Empire; thus when Lord Byron wrote to his mother from Ottoman Albania in November 1809, he noted that 'I have been some time in Turkey: this place [Prevesa] is on the coast, but I have traversed the interior of the province of Albania on a visit to the Pasha.' It was common for Europeans to speak of the Balkan provinces of the Ottoman Empire as 'Turkey-in-Europe' and of Asia Minor and the Arab provinces as 'Turkey-in-Asia', when they described the geography of the empire.

The idea of nationalism made inroads into the Ottoman Empire after the French Revolution, first among the non-Muslim communities of the empire, and then among a minority of Muslim intellectuals who became conscious of their 'Turkishness', their language and their roots. But nationalism remained a concern of the minority, for the majority was still determined to maintain a multi-ethnic, multi-religious empire, right until the final defeat in 1918 during the First World War.

Only after total defeat and the realization that the victors were going to partition the empire and promote self-determination did the Ottomans realize that they too had to determine their identity on the basis of nationalism and 'nationhood'.

When the nationalists created their republic in 1923, they were careful to call it the Republic of Turkey, a territorial and therefore a patriotic description, and not the Turkish Republic, which would have defined the republic ethnically. Nevertheless 'Türkiye Cumhuriyeti' is often rendered incorrectly as the 'Turkish Republic' and not the 'Republic of Turkey', and the assembly in Ankara as the Turkish Grand National Assembly and not the Grand National Assembly of Turkey. The nationalists were aware of the difference in meaning and chose their words with care. There was even a discussion about describing the people of the new Turkey as 'Türkiyeli', as the land of Turks, Kurds, Arabs, Circassians, etc., reserving the term 'Turk' for the ethnically Turkish. Turk was retained but with the same kind of meaning as 'British' or 'American'. As with other national movements, having succeeded in creating the territorial state of Turkey and gaining it universal acceptance at Lausanne in 1923, the nationalists began the task of creating the nation of Turkey and the Turk.

By the late 1930s, the nationalists had partially succeeded in creating a new identity for most of the population of Anatolia, with only the Kurdish population in the east and the Alevis of central Anatolia remaining disaffected, the former on ethnic-linguistic grounds and the latter on religious grounds. These problems of identity remained dormant until the early 1960s when they began to emerge in the more liberal political environment created by the new constitution of 1961. They remained unresolved, though progress was made during the nineties when the state began considering the liberalization of the regime and the reforms that were required by the European Union in order to meet its criteria for membership. The new Justice and Development Party (AKP) claims to be more determined than ever to introduce and implement these reforms after its efforts to gain admission were foiled at the EU summit in Copenhagen on 12–13 December 2002.

Acknowledgements

This book has grown out of a long-standing involvement with the history of the Ottoman Empire and modern Turkey. Since it is a work of synthesis, I stand on the shoulders of the scholars who have inspired me over the years, as well as students who forced me to reconsider the subject with questions I had not thought to ask. I should like to thank the two readers who read the work for Oneworld while it was in draft form and made helpful comments; my editors, Rebecca Clare and Judy Kearns, at Oneworld for their professionalism and patience; and my colleagues, especially Leila Fawaz, at the Fares Center for Eastern Mediterranean Studies at Tufts University, for their encouragement and support. However, I alone remain responsible for any errors of fact or omissions.

Notes on transcription

I have used the official modern Turkish when transcribing Turkish words and names in Roman script. Some indications on pronunciation are given to assist the reader not acquainted with Turkish.

c   *j* as in *jam*

ç   *ch* as in *church*

ğ   soft g lengthens the preceding vowel and is not sounded, thus Erdoğan is pronounced Erdoan

ı   (dotless i) something like *u* as in *radium*

ö   French *eu* as in *deux*

ş   *sh* as in *shame*

ü   French *u* as in *lumière*

Abbreviations

AFU	Armed Forces Union
AK Parti and AKP	The Justice and Development Party founded in August 2001
ANAP	Turkish acronym for the Motherland Party founded in 1983
COGS	Chief of the General Staff
CUP	Committee of Union and Progress
DLP	The Democratic Left Party founded by Bülent Ecevit's wife when he was banned from politics
DP	Democrat Party and Demokratik Party after 1969
DISK	Turkish acronym for the Confederation of Revolutionary Workers' Unions of Turkey
EEC, EU	The European Economic Community, later the European Union
FP	The Felicity (Saadet) Party founded in 2001 as the party of political Islam
FRP	Free Republican Party
GNAT	Grand National Assembly of Turkey
GNP	Gross national product
HADEP	People's Democracy Party formed by moderate Kurds in May 1994
IMF	International Monetary Fund
JP	Justice Party founded in 1961

MÜSİAD   Turkish for the 'Association of Independent Industrialists and Businessmen', though the 'M' was said to stand for 'Muslim' not 'Independent'

NATO   North Atlantic Treaty Organization

NSC   National Security Council – established in 1961, it gave senior generals a political role; also the body that governed after 12 September 1980

NUC   National Unity Committee, the junta that governed after the 1960 coup

NOP   National Order Party – founded in 1969, it was the first party representing political Islam

NSP   National Salvation Party, founded in 1972 after NOP was closed down

NAP   Nationalist Action Party

NDP   Nationalist Democracy Party founded in 1983

NGOs   Non-governmental organizations

NTP   New Turkey Party founded in 1961; another party using the same name was founded in 2002

OYAK   Turkish acronym for the Army Mutual Assistance Association created in 1961

PKK   Kurdish initials that stand for the 'Workers' Party of Kurdistan'

PRP   Progressive Republican Party founded in 1924

RPP   Republican People's Party

SHP   The Social Democratic People's Party after it merged with the Populist Party

SODEP   Turkish acronym for the Social Democratic Party founded in 1983

SPO   State Planning Organization established in 1960

TPP   True Path Party founded to replace the banned Great Turkey Party in 1983

Türk-İs   Turkish acronym for the Confederation of the Workers' Union of Turkey

TÜSİAD   Turkish acronym for the Association of Turkish

Industrialists and Businessmen

TPLA	Turkish People's Liberation Army
VP	Virtue (Fazilet) Party founded in December 1997 just before the dissolution of the Welfare Party; it was the fourth Islamist party
WP	The Welfare Party, the party of political Islam which was formed after the NSP was dissolved in September 1980
WPT	Workers' Party of Turkey

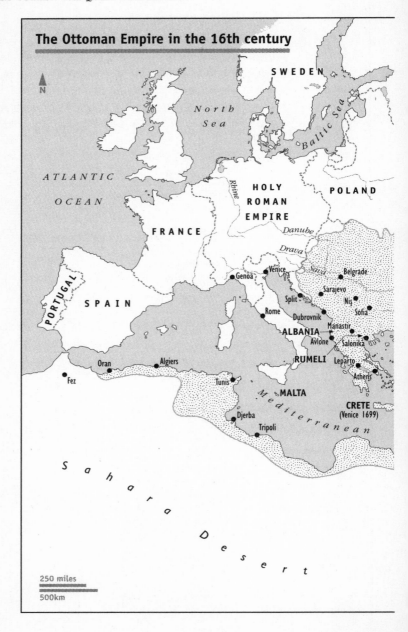

The Ottoman Empire in the 16th century

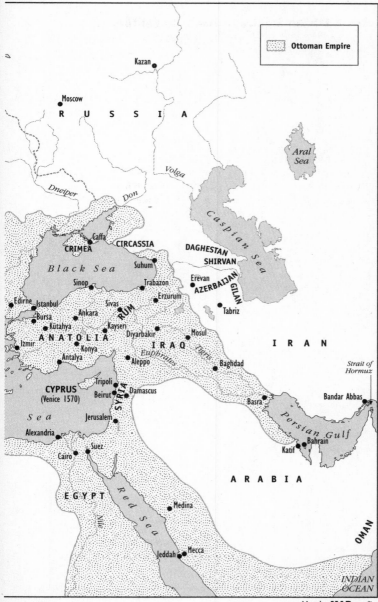

Ottoman Empire

Kazan

Moscow

R U S S I A

Aral Sea

Volga

Dneiper

Don

Caffa

CRIMEA   CIRCASSIA   DAGHESTAN

Black Sea   Suhum   SHIRVAN

Sinop   Trabazon   Erevan

Erzurum   AZERBAIJAN   GILAN

Caspian Sea

Edirne   Istanbul   Sivas   RUM   Tabriz

Bursa   Ankara   Kayseri

Kütahya   Diyarbakir   Mosul   I R A N

Izmir   ANATOLIA   *Tigris*

Konya   IRAQ

Antalya   *Euphrates*   Baghdad   *Strait of Hormuz*

Tripoli   Aleppo   Bandar Abbas

CYPRUS   Beirut   SYRIA   Damascus

(Venice 1570)   Basra   *Persian Gulf*

Sea   Jerusalem   Bahrain

Alexandria   Katif

Cairo   Suez

EGYPT   A R A B I A

Red Sea   Medina   OMAN

Nile

Jeddah   Mecca   *INDIAN OCEAN*

Map by **MAP**grafix

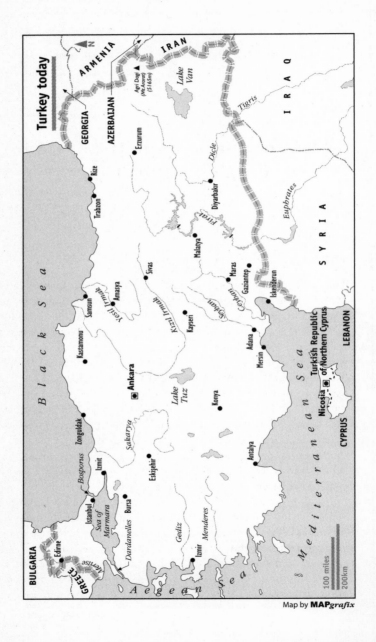

1

The Ottomans: from Statehood to Empire, 1300–1789

THE EMERGENCE OF THE HOUSE OF OTTOMAN

The Turkic tribes, under the leadership of the Seljuks, established their foothold in Anatolia in 1071, five years after the Norman invasion of England. Alparslan defeated the Byzantine emperor Diogenes at the battle of Manzikert and laid the foundations of the Seljuk Empire, the Seljuks of Rum, with their capital at Konya. Rum was the term used by early Muslims to describe the Byzantines as 'Romans' and their empire was called the 'land of Rum'. Later the term was applied to Asia Minor or Anatolia and, until the present, to the Greeks of Turkey. The Seljuk Empire was a federation of Turkish tribes, each led by its own bey, or leader, who recognized the sovereignty of the Seljuk dynasty. But when the Seljuks were defeated by the Mongols in 1243 and became their tribute-paying vassals, the beys began to break away from the Seljuks and declared independence for their principalities or *beyliks*.

The Ottomans had their origins in a clan that was loyal to the Seljuks, who rewarded their leader, Ertuğrul, with lands near Ankara which were extended further west to the region of Söğüt near modern Eskişehir. Ertuğrul is said to have died in 1288 at the age of 90 and was succeeded by his son Osman, whose name was adopted by his followers who called themselves *Osmanlı*, anglicized to Ottoman. As most vassals seized the opportunity to declare their independence as the Seljuks declined, Osman remained loyal until the death of Sultan Kaikobad II in 1298. Osman then declared his independence, marking the beginnings of the Ottoman state. Osman's principality abutted the Byzantine empire and he was able to wage religious war, or *gaza*, against the Christians, enabling him and his successors to become religious warriors (*gazi*s) par excellence and attracting followers from all over Anatolia. This was a great advantage that the Ottomans had over most of the other principalities. Osman Gazi died in 1326 and was succeeded by his son Orhan Gazi (r.1326–59), who captured the strategic city of Bursa in the same year, making it the first capital of the Ottoman state. At this stage the leaders enjoyed the title of *gazi* which made them little more than first amongst equals. They had yet to become sultans.

By 1326, there were a number of successor states to the Seljuks in Anatolia, although Karaman claimed recognition as the true successor to the Seljuks. The other beys – of such principalities as Aydın, Saruhan, Menteşe, Kermiyan, Hamid, Tekke, Karesi and Kastamonu – refused to grant such recognition. For the time being, the Ottomans were too small and weak and therefore preferred not to join the struggle for Seljuk succession. Orhan had the good fortune of being located adjacent to a rapidly declining Byzantine Empire and of capturing some of its territory while other Muslim emirs fought against each other. He extended his state along the southern coast of the Sea of Marmara and in 1345 captured Karesi from its Muslim ruler, thereby opening a way to cross the Dardanelles and begin expansion into Europe.

In 1341 Orhan intervened in the affairs of Byzantium, answering Cantacuzenus's appeal for help against his rival. Orhan saved the throne for Cantacuzenus and was rewarded with the hand of his daughter, Theodora, in marriage. Thereafter, it became almost a tradition for Ottoman sultans to take Christian wives, at least until the reign of Murad III (r.1574–1595). Orhan had already captured the strategic fortress of Gallipoli on the Dardanelles straits and secured his hold on the northern shore of the Marmara, capturing Tekirdağ. The Ottomans were poised to cross the straits and raid into the Balkans. When Orhan died in 1359, he had laid not only the territorial foundations of the state, but he had also begun to lay its institutional foundations by creating the institution of the *Yeniçeri*, or 'new troops', better known in the West as the janissaries.

The world of Islam was familiar with slave armies, but not the innovation of collecting (*devşirme*) youths from Christian communities and training them to become an elite of soldiers and administrators. Hitherto, the Ottomans had had no regular or standing army and had relied on tribal levies loyal to their own leaders. As the Ottomans were a federation of clans, each with its own leader, the sultan was still little more than the first among equals, dependent on his personal qualities and his success as a conqueror. Orhan tried to overcome this shortcoming by recruiting a regular army of his own from among Turkoman tribesmen. But his experiment failed because the Turkomans were essentially horsemen and did not take to the discipline of fighting in the infantry.

GROWTH OF THE MILITARY

Around 1330 Orhan began to take Christian youths aged between twelve and twenty from their families, converting them to Islam, and then training them as his 'new troops'. They were apprenticed to Turkish farms where they learned the language and the religion before being given a rigorous education in the palace school where they joined the state's ruling elite. Haji Bektaş (1242–1337), the founder of the Bektaşi order of dervishes, blessed the first janissary corps and became the patron saint of the janissaries until their dissolution in 1826.

This military innovation took generations to mature and, in time, the recruits of the *devşirme*, both as soldiers and administrators, strengthened the power of the sultan at the expense of the chieftains of the clans. These men recognized only one loyalty, to the ruling sultan, who was their master and they his *kul* or servitors, though the term *kul* is often rendered 'slave'. The sultan had the power of life and death over them. In theory, they were cut off from their origins and therefore from loyalty to their original community. In practice, such ties were not always forgotten and there are cases of men of the *devşirme* who rose up to become provincial governors and grand viziers, and who rewarded the communities from whence they came with mosques, libraries and bridges. The privilege of being a janissary could not be inherited by an heir, who would be a free-born Muslim.

The legality of the *devşirme* was raised under the Sharia or Islamic law. The Sharia granted non-Muslims who had submitted to Islamic rule and paid the poll tax, or *jizya*, the status of *dhimmi*, or protected people. They were allowed to practice their faith and live according to the rules of their communities. The sultan was forbidden to persecute them in any way, and taking away their male children was illegal. However, some parents understood that their children were destined for a comfortable and bright future and gave them up willingly. Sinan, the great Ottoman architect who was himself a *devşirme* recruit, is said to have used his influence to have his brother taken into the system. But the sultan, bound by the Sharia, could not violate it unless the *ülema*, the doctors of Islamic jurisprudence, found a loophole and legalized the practice. To do so, the ulema invented the fiction that if the sultan returned the poll tax to the community, the community would no longer be protected and the sultan could then legally take 'prisoners of war', and that is what the sultans did. The practice may sound harsh and even barbarous to our modern sensibilities, but the idea of being recruited into the *devşirme* was so attractive to some that an occasional Muslim family would even ask their Christian neighbours to pass off their Muslim children as Christians so that they could be recruited!

The *devşirme* operated in Anatolia, but the Balkans and Albania, Bosnia, and Bulgaria were the preferred provinces. The recruits were also taught a craft: for example, Sinan (1490–1588) learned about construction as a janissary, and served in the army building roads and bridges before becoming architect to the sultans. Janissaries were taught according to a very strict discipline: to obey their officers, to be totally loyal to each other, and to abstain from all practices that might undermine their ability as soldiers. That is why they were such a formidable force at a time when they were fighting against feudal levies and were therefore superior to armies of Western Europe.

The *devşirme* introduced the principle of 'meritocracy' into the Ottoman system. *Devşirme* recruits were taken purely for their abilities and usually came from modest, rural backgrounds, unlike feudal Europe where birth determined one's status in life. The *devşirme* proved to be a method of integrating the conquered

Christian communities into the imperial system, especially during the early centuries of expansion when Ottoman rule was usually lighter than the one it replaced.

EARLY OTTOMAN CONQUESTS AND EXPANSION

According to contemporary accounts, the Ottomans in the fourteenth and fifteenth centuries had a well-organized and disciplined force consisting of about 12,000 janissaries, who constituted the infantry, about 8000 *sipahis* or well-trained cavalry, 40,000 troops, feudal in character, supplied and led by rural notables and tribal clans, as well as many thousands of irregulars. European soldiers captured in battle and mercenaries tended to form the artillery. From the time of Orhan's reign, Christian vassals also supplied troops to fight both in Anatolia and Europe. As late as 1683, during the second siege of Vienna, a Wallachian corps was given the task of bridging the Danube. A Muslim Ottoman army, supposedly waging 'holy war' was willing to use Christian troops!

The Ottoman conquests continued under Murad I (r.1359–89). He fought on two fronts: in Anatolia, where he took advantage of the divisions among the Muslim principalities, and in the Balkans against the Christians – Greeks, Bulgarians, Serbs, Bosnians, and Albanians – who were equally divided. The Ottomans entered the Balkans at the invitation of the Christian rulers who were fighting against each other and sought Ottoman help. In 1361, Murad captured Ankara from the Turkomans and Adrianople (Edirne) from the Byzantines, making it second capital of the Ottoman state in 1367. The Ottoman victory at the battle on the River Maritza in Bulgaria in 1371, where Murad defeated a Serbian coalition, opened the road to the conquest of the Balkans just as the battle of Manzikert in 1071 had prepared the way for expansion into Anatolia. The Byzantine emperor and the Christian princes in the Balkans agreed to accept Ottoman suzerainty and to serve in the Ottoman armies as the sultan's vassals.

Murad also acquired territory by forming matrimonial alliances as, for example, when his son married into the Germiyan family and the Ottomans were given Kütahya and its six provinces as dowry. He also purchased lands from the principality of Hamid, but, in principle, conquest remained the main method of expansion. However, the two-front campaign was difficult to maintain and occasionally a Muslim–Christian alliance (as between Karaman and Bosnia) was capable of inflicting defeat on the Ottomans. Sensing weakness, Ottoman vassals in the Balkans rebelled and forced Murad to confront them in battle. The Balkans, and not Anatolia, had become the Ottoman's heartland and Murad took the challenge very seriously. On 15 June 1389, Murad, with an army of 60,000, met a force of Serbs, Bosnians, Wallachians, Moldavians, and Albanians, estimated at 100,000, and defeated them at the battle of Kosovo. His army was a mixed force of Muslims and Christians and included Bulgarian and Serbian princes, as well as levies for Turkoman principalities. The Serbian King Lazarus was killed in battle and Murad was assassinated by a Serb who came to pay homage as he reviewed his victorious army. The defeat of the Serbs acquired mythical proportions in Serbian poetry and folklore; in the nineteenth century, the battle became a source of nationalist inspiration and was put to political use, as it is today. The battle of Kosovo secured Ottoman power in the Balkans, and Kosovo acquired an important place in the Ottoman economy for it held vast deposits of minerals and was a major supplier of lead and zinc, necessary for the artillery. That is why the Ottomans and Hapsburgs fought over it for many years.

As the power of the Ottomans grew, the Byzantines tried to maintain cordial relations with Murad. Emperor John Palaeologos gave one of his daughters in marriage to Murad, and two other daughters to his sons, Bayezid and Yakub Çelebi. These beys were sent as governors to Germiyan and Karesi, with their own janissaries, where they gained experience of warfare and administration. The youngest son, Savcı Bey, who ruled over Bursa during Murad's absence, plotted with Andronicus, the Byzantine emperor's son, to overthrow their fathers and seize power. The plot was discovered and Savcı Bey was executed while Andronicus was blinded, following the Byzantine tradition.

Bayezid I (r.1389–1403) was proclaimed sultan at Kosovo; his first task was to execute his brother Yakub Çelebi, in order to guarantee his own succession, thereby establishing the tradition of fratricide within Ottoman politics. This practice violated the Sharia and it was legitimized only during the reign of Mehmed the Conqueror. He pronounced that if God had bequeathed the sultanate to one of his sons, that son could put his brothers to death for the sake of the order of the realm. The *ülema* legitimized the practice by issuing a *fetva* – legal opinion – arguing that fratricide was justified by *raison d'état* as the practice produced stability and therefore strengthened the state. Savcı Bey was executed because he had conspired against the sultan; Yakub Çelebi and other fratricides over the years were carried out as preventive measures!

Ottoman expansion continued under Bayezid's brilliant command and he consolidated his rule in Anotolia, subduing the *beylik*s of Aydın, Menteşe, Saruhan, Germiyan and Karaman. He laid siege to Constantinople in 1391 on the death of Emperor Palaeologos and defeated a European crusade, launched to save Constantinople, at Nicopolis in 1396. Having captured Salonika, he resumed the siege of Constantinople until he was bribed into raising it.

During the fourteenth century the Ottomans had begun to weaken tribal power by instituting the *devşirme* system, thereby recruiting Christian youths from outside the tribes and converting and training them so that they were totally loyal to the house of Osman. Therefore, by the fifteenth century, there was no unified sentiment in Anatolia, no sense of political unity or what would later be described as 'national' cohesion that inspired the various tribes. In fact, they were jealous of each other's growing power, and especially alarmed by the growing power of the Ottoman dynasty. Anatolia was divided into rival and conflicting tribal confederations, struggling to survive against the expansion of a neighbour.

The defeated and dispossessed beys of Anatolia appealed to the Mongol leader Timur – known in the West as Tamerlane – to stop Bayezid waging war against Muslim rulers and to reinstate them. Timur, the most powerful Mongol ruler since Genghis Khan and one of the greatest conquerors of world history, had subdued Central Asia and the Golden Horde in southern Russia, invaded India in 1398 and overran Iran, Iraq and Syria. He then advanced into Anatolia and defeated the Ottomans at the battle of Ankara in 1402. Bayezid was captured and died in captivity eight months later.

Timur's intervention in the affairs of Anatolia was brief but had the most momentous consequences. He had destroyed Ottoman power, given a temporary lease of life to the Anatolian beys and prolonged the life of Byzantium for a further fifty years. Timur died in 1405, leaving the Anatolian *beyliks* to fend for themselves while the Ottomans regrouped. Ottoman succession was disputed by Bayezid's sons and Mehmed I (r.1413–21) was finally recognized as the new sultan in 1413. By the time of his death in 1421, he had recovered most of the lands lost to Timur, and even organized a small navy to protect his domain from Venetian raids.

Murad II (r.1421–51), who had served as governor of Amasya, succeeded Mehmed. But before he could consolidate his power, he had to deal with two pretenders to the throne, supported by the Byzantines and the beys of Germiyan and Karaman. By 1426, both of them had become Murad's suzerains and paid tribute to him. Thereafter, Murad advanced into Macedonia and captured the strategic port city of Salonika from Venice in 1428. Murad was forced to fight a double-fronted war, against the Europeans, who organized an army led by the Hungarian Janos Hunyadi (c.1387–1456), as well as Karaman, which rose up in rebellion. Murad defeated Karaman in July 1444 but was forced to sign a ten-year truce with Hungary. He then abdicated in favour of his son, Mehmed, and retired to Manisa. The Hungarians, sensing Ottoman weakness, broke the truce and advanced into Ottoman territory. The janissaries brought Murad out of retirement to lead his army and the Christian force was routed at Varna in 1444. The war with Hungary continued until Hunyadi, at the head of a large army, was defeated at Kosovo in 1448. Murad died at Edirne and Mehmed II, known as the Conqueror (r.1451–81), finally came to the throne.

MEHMED THE CONQUEROR AND HIS INFLUENCE

Mehmed's fame rests on the conquest of Constantinople on 29 May 1453. Important though that was, his reign is more significant in Ottoman history for his decision finally to break the power of the Anatolian beys in his entourage and to establish the hegemony of the men of the *devşirme* who, unlike the beys, were his servitors and totally loyal to him, and over whom he had the power of life and death. As a result, the Ottoman Empire became more autocratic and bureaucratic, with the sultan relying on his grand vizier to conduct day-to-day business and even lead the army. The notables whose power was based on their tribal affiliation lost much of their political influence, their lands and property, and became dependent on the state. Perhaps it was this that ended any possibility of an independent landed aristocracy as a counter-force to the Palace emerging in the Ottoman Empire as it did in Europe. The sultan became an absolute autocrat, supported by loyal servants who in time became kingmakers. However, Islamic ideology required that he remain accountable to the Sharia and therefore the *ülema* of freeborn Muslims remained an autonomous political force in the empire.

Constantinople, which the Ottomans continued to call Konstantiyye until 1915, as well as Istanbul and *Dersaadet* (the abode of felicity), gave them an imperial mission as they believed that they had acquired the mantle of Rome. Though the city fell after a difficult siege, many Greek Orthodox subjects welcomed the Ottomans as they allowed them to practise their faith, unlike the Catholics who had wanted to restore papal hegemony by reuniting the two Churches. Mehmed granted the Orthodox Church a charter that gave the patriarch total jurisdiction over his community in return for the payment of a poll tax. The Armenian Church was also brought to the new capital and granted religious and cultural autonomy. Within a short time, a relationship was established between the state and the religious communities that developed by the eighteenth century into the *millet* system, or virtually autonomous religious communities. In pre-secular Ottoman society, religious allegiance was not a private matter but a matter of communal concern. People were organized according to the Church into which they had been born, regardless of the language they spoke or the ethnic group they belonged to. The religious and social life of each community was organized according to its traditions and individuals were bound by its laws. The Muslim *millet* included all Muslims (Turks, Kurds, Arabs, and converts) regardless of their ethnicity or language; the same was true for the Greek Orthodox *millet* that included not only Greeks but Slavic peoples of the Balkans and, later on, the Arab world. The same was true for the Jewish and Armenian communities. Only in the nineteenth century, with the advent of nationalism, did the *millets* begin to acquire an ethnic colouring and Serbs,

Bulgarians, Catholics, and Protestants acquired their own communal organizations. However, even in 1919, Greek Catholics felt more akin to Italian Catholics than to the Greek Orthodox army that invaded Anatolia! The *millet* system suggests that the Ottomans made no attempt at assimilation, only a pragmatic integration that allowed the empire to function smoothly.

Istanbul was refurbished after the conquest of 1453 as befitting the capital of a world empire. Mehmed imported craftsmen from all over the empire and settled them in the city in order to rebuild it. Its population increased substantially, especially after the expulsion of the Jews from Spain in 1492, when they were invited to settle in the empire and many chose the capital. Between 1500 and 1600, Istanbul became one of the most important cities of Europe; around 1600 it was still one of the most populous cities until it was overtaken before the end of the seventeenth century, first by Paris and then London.

The imperatives of empire also led Mehmed to extend his territories in all directions. He conquered southern Serbia and extended Ottoman influence in Wallachia. Commerce had been important to the Ottomans ever since their rise to power in the fourteenth century, but with the acquisition of Istanbul, sea power and international trade became crucial for Ottoman security and economy. Venice had become a rival and the Ottomans were forced to pay attention to their fleet and the defence of the city. Mehmed therefore captured the island of Mytilene (Midilli) and fortified the straits. He pressured Venice in the Mediterranean until she was forced to sign a treaty in 1478. He then conquered the Crimea making the Crimean Tatars his vassals and the Black Sea an Ottoman lake. Ottoman expansion continued until Mehmed's death in 1481, with attacks on Rhodes and even southern Italy, where the Ottomans seized Otranto.

Bayezid II (r.1481–1512) was forced to contest the throne with his brother Cem Sultan (1459–1495). First, he had to bribe the janissaries by granting an 'accession present' in order to win their loyalty; thereafter it became a tradition with which every sultan complied at the beginning of his reign. Cem was defeated and sought asylum with the Knights of Rhodes, who were paid in gold to keep him hostage. Cem went on to Naples where he died as a captive of the Pope, who was also able to blackmail Bayezid and force him to pay to keep Cem in captivity. Scholars have speculated as to what Bayezid might have achieved had he not been distracted by Cem's challenge to the Ottoman throne and the manipulation of the Christian powers. Given the anarchy ruling in Italy at the time and the ease with which the French conquered Italy in 1494, the Ottomans might have subjugated Italy, altering the course of world history. In Rome, it was feared that that city might share the fate of Constantinople.

EXPANDING OTTOMAN POSSESSIONS

By the fifteenth century, the Ottomans had reinvented themselves from being a tribute-levying empire to one dependent on world trade. Recent research in the Genoese and Venetian archives shows that the Ottomans took trade in the region seriously. From the early fourteenth century their conquests were based largely on the capture of strategic points, such as Gallipoli and the Dardanelles, which provided revenues from trade in the region. After inflicting a defeat on Venice in July 1496, they not only exempted the Venetians from paying an annual tribute, but agreed that Venice pay a four per cent tax on its exports to the Ottoman empire; trade had become as important as tribute.

Apart from waging war in Europe, the Ottomans were faced with the threat of such rivals as the Mamluks in Egypt and Syria, and the Safavids in Iran. The struggle with the Safavids assumed an ideological character, as a contest between the Sunni or orthodox Islam of the Ottomans and the heterodox, Shia Islam of the Safavids. This long-drawn-out conflict sapped the energies of both empires and was responsible for the relative decline of both in comparison with the rise of European power.

Having deposed his father Bayezid, Selim I (1512–20) was forced to turn his attention to the east and meet the rising power of Shah İsmail. In 1514, Selim defeated the Safavids at Chaldiran and acquired Azerbaijan and Kurdistan. Two years later, Selim advanced against the Mamluks and conquered Syria in 1516 and Egypt the following year. Egypt's agriculture and commerce provided Istanbul with considerable wealth as well as revenues from trade with India and Asia. The Ottomans also became the guardians of the two holy cities of Mecca and Medina and were elevated to the status of the most powerful Muslim state in the world. Jerusalem, or Kudus, became the third holy city of Islam; the Ottomans built great bazaars to enliven commercial life and Selim's successor, Süleyman, built the city's distinct white walls. Jerusalem did not become a major regional capital such as Damascus or Aleppo, but it was one of the three Holy Places of Islam and enjoyed great religious significance. The empire had doubled in size and its Islamic element was strengthened by the addition of the Arab provinces. Moreover, Egypt brought the Ottomans into direct contact with the Portuguese in the Red Sea and the Indian Ocean.

In the sixteenth century, the balance in the world had shifted from the Mediterranean to the Atlantic. Christopher Columbus's discovery of America in 1492 and Vasco da Gama's voyage around southern Africa to reach India in 1498 diminished but did not end the importance of the Islamic world. Trade with Asia did not dry up as a result, but the Ottoman treasury received less revenue. The empire also became too large and unwieldy to be ruled by the sultan alone and he was forced to rely more and more on his bureaucracy. The men who rose through the *devşirme* became more influential, as did the women in the Palace.

SÜLEYMAN THE MAGNIFICENT

Süleyman I (r.1520–66) is perhaps the most famous of the Ottoman sultans. He is known as *Kanuni* (the lawgiver) to the Turks, and 'Süleyman the Magnificent' in the West. He continued to expand and consolidate his empire in the tradition of his predecessors, capturing Belgrade in 1521 and besieging Vienna in 1529. The Ottomans actively participated in the European conflict between the Holy Roman Emperor Charles V and Francis I of France; the Ottoman role was partially responsible for Charles's failure to crush Martin Luther's Protestant Reformation. Wars in Europe continued until Süleyman's death in 1566, when he died leading the campaign into Hungary. He also fought against the Safavids, capturing Baghdad in 1534.

Commerce had become an important part of the Ottoman economy and Ottoman merchants – Muslim and non-Muslim – traded in Europe, especially Italy, and Asia. As a result of this, in 1535, Süleyman granted certain privileges, known as 'capitulations', to French merchants. They were permitted to live according to their own laws and customs while they resided in the empire, so long as Ottoman law was not violated. Over time, these capitulations were extended to other European states, leading to an expansion of commerce between Europe and the Ottomans.

The expansion of the Ottoman navy may also be explained as a measure to control the Mediterranean in order to secure commerce in the region. Thus Süleyman used Barbarosa Hayrettin to seize control of the North African coast from Charles V, establishing Ottoman rule over Algiers, Tunis and Libya. A serious attempt was also made to destroy Portuguese power in the Arabian Sea, but the Ottoman fleet was destroyed at the battle of Dui in 1538. Ottoman ships were constructed for the calmer waters of the Mediterranean and were no match for Portuguese galleons. Perhaps that is why the Ottomans made no attempt to sail in the Atlantic, though they mapped it and knew much about it. Like the Chinese in East Asia, the Ottomans were content with their empire in the eastern Mediterranean.

By Süleyman's reign, the Ottoman Empire had developed into a stable form with a military-bureaucratic ruling class, tempered by the free-born *ülema*, that ruled over a multi-religious population of peasants, merchants, and artisans, organized into virtually autonomous religious communities. Executive and legislative power resided in the sultan, who was aided by ministers who assumed more of the sultan's prerogatives as the empire expanded and became more bureaucratic. After Süleyman's reign, the grand vizier began to assume many of the sultan's duties and the sultan became more palace-bound. The patriarchs, as leaders of the non-Muslim communities who tended to the religious and communal needs of their flocks, enjoyed the protection of the sultan. No attempt was made to assimilate the various communities; they were integrated to the extent that day-to-day interactions were normalized and provided a social context for cultural exchange. The system worked well until the introduction of nationalism in the nineteenth century, enabling each community to go its separate way, something that they could not have achieved had they been assimilated.

Ottoman administration was advanced for the time in comparison with contemporary Europe, and Christian peasants found Ottoman rule to be lighter than that of their feudal co-religionists. Martin Luther (1483–1546), who had no sympathy for the 'Turks' whom he considered barbarous, agreed that the peasants yielded to the Ottomans because their taxes were lighter. Ottoman taxation continued to be light while the sultan conquered prosperous lands, but became heavier when the conquests ended.

With the conquest of Constantinople, the Ottomans acquired some Byzantine administrative practices. The sultan became increasingly distant, leaving day-to-day affairs to his imperial *divan* which was presided over by his grand vizier and was composed of other ministers. His principal ministers were the military judges (*kadıasker*) of Rumelia and Anatolia, the judge of Istanbul, the minister of finance, the keeper of the seal and the chief of the janissaries. Later, the offices of *Şeyhülislam*, the supreme religious authority, the *reis-ül kuttub*, the minister in charge of foreign relations, and *kapudan* pasha, admiral of the fleet, were added to the *divan*. A military officer, a pasha with two horsetails designating rank, was appointed governor of a province, which was subdivided into *sanjak*s governed by a pasha with one horsetail. Below him there were districts, or *kaza*s, governed by a *kadı* and landlords who represented the local people.

Land belonged to the state and the empire's economy depended on the state's control of both the land and agricultural production, the principal sources of revenue. Land was divided into a variety of fiefs (*tımar*s) whose revenues were allotted to the administrators – the beys and viziers – as their salaries. These fiefs were not hereditary and could be confiscated on the holder's death. As they could not be passed on to the landholder's beneficiaries, it was not possible to create a landowning class as in Europe. In theory, peasants could not be evicted from the land they cultivated so long as they paid the tithe to the landlord. That measure gave peasants security of tenure and may explain the general absence of peasant rebellions in Ottoman history.

The reign of Süleyman the Magnificent is traditionally described as the 'high noon' of the Ottoman Empire. He was described as the last of the great first ten rulers who had established and laid the foundation of a world empire. These rulers were not only great conquerors but wise and talented administrators, who ruled over their territories with ruthless sagacity. After Süleyman, it was said, the sultans were often incompetent, mediocre and corrupt men who were more given to the pleasure of the harem than the battlefield; a sultan such as Murad IV (1623–40) was the exception rather than the rule. Incompetent rulers lacked the initiative and drive of such great sultans as Mehmed the Conqueror, and therefore tended to paralyse the administration and weaken the empire. But despite this shortcoming, the empire was able to rely on the exceptional talents of such grand viziers as Sokullu Mehmed Pasha and the Köprülü dynasty of grand viziers which controlled the empire for almost half a century, as well as the occasionally competent sultan, such as Murad IV.

As an explanation for Ottoman decline relative to the rise of Western Europe, this is only partially true and modern scholarship has sought other explanations. By the beginning of the sixteenth century, the Ottoman Empire was operating in a totally different environment, both internally and overseas. The empire had been transformed from a state whose primary goal was territorial expansion, which therefore created the need for an active sultan-general to lead the armies, to a bureaucratic state that had to deal with such economic factors as commerce and relations with an expanding Europe. The Ottomans had created a world empire that was far too complex to be ruled by an individual, however gifted. Power had to be delegated and the sultans were forced to create a *divan*, an early cabinet, with a grand vizier and other ministers. During Süleyman's reign, the situation remained ambiguous and he executed his grand vizier, İbrahim Pasha, because he had become jealous of the growth in the latter's power. But his successor, Selim II, came to depend on his grand vizier and his bureaucracy, which then acquired its own residence known as Babiali or the Sublime Porte (similar to Number Ten Downing Street, the residence of the British prime minister).

For the same reason, the imperial harem also emerged as a focus of political power in the sixteenth century. The grand vizier was often related to the sultan by marriage and therefore directly connected to the harem and its powerful women, such as the *valide sultan*, the sultan's mother or the sultan's favourite concubine. Sometimes the sultan was a minor and therefore a regency headed by the sultan's mother had to be established until he came of age.

By the middle of the sixteenth century, the empire had reached the limits of expansion, especially of lands that could be profitably exploited to bring economic benefit. That was the difference between Ottoman imperialism and the imperialisms of such European powers as Spain, England, and Holland: their motives for expansion were largely economic and they plundered their colonies for all they were worth. The Ottomans presented a classic case of what has been described as 'imperial over-extension'. They had to maintain large armies in central Europe, North Africa, and Cyprus, as well as powerful naval forces in the Mediterranean, the Aegean, and the Red Sea. In addition to the Holy Roman emperor and his allies, the Ottomans began to face the threat of the growing power of Russia in the Crimea. In Anatolia, the Safavids posed a threat with their religious propaganda among the nomadic Turkoman tribes. All this was a great burden on the treasury, forcing the Ottomans to find new ways to meet their fiscal obligations.

Overseas, a great transformation was marked by a shift from the Mediterranean sphere to the world of the Atlantic. With the age of discovery, the former trade routes upon which the Ottomans had depended for centuries lost their prominence and the empire's revenues from commerce declined. But this was a gradual process and did not affect the empire immediately; however, due to the political and social structure of the empire, there was no obvious solution. The Ottoman economic system was incapable of withstanding the challenge of Western mercantalism and industrialization.

AN AGE OF REVOLUTION

In the Western world, the transition from feudalism to commercial capitalism was marked by revolution – the rising middle classes, the bourgeoisie, had to fight for political power. That was accomplished in England between 1640 and 1688, culminating in the 'glorious revolution'; in France, the revolution took place between 1789 and 1815. Where there was no bourgeoisie strong enough to challenge the power of the feudal class – as in Spain or Russia – there was no revolution and the old classes remained in power. That was the case with the Ottomans. While they maintained a government strong enough to preserve order and allow merchants and manufacturers to make their fortunes, they did not permit these merchants to emerge as a political force capable of promoting their own interests. This was made more difficult by the fact that the merchants were divided by religious affiliation – Greek Orthodox, Catholic, Armenian, Jew and Muslim – and could not act together as a class to protect their economic interests. The Ottomans, while aware of the importance of commerce for the economy, were never solely concerned with the interests of the commercial classes, nor did they take a conscious interest in the rapid growth of the economy. However, they were committed to defending the interests of the consumer, and one of the most important officials was the *muhtesib*, the inspector of the market place, who supervised prices and the quality of goods and weights and measures to see that consumers were not cheated. That in itself stifled the growth of capitalism and a market economy.

There were however a number of wealthy merchants who, in theory, might have played the role of carrying out a bourgeoisie transformation had they been given the opportunity. For example, a Greek merchant, known as Sheytanoglu, from a prominent Byzantine family, made a fortune from the fur trade and the imperial salt monopoly and, as a result, was able to fit sixty galleys for the Ottoman navy. But Murad II became suspicious of his increasing wealth and power and executed him in 1578. There were other prominent rich bankers and merchants, but the Ottoman ruling class never permitted them to alter the character of the state or economy. Even in Europe such change required a revolution, and the Ottoman state was too strong to allow any such radical political and social transformation. Thus there were rebellions and insurrections, but there was no single violent transformation of the political order and its supporting social system that would replace the existing ruling class with another, giving the empire a new look and direction.

It was not as though the Ottomans did not understand what was going on in the world around them; they were aware of the developments taking place in Europe. There was always a constant stream of visitors from Europe and some of these visitors stayed on and served the empire, especially as military experts. There were commercial contacts with the Italian city-states such as Genoa and Venice from the earliest days of the Ottomans, and

Muslim merchants resided in Italian cities. Mehmed the Conqueror had sent students to Italy to study the arts, and corresponded with the Pope. As a result, the Ottomans were well aware of developments in the world around them but were unable to absorb these developments into their own complex, multi-religious society. Nor did they realize how the changes in Europe were beginning to affect their own society, but that was the nature of empire and an imperial ruling class. They were conservative and bound to the status quo and would not permit the rise of a mercantile class that might transform the state and overwhelm the old ruling elites. The Ottomans had three principles that guided the state's economic policy: to provision the urban economy, especially that of Istanbul, and to keep the army, the bureaucracy, and the Palace well supplied; to provide the necessary revenues from taxation, urban and rural; and to preserve the status quo by maintaining strict controls in the towns and the countryside. The Spanish empire pursued a similar policy in the sixteenth century and later; despite her empire and her great wealth, Spain too failed to make the transformation to a bourgeois society, remaining a society dominated by the commercial classes, and therefore lagging behind such European states as Holland and England. It was not a question of religion (Islam or Catholicism), as some have suggested, but was rooted in the very nature of pre-Enlightenment imperialism.

But Ottoman decline was not precipitous. The empire was powerful enough to defend itself throughout the seventeenth century and was even able to launch a campaign that took Ottoman armies to the walls of Vienna in 1683 for the second time. In 1570–71 the Ottomans captured Tunis and Cyprus and the European power took the threat seriously enough to join forces and inflict a crushing defeat on the Ottoman navy at Lepanto in 1571. Such was the empire's wealth in the latter sixteenth century that Sokollu Mehmed Pasha, the grand vizier, informed Sultan Selim II that the fleet destroyed at Lepanto could easily be replaced with new and better galleys. However, as a result of the defeat, Selim was forced to make peace with Venice and the emperor.

By the reign of Selim II (1566–74) power had passed into the hands of other men, such as Sokullu Mehmed Pasha (1506–79), though they were not all as outstanding a statesman as he was. Born in the town of Sokolovic in Bosnia, he was recruited and trained in the *devşirme* system. He rose through the ranks until he was appointed grand vizier in 1564, having already married Süleyman's daughter and Selim II's sister. It was he, not the sultan, who administered the empire until he died in 1579.

Apart from the regular wars (with Iran, 1578–90, and Austria, 1593), the Ottomans had to cope with a situation that is described as the 'crisis of the seventeenth century'. This was marked by a number of factors that worked together and created a difficult situation that the Ottoman state found itself confronted with. Earlier scholarship argued that it was primarily the influx of American gold and silver that came into the Mediterranean world via its commercial connections with the West that created inflation and the pressure on the Ottoman economy. The treasury was forced to find more money to pay the salaries of its armies and administration. Recent research suggests that a cash economy had already penetrated large parts of the Balkans and Anatolia along the coast and the process was accelerated in the sixteenth century with the influx of New World silver, resulting in increased commercialization. Thus taxes were now collected in cash rather than kind, altering the method of landholding in parts of the empire. Inflationary pressures were aggravated by the growth in population, urbanization, and monetization of the economy that increased the demand for money and pressure on the empire's limited resources. The state was forced to finance larger armies to fight exhausting wars against the Hapsburgs and the Safavids, and one quick solution was to debase and devalue the currency, putting more brass than silver in the coins. The result was social turmoil and in 1589 the janissaries in Istanbul revolted in protest against their lower pay and declining standard of living. These revolts continued into 1592 before they were quelled. In the 1590s, central Anatolia began to witness social disorder with peasant unrest known as the *Celali* rebellions, named after the religious leader who began the first revolt. Serious dissatisfaction continued until the 1650s, undermining the authority of the state.

THE JANISSARY–ÜLEMA ALLIANCE

Despite all these problems and military setbacks, the Ottomans held their own throughout the seventeenth and eighteenth centuries. One of the most serious consequences of this prolonged crisis was the emergence of an alliance between the *ülema* and the janissaries that prevented the possibility of any structural reform in the state and society. The military provided the power, literally from the barrels of their guns, while the *ülema* provided ideological legitimacy. For example, the Ottomans were unable to follow the example of the Greek community which established a printing press in 1627, because the *ülema* objected that the printing press was a violation of the Sharia. When İbrahim Müteferrika, a Hungarian convert, set up the first Ottoman printing press a hundred years later, it survived only until 1742, when it was again shut down because of strong opposition from the reactionaries. The press was finally able to reopen in 1784! Even reformers who often diagnosed the problems of the empire correctly generally proposed a solution that asked the sultan to restore the practices of Süleyman the Magnificent, during whose reign the empire was thought to be at its peak.

When the situation seemed critical, such as during the reign of Murad IV (1623–40), a strong ruler was able to restore order but could not carry out fundamental reform. He ended fratricide in 1623 because his brother İbrahim was the last surviving Ottoman apart from Murad, and killing him would put the dynasty at risk. İbrahim was therefore isolated in the Palace and allowed to lead a passive and degenerate life away from political power. By 1632, Murad had established control over the state and continued a policy of conquest, capturing Baghdad from the Safavids in 1638.

The stability proved temporary for, in 1648, when Mehmed IV, a minor, came to the throne, the capital was in a state of anarchy, dominated by the janissaries, while rebel pashas controlled much of central Anatolia and the Venetians blockaded the Dardanelles. But in 1656, Mehmed Köprülü (d.1661) was appointed grand vizier and given absolute power. He is an example of Ottoman meritocracy, an illiterate rising from the sultan's kitchen to the rank of provincial governor and grand vizier, thanks to his own talent and patronage in the Palace. He remained in power for only five years until his death in 1661. During his brief tenure, he restored control over the janissaries and the rebels in Anatolia, lifted the Venetian blockade at the Dardanelles and restored Ottoman control over Transylvania and Wallachia. Mehmed Köprülü's aggressive policies were continued by his son, Fazıl Ahmed Köprülü (1635–76) and Kara Mustafa Pasha (1676–83). But the political stability of these years did not survive long and the long exhausting wars with the Hapsburgs, marked by the second siege of Vienna in 1683, hastened Ottoman decline.

GROWING EUROPEAN INFLUENCE

The Treaty of Carlowitz, signed in January 1699, was a turning point in Ottoman–Hapsburg relations. From being the aggressors, the Ottomans were forced to go on the defensive, and they began to take the European example seriously. Sultan Ahmed III (1703–30) led the reform drive during what is known as the 'Tulip Period'. But his attempts to introduce European methods into the army were thwarted by the *ülema*–janissary alliance. In 1729, faced with the threat of Austrian and Russian armies, the Ottomans invited Western experts to introduce modern methods of warfare. Count Alexander de Bonneval, a French officer, came to Istanbul to modernize the engineer and bombardier corps. Possibly to facilitate his work, he converted to Islam so that a Muslim, not a Christian, might be responsible for the reforms. Known as Ahmed Bey, he entered Ottoman service in 1731 and established a school of military engineering in 1734. He was given the rank of pasha and the title 'Bombadier' (*Humbaracı*) the following year. But his reforms did not take root and when another European reformer, Baron de Tott, arrived in Istanbul in 1768, he found hardly any evidence of *Humbaracı*'s efforts, as though he had failed totally to reform the army.

Baron de Tott arrived to carry out military reform while the empire was at war with Russia. The Russian fleet dominated the Aegean Sea by 1770, defeated the Ottoman army on the Danube and invaded the Crimea. The Ottomans suffered such crushing defeats that they were forced to sign a humiliating treaty with Catherine the Great in 1774. The Treaty of Küçük Kaynarca made the Crimea and northern coast of the Black Sea independent of Ottoman rule.

Catherine was also given the right to protect the Orthodox Church in Istanbul, thereby giving Russia the excuse to intervene in Ottoman affairs. The treaty marked the beginning of what has come to be known as the 'Eastern Question', the attempts by the Great Powers to exploit the multi-religious character of the Ottoman Empire by acting on behalf of the Christian communities. In return, Sultan Abdülhamid I (1774–89) was recognized by Russia – and soon after by other European powers – as the Caliph of all Muslims. According to Article 3 of the Treaty, the Sultan retained his spiritual authority over Muslims in the Crimea, by now ceded to Russia. The Sultan's claim to the caliphate was confirmed under subsequent treaties with the Powers.

The claim to the caliphate was an important innovation and had considerable influence on the future policy of the empire, strengthening the conservatives and enabling them to manipulate Islam in order to forestall reform. After the fall of the Abbasid caliphate in 1258, a number of independent sultans had assumed the title, and even Murad I had used it as early as 1326. However, the Ottomans began to attach importance to both the title and its prerogatives after 1774, in order to counter Tsarina Catherine's claim to be the protector of Orthodox Christians in the Ottoman Empire. The sultans in turn claimed spiritual authority over Muslim communities under Christian rule and found that this was a useful tool to use in their relations with Europe.

Piecemeal reform during the eighteenth century, obstructed by the reactionaries, had failed to improve the situation of the empire against the growing power of the European states. The treaty with Catherine did not bring peace or satisfy Russia's appetite for expansion. In 1783, she annexed the Khanate of Crimea, and three years later the Ottomans were again at war with Russia. When Selim III came to the throne of the troubled empire in 1789, his reign began the empire's longest century of continuous reform, culminating in 1908 with revolution.

SUGGESTED FURTHER READING

Stanford J. Shaw, *History of the Ottoman Empire and Modern Turkey, vol. 1: Empire of the Gazis – the Rise and Decline of the Ottoman Empire 1280–1808* (Cambridge University Press, 1976).

Halil İnalcık, *The Ottoman Empire: the Classical Age 1300–1600* (Weidenfeld and Nicolson, London, 1973).

Leslie Pierce, *The Imperial Harem: Women and Sovereignty in the Ottoman Empire* (Oxford University Press, 1993).

Daniel Goffman, *The Ottoman Empire and Early Modern Europe* (Cambridge University Press, 2002).

2

From Reform to Revolution, 1789–1908

REFORM OF THE MILITARY

When Selim III (r.1789–1807) came to the throne in April, revolution in France was just getting underway. His empire was in dire straits: he was at war with Russia, the Hapsburgs had taken Belgrade, Napoleon began the French occupation of Egypt in 1798, the Wahabbis, the founders of religious fundamentalism, were gaining strength in the Hijaz (today's Saudi Arabia), attacking the Ottomans for their lax religious practices, while in the Balkans, Tepedenli Ali Pasha of Janina – in present-day Greece – was in rebellion. He was a local notable (*ayan*) who, like many others throughout the empire, challenged the power of Istanbul and sought autonomy, if not independence, depriving the sultan of revenues. But a recurrent problem for the state was how to curb the power of the janissaries. During the crisis of the seventeenth century, the *devşirme* had fallen into disarray. The janissaries, adversely affected by inflation and the debasement of currency, enrolled their sons and relatives into the corps so that they too could obtain a salary. Moreover, they joined various guilds of artisans and began to ply a craft in order to augment their pay. As a result, the old discipline and esprit de corps that had made them the envy and the scourge of Europe disappeared, and the janissaries became a menace to the sultans. In alliance with the *ülema*, whose ranks had also swelled as a result of the economic crisis, the janissaries became opponents of any social or military reform that would threaten their position in society. Selim realized that military reform was critical if he were to wage successful warfare at the same time as curbing the growing power of his provincial notables. In 1801, peasants in Serbia revolted because the Ottoman officials and janissaries had seized their land. Istanbul attempted to arm and grant property rights to the peasants but to no avail. In 1815 the principality was granted autonomy. In 1804, the Russians annexed Armenia and northern Azerbaijan and advanced to the very borders of Anatolia. The following year, Mehmed Ali Pasha established his authority in Egypt and soon founded a dynasty that survived until its overthrow by a military coup d'état in July 1952. Mehmed Ali had been sent by Selim to drive out the French army that had destroyed the Mamluks and entered the heartlands of Islam for the first time since the eleventh century.

Selim introduced military reform in these inauspicious times. Inspired by the example of the French Revolution, whose impact was felt in Istanbul, Selim called his new army the 'new order' (*nizam-I cedid*). He invited experts from France, built new barracks and training schools and moved forward cautiously. But he had to raise taxes in order to finance his reforms and this measure met with opposition. When, in 1805, he wanted to create his new army in the Balkans, the notables rose up in rebellion. Unable to crush the rebels, Selim found that the janissaries had overturned their soup cauldrons in rebellion as well. The reformers were isolated and once again the janissary–*ülema* alliance had triumphed. Selim was deposed in 1807 and his 'new order' army was disbanded.

Selim's reformers, mainly bureaucrats, men of the Sublime Porte who survived slaughter by the janissaries, took refuge with Alemdar Mustafa Pasha (1750–1808), a notable of Ruscuk in the Balkans. Mustafa Pasha decided to support reform and restore Selim, who had been replaced by Mustafa IV (r.1807–8). He marched on Istanbul, but Selim was murdered in the palace and Alemdar Mustafa brought Mahmud II (1808–38) to the Ottoman throne and became his grand vizier. His goal was to integrate provincial notables into the imperial system by creating a charter that would be honoured by the sultan, giving them rights and obligations. The result of his consultations with the empire's notables and the reformers was the signing of the 'Deed of Agreement' (*Sende-i İttifak*), sometimes described as the Ottoman Magna Carta. The notables swore to be loyal to the sultan so long as he did not violate the law. They agreed to supply troops and to the establishment of a modern army, and also to pay taxes levied after consultation with them. Finally, they demanded an end to arbitrary punishment inflicted by the sultan. It seemed as though the provincial notables and the bureaucrats were gaining the recognition they had failed to win when their power was checked by the *devşirme* some centuries before. But that proved to be illusory, for the janissaries revolted again and killed Alemdar Mustafa. Mahmud was saved because he had executed Mustafa IV and had thus become the last surviving Ottoman. The janissaries were forced to accept Mahmud but he, in turn, agreed to disband the new army. For the moment, military reform was halted until the historical circumstances favoured it a few years later.

Historic conjunctions appear at rare moments in a country's history when the usual forces that provide social balance and maintain the status quo break down. War and defeat are often the cause of such breakdowns – which is what happened in Egypt when this Ottoman province was invaded by Napoleon in 1798. Napoleon had defeated the Mamluks and had destroyed their social power, which had left the *ülema*, another source of conservatism, defenceless and impotent. Thus when Mehmed Ali assumed political authority in 1805, he inherited a virtual political *tabula rasa* upon which he could write his own programme. What little threat the Mamluks posed to his regime he destroyed when he massacred their leaders in the citadel of Cairo in 1811.

Mahmud's moment in history arrived in the 1820s, during the Greek war of independence. He defeated Tependeli Ali's rebellion in 1820 with some difficulty, but in so doing he weakened his position in the region, and the Greeks of the Danube provinces and Morea seized the opportunity to rebel and fight for their independence. The janissaries failed to defeat the rebels, resulting in the capture of Athens by Greek insurgents. In 1824, Mahmud appealed to Mehmed Ali of Egypt, his suzerain, to send his modern army against the rebels and Ibrahim Pasha, Mehmed Ali's son, quickly quelled the rebellion. But the Great Powers – England,

France, and Russia – intervened on behalf of the Greeks and destroyed the Ottoman-Egyptian fleet in October 1827. Russia declared war on the Sultan and the war was concluded with the Treaty of Adrianople in 1829. As a result, Mahmud was forced to give autonomy to Greece, Serbia, and Rumania, and the Kingdom of Greece was established in 1830 with the consent of the Powers.

The Greek war revealed to Ottoman Muslims the impotence of the janissaries – who could not even overcome rebel insurgents let alone an organized army – without the assistance of a modern army organized by the empire's governor in Egypt. For Mahmud, this was a historical conjunction similar to the defeat of the Mamluks in Egypt. The janissaries had lost face, as well as the support of the artisans of Istanbul. When they rebelled in 1826, the janissaries no longer had any popular support in the capital and even the *ülema* held back; both artisans and *ülema* welcomed the elimination of the janissaries and the creation of a modern army. The massacre was described as an 'auspicious event' and Mahmud created his new army which, in order to appease conservative elements, he called the 'Victorious Army of Muhammad' under a '*ser'asker*' (war minister) and not under the ağa of the janissaries. Janissary standards, usually decorated with pictures of various animals, were replaced by a single flag decorated with the star and crescent, a symbol adopted later by the republic. Mahmud also introduced modern uniforms, a frock-coat to be worn by his bureaucrats, and the fez hat to mark his new order – the rise of a new class and the demise of the old. The establishment of the empire's first newspaper in 1831, emulating Mehmed Ali's example, was also an important step in the modernization of society. The paper, though only read by the elite, influenced the creation of 'public opinion' and the development of the language.

Without the support of the janissaries, the *ülema* no longer had the influence to prevent reform, and reforms came fast and furious. Students were sent to Europe to learn modern methods. New schools were set up, including a school of medicine (1831) and the War College in 1834; the entire governmental structure was bureau-cratized. The new army was trained in an entirely new tradition, breaking all ties to the past; the link between the army and religion – the Bektaşi order of dervishes – was broken when the order was abolished. Ottoman officers, with their modern education and outlook, became the vanguard of secular progress. The financial independence of the *ülema* ended with the creation of the inspectorate of foundations, or *vakf*s, and the Şeyhulislam virtually became a civil servant, acquiring his own office. The Sublime Porte, the heart of Ottoman government, was modernized with bureaux that were later transformed into ministries – civil affairs, the interior, and foreign affairs – led by a grand vizier. Mahmud also set up a translation bureau to train Muslim interpreters or dragomans, a task that had been performed by the Greek aristocracy, the Phanariot Greeks, before the Greek war of independence. Ottoman Greeks and Armenians continued to play a prominent role in the conduct of foreign affairs as ambassadors and even as a foreign minister, but Muslims began to learn European languages and that was an important innovation which had radical consequences, as these languages, especially French, brought them in contact with new ideas such as liberty and constitutionalism. Embassies in the major European capitals, established by Selim III, were restored, permanently enhancing the impact of the West on the bureaucratic class.

THE SUBLIME PORTE AND MEHMED ALI

The class that gained from these and later reforms was the men of the Sublime Porte, who began to curb the autocratic powers of the Sultan by forcing him to adhere to 'constitutional' forms. Like the men of the *devşirme*, who had come to the fore in the second half of the sixteenth century, the men of the Sublime Porte were establishing their claim to power in the nineteenth. As there was no rising middle class in Ottoman society demanding change, the bureaucrats used the threat of European intervention to force the sultan to succumb to their schemes. The Great Powers of Europe – England, France, Austria, Russia, Prussia and Germany, and Italy after 1870 – were crucial players in the development of the 'Eastern Question'. They brought about the creation of an independent Greek state, and the Porte required their support to control the ambitions of Mehmed Ali of Egypt, the first successful modernizer of the non-Western world.

In the first quarter of the nineteenth century, Mehmed Ali had created a state with a modern army and an industrial economy. He had regional ambitions that clashed with those of Mahmud and

Great Britain, for the British could not permit a strong modern state to control such a strategic country as Egypt and threaten Britain's route to India and the east. The Egyptians went to war against the Ottomans in 1831, advanced into Anatolia, defeated the Ottoman army led by the grand vizier, and threatened the capital. Mahmud was forced to appeal to Russia, and the tsar responded by sending naval squadrons and troops to defend Istanbul. Russian military help against a fellow Muslim required a *fetva*, a religious injunction from the Şeyhulislam, to make it acceptable to the people! Mahmud then signed the Treaty of Hünkar İskelesi with Russia on 8 July 1833, marking the zenith of Russia's influence in Istanbul. But Britain and France refused to accept Russian hegemony at Istanbul and after the Ottoman–Egyptian war of 1839–41, they intervened and forced Mehmed Ali to restore Syria to the Porte, while he was recognized as the hereditary ruler of Egypt.

Apart from the empire's diplomatic dependence on Europe during these years, its economic dependence on Europe, especially Britain, also increased. The Porte had begun to surrender its economic monopoly in the eighteenth century, when it was forced to allow its provincial notables to sell directly to European merchants. In 1829, the Treaty of Adrianople forced it to permit the notables of Wallachia and Moldavia, the emerging agrarian middle class, to sell their agricultural produce to foreign merchants at higher market prices rather than the lower prices set by the state. The Anglo-Ottoman Commercial Convention of 1838 established Ottoman economic policy until the abolition of capitulation in September 1914. It gave important commercial privileges to Britain, which at that time was embarking on the second phase of its industrial revolution; Britain required markets for her goods and she therefore engaged the Ottomans in the economic and political network of an emerging industrial civilization. The convention removed all state monopolies and allowed British merchants to purchase goods throughout the Ottoman Empire, including Egypt, which remained nominally part of the empire until 1914 when it became a British protectorate. As a result, Egypt's state-driven economy was destroyed. Duties were limited to 5 per cent on imports, 12 per cent on exports, and 3 per cent on transit. Initially, the convention was signed by Britain, but other European powers were soon given the same privileges. The Porte was able to have import duties raised to 8 per cent in the 1861–2 negotiations and to 11 per cent in 1907. The attempt to raise these duties by a further 4 per cent failed dismally. In short, the duties established by the regime of the capitulations did not provide the protection the domestic market needed to industrialize, and the attempt to industrialize after 1847 ended in abject failure and was never made again.

Duties could not be raised unilaterally by the Porte and required the consent of all the signatories. That was the stipulation that Britain imposed on the capitulation after she signed a treaty with the Ottomans in 1809; the capitulations were no longer seen by Europe as privileges granted unilaterally by the sultan, but rights negotiated by the Powers, rights that could be altered only by multilateral agreement. The capitulations and other treaties became a heavy burden on the Porte, a burden that the Ottomans were only able to shed after Europe was at war in 1914.

THE MOVEMENT TOWARDS WESTERNIZATION

Apart from a desire to destroy Mehmed Ali's experiment in modernization, Ottoman statesmen believed that the Ottoman Empire would benefit greatly by being integrated into the world market that the British were in the process of creating. In 1824 Mahmud had taken away the privileges that protected Ottoman merchants, forcing them to compete with foreign merchants without state protection. That measure began to undermine Ottoman commerce and manufactures, a process that was completed by the 1838 convention. The new agrarian middle class benefited from the liberalization of trade, for they were able to sell their produce at prices higher than those paid by the state. Merchants who sold foreign imports and acted as middlemen on behalf of European companies also prospered. But the crafts withered, unable to withstand the competition of cheaper, machine-made goods from Europe. Such ports as İzmir, Istanbul, Salonica, and Beirut prospered as more and more goods were imported and exported, and that created a vibrant economic climate that led to the immigration of Greeks from a stagnant Greece to a dynamic Ottoman Empire.

The benefits of free trade went disproportionately to the Christian communities of the empire because they were able to become the protégés of foreign merchants residing in Ottoman lands. As interpreted by the Powers, the capitulations permitted them to sell protection to their co-religionists and to make them protégés, thereby giving them the same protection they had enjoyed under the capitulations. The French consuls were able to make protégés, of Ottoman Catholics, the British of Protestants, and the Russians of Orthodox Christians. Only Jewish Ottomans were excluded because there was no Jewish nation. With the creation of a united Italy, Italian consuls took it upon themselves to sell Italian protection to a few Ottoman Jews. Consequently, the Jewish community tended to identify with the problems of the Muslim Ottomans, including their quest for a new patriotic identity. Not only did such a status allow Ottoman Christian merchants to benefit from lower taxes, it also meant that Ottoman authorities were unable to apply Ottoman laws since they could be brought only before consular courts.

EMERGENCE OF A NEW MIDDLE CLASS

Since a commercial/industrial Muslim middle class did not emerge as a result of the liberalization and the integration of the empire into the world economy, the Porte turned to the landlords to create a class that would be totally loyal to the new state that the bureaucrats were fashioning. The land code of 1858 was a step towards legalizing the private ownership of land. Earlier, in 1847, the Porte had passed a law whose aim was to encourage cultivators to farm unused state lands. Instead of being used by landless peasants, this law was manipulated by local landlords to augment their holdings, making them more prosperous and politically powerful. In regions where tribal life was prevalent, land was registered in the name of the tribal leaders, who became the landowners and their clansmen the peasants. One of the aims of this land code was to settle the tribes. Most of these landlords farmed their lands using peasants as share-croppers, hardly encouraging innovation on the land. However, some became capitalist farmers and grew such cash crops as tobacco and cotton, and prospered especially during and after the American civil war, when demand for their cotton grew on the European market. These are the men who emerged as the new middle class in the twentieth century, after the constitutional revolution of 1908.

The initiative for reform passed entirely to the bureaucrats on the death of Mahmud II on 30 June 1839. His successor, Abdülmecid I (1839–61), was only sixteen when he came to the throne and was guided by Mustafa Reşid Pasha, one of the great reforming statesmen of the era. Abdülmecid became sultan at a critical juncture during the crisis with Mehmed Ali, and Reşid Pasha persuaded him that if he carried out reforms that modernized the empire he would win the support of Europe, especially that of Great Britain. Abdülmecid agreed and launched an era of reform (1839–76) known collectively as the *Tanzimat*.

TANZIMAT (RESTRUCTURING)

The first proclamation (the Charter of the Rose Chamber) was announced on 3 November 1838. This promised the beginning of a new age with equality for all – Muslim and non-Muslim – the end of bribery and corruption and no punishment without trial, that is to say, it established the rule of law. The lives, honour and property of all Ottoman subjects were guaranteed, putting an end to the status of *kul* under which the sultan's servants could be executed at the ruler's whim and their property confiscated. The last such political execution had taken place in 1837, when Mahmud II had Pertev Pasha killed because of palace intrigue, and the lesson was not lost on Reşid Pasha. The charter gave state officials the security of life and property and they came into their own. Tax-farming was also abolished, but within a few years the law was sabotaged by tax-farmers who had much to lose and the practice continued until the end of the empire.

The Charter of 1839 was a crucial step in the process of secularization, which continued until the dissolution of the empire and beyond. While it undermined the principle of the traditional *millet* system, based on privileges for religious communities, the communities were unwilling to abandon their privileges at the same time as welcoming the equality. The Great Powers were asked to observe its implementation; in fact, they were invited to implicitly supervise Ottoman affairs if the Porte did not live up to its promise. They were being made the guarantors of reform. The *Tanzimat* statesmen calculated that if the sultan strayed from the path of reform, the European ambassadors would bring him back to the path since there was no internal social force that could do so. They relied on the support of the foreign embassies to keep up the pressure for Westernization. Stratford de Redcliffe (1786–1880), Britain's ambassador at the Porte, played a particularly important role in the Westernization movement of the bureaucracy; in fact, some scholars claim that the charter was largely his work, as he was considered to be a most influential figure among the Ottoman Westernizing reformers. He had spent much of his professional life in Istanbul before he became Britain's ambassador in 1847 and remained in Istanbul until 1858 where he was known as the 'Grand Ambassador', the doyen of the diplomatic corps. He disliked Russia and her influence, as directed through the Orthodox Church, and he promoted Protestantism as an alternative. He succeeded in having the Protestant Church and community recognized as a separate *millet* in 1850, even as he promoted Westernization and reform.

Just as the Charter of 1839 followed the Mehmed Ali crisis, the second Royal Charter was proclaimed on 18 February 1856, while the Congress was meeting in Paris (February–March 1856) to settle the Eastern Question after the Crimean War. The Crimean War broke out when the Sublime Porte refused to accept a proposal by Russia that she be allowed to protect Orthodox Christians in the empire. Supported by Britain and France, the Ottomans declared war on Russia on 23 September 1853. The British and French joined the war in March 1854 and the fighting took place on the Crimean peninsula. The Tsar agreed to make peace on 1 February 1856, when he was faced with defeat and the threat of Austria joining the anti-Russian coalition.

The Crimean War had other local results. Trade in Western commodities increased dramatically as European armies camped in the environs of the capital. The first telegraphic lines were laid between Europe and the Ottoman Empire, revolutionizing communications, especially for commercial purposes. Modern war and the example of Florence Nightingale's work in the Crimea led to the founding of the Ottoman counterpart of the Red Cross Society, in June 1868. Called simply the 'Society for helping sick and wounded Ottoman Soldiers', it was renamed 'the Ottoman Red Crescent Society' in June 1877 and continues as such to the present.

By the Treaty of Paris, Russia surrendered the mouth of the Danube and a part of Bessarabia to the future Rumania; the province of Kars in the Caucasus was given to the Porte, and Russia agreed to renounce her claim to protect the Orthodox Church in the Ottoman Empire. The Black Sea was neutralized until the treaty was revised in 1871. The Ottoman Empire was included in the European Concert system and the Powers guaranteed its independence and territorial integrity. But the Ottomans were not considered a European state and so were not granted equality. The Ottoman proposal to abrogate the capitulations was ignored, as the Powers claimed that Ottoman society and its laws were too alien for Europeans to live under. Nevertheless, in order to further the process of Westernization and secularization, the royal charter of 1856 reaffirmed the terms of the 1839 charter and defined in more precise terms equality between Muslim and Christian subjects. But the European powers saw the question of equality totally differently. The Porte saw equality as equality before the law for all Ottoman subjects, with communal privileges restricted to religious affairs, and the religious community (*millet*) reduced to a congregation (*cemaat*). For Russians, equality meant the extension of the religious communities' right to autonomy if not independence. For the British, equality meant the equality of the *millets* as corporate communities and not equality between Christians and Muslims as Ottoman subjects as the Porte proposed. The Porte also carried out educational measures that would promote understanding between the communities and lead to the success of Ottomanism, an ideology that focused loyalty around the person of the sultan and the dynasty. The opening of the Lycée of Galatasaray in 1868 was intended to bring together the intelligentsia of all communities in a secular environment to promote unity. After initial resistance from virtually all the communities, the institution flourished and was followed by other foreign religious institutions, such as Robert College, founded by American missionaries. These institutions stimulated the growth, not of Ottomanism but of national sentiment, among the cosmopolitan student body of the empire.

The Charter of 1856 strengthened the position of the Christian population, especially that of the rising middle class, while that of its Muslim counterpart became weaker. The Christian communities were secularized and the hold of their clergy weakened. The communities began to acquire the characteristics of individual 'nations' and began to undergo a 'renaissance' during which they recovered their history, language, and literature. In 1863, the Armenian community had its own constitution and a 'national' assembly, which heightened national aspirations. In February 1870, the Porte permitted the creation of the Bulgarian Church, independent of the authority of the Greek Orthodox Church. The Bulgarian Exarch was appointed head of the Bulgarian *millet* and the Exarchate began the task of creating the Bulgarian state and the Bulgarian individual. Services were thereafter conducted in Bulgarian, the language of Sofia, and local dialects were discouraged, especially when the language was introduced in schools.

The Muslims received none of these benefits from the *Tanzimat* reforms. There was no 'national' Church with which they could identify, as Islam remained a universal religion. Economically they found it more difficult to compete against the protected Christian merchants. Therefore they began to abandon commerce and industry and seek employment in the state bureaucracy and army. Initially, after the reforms of Mahmud II, the bureaucracy grew and absorbed this population, providing it with a modern education and secure employment. But by the 1860s, the Ottoman bureaucracy had reached saturation point; not only was it more difficult to find work in the bureaucracy, but promotion came to depend on patronage. Those who were affected by this new trend – the new intelligentsia – blamed the *Tanzimat* statesmen for the deterioration of the empire and for their own plight because of the concessions they had made to Europe and to Ottoman Christians.

THE YOUNG OTTOMANS MOVEMENT

A new movement known as the 'Young Ottomans' rose out of this popular discontent. This was the first modern opposition movement critical of the regime. The Young Ottomans rebuked the high bureaucrats, the pashas, for making the Europeans, the Levantines (people of European origin who settled in the empire), and some Christians, a privileged group while neglecting the Muslim population. They criticized the Porte for making economic concessions to Europe and undermining the empire's economy. All the reforms of the *Tanzimat* had not led to the creation of a modern economy; they had merely led to the subordination of the Ottoman economy to that of Europe. Some regions of the empire had been totally integrated into the economy of a European country and their links with Istanbul were weakened. Syria's economy was integrated into that of France and Iraq's into that of Britain, so that when the Ottoman Empire was partitioned after the First World War, these regions were mandated to these countries.

But the Young Ottomans were also the products of the *Tanzimat* era. They emerged out of the influence of the press and education of those years, which permitted the growth of an intelligentsia. Such intellectuals as İbrahim Şinasi (1824–71) expressed novel ideas in the journals that were read only by the literate few, but heard by the many when their ideas were read in the coffee houses of the cities and towns. The Porte responded by trying to curb the press and introducing laws which punished ideas critical of the regime. This led the intelligentsia to found secret societies devoted to the fall of the regime.

The recognition of Ismail Pasha as the hereditary Khedive (ruler) of Egypt in 1867 had unintended consequences for the Young Ottomans. The introduction of primogeniture alienated his brother Mustafa Fazıl, who was next in line to Ismail, and made him a dissident and one of the leaders of the Young Ottomans movement. While in exile in Europe in 1867, he wrote an open letter to Sultan Abdülaziz (r.1861–76) recommending constitutional monarchy as a solution to the empire's problems and calling for a government that guaranteed all liberal freedoms. The Young Ottomans wanted to end the autocracy of the sultan and his bureaucrats, convinced that the laws of the state could not be reformed under absolutism. The Porte responded by taking harsh measures against its critics, and such journalists as Namık Kemal (1840–88) and Ali Suavi (1838–78) were forced to leave Istanbul. Having failed to take over the government in Istanbul, the opposition regrouped in France, where they formed the Young Ottomans Society and continued their opposition to the Porte in a more sympathetic environment.

In their journals the Young Ottomans repeatedly called for a constitution and representative government, the first to establish a contract between the sultan and his subjects, and the second to discuss and legislate on the affairs of the empire. They emphasized the deterioration in the economic life of the people and the financial situation of the state, and lamented the Porte's dependence on the Great Powers and their increasing interference in Ottoman affairs. These factors were undermining the relationship between Muslim and non-Muslim subjects, all of which did not bode well for the future. For them, the solution was to establish a government in which the people participated and in which the sultan was subject to law.

But the Young Ottomans did not propose revolutionary change. Their objective was not to overthrow the system, but merely to reform it so that it was more inclusive and capable of standing up to European expansion. They belonged to the intelligentsia and lacked a social base that was radically different from the elite. Education and culture alienated them from the peasantry and the urban classes of artisans and merchants of the bazaar. Far from wishing to incite revolution, they were convinced that the only way to bring about real change was to bring to the throne a ruler sympathetic to their ideas.

Namık Kemal expressed the ideas of Ottoman liberalism coherently and consequently became the most influential thinker among the Young Ottomans, with ideas that were significant during his lifetime and long after his death. His poetry, plays and essays were widely read by the intelligentsia, even though they were banned by the regime. Apart from developing the notion of liberty, he introduced the doctrine of natural rights, perhaps for the first time in Islamic thought, as well as the idea of *vatan* (*patrie* or fatherland) and territorial patriotism, and the sovereignty of the people. Patriotism/Ottomanism was the most potent of his ideas: all Ottomans, regardless of their religion or language, owed loyalty not to the Ottoman dynasty but to their Ottoman fatherland. His ideas came mainly from post-revolutionary France, but were expressed in terms that would be comprehended by his Islamic milieu because he was able to reconcile them with the Sharia. Rousseau's social contract was explained as the Islamic oath of allegiance (*biat*) that established a contract between the ruler and the ruled. The Sharia was malleable and capable of adapting to progress no matter where it came from. Unlike earlier critics of

Ottoman decline, Namık Kemal argued that it was impossible to go back to an imagined glorious past, but legitimate to adopt such practices as constitutionalism that had been already tried successfully in he West.

While in exile in Europe, Namık Kemal came to fully understand the importance of contemporary Western advances in technology. But he realized that the Ottomans could only make material progress after they had abandoned the traditions of fatalism and adopted the ideas of freedom and progress. The Ottomans had failed to make rapid progress, not because Islam was the barrier, but because the empire had become part of the world market and its economy and political life was dominated by Europe. That was the shortcoming that had to be rectified.

BANKRUPTCY AND UPHEAVAL: UNRAVELLING OF THE OTTOMAN EMPIRE

While the Young Ottomans criticized the results of the *Tanzimat* reforms, the empire was heading for a financial crisis that forced the Porte to declare bankruptcy in October 1875. The empire had remained financially solvent until the government had to borrow money from Europe in 1854 during the Crimean War. The money raised from European loans was not used productively to create an infrastructure for a modern economy by building roads and railways so as to create a 'national' market. Instead the Court spent huge sums in ostentatious consumption, building modern palaces, buying arms from Europe and building a large navy. Huge sums of borrowed money were spent on royal weddings. When a royal princess died in 1880, she left behind the considerable debt of 16,000 gold liras, money borrowed from the Galata bankers.

The empire's economic, financial, and political situation was adversely affected by the outbreak of peasant rebellion in Herzegovina in 1875. What began as a peasant uprising against abuses by landlords, soon acquired religious and national overtones, of Christian Slavs against their Muslim overlords. The leadership of the movement began calling for union with their Slavic brothers in Serbia, and this won them the support of the pan-Slav movement in Russia which hoped to expand its influence in the Balkans. That is precisely what the Austrians feared, as

Slavic nationalism would block Vienna's expansion to the Aegean Sea and the port of Salonika. The situation became even more complicated in May 1876, when the Bulgarians revolted against the Ottomans and Serbia and Montenegro declared war. The strategic interests of the Great Powers clashed and they were therefore unable to resolve the conflict diplomatically. The Russians supported the rebels; the Austro-Hungarians opposed them, fearing the impact of the pan-Slavic movement in their own empire. Britain was fearful that Russia's growing influence in the region would adversely affect her own position. German unification in 1870/71 added a new player to the diplomatic game, making it even more complex.

The Ottomans suppressed the rebellion with great ferocity, soundly defeating the Serbs and Montenegrins. In Britain, William Gladstone, the leader of the Liberal Party, exploited the Ottoman suppression of the Bulgarian rebellion against Prime Minister Benjamin Disraeli, his pro-Ottoman Tory rival. He denounced the Ottomans as barbarians who had committed atrocities against Christian Bulgarians, and appealed for British support for the rebels. In that climate, the Russians declared war in April 1877, captured Plevna after a long siege that delayed their advance, and arrived at the outskirts of Istanbul during the spring of 1878. There, at the village of San Stefano (today's Yeşilköy), Russia dictated peace terms to the Porte: an enlarged Bulgaria, extending to the Aegean Sea, was to become autonomous, cutting off Ottoman access to the provinces of Albania and Macedonia; Rumania, Serbia, and Montenegro were to be granted independence, while Russia annexed the provinces of Kars, Ardahan, and Batum in the Caucasus; as compensation, Vienna was to be allowed to administer Bosnia-Herzegovina.

Britain was unwilling to accept these Russian gains and sent warships to Istanbul. Bismarck, the German chancellor, fearing a Great Power confrontation, acted as 'honest broker'. He convened the Congress of Berlin (June–July 1878) and revised the Treaty of San Stefano, settling the Eastern Question by achieving a balance in the region between Russia, Austria-Hungary, and Britain. Autonomous Bulgaria was reduced in size and the province of Eastern Rumelia, nominally Ottoman but with a Christian governor, was established south of Bulgaria; it united with

Bulgaria in 1881. The independence of Serbia, Montenegro, and Rumania was confirmed, as was Russia's annexations in the Caucasus and Vienna's administration of Bosnia-Herzegovina. With the Cyprus Convention of 4 June, the Ottomans ceded the strategic island of Cyprus to Britain in return for the promise of British protection against further Russian encroachments in Anatolia. Other lands ceded by the Porte at San Stefano were restored to the Ottoman Empire. The Treaty of Berlin also included Article LXI, by which the Porte undertook to carry out, under the supervision of the Powers, 'the ameliorations and the reforms ... in the provinces inhabited by the Armenians and to guarantee their security against the Circassians and the Kurds'. That was a crucial provision that had dire consequences for the future of the Ottoman–Armenian relationship. As a result of the congress, the Ottomans lost about 40 per cent of their empire and about 20 per cent of their population (about two million Muslims). Many fled to Istanbul and Anatolia as refugees from the Balkans, and the population of Istanbul is thought to have doubled as a result of the crisis and war.

FROM AUTOCRACY TO CONSTITUTIONALISM

Rebellion and war confronted the Porte with a severe conundrum. It was able to crush the rebellion and wage war successfully against its enemies in the Balkans, but was in a dilemma as to how it should deal with the Great Powers. The reformers decided that the empire required a constitutional monarchy so as to win the sympathy and support of Europe. Such a regime would not be possible under Sultan Abdülaziz and he was therefore forced to abdicate on 30 May 1876, committing suicide four days later.

Midhat Pasha (1822–84) the great reforming statesman, believed that under the new sultan they could establish a constitutional regime with an elected assembly that would curb the corruption of the Palace and bring financial order to the empire. But Murad V turned out to be mentally impaired and was therefore dethroned and replaced by Abdülhamid II (r.1876–1909). He came to the throne on 31 August, having promised Midhat that he would rule as a constitutional monarch. He ordered the preparation of a constitution, calculating that a constitutional regime would prevent European intervention and that the Powers would allow the empire to manage its own affairs. But the Great Powers had already decided to hold an international conference in Istanbul to discuss the crisis in the Balkans and the measures necessary to resolve it.

The conference met on 23 December 1876 and the Porte proclaimed the inauguration of the constitutional regime on the same day, suggesting that the conference had become redundant. But the ambassadors refused to accept this logic and proposed a plan of reform for the Balkans that granted autonomy for Bulgaria and Bosnia-Herzegovina. When the Porte rejected this proposal, the ambassadors issued the warning that they would leave the capital and that, in such circumstances, Russia might declare war. The Porte reconsidered the plan and rejected it once more, whereupon the ambassadors left Istanbul, leaving the situation up in the air. But the constitutional experiment continued even though its principal architect, Grand Vizier Midhat Pasha, was dismissed by the sultan and exiled. Elections were held on 20 March 1877. They were indirect, two-tiered elections in which the notables of each religious community elected its own representatives to the assembly; in the upper house or the Chamber of Notables, members were appointed by the sultan.

The rapid transition from autocracy to constitutionalism was quite an accomplishment for the reformers. In less than a decade they had apparently managed to accomplish what had taken centuries in Europe, and what the Russian reformers were able to achieve a generation later, and then only after a revolution. Moreover, the Assembly, representing the various *millets*, acted with surprising patriotism in the face of an ongoing crisis and war. While there was criticism of the government, it was couched in constructive and rational terms, which betrayed loyalty to the idea of Ottomanism and the state. But war turned out to be inauspicious for the continuation of constitutional government. Russia declared war on 24 April 1877. When the Russian army advanced towards the capital the following year, the sultan was given a pretext to suspend parliament. In February 1878, parliament was suspended and did not reconvene for the next thirty years, until the restoration of the constitution in July 1908. But Abdülhamid maintained the fiction that he was acting according to the constitution throughout his reign. Laws that he enacted, he said, would be debated by the Assembly when it met again, and he did his constitutional duty and appointed members to the Chamber of Notables until 1880. The war against Russia, Europe's partisan attitude towards the Ottomans and the crisis in the Balkans shattered the illusions of the reformers with regard to Europe's attitude towards the Muslim world. The reformers were faced with the contradiction of adopting Western ideas and institutions while struggling against Western imperialism.

European hegemony around the world during the second half of the nineteenth century alienated people from the West and Westernization and encouraged them to turn to their indigenous traditions and nativism. This was as true for India and Asia as for the Islamic world. Such Ottoman thinkers as Namık Kemal were in the forefront of this movement, and Abdülhamid encouraged this trend, for it added to his popularity throughout the Muslim world and weakened the arguments of the opposition. Islam was under pressure from Western imperialism in Iran and India, North Africa and South-East Asia. Muslims around the world saw the Ottoman Empire as the last remaining Islamic power capable of standing up to the West, and Sultan Abdülhamid as the universal caliph of the Islamic world leading the resistance. The sultan exploited the office of caliph to bolster his position against the West, and used political Islam as an ideology in the struggle against imperialism. He is described as a pan-Islamist, but his purpose was to use Islam for a defensive, not aggressive, purpose; he called for Islamic unity and solidarity and in that he was partly successful. Abdülhamid's policy was facilitated by the historical conjunction that was marked by the rise of imperial Germany. He won the support of the German kaiser, who had no Muslim colonies and who could therefore befriend a Muslim ruler and use this friendship against Germany's imperial rivals – Britain, France, and Russia. Kaiser Wilhelm II paid a state visit to the Ottoman Empire in October 1898, the only European ruler to do so. After Istanbul he went to Jerusalem, riding into the city on a black charger, and placed a wreath on the tomb of Saladin, the great Muslim hero who had defeated the crusaders. The kaiser then proclaimed himself a friend of the Muslim peoples, cementing a relation that led to the German–Ottoman alliance during the First World War.

EMERGING TRADITIONALISM

Compared to Ottomanism and Islam, the ideology of Turkism remained marginal and restricted to a small minority of intellectuals who were familiar with the works of or personally knew such European Turcologists as the Frenchman Leon Cahun (1841–1900) or the Hungarian Arminus Vambery (1832–1913); the latter was a friend of Abdülhamid and is alleged to have acted as his spy among the dissidents! Muslim intellectuals who came to Istanbul from Russia were more conscious of being 'Turks'. They brought with them the idea of nationalism for they had confronted the ideology of Slavism on a daily basis in the Russian Empire. Such activists as İsmail Gasparinski (1851–1914), Yusuf Akçura (1876–1935) and Ahmet Ağayev (1869–1939) popularized the ideology of Turkism. But they could not make it the dominant ideology and replace Ottomanism/Islamism while Turks ruled over a multi-ethnic, multi-religious empire.

Even after the settlement of the Congress of Berlin, the Great Powers continued to pressure the Ottoman Empire as they consolidated their hold on the region. In May 1881 France established a protectorate over Tunisia to forestall Italian ambitions, totally disregarding the promise of Ottoman territorial integrity made at Berlin. Egypt's financial troubles, the declaration of bankruptcy, and the anti-regime rebellion in the army led to British intervention in September 1882, followed by an occupation that lasted until 1954. In the Balkans and Greece, the struggle to satisfy national aspirations continued. The Greek attempt to wrest the island of Crete in 1897 led to a war that the Ottomans won on the battlefield but lost at the peace table. Thanks to Great Power intervention, the sultan was forced to give up Thessaly and establish an autonomous regime in Crete, the prelude to the island's annexation in 1912.

Macedonia, the region between Albania and Thrace, was contested by Greeks, Bulgarians, Serbs, and Muslims. Macedonia's principal city, Salonika, was predominantly Jewish, inhabited by Jews who had been expelled from Spain after 1492 and who were pro-Ottoman. All the communities organized guerrilla bands to fight for their own national cause, creating a situation of political confusion that invited foreign intervention. The Powers called for reform and the Porte agreed to take measures that would appease the Christian population. But Russia and Austria, who had conflicting interests in the region, found the Porte's reform measures unsatisfactory and made proposals of their own. In 1903, they succeeded in establishing quasi-foreign control over Macedonia, but violence continued until the constitutional revolution of July 1908, which established temporary harmony between the communities.

The Armenian community in Asia Minor was affected by the growth of nationalism in the region throughout the nineteenth century. Missionary activity stimulated a cultural renaissance, leading to a revival of the classical language and literature, as well as the secularization of communal life. The Armenian intelligentsia began to agitate for representative government within the community, as well as protection from tribal and feudal elements which dominated the region. Russia patronized the reform movement and Article LXI of the Berlin Treaty promised joint action if the Ottoman government failed to satisfy Armenian demands. The Armenians organized themselves to struggle for national rights and found support from neighbouring Russia. But the Armenian movement was divided, with some willing to struggle alongside the Young Ottomans, later the Young Turks, so as to bring about a liberal regime that would satisfy Armenian aspirations. These were members of the class of notables, mainly merchants, bankers and professionals, who benefited from being part of a large empire rather than members of a small national state. Those who wanted to create a nation state in Asia Minor were farmers and provincial merchants, and they emulated the Balkan example of provoking European intervention on behalf of their cause. The attempt to provoke intervention failed when they seized the Imperial Ottoman Bank, an Anglo-French institution, in Istanbul in August 1896, but the Great Powers were too divided to act in concert and intervene. As a result, the Armenian movement was crushed for the moment.

Apart from dealing with Great Power involvement in the affairs of his empire, Abdülhamid carried out reforms in many areas in order to put his house in order. Finance was a principal concern, and the possibility of European financial control, as in Tunisia and Egypt, leading to occupation, seemed real. So in November 1881, the sultan agreed to the creation of the Ottoman Public Debt (OPD), an institution independent of the finance ministry, to service the empire's loans. The delegates to the OPD were provided by England, France, Germany, Holland, Italy, and the Ottoman Empire, and the Ottoman Public Debt soon had a staff larger than the Ottoman finance ministry. It collected some of the most important taxes and paid the foreign bondholders from its receipts. The sultan introduced new taxes to make up for the shortfall, but he failed to tax the incomes of thousands of foreigners, as well as the thousands of protégés, who were able to take advantage of the capitulation treaties.

As a result of the creation of the OPD administration, foreign investors had greater confidence in the sultan's financial regime and the future of the empire. Consequently, foreign capital was invested in the empire to create an economic infrastructure of railways, roads, mines, and steamships, integrating the empire more closely into the expanding world market. Limited progress was made with the telephone system because Abdülhamid feared that it would be used for subversive purposes, but railway, road, and port construction increased dramatically during his reign, though never sufficiently to meet the needs of empire.

Abdülhamid understood the importance of agriculture and therefore promoted its development by founding specialist societies. The founding of the Agricultural Bank in 1888 was of great significance, for its aim was to regulate credit to farmers and cut out the moneylenders. Unfortunately, only the large landowners benefited by obtaining loans to enlarge and improve their holdings, while the small subsistence farmer could not obtain money and therefore stuck to old methods of cultivation. There was an expansion of large farms and farmers growing cash crops such as tobacco, cotton, figs, and olives that could be marketed for export. These prospered and became the rural bourgeoisie, influential in political life after 1908.

Commerce benefited from the export of agricultural goods and minerals. Unprotected industry, on the other hand, could not compete against the imports from Europe. Consequently, industry was local and small scale and artisans concentrated on such goods as leather, glass, cloth, paper, and hand-woven carpets. As a result, Ottoman industry remained underdeveloped, and only during the republic were measures taken to industrialize.

Politically, Abdülhamid's educational reforms proved to be the most significant, for they helped to undermine his regime. By introducing these reforms, the sultan dug his own political grave! Thus during his reign, education among the Muslim population expanded dramatically, though not as rapidly as among the non-Muslim communities. Attention was focused on middle and high schools and primary education was neglected so that overall illiteracy remained high. But secular education, especially for military and bureaucratic careers, became the ladder of upward mobility for the urban lower middle class. The Hamidian schools allowed people of the lower middle class to rise up the social ladder by joining the army. Many members of the Young Turks movement came from this social class and education enabled them to enter the bureaucracy. However, many in the same social group preferred the religious schools, the *medrese*, and opted for careers as lower *ulema*, as preachers in mosques. The secularly educated officers tended to be anti-Hamidian, and the sultan was always wary of the so-called *mektepli*, that is to say, the academy-trained, secularized officers. He therefore promoted officers who lacked such education but had risen from the ranks, their principal quality being their loyalty to the Ottoman throne. This duality in education continued until the end of empire and the two societies – the secular and the religious – lived side by side.

Education was the catalyst that produced the new and potentially revolutionary movement. Prior to the Hamidian reforms, members of the opposition belonged to the counter-elite. Such people – Ahmed Rıza (1859–1930) and Prince Sabaheddin (1877–1948), and many Young Turks in exile – did not want to change the political and social system, but merely to make it more inclusive and modern. Ahmed Rıza was extremely wary of Western involvement in Ottoman affairs, while Prince Sabaheddin was willing to use Western intervention to overthrow the sultan and establish a new regime. Abdülhamid was able to buy off many exiles by offering them sinecures in his regime; for them that was inclusion!

But members of the lower middle class, born in the 1870s and 1880s, who benefited from the new secular schools, considered the restoration of the constitution as just the beginning. They wanted to transform not just the political but the social, economic, and cultural life of the empire and turn their movement into a revolution. Not surprisingly, the older leaders – Ahmed Rıza and Prince Sabaheddin – who were socially conservative, played only a minor role after 1908, Sabaheddin as the leader of the Liberal opposition. The political initiative passed to a different social class in 1908, opening a new page in Ottoman history.

SUGGESTED FURTHER READING

Stanford Shaw and Ezel Kural Shaw, *History of the Ottoman Empire and Modern Turkey, vol. ii: Reform, Revolution, and Republic, 1808–1975* (Cambridge University Press, 1977).

Niyazi Berkes, *The Development of Secularism in Turkey* (Hurst and Company, London, 1998; first edn, Montreal, 1964).

Bernard Lewis, *The Emergence of Modern Turkey*, 3rd edn (Oxford University Press, 2002).

Donald Quataert, *The Ottoman Empire, 1700–1922* (Cambridge University Press, 2000).

3

The Constitutional Revolution, Reform, and War, 1908–1918

RESTORATION OF THE CONSTITUTION

Figuratively speaking, the Ottoman Empire entered the twentieth century on 23 July 1908, the day Sultan Abdülhamid II (r.1876–1909) restored the constitution he had shelved thirty years earlier. His decision generated great optimism and euphoria throughout the empire, as the new era held the promise of 'liberty, equality and justice' for all its citizens. Muslims and non-Muslims, as well as the various ethnic communities – Greeks, Bulgars, Macedonians, Armenians, Arabs, Kurds, Jews and Turks – embraced each other in the streets in anticipation of the constitutional age. Overnight, the press was free to publish without fear of censorship; people congregated in coffee houses, knowing that there were no Palace spies in their midst. In towns and cities, crowds marched with banners and musical bands to the governors' offices and made speeches in praise of the new order. An amnesty was declared for political prisoners, and exiles began to return to Istanbul from Europe, Egypt, and other parts of the far-flung empire.

In the provinces, the event was celebrated with equal gusto. The heads of various committees who had opposed the sultan's autocracy promised to cooperate and swore oaths of loyalty to the empire. The sultan's advisers, though not the sultan himself, were held responsible for the autocracy; by restoring the constitution without a struggle, Abdülhamid had succeeded in hijacking the movement. The Committee of Union and Progress (CUP), the principal architect of the constitutional movement, halted the insurrection and threatened to renew the struggle should Abdülhamid go back on his word. As the old regime collapsed, there was a breakdown of law and order. The Committee attempted to assume control; for the time being it was the only body that had the prestige and authority to support the government.

But the CUP had always been a secret organization with its roots in Macedonia. There was no hierarchy in which responsibility proceeded up and down the pyramid instead of outwards. There was no recognized leadership, and the CUP has therefore been described as a 'party of leaders' who made decisions by consensus in the central committee elected by the general congress. It had no well-defined ideology; its goal was to 'save the empire', and to reform it so that its multi-religious, multi-ethnic society could survive in the world of the twentieth century. Because Ottoman society was predominantly Muslim, Unionist liberals could not secularize the constitution by removing the Clause XI that declared that Islam was the religion of the state. Islamists among the Unionists argued that the constitution was in accord with the Sharia, the holy law of Islam, because the Sharia sanctioned consultation or *meşveret*. Thus the Unionists maintained the fiction that the Sharia prevailed under the constitution, though conservatives claimed that it did not. For the moment, the Unionists had succeeded in carrying out a coup d'état within the ruling elite rather than a revolution among the social classes. But within a year, they began to introduce reforms that shook society. By calling for elections to elect the assembly, they changed the social composition of parliament and the cabinet, giving representation to local elites – Muslim and non-Muslim, Turk and non-Turk. These elites, in turn, altered the character of the legislation.

The period of celebration came to an end in late August. There followed a spate of strikes by workers who believed that the constitution would also ameliorate their situation. However, they were wrong, for the constitutionalists believed that the economic order required social peace with disciplined and subservient workers. The constitutional regime also alarmed foreign powers, who feared that a resurgent Ottoman empire would naturally try and curb their imperialist ambitions. The British were concerned about the impact of successful constitutionalism on Egypt and India, and therefore adopted a cautious, and sometimes hostile, attitude towards the constitutionalists. Other powers acted more vigorously. In October, Bulgaria declared its independence and Vienna annexed Bosnia-Herzegovina, while the island of Crete announced its decision to unite with Greece. These events were serious blows which struck at the new regime and undermined its prestige.

In Istanbul, the Liberals who dominated the bureaucracy of the Sublime Porte – the seat of government – pressured the CUP to vacate the political stage now that power had been wrested from the Palace. But the Unionists refused to leave, convinced that they would be able to exert even more influence after the December elections that they intended to win. The Unionists, coming from the lower middle class of Muslim society, realized that they lacked the social status to rule directly by taking over the cabinet. They therefore counted on controlling the government by dominating parliament.

The results of the 1908 elections disappointed Liberal hopes and confirmed Unionist expectations. They seemed to win an overwhelming majority, though Grand Vizier Kamil Pasha was sure that the CUP would not command a majority when parliament convened. For the moment, the sultan acted as a constitutional ruler, while the cabinet set about reforming unconstitutional laws and reorganizing the state so as to create a modern, centralized structure. The aim was to establish a system that would be accepted by the Great Powers, who would then abandon the extra-territorial privileges they enjoyed by virtue of the capitulations. The Palace had been subdued, but the Sublime Porte, that is to say, the bureaucrats supported by the Liberals, hoped to monopolize political power by marginalizing the CUP. Kamil Pasha believed he could do that by gaining control of Ottoman armed forces, a crucial force in the power structure. Consequently, in February 1909, he replaced the ministers of war and marine with his own men, convinced that he had the support of parliament. But members of his own cabinet resigned on the grounds that Kamil had made changes in the cabinet without consulting his colleagues. Parliament met on 13 February in order to question Kamil, claiming that his actions had been unconstitutional. Kamil threatened to resign; instead parliament passed a vote of no confidence against him and his cabinet fell. Hüseyin Hilmi Pasha, an official who had served the old regime but was sympathetic to the Unionist programme of reform, succeeded Kamil.

Kamil's fall was a major setback for the Liberals and for all anti-Unionist elements. They included the non-Muslim elites, particularly the Greek patriarchate, the Palace and the reactionaries, as well as the British embassy. The opposition mounted a bitter press campaign against the CUP and were heartened by the support they received from the embassy. In April, reactionaries came out in opposition to reform and called for a union based on Islam. Through their paper, the *Volkan* ('Volcano'), they appealed to the clerics in parliament, the rank and file in the army, and the urban lower classes.

COUNTER-REVOLUTION

As a result of the anti-Unionist propaganda, the troops of the Istanbul garrison, led by students from the religious schools, mutinied on 13 April 1909. They demanded the restoration of the Sharia (the holy law of Islam), the dismissal of the cabinet, and the seclusion of Muslim women, liberated by the new regime. Hilmi Pasha resigned while Unionist deputies went into hiding, fearing for their lives. Abdülhamid seized the initiative. He accepted all the demands of the rebels and on the following day appointed his protégé, Tevfik Pasha, as the new grand vizier.

It seemed as though the counter-revolution had triumphed and the CUP had been routed. That was the case in Istanbul where the CUP had no roots. But in Macedonia, the situation was different. The Third Army and its Unionist supporters denounced the mutiny as unconstitutional and bombarded the Palace with telegrams threatening retaliation unless the constitutional regime was restored. They demanded the arrest of certain prominent Liberals who they claimed had fanned the flames of counter-revolution. Meanwhile, officers loyal to the constitution organized a force known as the 'Action Army' (*Hareket Ordusu*) and set out from Salonika to restore order in the capital and punish the mutineers.

The Action Army was led by General Mahmud Şevket Pasha, a strict disciplinarian who stood above politics. He refused to be placated by the deputation sent to assure him that the constitutional order was intact and all would be well once order was restored. He invested the capital and occupied it on 24 April after some light action. Meanwhile, the Senate and the Chamber of Deputies formed a 'National Assembly' and convened on 22 April at San Stefano, a Greek village on the Sea of Marmara outside the city. They guaranteed the constitutional regime and went on to depose Sultan Abdülhamid; the Assembly's decision was ratified by the *fetva*, a legal opinion, issued by the *Şeyhulislam*.

In the event of failure in Istanbul, the counter-revolutionaries had intended to provoke foreign intervention by staging the massacre of Armenians in Adana province, a province accessible by sea through the port of Mersin. Hagop Babikian, deputy for Edirne and a member of the commission sent to investigate the massacres, stated the Adana massacres took place because the counter-revolutionaries hated the Armenians for their loyalty to the new regime and the constitution. Therefore they had to destroy the Armenians if they wanted to destroy the constitutional order. But despite the massacres, there was no foreign intervention, though French warships sailed towards Mersin. The balance of power in Europe had changed dramatically after German and Italian unification; unilateral Great Power gunboat diplomacy was no longer possible without threatening the peace of Europe. For its part, the new regime was determined to foster good relations with the non-Muslims. Therefore, on 5 May, the cabinet approved a sum of TL 30,000 for the victims of the Adana massacres; on 12 May the chamber approved a proclamation expressing regret for the events in Adana and enjoining accord and fraternity on all elements of the population in all Anatolian provinces. Colonel Ahmed Cemal Bey (1872–1922) was sent as governor of Adana. Cemal was a leading Unionist officer and often described as one of the Young Turks 'triumvirate', the other two being Enver (1881–1922) and Talat (1874–1921). He took harsh measures against the counter-revolutionaries in order to restore order; for the first time in Ottoman history, a number of prominent Muslim notables were hanged for their role in the massacres.

The restoration of the constitutional regime proved to be a mixed blessing for the CUP. Though the liberal and conservative opponents of the CUP had been crushed as an organized body, they remained alive in spirit. Moreover, the counter-revolution had been suppressed under Mahmud Şevket Pasha's command and he therefore became the dominant force in the government. Unionists became his junior partners, especially after he ordered the army to become independent of all political influences. He was appointed Inspector-General of the First, Second, and Third Army Corps, an appointment that made him independent of the war minister and the cabinet and therefore the virtual dictator of the new regime.

THE ACCESSION OF MEHMED V

Mehmed Reşad, known as Sultan Mehmed V (1844–1918), succeeded Abdülhamid in 1909. Son of Abdülmecid (1839–61), he was considered to be the ideal constitutional monarch. He was sixty-five when he came to the throne and bereft of political experience and personal ambition. He was therefore willing to do the bidding of the government while the CUP maintained their influence in the Palace by having their members appointed to his entourage. Hüseyin Hilmi Pasha was again appointed grand vizier, but his cabinet did not include a single Unionist. Society was not ready to accept members of the lower middle classes in government! The Unionists attempted to have a law modified that would permit deputies – their deputies – to be appointed as under-secretaries to various ministries. In that way, they hoped to influence the working of the cabinet. But parliament refused to modify Article 67 of the constitution and the Unionists were forced, against convention, to place their members directly into the cabinet. Mehmed Cavid (1875–1926), an economist and deputy for Salonika, became finance minister in June 1909 and played a significant role in the years that followed. In August, Mehmed Talat, perhaps the most prominent member of the CUP and grand vizier in 1917, was appointed interior minister, replacing Ferid Pasha who was intimately associated with the old regime.

The Unionists were now secure in the cabinet, but their position in parliament was weak. The committee was unable to exercise discipline among members elected on its platform but who voted against its wishes. It is worth emphasizing that the CUP was not a political party and therefore lacked party discipline. It was a movement that included a variety of interests that competed against each other and often clashed. In March 1909, the CUP had agreed to allow the formation of a parliamentary group or 'party', hoping thereby to instil discipline. But the idea had not worked and deputies belonging to the 'party' had voted against amending Article 67. In February 1910, a splinter group broke away from the CUP and formed the People's Party, destroying the myth of a monolithic committee.

Under Mahmud Şevket's watchful eye, political activity was neutralized. The Liberals were discredited and temporarily eclipsed, while the Unionists were forced to work as the Pasha's junior partners, though he was won over to their programme of reforms and modernization. Meanwhile, the Liberals licked their wounds, reorganized and in November 1911 formed the Party of Freedom and Accord, a coalition of all the anti-Unionist groups in the empire.

After the abortive counter-revolution, the reformers were without opposition and therefore able to pass important laws whose purpose was threefold: first, to write into the constitution the political changes that had taken place since July 1908; second, to modernize and unify the empire and its administrative machinery; and third, to pass legislation that would be acceptable to the Great Powers so that they would agree to the abolition of the capitulations that gave foreigners in the empire a privileged position, placing them outside Ottoman law. The 1909 constitutional amendments took away power from the sultan and vested it in the legislature and the cabinet. But legislation that aimed at unifying and modernizing the empire caused disaffection among the non-Turkish, non-Muslim communities and led to serious revolts in Albania. Nor were the government's attempts to overcome the capitulations any more successful. The Powers temporized, refused to make any concessions and demanded economic concessions from the Porte. Because of these treaties, the empire remained a virtual semi-colony until the Porte abolished the capitulations unilaterally in September 1914, while Europe was at war. Meanwhile, the capitulations obstructed reform, violating Ottoman sovereignty and the very concept of a modern, independent state. Despite all the difficulties, the reforms, especially those of the financial regime under the stewardship of Cavid Bey, made considerable progress. Revenues increased from 148 million liras in 1909 to 184 million in 1910. Even the Ottoman Public Debt administration, a precursor of today's International Monetary Fund, was full of praise for the regime's administrative achievement. In Anatolia, and even in the lawless east, conditions had improved dramatically. The British vice-consul noted that in the province of Van conditions had improved since the constitution and that the peasants no longer feared attacks by Kurdish tribesmen, and were no longer arrested on political grounds, nor did they have to billet government officials and gendarmes.

Despite the reforms and improved conditions, there was considerable political tension, caused partly by Şevket Pasha's capricious behaviour and partly by dissension within the CUP that led to factionalism. The dissension became so acute in 1910/11 that Talat Bey was forced to resign as minister of the interior on 10 February 1911, to be replaced by the more moderate Halil Bey. Such concessions did not lead to political stability and the Committee soon lost control of the assembly. The political situation was aggravated by Italy's declaration of war against the Ottoman Empire and her attack on Tripoli in Libya on 29 September 1911. Grand Vizier İbrahim Hakkı Pasha, who had been ambassador in Rome and had replaced Hilmi Pasha, was forced to resign, to be replaced by the octogenarian, Said Pasha. Mahmud Şevket and the CUP lost much prestige as a result of the war, especially when the Italians captured some of the Greek islands and blockaded the Dardanelles. The Unionists therefore decided, while they had the means to impose their will throughout the empire, to have the Assembly dissolved and to hold early elections in the spring of 1912. The 1912 elections are known as the 'big-stick elections' because the Unionists resorted to coercion and manipulation during the campaign. The CUP won an overwhelming victory but at the expense of alienating their supporters in Macedonia. But the Unionists were not permitted to enjoy power for long. In July 1912, a military group, known as the 'Group of Saviour Officers' and reminiscent of the one that had carried out the coup in 1908, gave an ultimatum to the government and forced Said Pasha's resignation.

BALKAN WARS AND OTTOMAN DEFEATS

The Liberal cabinets that the Saviour Officers brought to power (Ahmed Muhtar Pasha, 21 July to 29 October 1912, and Kamil Pasha, 28 October 1912 to 23 January 1913) were both anti-Unionist and determined to destroy the CUP. Had the Liberals had more time, and received sufficient diplomatic support from the Powers, especially Britain, following Ottoman defeats in the Balkan War, they might have succeeded in destroying the CUP and surviving military defeat. The Balkan allies, Serbia, Montenegro, Bulgaria, and Greece, took advantage of Ottoman political dissension and the ongoing war with Italy and attacked the Ottomans in October 1912. Within weeks, Ottoman armies had been routed and the Balkans lost. Before the outbreak of hostilities on 9 October, Britain's Foreign Secretary, Sir Edward Grey, had declared in the House of Commons that 'Whatever the outcome might be of the hostilities, in no case would the Powers permit any alteration in the status quo.' But such declarations were quickly forgotten following the Ottoman rout. The Bulgarian army was halted at Çatalca, on the very outskirts of Istanbul, in mid-November, and an armistice was concluded on 3 December. Negotiations opened in London in January 1913, but failed because the Porte refused to surrender the town of Edirne or the Aegean islands. Edirne had been the empire's capital before the conquest of Constantinople and was considered vital for the defence of the city and Ottoman morale.

Kamil Pasha was unwilling to take responsibility for ceding Edirne and the Aegean islands in the teeth of opposition in the army. The officers, who had not yet engaged in battle, wanted another round, convinced of victory in the final encounter. The press also opposed surrender while the CUP encouraged popular resistance. On 13 January, the Powers again urged the Porte to cede Edirne and leave the question of the islands to be settled by the Powers. The Porte was warned that renewed hostilities would expose the Empire to even graver perils, and that at the conclusion of peace the Ottomans would need the 'moral and material support' of the Great Powers; such support would be forthcoming to the extent that the Porte listened to the advice of Europe. However, Germany and Austria supported Ottoman resistance because the Unionists argued that Edirne was essential for the defence of the capital and therefore could not be surrendered. Before the cabinet could reach a decision, the Unionists forced Kamil's resignation at gunpoint and seized power on 23 January 1913. Talat declared that 'this movement means that we are going to save the national honour or perish in the attempt. We do not want a continuation of the war, but we are determined to keep Edirne. That is a *sine qua non*'. Şevket Pasha formed the new, moderate cabinet and such prominent Unionists as Talat, Cavid, and Enver were conspicuous by their absence. Mahmud Şevket Pasha remained the dominant political figure.

The situation of the new cabinet was critical. Apart from an empty treasury, the Balkan states were threatening to break off negotiations and resume hostilities. Given the political uncertainty, the Unionists adopted a conciliatory attitude towards the opposition, buying off such prominent leaders as Ali Kemal and Rıza Nur, and sending them to sinecures in Europe. Hostilities were renewed when the armistice expired on 3 February. The Porte appealed for Great Power intervention but was told that Edirne had to be ceded before Europe would intervene. By the end of February, Edirne was ready to fall and the government took measures to foil a Liberal coup whose aim was to make Prince Sabaheddin grand vizier. But the coup d'état had also radicalized the CUP. Contemporaries noted how, since seizing power, the Unionists had begun to emulate the French Commune of 1870, and how Edirne had become the equivalent of Alsace-Lorraine for the Ottomans. Edirne fell on 26 March after a six-month siege, and the fall of the city freed the CUP of the odium of surrendering the Ottoman's second capital without a fight. Nevertheless, the CUP lost some of its prestige. Once again, negotiations were opened and the Porte was offered terms worse than those offered to the Kamil Pasha Cabinet.

After the coup of 23 January, Kamil had gone to Cairo, where he discussed with Lord Kitchener the situation in Istanbul. Kitchener was told that 'he [Kamil] did not expect the present Turkish Government to last very long, and that information had reached him as to the probability of another revolution in the very near future'. Kamil then expressed his willingness to come to power in Istanbul, providing 'he could count on the support of the Entente Powers, and more especially of England'. He asked that Grey consider 'the question whether some adequate foreign control might not be established in regard to administration in Turkey. Such a course was, in his opinion, the only means of preserving Turkey from extinction, and he would be very glad to undertake the task. He added that it would of course be necessary for England and the Powers of the Entente to impose foreign control, as he could not undertake to introduce it himself. Were they, however, to adopt such a policy he would gladly carry it out.'

The Unionists suspected a conspiracy and when Kamil arrived in Istanbul on 28 May he was placed under virtual house arrest. Ahmed Cemal Bey, military governor of the city, recalled in his memoirs that 'The arrival of the Pasha in Constantinople was the surest sign that the insurrection was immediate', and he assured Şevket Pasha that Kamil had 'been brought to Constantinople in order to be made Grand Vizier over your corpse. The arrival of the Pasha is the secret sign that a revolution is imminent.' Sure enough, on 11 June, the Liberals, convinced that the loss of Edirne had undermined Unionist prestige, assassinated the grand vizier, but failed to seize power. The plot was foiled and the opposition eliminated soon after, marking a new phase in Ottoman political life.

By the Treaty of London on 30 May, the Porte surrendered Edirne to Bulgaria, along with all territory west of the Erez-Midya line. For the moment, Enver Bey, the hero of the 23 January coup, lost prestige and his position in the CUP, and Ali Fethi (Okyar, 1880–1943) became the general secretary. After Şevket Pasha's assassination, the Unionists were finally in power. The cabinet, formed by the Egyptian prince, Said Halim Pasha (1863–1921), who also held the portfolio of foreign affairs, was still moderate. Its aim was to conciliate the Arab provinces and the Armenian community by including an Arab grand vizier, as well as Süleyman al-Bustani, a Lebanese-Christian, and Öskan Efendi, an Armenian member of the Dashnak nationalist movement. That there was no Greek minister in the cabinet simply shows that the impact of the Balkan War had heightened Greek nationalism and the Greek community was no longer considered reliable and part of the Ottoman commonwealth. The cabinet also included such prominent Unionists as Talat (Interior) and Halil (President of the Council of State), İbrahim (Justice), Şükrü (Education). The government took harsh measures against the opposition and over

300 were sent into internal exile to Black Sea ports as a preventive measure. A number of plotters, including Damad Salih Pasha, a relative of the sultan, were hanged.

Differences between the Balkan allies soon led to war. On 28 June 1913, the Bulgarians attacked the Serbs and Greeks, and on 11 July Rumania declared war on Bulgaria; the next day the Ottomans took advantage of the situation and joined the war, acting independently of the Balkan states. Finding Thrace undefended, the Ottomans began to occupy territory they had only recently lost. An imperial *iradé*, decree, authorized the reoccupation of territory belonging to the Empire and the press urged the retaking of Edirne before the Greeks, flushed with victory, did so. But the cabinet was divided, fearful that the violation of the Treaty of London might lead to Great Power intervention. The Unionists called for action arguing that Edirne had been the reason for the coup d'état of 23 January and that the CUP would lose its moral right to rule unless it attempted to regain the city. On 22 July, the day before the fifth anniversary of the revolution, Enver led the army into Edirne and the Unionists fulfilled their promise, regaining some of their lost prestige. Despite foreign pressure and promises, the Porte refused to surrender Edirne again. Talat, whose constituency was Edirne, told the press that 'Ottoman patriotism is not for sale for the price of an increase on customs duties ... Edirne can be bought only at the price of the blood of our devoted and courageous army, ready to sacrifice itself to the last man in order to defend the town.' The Great Powers – Britain, France, Russia, Germany, Austria-Hungary, and Italy – failed to present a united front in Istanbul. Italy assumed a Turcophile attitude, while the German ambassador said he had no instructions from Berlin. Sofia was isolated and forced to negotiate directly with the Porte. Finally, on 29 September, a treaty was signed between the Ottomans and Bulgarians ceding eastern Thrace – including Edirne and Dimotoka – to Istanbul, and included terms for the exchange of populations, an ominous development that had grave implications for the future.

THE REPERCUSSIONS OF DEFEAT

The crushing defeats of the Balkan War ushered in a period of self-doubt and introspection among the Unionists. While they had been unwilling to simply surrender to the Balkan alliance, they were more amenable to the dictates of the Great Powers. They became convinced of the need to have foreign expertise to reform Ottoman institutions. Thus in October, the Porte signed a contract with Germany, defining the functions of the military mission that would reform the Ottoman army. The naval agreement with Britain, according to Admiral Limpus who headed the British naval mission, would lead to the renaissance of the navy, but more important still, it would lay the foundations for the creation of heavy industry in the empire. Ahmed Cemal confided to Sir Henry Wilson that while the 'Turks could not change their military teachers [the Germans], [but] in all else, in finance, administration, navy, they wished to be under British guidance'. But the British were unable to alienate Russia by taking the Ottomans under their wing, and were fearful of the consequences in the European balance of power.

In June 1913, the Russians had proposed to the ambassadors of the Great Powers that the grievances of Ottoman Armenians be met, and the so-called Armenian provinces in eastern Anatolia be placed under a Christian governor on the model of Lebanon. In July, the Porte sent a mission composed of Captain Deedes and three Muslims to study the demands of the Ottoman population. Meanwhile a Colonel Hawker, known for his honesty and fairness, was placed at the head of the gendarmeries of Erzurum, Trabzon, and Van. According to Count Ostrorog, who had served as adviser to the ministry of justice and knew the empire intimately, 'The Turks, aware that the Armenian question had absolutely to be settled by means straight and effective, were desirous of executing the work of Armenian reform under British control. Diplomatic considerations alone prevented the scheme from being carried out'.

In February 1914, the Porte adopted Great Power proposals to divide the provinces of eastern Anatolia into six zones, with a foreign inspector-general chosen from small, neutral states in each zone. The inspectors-general would be charged with the reforms necessary to establish an efficient administration. But such reforms, under foreign supervision, observed the journalist Ahmed Emin [Yalman], meant 'in the phraseology of the Eastern Question, a preliminary to amputation. The fiction of the maintenance of

Turkish sovereign rights was, in every case, offered merely as an anaesthetic.' In April 1914, when Kurdish tribes, encouraged by Russian agents, attacked the Armenians of Bitlis, the Porte sent troops and gave arms to the Armenian community so that they might defend themselves. An Armenian paper praised the Porte for the complete confidence it had shown in the Armenian community by distributing arms so that they might defend the city against the reactionaries. In fact, arming the Armenians of Bitlis showed the weakness of the Unionist state; it was a candid confession that the state was unable to defend its citizens in eastern Anatolia, the principal function and claim of any modern state. However, the rebellious Kurds were punished so as to prevent further outbreaks of violence. In May, eleven were found guilty and hanged, and their bodies were displayed in the city for all to see. In July, the Chamber voted 40,000 pounds for the salaries and expenses for the two inspectors-general and their staffs so that the reform programme could progress.

Ever since the diplomatic isolation the Ottomans had experienced during and after the Balkan War, the Unionists decided that they must form an alliance with one of the two European blocs: the Triple Entente composed of Britain, France, and Russia, or the Triple Alliance of Germany, Austria and Italy. The Unionists preferred the Triple Entente and approached, in turn, England, France, and Russia, only to be rebuffed by each. Germany was equally reluctant to form an alliance with Istanbul after the dismal Ottoman performance in the Balkan War; the Ottomans were likely to be both a diplomatic and military liability. But after the outbreak of the Austro-Serbian war in July 1914, Berlin calculated that there was little to lose and much to gain from an Ottoman alliance. Only when Berlin seemed sure of entering the war did it turn to Istanbul. On 28 July, Berlin offered the Porte definitive terms for an alliance, guaranteeing Ottoman territorial integrity vis-à-vis Russia *if the Porte would place her army under German military command in case of war* and would further bind herself to take Germany's side if Russia entered the war as a belligerent. The kaiser saw the empire and the caliphate as the basis from which to foment *jihad*, or holy war, against England. He wrote to his ambassador: 'England must ... have the mask of Christian peaceableness torn publicly off her face ... Our consuls in Turkey and India, agents, etc., must inflame the whole Mohammedan world to wild revolt against this hateful, lying, conscienceless people of hagglers; for if we are to be bled to death, at least England shall lose India.'

ALLIANCE WITH GERMANY

The secret alliance was concluded on 2 August 1914. The Porte assured the military mission 'effective control in the conduct of the war', placing the Ottoman army under its control. Fritz Fischer, the German historian, wrote that the alliance 'was concluded with an eye to the unleashing of a pan-Islamic movement, which was to lead off with a "Holy War" ... Turkey thereby acquired an important dual role in Germany's war strategy. Guardian of the Straits, with the duty of severing communications between Russia in the Black Sea and the western allies, and of exercising a constant threat against Russia's southern flank, she was also meant to act as a springboard from which Germany should attack Britain at her two most vulnerable points, India and Egypt.'

The Unionists saw the alliance with Germany as an insurance treaty designed to protect the empire from the ambitions of European imperialism. Like most observers at the time, they expected a war of short duration to be concluded with a negotiated peace in which they expected to be protected by their German patron. Britain's decision to confiscate two warships built for the Ottomans in British yards had a profound effect on the mood in the country and strengthened Germany's position in the empire. The British fleet had begun to blockade the straits long before Istanbul entered the struggle. The cabinet responded by mobilizing and declaring martial law on 3 August. Talat explained that mobilization was a defensive measure and the Porte would remain neutral until the end of the war if England and France gave separate guarantees to protect Ottoman territorial integrity and independence and accepted the abolition of the capitulations. London and Paris were unwilling to do that; the promise of dividing and sharing Ottoman territory was one of the principal means of keeping the Entente together.

The mobilization had grave consequences for the economy, especially for agriculture. Men between the ages of 18 and 40 were called up just when they were needed to harvest the crops, and women were forced to take over their labour. The country's finances, already in a poor state, were also adversely affected, making the government even more beholden to Berlin. On 10 August, the escape of the two German warships, the *Goeben* and the *Breslau*, into the Sea of Marmara, strengthened Germany's hand even more, especially over the Ottoman navy that had hitherto been controlled by the British naval mission. The Ottoman cabinet proposed disarming the ships. But Baron von Wangenheim, German ambassador at the Porte, refused to consider such a measure; he threatened to join the Russians and partition the empire if the Ottomans failed to comply. The cabinet refused to be intimidated and settled for the fiction that the Germans had sold the ships to the Porte. The Unionists were not timid men and they exploited the crisis to strengthen their position vis-à-vis the Powers. In September, they abrogated the capitulations unilaterally, despite diplomatic protests. At the same time, they hung on to their neutrality, arguing that they could not go to war until Bulgaria and Rumania had been won over to the Triple Alliance. French success at the battle of the Marne in September 1914 strengthened the hand of the neutralist faction in the CUP. After the setback in France, the German general staff was forced to make fundamental changes to its war plans and required a holding operation against Russia. That involved the Ottomans opening a front on the Caucasus against Russia. Thereafter, pressure on the Porte increased day by day; Berlin exploited the Porte's need for money, as the government had begun to feel the cost of six weeks of mobilization. Germany acquired total control of the Ottoman navy when Admiral Wilhelm Souchon was given command and the British naval mission under Admiral Limpus was recalled. Richard Crawford, who had served as adviser since 1904 at the Ottoman ministry of customs and later finance, also resigned. German experts virtually took over the Ottoman state! The American ambassador wrote that '... Germany has absolute control of Turkish Navy; their military mission almost controls Turkish Army. They have von der Goltz in the palace and German Ambassador advising the cabinet'.

On 27 September 1914, Cavid confided to his diary: 'I am certain Germany will never give us any money until we enter the war'. Berlin was told of the country's dire financial situation and in

October the first instalment of the loan arrived, with promises of more to come when the Ottomans entered the war. On 29 October, Admiral Souchon, supported by Enver Pasha's war party, attacked Russian shipping and ports on the Black Sea and the Ottomans became belligerents. The timing of the incident was determined by German strategy. The Germans had just launched an attack in Poland and they wanted to tie down Russian forces in the Crimea and the Odessa region. After the Black Sea incident, the Russians were forced to launch an offensive in the Caucasus and diverted troops from European fronts. The Ottoman entry had a similar impact on British forces in the Middle East, especially in Egypt, to which the Ottomans had a historic claim. Once Russia, Britain, and France had declared war on the Porte, the Ottomans were able to proclaim a *jihad* on these powers, declaring that it was a sacred duty of all Muslims to fight the enemies of the sultan-caliph. The goal was to foment rebellion among the Muslim population in the colonies and to motivate Muslim soldiers at home.

Guided by Germany's strategic needs, the Ottomans launched a major offensive in December 1914. The British responded by bombarding the outer forts at the Dardanelles, causing great anxiety in Istanbul that led to talk of moving the government to Anatolia and Thrace, to Konya and Edirne. The Sarıkamış offensive proved to be a military disaster for the Ottoman army, which was totally unprepared for such a campaign in the middle of winter. The army, led by Enver Pasha with Bronsart von Schellendorff as his chief of staff, was decimated, and Enver returned to Istanbul in January 1915 a chastened man.

THE OTTOMAN ROLE IN THE FIRST WORLD WAR

The Ottoman war may be divided into two principal phases: from November 1914 to March 1917, the outbreak of revolution in Russia, a period that may be described as the 'Years of Crisis and Revival'; and from March 1917 to October 1918, a period of 'Resurgent Ambition and Defeat'. During most of the first phase, the situation of the empire was often precarious. The Dardanelles campaign of 1915, launched by the British and French in order to lessen the pressure on Russia and open a supply line to southern Russia via the Black Sea, threatened the very existence of the empire. By January 1915, the situation had become sufficiently dangerous for the Unionists to consider making a separate peace. They approached the British but were rebuffed. The first major bombardment of the outer forts began on 19 February 1915. Such was the fear that the Entente would break through the straits and reach the capital, that the Unionists began to prepare to retreat into Anatolia and Thrace in order to continue the struggle. By March, the situation had become quite desperate, though it eased when the French battleship, *Bouvet*, was sunk at the mouth of the straits on 18 March. Churchill's bombardment of the straits from the sea was essentially a political act designed to bring Greece and Bulgaria into the war on the Entente side. Churchill even hoped that the bombardment would provoke an uprising of the Greek and Armenian communities in the capital and a Muslim movement against the Unionists, who were described in British propaganda as atheists and freemasons, under the control of Ottoman Jews. The British were relying on the Liberal opponents of the CUP, led by Prince Sabadeddin, to overthrow the government in Istanbul should the opportunity arise. Thus apart from waging war on two fronts, the Unionists had to contend with the possibility of an internal coup d'état. The news from the other fronts was equally discouraging: in May 1915, Russian forces advanced into eastern Anatolia, captured Tutuk, Malazgirt, and Van, and began preparations for a major winter offensive. The British continued to advance in Iraq, capturing Kut on 3 June. The Ottomans, on the other hand, failed to make any impression on the Egyptian front. To make matters worse, Italy, which had remained neutral so far, seemed about to join the Entente.

The relocation and massacre of the Greek and Armenian communities in Anatolia began precisely at this point, the Ottomans convinced that the Greeks and Armenians had thrown in their lot with the enemy. As the Ottoman parliament had been adjourned in March 1915, the cabinet issued a temporary order on 27 May 1915 to relocate the Armenian, and later the Greek, population away from regions in the war zones to areas where they could not aid the enemy. In 1918, during the armistice period, Greek deputies in the Ottoman parliament held General Liman von Sanders and the German military responsible for implementing the policy of relocation against the Greek community of western Anatolia. When the grand vizier asked him to explain the deportations of Ottoman Greeks from the *vilayet* of Aydın, von Sanders claimed that 'if these deportations ceased, he could not guarantee the security of the Turkish army and stressed that military necessities in time of war outweighed political motives. He also stressed that the German General Staff approved entirely of his activities concerning the expulsion of the Greeks from the Aivalı [Ayvalık] district.' The policy led to massacres and great suffering on the part of the non-Muslims. But Dr Harry Stuermer, the correspondent for the *Kolnische Zeitung* in the Ottoman Empire in 1915–16, wrote in his memoirs, *Two War Years in Constantinople* (London, 1917, 59–61), that 'deportations began to abate in the summer of 1916 after the fall of the Armenian Patriarchate and more or less ceased in December 1916 with the gathering-in of all those who had formerly paid the military exemption tax.' The situation deteriorated again in 1917 after the outbreak of revolution in Russia.

It is worth noting that the ideology that was promoted by the state was principally pan-Islamism and Ottomanism, and not, as is often claimed, Turkish nationalism. There was a growing awareness of nationalism in Unionist circles, manifested in the *Türk Yurdu* (The Turkish Homeland) group around people like Yusuf Akçura, a Turk from Russia. But this group, though extremely articulate, with a loud voice in the press and among the intelligentsia, did not influence the ideology or the policy of the government, especially in the field of foreign policy. The reason for this was only partly pragmatic and had to do more with the consciousness of both the ruling elite as well as the mass of the people who had to be mobilized. The majority of the population in the empire was Muslim and was therefore more likely to be swayed by an appeal to religious rather than national solidarity, for which there were as yet no symbols. The charisma of the Ottoman dynasty that united the sultanate and caliphate for generations facilitated the appeal to religion. Moreover, the appeal to Islamic solidarity was expected to be effective not only in the Arab provinces and North Africa but also in Iran, Afghanistan, and India – regions where the Germans and the Unionists hoped to foment rebellions against their enemies.

Throughout the second half of 1915, the military situation remained desperate. The success of the expedition at Gallipoli and the threat of an Anglo-French breakthrough continued to hang over the capital, aggravated by the fear of a Bulgarian attack. 'Had the Bulgarians attacked us from the rear while we were fighting ... at Gallipoli, our situation would have been disastrous', wrote Foreign Minister Halil Menteşe in his memoirs. The situation had become so desperate that in September, the Unionists agreed to surrender territory to Sofia in order to win her over to the Triple Alliance. This was seen as a turning-point in the war, an event that altered the balance of power in the Balkans. The Serbo-Bulgarian war that followed ended in Serbia's defeat, enabling Berlin to establish for the first time a direct road link with Istanbul. Moreover, the Dardanelles campaign seemed to be failing as well.

In January 1916, the Entente began to evacuate the Dardanelles peninsula. As soon as the news of the evacuation was announced, there were public celebrations in the capital, organized by the CUP. But the lasting significance of this event, described in the press as 'The Great Victory', was a tremendous boost to Ottoman/Muslim morale. In a single stroke, the trauma of the Balkan Wars was purged and with it the sense of inferiority. The Ottomans were convinced that they had won a decisive victory, having defeated the British fleet (and army) that had threatened their capital for a century. They were also sure that they had done more than their share within the alliance and expected the Germans to recognize and remember to reward their contribution.

However, the British evacuation of Gallipoli did not end the crisis; it now assumed a different form. In January 1916, the Russian army of the Caucasus launched a new offensive and captured Erzurum on 16 February, opening the road into Anatolia. Trabzon fell in April and Erzincan in July. Prior to the fall of Erzurum, General Falkenhayn had noted the precarious situation of the allies, particularly Turkey, observing that she 'would not be able to hold out much longer and already showed signs of wanting to make peace'. It was ironic that with the loss of these Anatolian towns, the chances of peace for the Unionists had become more remote. The Ottoman capture of the Iraqi town of Kut-ul-Amara from the British expeditionary force on 29 April 1916, and the surrender of General Townsend and his army, was the only bright spot in the Ottoman war effort in 1916. But what rejoicing there may have been over this triumph soon gave way to despair and anger when the Unionists learned of the Arab revolt in the Hijaz in late June 1916. Given all the territory the Ottomans had lost in Anatolia and the Arab provinces, there was no question of making peace until this territory had been recovered. In September 1916, both Berlin and Istanbul promised not to sign a peace treaty so long as the territory of one was occupied by the enemy. The Unionists were now more dependent than ever on Germany. This was symbolized by the decision to send Ottoman troops to the European theatre, even though Anatolia was partially occupied by the Russians. The Porte recognized that if victory were to be won, it would only be won on the battlefield in Europe.

The general crisis continued to deepen into 1917. The continuation of the war became a heavy burden that might have been lifted by a mediated peace under the auspices of a neutral Washington. But Britain and France rejected President Wilson's peace proposals while Russian and British armies continued to advance into Anatolia and the Arab provinces, meeting resistance that grew weaker by the day. By 1917, the Ottomans had lost almost one-third of a million men and were quite disorganized. The Russian advance was also hampered by poor communications, by war weariness and the onset of revolutionary discontent. Had there been no revolution in March 1917, the Ottomans might well have collapsed before the Russian advance. The collapse of the tsarist autocracy gave a new lease of life to the Unionist regime, itself on the verge of collapse.

Talat, elevated to the rank of pasha, replaced Said Halim as grand vizier on 3 February 1917. But he could do little to resolve the internal contradictions of an exhausted state. Revolution in Russia revived hopes of an early peace, alarming the generals in Berlin, who still believed in victory. Enver Pasha assured them that the Ottomans would continue to fight. On 6 April, Washington's declaration of war on Germany and, under German pressure, the Porte's rupture of relations with the United States, was another demoralizing blow. Berlin pleaded with Istanbul to hold on until German submarines had brought Britain to her knees and forced her to negotiate an honourable peace. As a result of war weariness, the position of the war party, led by Enver, declined and political power shifted back to other factions in the CUP. Enver Pasha was challenged within the CUP by such rivals as Fethi Bey [Okyar], a patron of Mustafa Kemal [Atatürk]. There was now some talk of Turkish Anatolian patriotism (*Türk Anadolu milliyetçiliği*) rather than the ideology of Ottomanism. But Ottomanism/Islamism remained the dominant ideology.

As the situation in Russia deteriorated throughout 1917, the Ottomans recaptured territories that had been under Russian occupation since 1915. The Unionist press no longer spoke of peace at any price, hopeful of a negotiated peace that would restore lost territories to the empire, especially after the Porte sent troops to Galacia to support the Austrian army. After the Bolshevik revolution and what seemed like the impending defeat of the Entente, Unionist war aims became more ambitious. The government demanded the restoration of Egypt, the Arab provinces, and Cyprus, while the pan-Turkish press looked to the Caucasus and spoke of the union of Turkic/Muslim peoples of Russia, Persia, and even Afghanistan.

The Unionists viewed themselves as a potentially great regional power, the 'Japan of the Middle East'. They believed that the empire's geo-political position in the region required that she possess a powerful fleet, and they argued that the Porte ought to be given the lion's share of Russia's Black Sea fleet captured by the Germans. This self-image clashed with Germany's imperial ambitions and with the role she had assigned to the Ottomans in the new world order that she intended to establish after winning the war.

However, there was no change in the deplorable state of the country's economic situation. Food and fuel were virtually impossible to obtain and the people in the capital suffered great hardship but were not organized to resist. The treasury was empty and in October 1917, the government printed 50 million liras against the German deposit of the same amount in the Ottoman Public Debt. The Treaty of Brest-Litovsk, signed in March 1918 between the Bolsheviks and the Germans, suggested that the Unionist gamble to enter the war had paid off. They had not only regained territory but seemed to have acquired a sphere of influence in the Caucasus that served 'as a rampart between us and the Russian provinces to the north'. The growth in Ottoman influence was an illusion that the Unionists could not sustain, for they were now totally dependent on Germany.

The war weariness and demoralization that the Ottomans had suffered at the beginning of 1917 returned to haunt the Unionists after the failure of the German offensive of 1918. The problem of feeding the capital was more acute than ever. British aerial bombardments that began in July increased the demoralization and the yearning for peace. The civilian element in the CUP gained strength by the day. Political censorship was abolished on 11 June 1918, followed by military and postal censorship. The death of Sultan Mehmed Reşad on 3 July brought the anti-Unionist Vahdettin Mehmed VI (r.1918–22) to the throne. He immediately asserted his constitutional authority by declaring that he was the supreme commander and replacing Unionist appointees with his men as his personal aides-de-camp.

At the beginning of September, Berlin was forced to provide a loan so as to feed the people of Istanbul. So desperate was the situation in the empire that Talat Pasha went to Berlin to explain just how terrible it was at home. On his way back to Istanbul, Talat stopped off in Sofia to see Tsar Ferdinand of Bulgaria. But his audience was cancelled as Bulgaria was suing for peace. He realized that the war was over for the Ottomans, and the Unionists had to make way for a government not tarred with the brush of Unionism and the German alliance. Talat resigned on 8 October and was succeeded by Ahmed İzzet Pasha. After discussions in the assembly about the futility of carrying on the war, the government decided to sue for peace and signed the armistice of Mudros on 30 October.

It was this event that marked the end of the Great War for the Ottoman Empire. The war ended in defeat, but the ten years of constitutional rule, especially the war years, had transformed Ottoman society. For the Unionists, war had defined all that was social; it had defined society. By its very dynamic, war became the most all-encompassing phenomenon of a country's situation, the dominant process to which all other social, political, economic and cultural processes were subordinated, and which, directly or indirectly, affected all members of society. But this same absorbing quality of war should not lead us to ignore the different ways in which diverse groups and individuals were affected: what represented ruin for most, proved to be a boon for a minority of Muslims. They enriched themselves and emerged as businessmen who constituted a new class, a nascent bourgeoisie.

The emergence of this 'new class' was perhaps the most significant development of the decade. Soon after restoring the constitution, some intellectuals had observed that the Ottomans would not survive in the world of the twentieth century unless they established capitalism and created their own bourgeoisie. The attempt to do so became one of the main tasks of the Unionists. The CUP led the campaign to establish a 'national economy' by founding small, private trading companies and banks throughout the empire, and in doing so created a small nucleus that had a vested interest in the new regime. After the capitulations were abolished in September 1914, capitalist landowners were able to sell their produce – wheat, cotton, tobacco, etc. – directly to the Germans and Austrians, and prosper. Such people became the backbone of the nationalist movement that was launched after the war to prevent the implementation of the Treaty of Sèvres.

Apart from the emerging bourgeoisie, the war also produced a small working class in the factories that had been established under German auspices for the purpose of war production. Artisans had been sent as apprentices to Germany to work in factories and learn new skills and methods of modern production. Not only did they acquire these skills, they acquired a new political consciousness and some even joined the communist revolution that broke out in Germany in late 1918.

Women also played a significant role during the constitutional period, especially during the war. A number of women's journals appeared, encouraging Ottoman women to liberate themselves from some of the most obscurantist practices of their society. They were told to educate themselves and play an active role within the family and society. It was generally agreed among the modernists that Ottoman society would make slow progress unless women were brought in as active partners. Beginning with the Balkan war in 1912, urban women began to work as nurses, and later to replace Christian women in such institutions as the telephone exchange. Peasant women had always worked in the fields, but in wartime they were made to work even harder when their men were conscripted and sent to the front. Women continued to play a critical role when the new Turkey was created.

In short, the constitutional period had transformed the mentality of the Ottoman peoples, especially those who now began to see themselves as Turks rather than Ottomans. Writing on the 46th anniversary of the revolution, the author, Vala Nureddin observed: 'if the Turks had had no experience of the second constitutional period, the ideas of "country and nation" (*vatan ve millet*) would not have become widespread. The country and the people would have remained the "Sovereign's domain" (*Padişahın malı*). People would have continued to think in terms of "His Royal Highness does what he knows to be best; it is not for us to question his wisdom". Under such conditions a national struggle would have been impossible. It is quite possible that there would have been no Republic of Turkey today, and Turkey may have been a monarchy in the Middle East.'

SUGGESTED FURTHER READING

Ahmad, Feroz, *The Young Turks: the Committee of Union and Progress in Turkish Politics 1908–1914* (Clarendon Press, Oxford, 1969).

Idem, 'The Late Ottoman Empire' in *The Great Powers and the End of the Ottoman Empire*, ed. Marian Kent (Allen & Unwin, London, 1984; reprinted, Frank Cass, London, 1996), pp. 5–30.

Idem, 'War and Society under the Young Turks, 1908–1918' in *The Modern Middle East*, ed. Albert Hourani, Philip Khoury and Mary Wilson (University of California Press, Berkeley and Los Angeles, 1993), pp. 125–44.

Kansu, Aykut, *The Revolution of 1908 in Turkey* (Brill, Leiden, New York and Cologne, 1997).

Idem, *Politics in Post-Revolutionary Turkey, 1908–1913* (Brill, Leiden, Boston and Cologne, 2000).

Turfan, M. Naim, *Rise of the Young Turks* (I.B. Tauris, London and New York, 2000).

4

The Kemalist Era,
1919–1938

ATATÜRK'S BACKGROUND AND RISE TO POWER

The Ottoman Empire lay prostrate at the end of the war, its old ruling class willing to accept the dictates of the victors as long as they allowed the sultan-caliph to reign. But the Young Turks era, despite its many failings, had created a Muslim counter-elite and a nascent bourgeoisie that was willing to fight for the gains it had made, and to create a new patriotic state. Such elites set up the Defence of Rights Association throughout Thrace and Anatolia, demanding 'justice' for the Muslims from the victors. They were local bodies articulating local demands, for there was as yet no conception of a nation or even the territory the 'nation' would embrace. The Greek landing at İzmir in western Anatolia on 14 May 1919, proved to be the catalyst that launched broader resistance that soon became 'national'. Mustafa Kemal (1881–1938), who assumed the name Atatürk or 'Father Turk' in 1934, came to play a crucial role in mobilizing the Muslims of Anatolia and organizing the resistance.

Mustafa Kemal was born in the cosmopolitan port city of Salonika (today Greece's second city) in 1881, into a family of modest means. Given the lack of opportunity for Muslim youths of the lower middle class, Kemal could either opt for a religious education and become a member of the clerical class, the *ülema*, or could opt for a military education, perhaps the easiest way for a Muslim boy to acquire a modern education and upward mobility.

The Hamidian army was divided between the *mektepli* (schooled) and *alaylı* (commissioned) officers. The former were educated in the modern military schools and academies and were taught modern methods of warfare, often by foreign military advisers. They also acquired such secular values as patriotism and nationalism, liberty and fraternity, and the rule of law; in short, ideas that had emerged from the French revolutionary tradition. The *alaylı* were officers who were promoted from the ranks because of their loyalty to the sultan-caliph and the institutions he represented. They were tradition-bound and found ideas that flourished after the constitutional revolution to be repugnant to their upbringing. The *mektepli* officers were the 'enlightened' men who came to form the backbone of the army and who supported the reforms of the CUP. But many of them had died in the wars the empire had been forced to wage between 1908 and 1922, weakening the reformist element in the army and in the Unionist and Kemalist movements.

Kemal entered the military preparatory school in Salonika in 1893, from whence he went on to the military high school in Monastir in 1895, and the War College in Istanbul in 1899. He was commissioned second lieutenant in 1902 and sent to the Staff College. From there he passed out as staff captain in 1905 and was posted to the Fifth Army in Damascus. In Syria, Kemal became active in military politics and conspired against the regime. But the real opposition to the Hamidian regime was taking place in Macedonia under the auspices of the Committee of Union and Progress, so that when he was posted to the Third Army HQ in Salonika in October 1907, he was already on the fringes of the movement. That is where he found himself when the constitution was restored in July 1908 and the CUP suddenly found itself in a position of power.

Mustafa Kemal never became part of the inner circle of the CUP and was opposed to army officers engaging in politics. He came as a staff officer to Mahmud Şevket Pasha's Action Army that crushed the counter-revolution of April 1909. Thereafter, he concentrated on military matters, following foreign literature on the subject, and translated some training manuals into Ottoman

Turkish. In September 1910, he was sent to observe manoeuvres of the French army and the following year, he was promoted to the rank of major. When Italy invaded the Ottoman province of Tripoli (today's Libya) in September 1911, Kemal was sent to organize local Arab forces for guerrilla warfare. In the Balkan War of 1912–13, Mustafa Kemal became involved only after the Ottomans had been routed. The recapture of Edirne from the Bulgarians enhanced the prestige of Enver Bey, who had been groomed by the CUP to become one of its leading lights. Enver, who was married to an Ottoman princess, was appointed war minister in January 1914; he then rejuvenated the army, purging many of the Hamidian generals who were thought to be out of touch with modern warfare. Meanwhile in October 1913, Ali Fethi [Okyar], a prominent Unionist officer, Enver's rival in the CUP and Kemal's patron, was appointed ambassador to Sofia. He took Mustafa Kemal as his military attaché. These were important appointments because Bulgaria's position in any future war was of the utmost importance for Istanbul and the reports sent by the ambassador and his military attaché were of great importance to the Unionist government. In Sofia, Mustafa Kemal was also impressed by the modernization that was taking place, and that was to influence his own views when he became president of Turkey.

The Ottomans entered the war in November 1914, and Allied forces began their bombardment of the Gallipoli peninsula in January 1915. Mustafa Kemal, who was now a lieutenant-colonel, commanded the 19th Division in Gallipoli. This is where he made his reputation as a successful general and became known in the country as one of the saviours of Istanbul. He played a crucial role in checking the Allied advance at Arıburnu, and later as commander of the Anafartalar group. On 1 June 1915, he was promoted to colonel. When he left Gallipoli in December for the capital, he hoped that his contribution would be recognized and rewarded by the Unionist government. But that was not to be. The Unionists honoured only officers totally committed to the movement and Kemal was not one of them.

Nevertheless, he was promoted to brigadier-general in April 1916, and sent to the front in eastern Anatolia, which was occupied by the Russian army. In August, he recaptured the towns of Bitlis and Muş from the Russians, though the recapture of Muş proved to be only temporary. But Kemal had established a reputation among his men as a charismatic officer, one who seemed to lead a charmed life and always won his battles. He continued to be given military commands – that of the Second and Seventh Armies in Syria – where he was successful even when he was forced to retreat. He resented Germany's exploitation of the Ottoman army for Berlin's ambitions, for that had been the case ever since the German military mission was placed in charge of the Ottoman army in 1913.

In October 1917, Mustafa Kemal resigned his command in Syria and returned to Istanbul. Known as a critic of Enver Pasha's pro-German policies, he was invited to accompany the anti-Unionist Vahdettin, the heir apparent, on his official visit to Germany. Kemal and Vahdettin became acquainted with each other and that proved useful later when Vahdettin came to the throne in July 1918 and chose Mustafa Kemal to supervise the demobilization of troops in Anatolia after the armistice. In August 1918, Kemal was appointed commander of the Seventh Army in Syria. He was not able to halt the British advance, but led an orderly retreat. By now, the war was irrevocably lost and the Ottomans were forced to sign an armistice with the Allies on 30 October, marking the end of the war. Kemal returned to Istanbul on 13 November.

The Allies – Britain and France – believed that they could impose whatever terms they wished on the defeated Ottomans and treat the empire like a colony. They had already signed secret agreements during the war, which partitioned the Ottoman Empire between them. Though these treaties no longer applied after the revolution in Russia, they were to be implemented under the new circumstances. For their part, the Ottomans were in an anomalous position, a defeated imperial people who had no 'homeland' to retreat to. The Spaniards had retreated to Spain, the British to Britain, etc. But where could the Ottomans go? They had come as Turkic tribes from Inner and Central Asia and had established a foothold in Asia Minor in 1071, just five years after the Norman invasion of Britain. They were regarded by Europe as conquerors who had come out of Asia and *occupied* lands in Europe, Asia Minor and the Arab world with no right to be there. They had been driven out of Europe during the nineteenth and early twentieth centuries, and from the Arab provinces during the First World

War. They held Asia Minor, or Anatolia, but that was land contested by other peoples – the Greeks, the Armenians, and the Kurds. The Ottomans believed that Wilson's 'Fourteen Points' applied to them, both as Muslims and Turks as well, and they therefore enjoyed the right of self-determination in territory where they were in a majority. But that was not the case. Judging by the terms of the Treaty of Sèvres, signed in August 1920 – terms that were to be imposed on the Ottomans – they were to be left only a part of Anatolia. When President Wilson was asked to fix the boundary between the sultan's Turkey and Armenia, he assigned some 40,000 square miles of Anatolia to Armenia, including the towns of Trabzon, Erzincan, Erzurum, Muş, and Van. The Armenian Republic claimed territory in south-eastern Anatolia that would link it to the Mediterranean; the territory allotted to Armenia would have amounted to one-third of Anatolia.

After the collapse of the Ottoman Empire and the flight of the most prominent Unionist leaders to Europe, the leadership was restored to the sultan and the palace. Initially, Mustafa Kemal hoped to pursue what may be described as a strategy based on Istanbul, salvaging the country's independence mainly by diplomatic means. The Sultan was expected to lead such a movement and Kemal Pasha expected to play a prominent role as minister of war in any Palace cabinet. Had such a strategy worked – and it was destined to fail, given the attitude of the Powers, especially that of Great Britain – it would have operated within the established framework of Ottoman institutions; it would have had a loyalist and politically conservative programme instead of a radical and secular one.

Despite his military and anti-Unionist credentials, Kemal was not given a cabinet post and soon became disillusioned with the Palace. The sultan seemed willing to do Britain's bidding simply to retain what little power was allowed him. Meanwhile, in Anatolia, local notables who had tasted political and economic power during the Young Turk era, began to organize local 'Defence of Rights Associations' to resist foreign and local non-Muslim aspirations. One of the first such bodies was founded in Trabzon on the Black Sea, to oppose the establishment of the Greek republic of the Pontus.

THE BIRTH OF THE NATIONAL LIBERATION MOVEMENT

The Palace, with British approval, appointed Mustafa Kemal as inspector of the Ninth Army in Anatolia, with the task of demobilizing Ottoman forces left intact after the armistice. He left Istanbul by boat and arrived at the Black Sea port of Samsun on 19 May 1919, four days after the Greek occupation of İzmir, a traumatic event in the history of modern Turkey. Instead of disarming Ottoman troops, Kemal met the military commanders and issued a joint declaration of resistance from the town of Amasya. The Palace decided to cashier him; instead Kemal resigned his commission. Thereafter, the Defence of Rights Associations coalesced around him. Congresses of such associations were held in Erzurum (27 July–7 August) and Sivas (4–11 September 1919), electing Kemal Pasha as their leader each time. In December, Kemal moved to Ankara in the centre of Anatolia and made it the headquarters of the national liberation movement.

A word ought to be said about the Ottoman-Turkish terms *millet, milli*, and *milliyetçi*, terms that are rendered into English as 'nation', 'national', and 'nationalist'. But during the war of liberation and after, the terms were intended to be more patriotic than nationalist, inclusive rather than exclusive. The terms embraced all the Islamic elements of Anatolia – Turks, Kurds, Circassians, Arabs, and Lazes – all of whom had identities of their own, and Kemal noted in October 1919 that the 'National Pact' border in Anatolia had been demarcated accordingly. 'Gentlemen', he lectured his audience, 'this border is not a line which has been drawn according to military considerations. It is a national (*milli*) border. It has been established as a national border. Within this border there is only one nation which is representative of Islam. Within this border, there are Turks, Circassians, and other Islamic elements. Thus this border is a national boundary of all those who live together totally blended and are for all intents and purpose made up of fraternal communities (*milletler*).' The National Pact defined the boundaries of the new state. The boundaries were agreed according to the peace treaties of 1913 and drawn up after the Balkan Wars, which gave the Ottoman Empire territories in Thrace, and the armistice lines of October 1918. The last Ottoman parliament, which unanimously adopted the National Pact on 17 February 1920, discussed the terms *Türk* and *millet* two days later and arrived at the consensus that the term *Türk* included all the different Muslim elements; some deputies even included Ottoman Jews within the term *Turk*! Kemal repeated these ideas on 1 May 1920: 'What is intended here ... is not only Turks, not only Circassians, not only Kurds, not only Lazes, but the Islamic ethnic elements of all of these, a sincere community ... The nation, the preservation and defence of which we have undertaken, is not only composed of one ethnic element. It is composed of various Islamic elements.'

The Ottoman or Kemalist notion of citizenship had never been ethnic. The Ottoman identity was focused around the dynasty, regardless of ethnic origin or religion, and Muslims, Christians or Jews could be Ottomans so long as they were loyal to the dynasty and the culture that had developed over time. In the same way, Turkish citizenship depended on residence (not birth) within the borders of the emerging state defined by the National Pact. During the national struggle, religion played an important role, as the non-Muslims (Greeks and Armenians) were also fighting for their own states; only Ottoman Jews as a community joined the Nationalists. according to the principle of birth, Kemal's enemies in the assembly even wanted to deprive him of his civil right to be elected to the assembly, claiming that he had not resided for five years within the new borders of Turkey, for he had been born in Salonika, a part of the new Greece.

The British responded to the Nationalist challenge by occupying Istanbul. The Istanbul parliament met for the last time on 18 March 1920, and adjourned *sine die* after protesting Britain's action. The sultan dissolved the chamber on 11 April, adding to the legitimacy of the Nationalists in Ankara, who had long claimed that the sultan was the prisoner of the Allies. Nevertheless, the Nationalists had to wage civil war against the sultan's supporters, especially after the Palace issued a *fetva*, a religious edict, denouncing the Nationalists as infidels and stating that it was the duty of believers to kill them. They responded by having the mufti of Ankara issue a counter *fetva*, declaring that the caliph was a captive of infidels and stating that believers were duty-bound to fight to save him.

The spring of 1920 marked the beginning of the most dangerous period for the Nationalists. They were engaged in a life and death struggle with the Palace and the foreign powers. Greek forces had occupied western Anatolia in 1919; they began to advance in June, occupying the town of Bursa and Edirne in July and August. The following year, the Sultan signed the Treaty of Sèvres on 10 August 1920, and signed away much of Anatolia to future Greek, Armenian, and Kurdish states, as well as territory to Syria, mandated to France by the League of Nations. Even Istanbul was placed under an international organization that was to administer the straits.

The Nationalists were convinced that the very survival of a Turkish–Muslim state was threatened. This threat persisted into 1921, when the Greek army launched a new offensive in June and advanced to the towns of Eskişehir and Kütahya and threatened Ankara's communications. By August, the military situation became so serious that the assembly allowed Kemal Pasha, as commander-in-chief, to exercise his authority in military matters. The victory at the battle of Sakarya on 13 September 1921, strengthened his hand against his opponents in the nationalist movement. Scholars have rightly concluded that had Kemal lost the battle, the leadership of the liberation movement would have passed to Kazım Karabekir, one of Mustafa Kemal's rivals and a general with excellent military credentials.

The battle of Sakarya was a turning-point in Kemal's career and the fortunes of the liberation struggle. He was promoted to the rank of marshal and given the title, Gazi – soldier in the holy war – a title he used until 1934, when he assumed the name Atatürk, or 'Father Turk'. His position vis-à-vis the Powers was also strengthened. He signed an agreement with Moscow and confirmed the Turkish-Russian frontier; the British released prisoners – Unionists and Nationalists – they were holding on the island of Malta in the Mediterranean. Eleven months later, in August 1922, Mustafa Kemal launched a general offensive against the Greek lines, forcing the Greek army to surrender on 2/3 September. Nationalist forces entered İzmir on the 9th and the Armistice of Mudanya was signed on the 11th. The war of national liberation had been won; now it was a question of reaching a consensus on the nature of the new state and the society the Nationalists would agree to.

Unwittingly, the British made the Nationalists' task easier by inviting delegations from both Istanbul and Ankara to discuss peace terms. Instead of dividing the Nationalists, the British forced them to unite and take decisive action. The Nationalists declared that the Ankara government was the new Turkey's only legitimate authority. In Istanbul, General Refet Bele, a conservative who favoured continuity under the sultan, tried to persuade the sultan to dismiss his government in Istanbul and to follow the Nationalists' lead. Had he done so, it is difficult to see how the Nationalists would have abolished the sultanate. But Vahdettin rejected Refet Bele's proposal and on 1 November, the Ankara assembly responded by abolishing the sultanate, arguing that the sultan's government had been a fiction since 16 November 1920, when the Allies had formally occupied the capital. Henceforth Istanbul was governed from Ankara, like any other province. Vahdettin fled the country on 17 November 1922, on a British battleship; the following day, the assembly elected Abdülmecit the country's new caliph.

The assembly had abolished the monarchy, but the caliphate continued to enjoy much popular support within the national movement and among the people. Kemal Pasha's position was far from secure. Some deputies wanted to disqualify him from being elected to the assembly by amending the electoral law so that only candidates who had resided in their constituencies for five years would be allowed to stand. This would disqualify Mustafa Kemal, who had been born outside the borders of the new Turkey and had never resided in any part of Turkey for a full five-year period. But the amendment was withdrawn in committee.

Kemal realized that he was isolated and had to broaden his base of support. Consequently, he formed his own political party, the People's Party, later renamed the Republican People's Party, which would represent all those who were opposed to the old order. The term *halk*, or people, included all those, regardless of their class, who were opposed to the old order; their principal task was to defeat the ancien régime and its supporters, and to establish the 'people's state'. The Kemalists had declared ideological war on his rivals and Mustafa Kemal then took his message to the country, making speeches and giving interviews to the press along the way.

Kemal's leadership was also threatened by his more conservative comrades-in-arms. They were officers he had known for many years, men such as Rauf Orbay, Ali Fuat Cebesoy, Kazım Karabekir, and Refet Bele, all of whom had fought bravely in the national struggle, but who wanted to utilize the moderation and legitimacy that came with the old constitutional order. The monarchy had been abolished, largely because of the sultan's tactical error. But these men saw no reason why the caliph should not lead the new Turkey as its president. They, like the Unionists before them, believed that Turkey could be ruled by a symbolic figure, formerly the sultan-caliph, now the president-caliph, who would be unassailable from below, yet easy to manipulate from above. The Kemalists, on the other hand, wanted a total social, economic, and political transformation. They no longer wanted to rule a state and society by traditionalist social conventions and symbols; they wanted to create a new, secular ideology that would allow Turkey to progress rapidly into the twentieth century. The Kemalists wanted to adopt the materialism of the West, its technology and its modern weapons, along with its ideas, so that society would be transformed in the broadest sense. This meant creating a secular society in which religion would be controlled by the state rather than separated from it. For them, modernity implied a broad totality and included political and cultural, as well as economic, dimensions. They wanted to accomplish both modernization and modernity, by radically reforming their traditional, patriarchal society.

If we examine the Kemalist record after 1923, we find that the regime moved aggressively away from traditionalism towards modernity. Government may not have been democratic, but it was no longer a neo-patriarchal sultanate. The Kemalists introduced 'laicism' (*laiklik*), that is to say, a state-controlled Islam and not 'secularism', i.e. separating religion from politics. They intended to use Islam to further their programme of reform and revolution by having it legitimized, when necessary, by the Directorate of Religion. Knowledge or science came to be defined as 'the best guide to life'. Urban women also benefited from modernity in a way they would not have done under a regime of modernization.

BIRTH OF THE REPUBLIC

The Lausanne Treaty of 24 July 1923, recognized the new Turkey and its borders and added to Kemal Pasha's prestige. Turkey acquired international recognition of its independence. At the time, there were only a handful of states in Asia and Africa that had the semblance of independence; the rest were colonies or dependencies of the imperialist powers. In Africa, there was Abyssinia (Ethopia), Iran and Afghanistan in West and South Asia, Thailand and China in South-East and East Asia. Abyssinia became an Italian colony in 1935; Iran was invaded by Britain and Russia in 1941 and enjoyed only nominal independence thereafter; Afghanistan served as a buffer between British India and Soviet Central Asia, as did Thailand between British India and French Indo-China; China was invaded by Japan. Only Kemalist Turkey retained its full independence after 1923.

Kemal was re-elected president of the assembly in August 1923 and in October, the assembly approved the resolution to make Ankara the capital of the new state, while retaining Istanbul as the seat of the caliphate. That was a significant blow to the conservatives, for it isolated Istanbul, their stronghold, from politics and shifted the centre of gravity of political life to Anatolia. In this favourable political climate, and with what amounted to a legislative coup d'état against his rivals, on 29 October 1923, the assembly proclaimed Turkey a republic and elected Mustafa Kemal as its president. By establishing a republic, the Kemalists were proclaiming their commitment to modernity and equality, rather than the modernization and hierarchy of the old order. They were rejecting hierarchy and tradition, the foundations on which the old order had rested and which many nationalists, who went on to form the Progressive Republican Party in 1924, wished to maintain with the caliph as the president of the republic. Istanbul was also the bastion of the rising bourgeoisie, many of whose members would have preferred an American mandate instead of total independence – for they claimed that Washington would 'civilize' Turkey rapidly, as it had the Philippines! The Nationalists disagreed and in November, the assembly dispatched an Independence Tribunal to Istanbul, reoccupied by Nationalist forces in October, to crush any opposition.

The opposition in Istanbul urged the government to maintain the caliphate as an institution treasured by the entire Islamic world, a kind of Muslim pope, who would project Turkey's influence far and wide. Ankara responded by arresting the dissidents and abolishing the caliphate on 3 March 1924, and sending members of the Ottoman dynasty into exile. This event marked the beginning of the campaign to introduce modernity and secularism into the country, a campaign that continued virtually until Atatürk's death.

Mustafa Kemal's leadership remained insecure while he had doubts about the loyalty of the army. The army had won the war of liberation and enjoyed great prestige among the people. Kemal, now a marshal, had the support of many officers. But so did such generals as Kazım Karabekir and Ali Fuat Cebesoy, for they too had held successful commands during the First World War and the national struggle. Moreover they supported some traditional symbols of the Ottoman past, and were therefore supported by the traditional elements, especially by the old elite and the bourgeoisie in Istanbul. Kemal Pasha undermined their influence in the army by having the assembly pass a law forbidding officers on active service from being deputies. After the law came into force, the conservative opposition came out into the open and formed the Progressive Republican Party (PRP) in November 1924, as a rival to Mustafa Kemal's People's Party, which responded by adding 'republican' to its own name and becoming the Republican People's Party, the RPP.

Had the Kurdish tribes not rebelled in eastern Anatolia under Sheikh Said in February 1925, it is not clear how the Kemalists would have dealt with the challenge from the PRP. Would they have been able to dissolve the party and force its leaders out of politics? It is doubtful whether Mustafa Kemal would have taken such a risk, as the Progressive Republican leadership had strong support in the army. The Kurdish rebellion provided the pretext to dissolve the PRP and crush all opposition; it also allowed the regime to introduce radical reforms – the Hat Law, the closure of the Dervish orders, the introduction of a new civil and criminal code – reforms which brought modernity to Turkey, but were opposed by the conservatives. But the Kurdish rebellion also culminated in the establishment of an autocracy and marked the end of the first attempt at multi-party politics.

Mustafa Kemal, fearing a reaction from the army, was therefore lenient with the Progressive Party generals, neither executing nor imprisoning them. He was not so lenient with former Unionists. When a plot to assassinate him in Izmir was uncovered in June 1926, there were arrests and a trial that led to the hanging of four leading former Unionists. That marked the end of any open opposition to Mustafa Kemal's rule.

REPUBLICANISM TAKES ROOT

The new regime was finally secure: the old regime had been defeated, along with the nationalist conservatives and former Unionists. By 1926, Kemal felt confident enough to have his statue unveiled in Istanbul, an iconoclastic gesture in a predominantly Islamic society where the representation of the human form was looked upon as sinful. The following year (15–20 October 1927), he addressed his party's congress and gave his 'great speech', which provided his interpretation of the war of liberation and against what great odds it was fought and won. As the regime became more confident, further measures were taken to secularize and modernize Turkey. The article in the constitution that described Islam as the religion of the state was removed in 1928. The Roman alphabet replaced the Arabo-Persian script, marking a major rupture with the Ottoman past. Those who had been educated in the old script became illiterate overnight and were forced to learn the Roman letters so as to keep their jobs. Literacy in urban society increased and a new generation schooled in the new script grew up with the new ideology.

By 1930, Kemal Pasha felt sufficiently confident to experiment with a multi-party system once again. The first attempt, in 1924, had not been of his making but had been launched by rivals to challenge his leadership. This time he asked his friend Fethi Bey [Okyar], to form the Free Republican Party and act as loyal opposition to the RPP. The party was formed in August. But Kemal had misjudged the mood of the country and had not bargained for the new party's popularity, and the unpopularity of his own party. There were clashes between Free Party supporters and the gendarmerie at party rallies, and charges of electoral fraud. Therefore in November, Fethi Bey, who was a close friend of

Mustafa Kemal and not a political rival, decided to dissolve his party rather than be forced to challenge Mustafa Kemal directly.

The 'Menemen incident' in western Anatolia in December 1930, proved to be even more traumatic than the popularity of the Free Party. In the provincial town of Menemen, a Dervish sheikh called for the restoration of the Sharia and the caliphate. To make matters worse, he won the support of the crowd, even when he beheaded a reserve officer who had been sent to investigate. The incident exposed the shallow rootless character of the reforms and suggested that the reforms would not take root in society on their own. They would take root only to the extent that they were explained to the people and enjoyed public approval and support. But the Kemalists, confident that their reforms were good for the country, had made no attempt to explain their programme to the masses in the provinces. The masses, who had as yet gained nothing from the reforms and were suffering the consequences of the worldwide depression of the 1930s, found solace in the traditions and symbols of the past to which they were still attached. The Free Party under Fethi Bey had offered a modern leader and modern ideas. But in Menemen, the crowd had opted for traditional, obscurantist religious ideas that the Kemalists believed were totally unsuited to republican Turkey. They were shaken by the incident, and after a soul-searching debate concluded that the revolution required an ideology that would guide the people towards modernity and win their allegiance so that they would be able to substitute patriotism for religion.

The ideology that came to be known as Kemalism/Atatürkism was the result of the debate. It was launched in May 1931, at the third party congress, and consisted of six 'fundamental and unchanging principles', namely Republicanism (*Cumhuriyetçilik*), Nationalism/Patriotism (*Milliyetçilik*), Populism (*Halkçılık*), Statism (*Devletçilik*), Laicism/Secularism (*Laiklik*) and Revolutionism/Reformism (*İnkilapçılık*). These 'principles' became the RPP's six arrows, the symbol of its emblem, and were incorporated into the constitution in 1937. But their interpretation remained fluid and pragmatic, changing according to the needs of the growing bourgeoisie.

There was no room for compromise on 'republicanism', for that could mean the restoration of the Ottoman house and the sultan-caliph. But nationalism/patriotism remained inclusive – territorial rather than ethnic. Kemal's aphorism of 1933 ('Happy is he who calls himself a Turk') opposed the idea of birth, blood, or ethnicity, an idea that was popular among the fascist regimes in Germany and Italy. Anyone who lived within the borders of the new Turkey could call himself a 'Turk'. That is how patriots interpreted *milliyetçilik* (patriotism/nationalism). The pan-Turkists on the other hand, possibly influenced by the fascist regimes in Europe, tended to adopt the dogmatic, ethnic, and linguistic interpretation of nationalism. The struggle between the two interpretations has continued to the present day. Atatürk was a patriot rather than a nationalist. Secularism or *laiklik* – the state's control of religion rather than its separation from the state – was equally open to interpretation and some took a liberal position, while others were militantly secular and shunned Islamic practice. *The Times* (London) of 14 May 1938 noted that the Turkish ambassador had chaired a meeting at the Ritz Hotel to celebrate the Prophet's birthday, hardly a sign of Kemalist militancy or dogmatism.

Statism had emerged as a principle of Kemalist ideology when the bourgeoisie had failed to support the Nationalists' economic programme, by failing to invest in the country's infrastructure; businessmen had bought foreign consumer goods while the Turkish government was forced to keep the tariffs low until 1929, as required by the Lausanne Treaty. The Nationalists were in the process of carrying out what was in effect a 'bourgeois revolution' – separating 'church and state'; introducing universal suffrage, including votes for women; a cabinet responsible to the assembly; and a secular educational system. Mustafa Kemal married into a prominent business family of İzmir, invested his own money in the newly founded Business Bank of Turkey, and encouraged local enterprise by passing laws to that effect. But all these measures were inadequate for the business community, which preferred quick, short-term profits to the long-term development the country required urgently. Statism, or state control, advocated a mixed economy, in which the state undertook to build the infrastructure (railways, mines, dams, industry, etc.) which private capital was too poor to invest in or did not find sufficiently profitable in the short term. By developing the infrastructure, the state subsidized the private sector and contributed to its growth. The

Kemalist regime that ruled Turkey was divided between statist bureaucrats and liberal free entrepreneurs; the latter viewed the regime as transitional and expected reforms that would hasten the progress of liberal capitalism rather than state capitalism in the country. Celal Bayar (1884–1986), a prominent liberal and the leader of the future Democrat Party (DP), was appointed minister of national economy in 1932. He recognized the importance of statism and was happy to see it included in the RPP's programme. But at the same time he was expected to discipline and control the statist element within the party. In November 1937, Atatürk replaced İsmet İnönü (1884–1973), his long-standing prime minister and a confirmed statist, with Celal Bayar. Throughout the thirties, Atatürk mediated between these two factions, but he tended to favour the liberals. Only after his death in November 1938, did the statists, led by İsmet İnönü, become dominant, until they were forced to liberalize after the Second World War.

ATATÜRK'S INFLUENCE ON THE NEW REPUBLIC

Kemalist reforms transformed, even revolutionized, the country. Atatürk also left his distinctive mark on Turkey's foreign relations. But here too he was a pragmatist, as his close relationship with the Soviet Union shows. Given the hostility of the West to both movements, the Kemalists and the Bolsheviks were natural allies. The Kemalists had no sympathy for communism at home and therefore crushed it ruthlessly, despite Kemal's good relations with Moscow, marked by the 1925 Treaty of Friendship. But Mustafa Kemal maintained Turkey's total independence, even if that meant angering Stalin by giving asylum to Trotsky, Stalin's arch-enemy, in 1929. His main concern was not to allow the West to treat Turkey as a semi-colony, as the West had treated the Ottoman Empire, or let the Soviet Union patronize Ankara and act as 'big brother'. Consequently, until Atatürk's death, Moscow dealt with Ankara on equal terms and the relationship remained cordial.

After Lausanne and the loss of Mosul in 1926 to British-mandated Iraq, Turkey's perception of geo-politics changed. Ankara turned away from the Arab Middle East, not because Turkey was hostile to the Arabs or to Islam, as conventional wisdom would have us believe, but because the Arab world had lost its independence to Britain and France and was incapable of acting independently. However, Turkey's relations with Iran – a Muslim and Middle Eastern state – remained cordial, as the shah's visit to Turkey in June 1934 demonstrated. Ankara even established friendly relations with distant Afghanistan, another Muslim country which tried to emulate the Kemalists. However, Turkey's primary concern was with the Balkans, because of what was described as the 'Mediterranean Question', namely, Mussolini's ambition to expand Italy's sphere of influence in the region. Atatürk took Mussolini's pretensions seriously. That is why he had signed the treaty with Greece in October 1930, during the Greek prime minister, Eleutherios Venizelos' visit, and entered into an entente with the Balkan states in 1934.

Turkey joined the League of Nations in July 1932 and lent its support to the principle of 'collective security' against aggression. Earlier, in 1929, the Franco-American Briand–Kellogg Pact that renounced war as an instrument of national policy was ratified by the Grand National Assembly of Turkey. An agreement with Rome on neutrality signed in 1928 and the June 1930 accord with Greece confirmed the desire for 'peace abroad'. But Atatürk's support for collective security went beyond words. When the League applied sanctions against Italian aggression in Ethiopia, Ankara agreed not to trade with Rome even although Rome, was an important trading partner during the depressed 1930s.

The Kemalists were critical of the West's policy of appeasing the dictators, Hitler and Mussolini. Atatürk used the threat of aggression to win support for the remilitarization of the straits. The Montreux Convention, signed in July 1936, was important because Turkey was treated as an equal for the first time by the Western powers, and freed from another restraint imposed by the Treaty of Lausanne. The Convention coincided with the outbreak of the Spanish Civil War and once again Atatürk supported collective security. In September 1937, the Mediterranean states convened the Nyon Conference and denounced 'Italian piracy'. The Turkish delegation, acting on Atatürk's personal instructions and not those of the İnönü government, permitted British and French ships to use Turkish naval bases to prevent Italian aggression in the Mediterranean; the İnönü cabinet was opposed to this measure on the grounds that Rome would find it provocative.

Though cordial relations with Moscow remained the corner-stone of Turkey's foreign policy, Ankara understood the value of a friendly Britain, the foremost naval power in the world. In September 1936, the unofficial visit of King Edward VIII was treated as a state visit, and Atatürk was photographed frequently with the king. The king's visit to Turkey suggested that the country was regarded in London as an important factor in international politics and worthy of being treated as an equal. Atatürk's desire to come closer to foreign democracies had an impact on domestic politics as well. It led to the dismissal of Recep Peker, the autocratic and statist secretary-general of the RPP, who is said to have given the regime a 'fascist colouring'.

Atatürk continued to oppose the aggressive policies of the fascist dictators. The press was critical of the Munich agreement of September 1938, by which Britain and France agreed to abandon Czechoslovakia to Hitler. Remembering their own national struggle, journalists lamented that the Czechs could have main-tained their dignity, if not their independence, had they fought against German aggression. Atatürk's policy of opposition to appeasement was so rare in the 1930s that the British author, George Orwell, wrote: 'In the years 1935–9, when almost any ally against Fascism seemed acceptable, left-wingers found themselves praising Mustafa Kemal'.

By October 1938, official bulletins based on his doctors' reports noted that Atatürk was very ill. He was too ill to participate in the celebrations of the fifteenth anniversary of the republic on 29 October. When the new session of the Grand National Assembly was opened on 1 November, the president's speech was read by the prime minister, Celal Bayar. Nine days later, on 10 November, the country learned that Atatürk had died.

In his fifteen years as president of the Republic of Turkey, Atatürk had succeeded in creating a nation that had acquired a new identity and was virtually self-sufficient and independent. He had begun the process of converting a country from its semi-feudal, agrarian base into a modern industrial economy. All the nation's energies had been directed to progress at home, while the goal of Turkey's foreign policy was to maintain the status quo. When the republic was founded in 1923, Turkey had been inca-pable of producing something as simple as safety matches. But by the mid-thirties, factories were producing textiles, sugar, paper, and cement, while a British company was in the process of setting up an iron and steel industry. Such foreign-owned enterprises as the railways were purchased by the state and nationalized, although the term adopted was not 'nationalization' but 'statification'. More railway lines were constructed and fused into a national system, whose aim was to create a national market. Turkey was now able to feed itself and export some of its produce to Europe. She was also self-sufficient in such raw materials as wool and cotton, for use by its nascent textile industry, as well as coal from the mines on the Black Sea.

In the mid-twenties, after the transfer of population between Greece and Turkey, people complained that Turks were incapable of doing the most modest technical tasks of plumbing or cobbling, because such work had been monopolized by the non-Muslims. But within a few years, the 'new Turk' had learned to take on all the professions required by a modern society, from railwayman to bank clerk, while women now worked in the textile mills and as secretaries, as well as in the professions.

Atatürk was not like the dictators of the thirties. He made speeches, but never in front of large crowds at organized rallies as Hitler and Mussolini had done. He wanted to mould his people rather than mobilize or energize them in order to manipulate them. He wanted to convince them to accept his reform programme, for he had no plan of irredentism or conquest. Unlike contemporary leaders, his charisma was not based on the promise of territorial expansion. His programme was principally domestic, and the only territorial gain the republic made was to obtain Iskendurun or Alexandretta in 1938 from Syria, which was then under the French mandate. But in 1926, he was forced to cede Mosul, with its oil, to British-controlled Iraq. He did not rule the society he came to lead by means of traditionalist social convictions and symbols as, for example, General Franco did in Spain after 1936. He preferred to create a new ideology and symbology which were in keeping with the needs of the twentieth century. Not being a conservative, he feared neither secular modernism nor liberal democracy, though he saw the latter as a brake on his own radicalism. Only Marxism, with its analysis of society based on classes and class conflict, provided an alternative to Kemalism and he refused to confront it.

Though he did not practise them fully in his own lifetime, Atatürk accepted the rationale of such liberal institutions as political parties, trade unions, a free press, and freedom of speech. The assumption of the regime was that these institutions would be introduced as soon as Turkish society had achieved the requisite stage of development. When Atatürk died in November 1938, the new generation that had grown up in the republic thought that everything they had known had died with him. It was difficult for many to imagine a Turkey without Atatürk, for he had become synonymous with the republic and the new Turkey. His successors were therefore faced with the difficult task of establishing their authority in order to rule a country that was still in the process of maturing.

SUGGESTED FURTHER READING

Andrew Mango, *Atatürk: The Biography of the Founder of Modern Turkey* (The Overlook Press, New York, 1999).
Ali Kazancigil and Ergun Özbudun, *Atatürk: Founder of a Modern State* (Hurst, London, 1981).

5

Towards Multi-Party Politics and Democracy, 1938–1960

İNÖNÜ'S NEW PRESIDENCY

The transition of political power following Atatürk's death was smooth, and any sign of infighting for the leadership within the RPP was hidden from public gaze. Thus on 11 November, the Grand National Assembly of Turkey elected unanimously İsmet İnönü as the republic's new president. İnönü's election surprised many observers, because in 1937 there was a rift between Atatürk and İnönü, and Atatürk had replaced him as prime minister with Celal Bayar, suggesting that İnönü was being bypassed in the succession. Some have even suggested that in his secret will, kept in the presidential library in Ankara, Atatürk is said to have declared: 'Let Marshal Fevzi Çakmak be the president after me'. If so, Atatürk's wish was disregarded and İnönü, supported by General Fevzi Çakmak, the chief of staff since 1923, was elected Turkey's second president. İsmet İnönü had managed to maintain his hold over the party machine, despite his fall, and as a result he was able to secure his election. But his position with the people of Turkey was weak, for he lacked the stature of Atatürk. Therefore in December, the RPP's Extra-Ordinary Congress met and declared Atatürk as the Party's founder and 'eternal leader', while İsmet Pasha was declared its 'permanent national chief', or *Milli Sef*. These changes suggested that İnönü was emulating the leadership principle prevalent in Nazi Germany and fascist Italy in order to bolster his position at home and abroad.

Given the tensions in Europe and the possibility of war, İnönü brought about political harmony at home by pursuing a policy of reconciliation with opponents of Atatürk and Kemalism. People who had lived in exile during Atatürk's rule returned to Turkey and became active in politics again. At the same time, he gave the government broad powers to regulate the economy by having the assembly pass the National Defence Law on 18 January 1939. The following week, Celal Bayar, a liberal, anti-statist politician, resigned as PM and was replaced by Dr Refik Saydam, who had been minister of the interior and general secretary of the RPP. Thereafter, the two offices of party secretary-general and minister of the interior were separated, suggesting that the RPP was giving up its control over the bureaucracy established in the mid-1930s. That was an illusion, for the party's hold over the state remained firm; only that of individual politicians was weakened. When general elections were held in March 1939, in a house of 424 deputies, there were 125 new faces; some men who had been close to Atatürk were not elected, while such rivals and opponents as Fethi Okyar, Kazım Karabekir, Hüseyin Cahid Yalçın, Refet Bele and Ali Fuad Cebesoy, entered the assembly. At the same time, Mustafa Kemal's landing at Samsun on 19 May 1919, was celebrated for the first time, suggesting that the post-Atatürk regime would continue to honour the republic's founder. The celebration became known as the 'Youth Festival' and has been celebrated each year thereafter.

İnönü continued to liberalize the regime, appointing Fethi Okyar as Minister of Justice in May. On 29 May, he permitted the formation of the 'Independent Group' in the assembly which was expected to act as the loyal opposition to the government. But this was a paper reform, for the group did not take its oppositional role seriously and allowed the government to ride roughshod, with the passage of certain completely undemocratic laws that were passed during the war.

President İnönü's principal task was to steer his country safely through the world crisis. He had still to prove himself in the wake of Atatürk's charismatic leadership. Though he had been Atatürk's right-hand man from the early twenties until 1937, he was thought to be neither imaginative nor dynamic. Hitler is said to have remarked to his commanders that, after the death of Atatürk, Turkey would be ruled by morons and half-idiots. Given his bullying policy towards post-Atatürk Turkey, Stalin may have reached a similar conclusion. But they were wrong. İnönü was a cautious man, unwilling to gamble the future of the republic by opting for the wrong side; the memory of the First World War was still fresh in the minds of that generation and they did not want to repeat the error of the Unionists. So when the Second World War broke out in September 1939, İnönü chose to remain neutral, even though Turkey had signed declarations of friendship and mutual assistance with Britain in May and with France in June 1939. In return for Turkey's pledge, France agreed to cede Alexandretta, a part of Syria (known in Turkey as Hatay) to Ankara. The German–Soviet Pact of 23 August 1939 marked the end of any possibility of a tripartite (Anglo-French-Soviet) guarantee against the threat of fascist aggression. Turkey was now more determined than ever to maintain its neutrality.

WAR IN EUROPE

Ankara watched the war in Europe closely, hoping that neither side would win an overwhelming victory and dominate Europe. An Allied victory would be to Moscow's advantage, while an Axis victory would guarantee Italian hegemony in the eastern Mediterranean. For the moment, Turkey's foreign policy seemed directed by her foreign trade, which she juggled between the two blocs. On 18 June 1941, three days before Germany invaded Russia, Turkey signed a non-aggression pact with Germany. The invasion gave Ankara breathing space – Germany having already invaded and occupied Bulgaria and Greece, was incapable of invading Turkey while she fought Russia. Many in Turkey believed that Hitler would knock out Russia in a short war and force Britain and France to make peace. Consequently, in the summer of 1942, Ankara announced that it would join the war on the German side if Russia were defeated.

War, neutrality and mobilization undermined whatever gains the economy had made during the thirties. The government had been forced to implement the 'national defence law' in January 1940, to counter the hoarding, profiteering and shortages that had resulted since the outbreak of war. Price controls were introduced and rents frozen to the April 1940 level, the working day was increased by three hours and the weekly holiday abolished in many workplaces. Indirect taxation increased sharply on such essentials as sugar, tea, and transportation. German successes in Russia encouraged the racist element in the Turkish elite to harass their own minorities, so much so that in November 1942, the assembly passed the notorious and controversial wealth tax law, known in Turkish as *Varlık Vergisi*. Its ostensible purpose was to raise around US $360 million from businesses that had profited from the war; but taxes were assessed according to the taxpayer's religion and not his wealth. There were separate lists for Muslims, non-Muslims, foreigners and for the Dönme, a sect of Jews who had converted to Islam in the seventeenth century. As a result of this tax, many non-Muslims were forced to sell their assets (real estate, factories, etc.), which were then purchased by members of the new Muslim bourgeoisie at well below market prices, enriching that class, at the same time as alienating it from the government!

Fortunately, the pressure on the minorities eased soon after the German army surrendered at Stalingrad in February 1943, and the tide began to turn against Berlin. The following month, Avram Galanté, a Turkish Jew, was elected to the assembly, while the pro-German journalist, Yunus Nadi lost his seat. These were signals that İnönü was abandoning Turkey's benevolent neutrality towards Germany and leaning towards the Allies. In September 1943, victims of the wealth tax who had been sent to a work camp in eastern Anatolia were pardoned and the tax was annulled in March 1944. The racist pan-Turkist movement that had been supported by German money and propaganda and had become influential even in government circles, was finally banned and prosecuted. In May 1944, its leaders were put on trial and İnönü personally denounced pan-Turkism in his 19 May Youth Day speech. The trials only ended in March 1947, during the cold war, when Moscow, not Germany, was the enemy. The accused were acquitted and lauded as nationalists who had struggled against a subversive ideology, i.e. communism! Pan-Turkism was an instrument to be employed in the game of international politics.

As the world war wound down, the İnönü regime found itself in a difficult predicament. The majority of the people in Turkey were suffering severe hardship. All the basic needs were in short supply. Bread rationing had been introduced in January 1942 and a law passed that virtually permitted the forced collection of agricultural produce. All classes except the bureaucracy were alienated from the regime: businessmen by the arbitrary wealth tax, which had enriched a few Muslims but revealed how autocratic the state could be; the landlords and peasants by the agrarian legislation and the harsh and arbitrary rule of the gendarmerie; and the urban masses by the labour legislation, which overworked them, gave low wages and left them hungry.

THE AFTERMATH OF THE SECOND WORLD WAR

İsmet İnönü understood that the world had changed radically as a result of the victory of the Allies over fascism, and that he had to respond to the situation before there was an explosion at home. On 1 November 1945, he declared that the political system would be reformed so as to bring it in line with the emerging world order of capitalism and democracy. The Turkish political system lacked an opposition party and he would permit the formation of such a body. Though the defeat of the fascists had undermined the legitimacy of a single-party state in Turkey, internal factors also made it untenable. The political alliance between the military-bureaucratic elite, the landlords, and the rising bourgeoisie had brought about the success of the war of liberation and the early Kemalist regime. The very success of the regime, the growth of capitalism, both urban and rural, eroded that alliance, and bourgeoisie and landlords were no longer willing to tolerate the system. Besides, the economy required a vast injection of capital, and that could only be provided by America. Washington, in turn, encouraged the anti-statist forces and the establishment of a free market. In Turkey, the problem could only be resolved with a struggle within the RPP, between the liberal and the statist wings; rather than liberalize the system, the statists wanted to strengthen their hold on the state even further.

The land reform bill of January 1945 polarized opinion in the country. The statists wanted to redistribute land, break the political and economic power of the landowners and transform Turkey into a republic of independent peasant proprietors, akin to the Balkan states. Though parliament passed the bill, the RPP was fragmented as a result, leading to the founding of the Democrat Party in January 1946. Its founders – Celal Bayar, businessman and banker; Refik Koraltan, a bureaucrat; Fuad Köprülü, a professor; and Adnan Menderes, a landowner – were all respected members of the RPP. They called for the implementation of a multi-party system, democracy, and the inviolability of private property. Three of the dissidents were expelled from the RPP and Bayar resigned. They responded by forming the Democrat Party, thus opening a new page in Turkey's political life.

THE FORMATION OF THE DEMOCRAT PARTY

Initially, the Democrats were seen as another loyal opposition, created by men who came out of the RPP. After all, its founding members were all Kemalists of long standing and offered virtually the same political and economic programme as the ruling party. Mahmud Celal Bayar had also paid his political dues. He was born in a village in Bursa province in 1884. In 1903, he joined the Bursa branch of the Deutsche Orient Bank and was an active member of the Committee of Union and Progress. After the Ottoman Empire collapsed in 1918, Bayar organized the national struggle in the İzmir region. In 1923, he was elected deputy for İzmir in the assembly and minister for reconstruction in the 1924 cabinet. He won the confidence of Mustafa Kemal and was hand-picked to lead the tiny private sector. He founded the Business Bank of Turkey (*Türkiye İş, Bankası*) in 1924, which became one of the engines of economic change and is still one of the principal economic institutions in the country. During the economic crisis of 1932, Bayar was appointed Minister of National Economy, and in 1937 replaced İnönü as Atatürk's last prime minister. When İnönü became president, Bayar resigned and was given no further ministerial post. He next appeared on the political scene in 1945, as leader of the dissident faction in the ruling RPP.

Mustafa İsmet İnönü came from a social background similar to that of Bayar. He was also born in 1884 and, as with so many youths of his class, had a military schooling, where he acquired a modern education that paved the way to social mobility in a society that offered few opportunities to Muslim youths. He graduated as a staff captain in 1905 and served in many parts of the empire. In the Greco-Turkish war, he won the Battle of İnönü (hence his surname) in 1921. İnönü became a loyal supporter of Kemal Pasha and was sent to the Lausanne conference as leader of the Turkish delegation to negotiate the peace treaty, establishing a reputation as a clever negotiator. He served as prime minister during the twenties and thirties, but was forced to resign in 1937. He had become one of the principal figures in the party–state bureaucracy and was therefore well situated to be elected president on Atatürk's death. As president, he kept Turkey out of the war but he became unpopular with the masses because of the virtual police state he established in which he was designated the 'national leader'. By 1945, İnönü had the foresight to see that times had changed and that he now had to preside over the dismantling of the single-party regime and the introduction of multi-party politics, though not necessarily democracy.

The mood in Turkey had changed dramatically since Atatürk's death, and the party that had played such a crucial role in the creation of the new Turkey was no longer trusted. The RPP was no longer seen as capable of leading Turkey in the postwar new world order. Initially, the Republicans were unaware of the changing mood in the country, convinced that all they needed to do in order to regain popularity was to carry out some reforms. The Democrats shared the same Kemalist philosophy, with perhaps a slight difference in emphasis: they were expected to enhance the government's legitimacy by acting as its official opposition. Initially, even the public did not take the Democrat Party seriously, for its programme hardly differed from that of the Republicans; after all, the constitution required that all parties adopt the six arrows of Kemalism. But the Democrats claimed that they would interpret these principles according to the new circumstances and that their aim was to advance democracy in Turkey. They wanted to curb the interventionist state and enhance individual rights and liberties. The Democrats were populists, who claimed that political initiatives should come from the people and not from the party or the state. They spoke for private enterprise and the individual, as the liberals had during the Young Turks era; very soon they had won over much of the bourgeoisie and the intelligentsia, the educated segment of the urban population, as well as journalists and academics. They already had the support of the landlords.

When the Republicans finally sensed hostility to their rule in the country, they began to liberalize the party and society. İnönü abandoned his titles of 'national leader' and 'permanent chairman' of the RPP and agreed that the party would elect a chairman every four years. But people saw these as cosmetic changes and they were right, for İnönü continued to lead the party until his ouster in 1972! The radicals in the RPP wanted their party to become a 'class party', to win over the peasants, workers, tenant farmers, artisans and small merchants and isolate the Democrats as the representatives of landlords and big business. However, despite these changes in the regulations, the conservatives remained dominant and the RPP continued to be a party that was all things to all men. As a result, the Republicans lost the support of most groups and were forced to rely on their traditional supporters in the most underdeveloped part of Turkey, in eastern and central Anatolia.

THE GENERAL ELECTIONS OF 1946 AND 1950

İnönü decided to hold an early general election, in 1946 rather than in 1947, before the Democrats had more time to organize and become a real electoral threat. But Bayar said that the Democrats would boycott the poll unless the laws were made more democratic. The DP's boycott would have robbed the government of its legitimacy and therefore İnönü was forced to amend certain undemocratic laws in order to appease the DP. The electoral law was amended and direct elections were introduced. After 1908, elections were two-tiered: voters elected representatives locally, who then elected the parliamentary deputies from the party list. Universities were granted administrative autonomy and the press laws were liberalized.

The Democrats knew that they would not do well in the 1946 election because they had not completed their organization throughout the country: bureaucracy remained hostile to them, and the voters were not sure whether the multi-party system would continue to function. Thus the RPP's victory in 1946 came as no surprise: it won 390 of the 465 seats, while the Democrats managed to win only 65 – not a bad showing in an election marred by corruption and state repression. But the political atmosphere was poisoned, which had a detrimental effect on the country's political life. The period after the 1946 election was crucial for the establishment of multi-party political life. The struggle between radicals and moderates within the RPP continued, but on 12 July 1947, President İnönü decided to support the moderates and undermine the radicals. Consequently, the pressure on the Democrats eased and they were allowed total freedom of action and equality with the governing party.

İnönü hoped to revive his party's political fortunes by adopting liberal measures. The economy was cautiously opened up to market forces; the currency was devalued, import facilities eased and banks were permitted to sell gold. These measures resulted in inflation, with the cost of living index rising from 100 in 1938 to 386.8 in August 1946, and to 412.9 as a consequence of the devaluation. The business community was encouraged by these measures but the voters were alienated even more. Bayar found that he could exploit economic discontent against the government. Although İnönü was known as a devout laicist/secularist, he allowed the government to restore religious instruction in schools. Religious concessions were considered of prime importance to isolate the Democrat Party as well as the Nation Party, formed in 1948 by conservative DP dissidents, who wanted even greater religious freedom. İnönü seemed to be abandoning three of the principal pillars of Kemalist ideology: statism, revolutionism, and laicism, and even embracing Islam. Having carried out these reforms, by 1950 the Republicans were so sure of success in the coming elections that they thought that the DP might become politically irrelevant; they even offered some seats to the Democrats so as to ensure the existence of an opposition in the new parliament!

İnönü's policy of pandering to popular sentiment and opening up the economy did little to enhance the party's reputation with the voters. When the general election was held on 14 May 1950, the voters delivered a devastating blow to the RPP and elected the Democrats with an overwhelming majority.

The Democrats had exploited the popular memory of past grievances inflicted during twenty-seven years of Republican rule.

Voters were told that nothing would change while İnönü remained in power; İnönü – not Atatürk – had come to symbolize single-party authoritarianism. The Democrats had also succeeded in winning over the bureaucracy by holding the party and not the state responsible for Turkey's problems. Without the tacit neutrality of the bureaucracy, if not its active support, the Democrats were unlikely to win, because Turkish people both feared and respected state officials and were often guided by them. When officials did not canvass for the governing party, the voters took note. Of the 90 per cent turnout, 53 per cent voted Democrat and gave them an overwhelming majority of 408 seats in parliament. The Republicans won a respectable 38 per cent of the vote, but only 39 seats; this was because they had instituted the winner-takes-all principle in the electoral system, a system that had served them well in the past.

The 1950 electoral triumph of the Democrats was seen, at the time, and is still described by some scholars, as a turning-point in the history of modern Turkey. The party in power had accepted the verdict of the voter, and this was seen as a great step forward for the democratic process, at a time when a struggle was raging between communist authoritarianism and the 'free world'. In actual fact, the change in Turkey was not as dramatic as it seemed. It is true that new political forces represented by the DP had entered the political arena, but in power they continued to work with the same instrument – the restrictive 1924 constitution – as had the Republicans. The great change in the 1950s resulted from the process of decolonization and the cold war, and that affected life in Turkey as well.

THE COLD WAR AND ITS EFFECTS ON TURKEY

As the Second World War ended, the Allies – Britain and the Soviet Union – were in the process of dividing Europe into spheres of influence. Until Germany's defeat at the battle of Stalingrad, Turkey had been benevolently neutral towards Berlin. After Stalingrad, Ankara began to favour the Allies. Stalin began to raise the question of the straits with Churchill, in Moscow in October 1944, and again in Yalta, in February 1945. The Allies agreed to discuss the question, to inform Turkey of their deliberations and to guarantee her independence. Recently opened Soviet archives inform us that, as early as May 1945, Turkey proposed a bilateral treaty of friendship with Moscow, sending, so Stalin thought, a clear message that Ankara was willing to alienate its ally Britain. Heartened by what Stalin considered Turkish timidity, in June, he verbally demanded the lease of a base on the Turkish Straits and the concession of two territories, Kars and Ardahan – territories conquered by Tsarist Russia in 1878, and ceded by Lenin to Atatürk under the treaty of 1922. Stalin, we are told, looked upon the straits, not only as an issue of Soviet security, but also as a matter of prestige. He believed that Turkey, impressed with the victories of the Red Army, would give in to his demands, and then Washington and London would accept it as a *fait accompli*. Later, Vyacheslav Molotov, commissar for foreign affairs, admitted that Stalin had overplayed his hand and had been too arrogant in 1945. Soviet demands, said Molotov, were ill-timed and unrealistic. But Stalin insisted that he push for joint ownership of the straits. By 1946, realizing its mistake, Moscow had abandoned its claims on Turkey. Recent American scholarship, based on US archival documents, agrees that there were no Soviet demands, only proposals and conditions – and there is a major difference between demands and proposals – for renewing the Turkish–Soviet Treaty of Friendship of 1925 that expired in November 1945. Even the Turkish foreign minister, Hasan Saka, was relieved when he read the Soviet démarche and saw that there was no explicit demand for bases on Turkish soil.

The cold war crisis between Moscow and Washington over Greece, Turkey and Iran, made Turkey an important regional player. The crisis also allowed the Truman administration to push its programme of rearmament through Congress and the Senate. In Washington there were two schools of thought about dealing with the Soviets: the State Department viewed the Soviet challenge as essentially political and economic, and therefore best met by political and economic means; the Pentagon viewed the Soviet threat as primarily military, to be met by a system of alliances, of which the North Atlantic Treaty Organization (NATO) was the first. The Pentagon school prevailed in US relations with Turkey.

The cold war climate accelerated Turkey's involvement with Washington. Both parties believed that Turkey required foreign capital investment for rapid economic growth, and this would only be forthcoming if Turkey joined the West and served its interests in the Middle East. Stalin's bullying tactics towards Turkey facilitated the rapprochement with Washington, especially as civil war broke out in neighbouring Greece. A friendly Turkey became a valuable asset for Washington, and was therefore included in the Truman Doctrine of 1947 and the Marshall Plan, designed to hasten the economic recovery of Europe. The statist faction in the RPP was finally defeated in 1947, with the resignation of Prime Minister Recep Peker; thereafter both parties pursued a bipartisan policy, designed to project a stable image of Turkey to the West.

Ankara was not happy about its relations with the West. The West had made no commitment to defend Turkey in the event of Soviet aggression, and after the formation of NATO in 1949, Ankara wanted a guarantee that the West would come to its defence in case of war with the Soviet Union. Washington was reluctant to make such a commitment. The Pentagon was content to use Turkey's armed forces, which it was rapidly modernizing to blunt any Soviet attack in that region, and to have bomber bases in Turkey.

But İnönü wanted a firm commitment from Washington and not just military and economic aid. By the late 1940s, there was talk of non-alignment in Ankara's political circles, a concept that became popular in parts of the postwar world. In April 1949, when Foreign Minister Sadak visited Washington, Secretary of State Dean Acheson was struck by his argument in favour of Turkey's neutrality if she were given no US guarantee. US diplomats and military officers feared that Turkey might seek a position of neutrality and the United States would be unable to capitalize on its investments in Turkey.

Turkey's considerable bargaining position proved insufficient to win any concessions from Washington, and İnönü made no headway in the negotiations. When the Democrats came to power in May 1950, they pursued the same policy and their initiatives were not taken seriously either. The contribution of Turkish troops in the Korean War and Turkey's participation in Washington's 'containment policy' against the Soviet Union seemed to make no difference. When Celal Bayar, now president of Turkey, saw the American ambassador in February 1951, he expressed his personal displeasure with the US–Turkish relationship and hinted at the possibility of neutrality in case of war with the Soviet Union. This had the desired effect. Despite British opposition (Britain wanted to restrict Turkey's membership to the Middle East Defence Organisation), both Turkey and Greece became full members of NATO in February 1952. Once in NATO, Turkey abandoned all her foreign policy options and became totally committed to the organization. Atatürk's policy of never wanting Russia and Turkey to be enemies again was abandoned; so was Kemalist geo-strategic thinking that Turkey was no longer a part of the Middle East. Inside NATO, Turkey assumed the role of 'bridge' between the West and the Middle East, a role that was institutionalized with the formation of the Baghdad Pact in 1955 between Turkey, Iraq, Iran, Pakistan, and Britain. Its alleged aim was to contain the Soviet Union, but it was directed also against the Arab nationalist movement led by Nasser of Egypt. Although Washington did not join the pact, it remained the material and moral inspiration behind it. The Baghdad Pact established Turkey's leadership of the conservative regimes in the region and it became a link between NATO and the Middle East. But it also meant that Ankara became isolated from the emerging third world, especially at the United Nations.

DOMESTIC POLITICS

In power, the Democrats aroused great hope in the country. They had brought to an end the era of authoritarian single-party rule. They promised to rule democratically and bring about modernization and prosperity. In actual fact, there was no real ideological difference between the governing party and the opposition: both parties were committed to the creation of a modern, prosperous Turkey. The Democrats employed the slogans of making Turkey into a 'little America', an idea put forward by a Republican politician in 1948, and of creating 'a millionaire in every quarter'. The opposition could not dispute a vision that they also shared; they only differed over the method of achieving these goals.

Perhaps the major difference between the Democrats and the Republicans was the speed with which the two parties wanted to develop Turkey. Having won such an overwhelming victory at the polls, the Democrats believed that the nation stood behind their programme. They believed in 'majoritarian democracy' – that the majority could do as it wished because it was the majority by virtue of its victory at the polls. They were therefore intolerant of criticism and any obstacles that might stand in the way of their programme. They subscribed to the ideology of Kemalism, but only in so far as it was interpreted according to the needs and circumstances of the times. Some of the 'isms', they argued, had served their purpose and had to be modified. For example, Turkey no longer needed a paternalistic state, and therefore statism had become redundant in an age of free enterprise.

The Democrats saw themselves as social engineers who understood their society and knew what was best for the people; this was in keeping with the Kemalist dictum: 'for the people, despite the people'. They agreed that the Republicans had made a vital contribution to the creation of Turkey during the early republic but the RPP had become an anachronism and was no longer in touch with the people or their needs. The RPP in opposition was therefore expected to play the role of official opposition and watch patiently as the DP transformed Turkey's economy and society. As for the Nation Party, formed in 1948 by conservative Democrats who wanted greater religious freedom, it too was redundant because the DP would pass laws to liberalize religious practice in order to meet the spiritual needs of the Turkish people. On 16 June 1950, barely a month after they came to power, they passed a law restoring the call to prayer (*ezan*) in Arabic; the *ezan* had been called in Turkish only since June 1941. The Democrats also restored the language of the constitution to its Ottoman original and away from the reformed Turkish of the Kemalist era, and began the process of coming to terms with Turkey's Ottoman past. In the prevailing climate of the cold war and anti-communism, all parties left-of-centre were made illegal, and many of their leading members put in jail or exiled. Nazım Hikmet, a communist poet, had to flee the country and live in exile in the Soviet bloc, while the left-wing writer, Sabaheddin Ali, was murdered by right-wing extremists.

Their electoral success in the 1950 elections led the Democrats to believe that the people supported their programme and that they represented the 'national will' (*milli irade*) to which they would be held accountable every four years at election time. For that reason, they did not take the opposition or its criticism seriously. During the early years of DP rule, the country seemed to be growing rapidly, thanks to the demand for Turkish products in Europe and the Korean War boom. Moreover Marshall Law aid also opened up the country to the West.

Turkey was led by Prime Minister Adnan Menderes (1899–1960). He was chosen by President Bayar as his prime minister over the older and more experienced Fuad Köprülü (1890–1966), the intellectual, because Menderes belonged to a younger generation and was thought to have a vision for postwar Turkey. He belonged to a wealthy landowning family in the cotton-growing province of Aydın, in western Anatolia. Menderes had matured during the Kemalist era and had entered politics by joining Ali Fethi's Free Republican Party in 1930. When the party was dissolved, he joined the RPP and, in 1945, sided with the dissidents against the land reform bill. He was expelled from the RPP and became a founding member of the Democrat Party.

Menderes viewed political power as the tool necessary for Turkey's rapid growth. He had no time for amending the anti-democrat laws or the establishment of a neutral administration that the Democrats had called for while in opposition. In keeping with the principle of an 'above-party' president, Celal Bayar resigned from the DP and Menderes was elected party chairman. But that was a cosmetic reform, for Bayar was too closely associated with the party to cut all his ties from it. In other areas, the DP government tightened its grip on the penal code adopted in the mid-1930s from the Italian model, and laws became more repressive, in keeping with the frigid political atmosphere created by the cold war. Moreover the Republicans were kept under constant pressure by the threat of liquidating the party's assets.

The situation worsened after Menderes's victory in the 1954 election. Turkey was going through a period of prosperity and there was a mood of optimism in the country. Voters had benefited from economic growth and showed their appreciation by supporting a government that had opened up the country and made it less bureaucratic. The Democrats had distributed state lands to some landless peasants, introduced mechanization on the farms by importing agricultural machinery from the US and increased production. The Agricultural Bank, founded in Ottoman times, extended credit to farmers, while the state subsidized wheat and cotton, as well as increasing storage facilities for farm produce. Weather during the first half of the 1950s had also favoured the farmer and world wheat prices were unusually high, thanks to the demand generated by the Korean War. As a result, the countryside, especially the big farmers, had benefited and were happy to vote for the DP.

The urban intelligentsia, the universities and the professionals, who had mostly supported the DP because it had promised political liberalization, were disappointed and became disillusioned with the party's performance in power. They saw that democratic and multi-party politics could not function with institutions inherited from the single-party period. Such institutions as the 1924 constitution and the penal code were anachronisms and had to be amended in order to suit Turkish society living during the second half of the twentieth century. The DP government showed no concern for such detail. Menderes became dismissive of critics as his power grew and smothered democracy within his own party. In opposition, the Democrats had won the support of the small working class in Turkey by promising them the right to strike, which had been denied them by the single-party regime. When Menderes was reminded of this promise, he replied: 'Is Turkey to have strikes? Let's have some economic development first and then we'll think about this matter'. That summed up his attitude towards democracy; for the time being, it was to be sacrificed on the altar of economic growth!

Despite their electoral strength, the Democrats suffered from an inferiority complex that left them feeling insecure. They may have won the support of the voters and were now the government, but they did not feel that the instruments of state – the bureaucracy, the judiciary and the army – stood behind them. These institutions were the creation of the RPP and were suspected of being loyal to the opposition. This was especially true of the army, which was thought to be loyal to İnönü, still known by his military title, İsmet Pasha. There were rumours of a military coup when the DP won the election in 1950, with subsequent great relief when the generals did not intervene. Nevertheless, Menderes carried out a purge in the top ranks of the army, and retired those who were considered

İnönü loyalists, replacing them with loyal Democrats. He did the same with a number of provincial governors and other senior positions in the bureaucracy. The Democrats suffered from what was described as the 'Pasha factor', an irrational fear that they would not be safe in office as long as İnönü led the opposition. They came to believe that İnönü, known as 'the cunning fox', was the cause of all their troubles, and that the Republican opposition would be ineffectual without him. Even the Republicans believed this myth, and no leader from within the party emerged to challenge İnönü's leadership, even though he was already 70 years old in 1954. Had İnönü retired from political life when his party lost the 1950 election, Turkey's history might have taken a different turn. Menderes and the Democrats would have felt more confident and perhaps would have behaved more fairly and justly towards the opposition. New leadership would have emerged within the RPP and the party would have reformed and adapted itself in keeping up with the needs of the times. While İnönü led the party, it was impossible to imagine any change; he was a figure from the past and cast a huge shadow under which nothing new could grow. For the Democrats, their ten-year rule was their failure to come to terms with the 'Pasha factor'.

After Menderes was hanged by the military junta that seized power in May 1960, there was a droll joke doing the rounds of Ankara. Menderes went to heaven and met Atatürk one day, and Atatürk asked him about political life in Turkey. Menderes then recounted in detail all that had befallen the country since Atatürk's death, ending with his own execution. Menderes concluded: 'Well Pasha, that's Kısmet (fate)'. 'No Adnan', replied Atatürk, 'that's İsmet, not Kısmet'!

Menderes's undemocratic rule cannot be explained away simply by the RPP and the 'Pasha factor'. However insecure he may have felt, he knew that the opposition was weak and disorganized and gave him nothing to fear. Menderes's political apprehension was founded on the makeup of his own party. The Democrats had never been as homogeneous as they appeared to be while in opposition. The top echelon of the party's leadership came out of dissidents in the RPP. But much of its provincial support came from people who entered politics only after the party was established in January 1946. Such people remembered the harsh rule of the provincial gendarmerie and had an irrational hatred for the RPP and İnönü. Many were blinded by the spirit of revenge and wanted the party to take a hard line with the RPP, even while it was the governing party. They accused their leader of colluding with İnönü, and some even left the DP and went on to form the Nation Party in 1948. In power, these DP dissidents accused Menderes of being no different from the Republicans and of offering virtually the same programme.

Menderes was confronted repeatedly with such criticism at provincial party congresses. He soon learned that his internal opposition was more troublesome than the opposition in parliament. He knew that he could appease DP dissidents by taking harsh measures against the RPP. That policy partly explains the anti-democratic laws his government passed against the RPP, as well as laws against such institutions as the universities and the press. Menderes may have won over some of his dissidents, but these measures alienated the liberal intelligentsia, who had supported the DP from the very beginning because of its promise of political liberalization. The intelligentsia, though few in number, were articulate and were a voice in the universities, the press, and the professions. The DP government was expected to strengthen civil society by furthering democratic freedoms instead of curbing them. But Menderes's measures against the press, the opposition, and university autonomy, all suggested that he was not committed to a more free and democratic Turkey. The government's ability to close down the opposition Nation Party in January 1954 revealed how fragile party politics could be.

Menderes was transformed by his success in the 1954 election. His popular vote had increased, as had his representation in parliament. He became convinced that he had chosen the correct policies because the people said so; he felt he no longer needed to consult even sympathetic journalists who had supported the DP since 1946. The only effective check on government was a strong opposition in the assembly. Since the founding of the Republic, the Grand National Assembly of Turkey was the most powerful institution of the state. National sovereignty was vested in parliament, which elected the president from among its members. The president then appointed the prime minister, who formed his cabinet from among the 'representatives of the nation' (*milletvekili*), as members of parliament are designated in Turkey. They were (and are) expected to represent the nation and not the constituencies from which they were elected.

Under the 1924 constitution, parliament passed laws and there was no upper house to review these laws or a constitutional court to assess their constitutionality. The president alone had the veto to suspend laws, but he was too intimately associated with the governing party to act independently. Without a strong opposition party, the government could do as it pleased, providing it could keep its own party in line. That became Menderes's principal concern after 1954, for his political problems stemmed largely from within his own party.

DP liberals, who supported free enterprise and political liberalism, came out strongly against the government's policy of state controls over the economy and curbs on political activity. Such liberal Democrats either resigned or were expelled from the party. They included such prominent democrats as Fevzi Lütfi Karaosmanoğlu, who formed the Freedom Party in December 1955. Menderes became totally dependent on his parliamentary group and agreed to the resignation of his cabinet while he alone remained to form a new cabinet. In agreeing to this political manoeuvre, parliament confessed that there was no one else in the party able to lead the government or keep the party together. Thereafter, Menderes treated his parliamentary group with great humility and respect.

ECONOMIC CONCERNS

The downturn in the economy after 1955 began to have an impact on Turkey's political life. Unfortunately, the economic miracle of the early fifties was based on flimsy foundations and was therefore doomed to collapse. Food and cotton production was based, not on improved agricultural techniques, but on an increase of acreage in cultivation. By 1954, the economy began to show signs of stagnation and the growth rate began to drop. The years 1956–9 were marked by spiralling inflation, with prices rising at 18 per cent per annum. Meanwhile the growth rate of the economy had levelled out to a mediocre 4 per cent, barely enough to keep up with the high birth rate. The economy had seen artificial growth and no sign of development that became self-sustaining. The constantly rising inflation undermined the living standards of salary and wage earners. Military officers were directly affected and resented the loss of prestige their profession suffered as a result of the decline in their living standard. They complained that they were no longer able to marry into middle-class families because such families preferred to give their daughters to the emerging business class. That had grave political consequences and was one of the factors that led to the military coup d'état in 1960.

There was also a great shortage of foreign exchange, thanks to the government's policy of over-pricing the Turkish lira. Until the devaluation of 1958, the lira was kept at 2.8 liras to the dollar, while its real value was around ten liras. As a result, imports were subsidized by the government and were very cheap, while exports were prohibitively expensive. This policy encouraged corruption on a large scale; if a businessman had political patronage he was able to acquire foreign exchange cheaply and make a small fortune. Fortunes were made during this period, but the treasury was left bankrupt.

We don't know how the Democrats would have fared had elections been held in 1958 when they were due. Realizing that the economy would have been in worse shape in 1958, Menderes decided to call them early, in October 1957. Even so, the election marked the decline of the DP, with Republican seats increasing from 31 to 178. The Democrats were still very much in command, though they were forced to pursue a more populist policy, with the exploitation of religion for political ends. That was especially true after Menderes survived the air crash at Gatwick in London on 17 February 1959. Menderes's supporters exploited his survival as a miracle (fourteen others were killed) and he was seen as a man of destiny, chosen by God to serve a higher purpose.

By the time of the 1957 election, the Democrats no longer controlled the economy. Menderes believed that he faced only a short-term problem and that all he needed was time before his policies showed results. He turned to the West to seek help and in July 1958, Washington agreed to provide a loan of US $359 million in order to consolidate Turkey's US $400 million debt. In return, Menderes agreed to 'stabilize' the economy by devaluing the Turkish lira from 2.8 to 9.025 liras to the US dollar. The stabilization programme did not have the desired effect, so in October 1959, Menderes went to America to seek more financial loans. But the Eisenhower administration refused to bail him out and Menderes returned empty-handed. He then decided to visit the Soviet Union in July 1960, to see if the cold war enemy would be more forthcoming with a loan. But he had decided late in the day to repair fences with Moscow; before any such visit could take place, Menderes was overthrown by his army.

THE ARMY ENTERS THE FRAY

Political tension had mounted after the 1957 election. The opposition was much stronger and had issues it could exploit against the government, but it lacked the means to bring down Menderes except by defeat in the general election. Menderes tried to bolster his authority by forming a nationwide front called the 'Fatherland Front', whose aim was to isolate his critics and disarm the opposition. Those who refused to join the front were denounced as 'subversives' and their names were broadcast in the media. Instead of bringing unity, the 'Fatherland Front' polarized political life. When this political manoeuvre failed to quell the opposition, the Democrats set up a committee, in April 1960, to investigate the opposition's 'subversive activities', whose aim, they claimed, was to engineer a military revolt. In Ankara, there were student protests, which spread to other parts of the country. Martial law was declared but to no avail; finally, on 24 May, Menderes declared that the investigating committee had completed its work and that he would hold early elections in September. But Menderes's declarations came too late. Groups of military officers, alienated from DP rule, had been conspiring since 1957 to bring about its end. They intervened on 27 May and dismissed the DP government.

Reform of Turkey's armed forces had been an important plank in the DP's programme. With the declaration of the Truman Doctrine in 1947, the Pentagon had begun to provide modern weapons to an army that was still equipped with First World War vintage arms. Modernization was accelerated when Turkey became a member of NATO in 1952, and Menderes seemed to favour military reform when he appointed retired Colonel Seyfi Kurtbek as minister of national defence to carry out the necessary reorganization. The Kurtbek reorganization plan was popular with younger officers, but not with the generals, who feared early retirement as they were considered incapable of mastering the new techniques of modern warfare. A hierarchical army, still Prussian in its attitudes, resented sharing power with junior officers. They came out in opposition to the reforms and spread rumours that Kurtbek was planning a military coup. Menderes responded by postponing the reforms and Kurtbek decided to resign in July 1953, realizing that his programme had been shelved.

For Menderes, reorganization of Turkey's armed forces was not a priority. He was happy to maintain the status quo and not challenge his top brass. He decided to win over some of the important generals to the party, one of the most prominent being General Nuri Yamut who had made his reputation in Korea and was well-known to the Pentagon. While such senior officers sided with the Democrats, Menderes felt secure from any threat from pro-İnönü generals.

Money for the armed forces was not on the Democrats' list of priorities; Menderes preferred to spend Turkey's limited resources on building the country's infrastructure, its roads and factories, in order to accelerate economic development. The country was already spending more in relation to its national income than most other NATO allies. Military expenditure had already risen substantially from US $248 million in 1950 to US $381 million in 1953, an increase of 54 per cent, and this figure kept growing throughout the 1950s. The Turks thought that the country's military expenditure would fall once they were members of NATO, for the alliance would subsidize Turkey's armed forces. That did not prove to be the case, and Menderes had no intention of spending more money from the budget to increase military salaries so that they would keep up with the spiralling inflation. Expenditure on military reform would have to wait until the economy generated a larger surplus.

Once Turkey joined NATO, not only did it spend more resources on the military, but the very character of its armed forces changed dramatically. The officers were exposed to new technology and methods of warfare, and ideologically they became more cosmopolitan, abandoning parochial nationalism in favour of Cold War anti-communism. They were sent for training to other

NATO countries, where the way of life was totally different from the one at home. They acquired a new world view and a desire to reform Turkey. They became politicized and resented the political strife in their midst. Membership of NATO also intensified the division within the officer corps, along both technological and political lines. The Democrats managed to co-opt the generals so thoroughly that the conspirators had difficulty in recruiting a full general to lead their conspiracy. Turkey's armed forces in the fifties had become divided along lines of rank and economic status.

Disaffection among the officers was triggered in the mid-fifties by the spiralling inflation, political instability, and a general sense of discontent in urban areas. Being mainly from the lower middle class, they shared the grievances of that class, whose position in society was being rapidly eroded by the free-market philosophy of the governing party. Such people deplored what they perceived as the erosion of moral, traditional values that had made the Turkish people what they were. The Democrats were undermining these values in favour of crass materialism that glorified wealth and ostentation. That is how Orhan Erkanlı, a radical member of the 1960 junta, expressed himself soon after the coup:

> The clique in power after 1954 trampled on all the rights of the people. They deceived the nation and dragged the country into economic and social ruin. Moral values were forgotten and people were made oblivious of them. The institution of the state was transformed into an appendage of the party organization. The pride of the Turkish armed forces, which are the only organized force in the country, was hurt on every occasion; the uniform which is the real legacy of our history brought shame to those who wore it. (*Cumhuriyet*, 20 July 1960)

Discontent in the armed forces took a political form, reflecting the inter-party struggle of those years. The officers came to see the problems of Turkey in the way they were articulated by the Republican opposition and the press. The solutions that were acceptable to them after they seized power were also borrowed from the intelligentsia that supported the opposition. Only a few officers with a radical bent, men like Alparslan Türkeş and Orhan Erkanlı, had an agenda for taking Turkey in a direction different from the one envisaged by the elite. These people may well have been influenced by what they were witnessing in such neighbouring countries as Nasser's Egypt, Syria, Iraq, and Pakistan – all under military rule in 1960. But in Turkey, the hierarchy was well established in the armed forces and the radicals were soon marginalized by the senior officers. Henceforth it was they who established the political agenda for Turkey for the rest of the twentieth century.

SUGGESTED FURTHER READING

Kemal Karpat, *Turkey's Politics: the Transiton to a Multi-party System* (Princeton, 1959).

B. Lewis, *The Emergence of Modern Turkey*, 3rd edn (London, 2001).

Feroz Ahmad, *The Turkish Experiment in Democracy, 1950–1975* (London, 1977).

Cem Eroğul, 'The establishment of multi-party rule: 1945–71' in I.C. Schick and E.A. Tonak (eds.), *Turkey in Transition* (New York, 1987), pp. 101–43.

Morris Singer, *The Economic Advance of Turkey, 1938–1960* (Ankara, 1977).

6

Military Guardians, 1960–1980

GOVERNMENT BY JUNTA

Rather than the election victory of May 1950, it was the period that followed the military coup of 27 May 1960, which marked the beginning of a new phase in Turkey's political, social, and economic life. Few of the 38 officers who constituted the military junta came to power with any preconceived notions of Turkey's political future. Such men as Colonel Alpaslan Türkeş (1917–97), who went on to play an independent political role as leader of a neo-fascist party, had their own radical agenda. Most simply followed the lead of the intelligentsia, to reform the country's politics in keeping with the needs of the times.

The aims of the junta were explained in the radio broadcast announcing the coup on the morning of 27 May 1960.

> Honourable fellow countrymen! [announced Colonel Türkeş] ...
> Owing to the crisis into which our democracy has fallen, in view of the recent sad incidents, and in order to avert fratricide, the Turkish armed forces have taken over the administration of the country. Our armed forces have taken this initiative for the purpose of extricating the parties from the irreconcilable situation into which they have fallen ... [and will hold] just and free elections as soon as possible under the supervision and arbitration of an above-party administration ... [They will hand] over the administration to whichever party wins the election.

This initiative is not directed against any person or class. Our administration will not resort to any aggressive act against individuals, nor will it allow others to do so. All fellow countrymen, irrespective of the parties to which they may belong, will be treated in accordance with the laws.

Most of the officers wanted to return to their barracks after holding 'just and free' elections and restoring power to the politicians. However, their plans changed when some law professors from the universities were called in to advise them. The 38 officers who formed the National Unity Committee (NUC) represented a broad coalition of factions in the armed forces. The reason why the Committee was so large was precisely because any number of secret factions claimed to be involved in the coup and wanted to be represented. Those left out of the junta were disgruntled and became an element of instability in the armed forces, and attempted to carry out coups during the next three years.

The NUC, having no plan of its own, took the advice of academics and formed a commission to prepare a new constitution. Professor Sıddık Sami Onar, professor of law and rector of Istanbul University, chaired the commission. Soldiers had captured political power, but it was intellectuals who turned the 27 May movement into a revolution, a 'revolution of the intellectuals'. The ideas that the Onar Commission put forward were not original; they had been in circulation since the mid-fifties when it was understood that there could be no true democracy under institutions inherited from the single-party period. Responding to the DP's autocratic rule, the opposition began to formulate reforms for when they came to power. The RPP promised to amend the constitution and establish a bicameral parliament, so that the upper house could monitor the legislation passed by the lower chamber. The Republicans made a number of promises: a constitutional court to test the legality of laws; proportional representation so as to prevent parliament being dominated by one party; the right to strike for the unions; the right to unionize for state employees; to repeal anti-democratic laws; and to establish a neutral bureaucracy.

The Onar Commission adopted most of these ideas; it also claimed that the DP had lost its legality because it had failed to respect the constitution and other institutions such as the press, the armed forces and the universities. Therefore their removal from power by the junta was quite legal. The professors legitimized the coup and allowed the junta to stay in power.

NATIONAL UNITY COMMITTEE: INTERIM GOVERNMENT

Having legitimized the coup, the commission recommended that the NUC create a new state structure and institutions before holding elections and restoring power to the civilians. It proposed a new constitution, a new electoral law, and new laws and institutions that were in keeping with Turkey's place in the democratic world. The NUC became the interim government legalized by a provisional constitution in June 1960. It began to exercise sovereignty on behalf of the Turkish nation, until an assembly had been elected under the new constitution. It held legislative power directly and executive power through the cabinet appointed by the Head of State, who was also Chairman of the NUC. Only the judiciary functioned independently of the junta.

There was much factionalism within the NUC. General Cemal Gürsel (1895–1966) was chosen as president, head of state, prime minister, and commander-in-chief, simply because he was amiable and without ambition and therefore stood above the factions. There were two factions that struggled for power: the moderates supported the Onar Commission's proposals and wanted to restore power to civilians; the radicals, mainly lesser officers, including Colonel Türkeş, wanted to retain power and restructure the Turkish state and society more radically than Professor Onar's proposals. They spoke of creating a 'new culture' and a populist political system without parties, akin to Nasser's Egypt.

The factional struggle lasted until 13 November, when the moderates ousted fourteen of the radicals and exiled many of them to embassies abroad. The purge of 'the fourteen' was welcomed by the bourgeoisie which disliked their collectivist radicalism, but it angered serving junior officers and cadets and created instability in the armed forces. Some officers who had been active in the 1960 coup, but had been kept out of the NUC, began to conspire again. One, Talat Aydemir, attempted two coups that were aborted, the first on 22 February 1962 and the second on 20/21 May 1963. The days of military coups from below were over. The military coup of 27 May 1960 was the first and the last successful military intervention made from outside the hierarchical structure of Turkey's armed forces.

THE 'SECOND REPUBLIC'

Active officers saw the danger of intervention from below or 'outside the chain of command' and took measures to prevent such occurrences in the future. They formed the Armed Forces Union (AFU) in 1961, a body that included all ranks and which monitored activities throughout the military. Within a short time, the AFU had become the arbiter of political power and the guarantor of the new constitution. Meanwhile, a new constitution had been written and put to a referendum on 9 July 1961. It received a lukewarm reception and almost 40 per cent voted against the constitution. People feared the return of the RPP and single-party rule, even although the new election law guaranteed proportional representation and therefore a multi-party parliament.

The 1961 constitution was radically different from its predecessor. There was now a bicameral parliament, with the lower chamber (the National Assembly) of 450 deputies, who were elected every four years by a system of proportional representation. The Senate consisted of 150 members, elected for a term of six years by a straight majority vote, with one-third retiring every two years. All the members of the NUC were made life senators, while the president nominated 15 senators. The two chambers in joint session constituted the Grand National Assembly of Turkey (GNAT). The assembly elected the president for a term of seven years, from among its own members, by a two-thirds majority. Cemal Gürsel was elected the first president of the Second Republic. He appointed the prime minister, who chose the rest of the cabinet. The cabinet was responsible to the assembly.

The Constitutional Court became one of the most controversial institutions of the Second Republic. It reviewed the constitutionality of legislation and sent back many measures, much to the annoyance of conservative governments. The guarantees of freedom of thought, expression, association and publication contained in the constitution were as important as the new institutions. The state became a 'social state' promising 'social and economic rights', with provisions for the State to plan economic development so as to achieve social justice, and individuals to have the right to own and inherit property and have the freedom of work and enterprise.

The military high command was also given a role in government. Article III created the National Security Council (NSC) which consisted of 'the Ministers provided by law, the Chief of the General Staff, and representatives of the armed forces'. The president (himself a retired general) or, in his absence, the prime minister, presided over the NSC. Its function was to assist the cabinet 'in the making of decisions related to national security and co-ordination.' The term 'national security' was so broad and all-embracing that the generals were able to interfere in virtually every question before the cabinet. In March 1962, the powers of the NSC were increased even further, and the chief of general staff became virtually autonomous of the minister of war because Article 110 made him responsible to the prime minister.

The armed forces were given autonomy and were recognized by the civilians as partners and guardians of the new order they had just created. The generals soon became a vital part of Turkey's political and socio-economic life. The pay and living standards of officers were increased substantially so that they were no longer affected by inflation. Retired generals were sent as ambassadors or were appointed directors of corporations and banks. In this way they were integrated into the system!

The military entered the world of business and industry in 1961, when the Army Mutual Assistance Association (generally known by its Turkish acronym OYAK) was created. Capital was generated by the contribution of ten per cent of officers' salaries and then invested in some of the most lucrative ventures in the economy. OYAK functioned as another corporation managed by civilian managers and technocrats, but it was attached to the ministry of defence. It provided loans and other benefits to its members and sold goods at discounted prices to soldiers and their families, in supermarkets called 'army bazaars'. This service was another hedge against inflation. OYAK has continued to expand and diversify so that it is now to be found in virtually every area of the economy from automobile production to insurance and banking; it is sometimes described as the 'third sector' of the economy, along with the state and private sectors.

The military had become the guardians of a system of burgeoning capitalism rather than such abstractions as the 'nation' or 'Kemalism', though the rhetoric of the past has been retained. The principal concern was with maintaining stability and to intervene whenever that was threatened, no matter where the threat came from. But the generals disliked movements of the Left for they threatened the system; but they were equally hostile to parties of the Right if they were the source of instability. While they were in sympathy with parties whose free market ideology they shared, the generals no longer allied themselves to specific parties or their leaders; parties and leaders now wooed the generals.

ECONOMIC REFORMS

While resolving political issues inherited from the DP decade, the NUC was forced to lay new foundations for the economy. The Democrats had pursued a haphazard economic policy that brought about growth rather than development; the NUC opted for a policy that would bring about development and growth. To accomplish this ambitious task they created the State Planning Organization (SPO), whose principal function was to supervise the economy according to a five-year plan. The SPO was created in September 1960, and was included in the new constitution. It was an advisory body, chaired by the prime minister and therefore influenced by the party in power. Moreover, the plan had to be approved by the cabinet and the assembly before it could be implemented; as a result, the entire process of planning became political and ideological. Under coalitions and neo-Democrat governments that ruled once multi-party politics were restored, Article 41 of the Constitution became a dead letter. It promised that 'Economic and social life shall be regulated in a manner consistent with justice and the principle of full employment, with the objective of assuring for everyone a standard of living befitting human dignity.' Such promises did not suit Turkey's nascent business/industrial community, who had become politically influential. Rather than the 'social state' promised by the 1961 constitution, they wanted a state that would discipline and control the workers; they believed that the right to strike or collective bargaining was a luxury for a country at Turkey's stage of development. For the moment, capital and labour were forced to coexist, but the coexistence came to an end in March 1971, when the military intervened in order to resolve the contradiction in favour of capital.

Meanwhile the five-year plan was launched in 1963, and Turkey embarked on a path of rapid industrialization based on the model of producing goods it had formerly imported. Goods such as automobiles, refrigerators, televisions, etc. were usually made in collaboration with such foreign firms as Ford or Philips; Turkish capitalists were not entrepreneurs who would risk creating anything original which could compete on the world market. They were concerned about making quick profits. They refused to permit structural change by allowing state economic enterprises to reorganize and become efficient competitors. They wanted the state to subsidize the private sector as in mixed economies. There was no land reform, no taxing of farm incomes, or measures to increase productivity. But despite the lack of structural reform in both sectors, the economy grew at the SPO's target rate of 7 per cent. The world economy was favourable, as it had been in the early fifties. There was a demand for Turkish workers in Germany, undergoing its 'economic miracle'. Export of labour helped Turkey in two ways: with employment, as peasants left the land, and with foreign exchange, as workers sent back remittances to their families in German marks. Turkey's economy soon became dependent on these remittances.

Despite the plan, economic expansion remained lopsided. The agrarian sector failed to grow as fast as the planners hoped, while the urban sector grew rapidly, but more in construction and services than industrial production. With low export earnings, the economy depended on the savings of Turkish workers in Europe. When the European economy entered a downturn in the early 1970s, the impact on Turkey was severe.

The planners had succeeded in transforming Turkey's economy and society within a few years. Turkey was no longer predominantly agrarian, with a small state-run industrial sector, as it had been in the 1950s. By the end of the 1960s, there was a dynamic private industrial sector, which contributed as much to the gross national product (GNP) as agriculture. But by 1973, industry had overtaken agriculture.

CHANGING SOCIETAL STRUCTURES

Industry led to urbanization as Anatolian peasants settled in shanty towns in and around the major cities. By the sixties, there was a small working class that became active politically, led by a class-conscious leadership free to act under the new constitution. Workers had acquired the right to bargain collectively and to strike, but they continued to be led by the conservative Confederation of the Workers' Union of Turkey (Türk-İs). This confederation, organized with the advice of the American Federation of Labour–Congress of Industry Organizations (AFL–CIO), chose to be 'non-political' and called only for economic gains. But in 1967, a few unions affiliated with Türk-İs broke away and formed the Confederation of Revolutionary Workers' Unions (DİSK). Their demands were both political and economic and they had the support of the recently founded Workers' Party of Turkey (WPT).

The bourgeoisie had also grown, both in size and in confidence, during the sixties. In the past it had relied exclusively on the governing party to further its cause. But in 1971, it found its own pressure group, the Association of Turkish Industrialists and Businessmen (TÜSİAD), which has played an important political role ever since. Consumption patterns changed as more goods became available, and the introduction of radio (in the fifties) and television in the seventies transformed social and political life. Both radio and television were important for the success of smaller political parties with limited financial resources, as they could appeal directly to voters through their broadcasts.

The process of monopolization under large corporations in partnership with foreign capital began to undermine local and much smaller enterprises, simply because they were unable to compete. This led to bankruptcies and the closure of thousands of workshops, threatening the livelihood of millions. Meanwhile, new patterns of consumption caused inflation and a demand for higher wages and salaries. All these changes in Turkey's economy and society aggravated an already unstable political situation when the NUC restored multi-party politics in 1961.

The 1961 Constitution provided the people of Turkey with a greater degree of political freedom than they had ever enjoyed since the creation of the Republic. The new state was described as a 'social state'; it gave greater civil rights than ever before, autonomy to the universities and the right for students to organize associations, and workers enjoyed the right to strike. In this environment of political freedom, workers and leftist intellectuals united to form a socialist party, the WPT, and provided an ideological alternative to the debate on political life framed in the past on Kemalist terms.

THE FORMATION OF NEW POLITICAL PARTIES

The 1961 Constitution and new laws had changed the political structure, but not the underlying structures. The DP had been dissolved; many of its leaders who were put on trial for violating the Constitution were imprisoned, and three ministers – Prime Minister Menderes, Finance Minister Polatkan and Foreign Minister Zorlu – were executed. The Democrats remained popular at a grass-roots level and the neo-Democrat parties that were formed in 1961 depended on that vote bank. In the 1961 elections, the Justice Party (JP) and the New Turkey Party (NTP) won 48.5 per cent of the vote between them (34.8 and 13.7 per cent respectively). İnönü's RPP won only 36.7 per cent, insufficient votes or seats in the assembly to form the government. As the generals would not permit a neo-Democratic government, İnönü was asked to form the first of three coalitions which governed Turkey from November 1961 to 1964.

These years were marked by political instability and it was only the threat of military intervention that kept the coalition together. The Justice Party gained strength, especially under the leadership of Süleyman Demirel (1924–), becoming the most popular party after the local elections of November 1963. When the third İnönü coalition resigned on 12 February 1965, because it had failed to win a vote of confidence, Demirel was ready to take charge. The last coalition was led by an Independent elected on the JP list and Demirel therefore ruled by proxy. The role of the coalition was to lead Turkey to the election of 1965; this brought the Justice Party to power and restored a semblance of stability.

The Justice Party was founded in February 1961 and was initially led by a retired general, Ragıp Gumüşpala, who had the trust of the armed forces. He was expected to keep the neo-

Democrats in check. When he died in June 1964, the party chose Süleyman Demirel, the least controversial candidate, as chairman. He was an engineer and a technocrat, who came to the top because the NUC had eliminated the top layers of DP leadership after the coup. Coming from a modest rural background, he was able to appeal to ordinary people, especially the Anatolian migrants of the shantytowns who were able to identify with him as someone who had succeeded by his own talents.

THE NEW POLITICS AND THE WIDER WORLD

Political life in the sixties was dramatically different from what it had been in earlier decades. The country had been politicized and the 1961 Constitution provided a new framework for ideological discourse. For the first time a Left emerged that challenged politics as usual, especially Turkey's foreign policy. The country no longer felt isolated and became conscious of what was happening in the world around, especially as students could now read left-wing Marxist literature, which was widely available, even in small towns. Conservative forces, alarmed by these trends, began to organize against the Left, describing their fight as a struggle against Moscow's communism.

Politics in Turkey were influenced by the cold war and events in the Middle East. Policymakers in Washington had been alarmed by the rise of nationalism in the Middle East and Asia and concluded that nationalism was as great a threat to Western interests as communism. Consequently, in November 1958, the US government issued an internal document – National Security Agency document 5820/1 – arguing that Islam could be used as an antidote to nationalism and communism. After 1960, many Turkish nationalists began to criticize US policy and their government's unquestioning loyalty to it. The NUC continued to reaffirm Turkey's commitment to NATO, and during the Cuban Missile Crisis in October 1962, İnönü stood by Washington, despite the Soviet nuclear threat. But Turks learned that the Kennedy Administration had bargained away the Jupiter missiles in Anatolia in its negotiations with Moscow. Soon after, it was revealed that in case of war with the Soviet Union, NATO planners had decided that much of Anatolia, apart from Istanbul and western Anatolia, was expendable! Turkey's foreign relations had become a major factor in everyday politics.

THE CYPRUS QUESTION

The crisis with Greece over Cyprus in the winter of 1963/4 brought the situation to a head. The Menderes government became embroiled in the Cyprus question wherein the Greek-Cypriot national movement sought independence from Britain and union with Greece. Initially, Ankara and the Turkish Cypriots – about 20 per cent of the island's population – supported Britain and the status quo. By 1955, when Britain's hold was weakening, Ankara asked that Britain return the island to the Turks from whom she had acquired it in 1878. Both Britain and Turkey were convinced that Greek Cypriots would prefer British to Turkish rule! When the Greeks found that proposal unacceptable, Ankara proposed partition; since that too was out of the question, Ankara proposed and pressed for partition in 1957. After prolonged negotiations, in 1959, the parties agreed to the creation of a republic in Cyprus, with Britain, Greece, and Turkey agreeing to guarantee the constitutional rights of the Turkish-Cypriot community. On 15 August 1960, the Republic of Cyprus came into being with a Greek-Cypriot president (Archbishop Makarios) and a Turkish-Cypriot vice president (Dr Fazıl Küçük).

President Makarios found the power-sharing constitution unworkable and said he would not be bound by the 1960 treaty guaranteed by Britain, Greece, and Turkey. Violence broke out on the island between the two communities in late 1963 and on 13 March 1964, İnönü, as one of the guarantors, threatened unilateral action unless there was an immediate cease-fire. Makarios rejected İnönü's note, though he lifted the siege from Turkish districts and hostages were released.

In Turkey, nationalist passions were aroused and there was overwhelming support for military intervention, as everyone believed in the justice of the Turkish cause. In January 1966, the publication of a letter from President Johnson to Prime Minister İnönü (sent in June 1964) created a furor throughout the country. İnönü was told that the Turks could not use arms provided by Washington without US consent, and he issued a warning that NATO would not come to Turkey's aid 'against the Soviet Union if Turkey takes a step which results in Soviet intervention without the full consent and understanding of its NATO allies.'

Anti-American demonstrations followed, to the extent that visits by the US Sixth Fleet to Turkish ports became virtually impossible. The demonstrations continued until the military intervention of 12 March 1971. The nationalists and leftists began calling for a non-aligned Turkey, and even the government asked the foreign ministry to re-examine the country's foreign relations in light of the prevailing world conditions. After due consideration, the foreign ministry proposed turning more to a Europe which was then in the process of forming a common market and political union. The Turkish general staff decided to create a division independent of NATO to be used when 'national interest' required, as in Cyprus.

Anti-Americanism polarized society into a conservative Right and a nationalist and radical Left, sometimes described as neo-Kemalist. The Left viewed the US as the leader of the capitalist world upon which Turkey had become dependent. They interpreted Turkey's history since 1919 as a struggle for independence against imperialism – independence that the sultan had been willing to abandon merely to remain in power. After the Second World War, both the RPP and the DP had betrayed Kemalism by accepting the Truman Doctrine and the Marshall Plan, joining NATO and the Baghdad Pact, and making Turkey an appendage of the West. Recent events had shown that such a policy was against the national interest and therefore had to be abandoned. Such was the criticism of students' clubs in the universities, the Workers' Party, and the unions. The RPP was influenced by some of these radical ideas and responded by adopting what was described as a 'left-of centre' political line and adopting the slogan that 'this order must change'.

The Right was alarmed by these radical nationalist ideas and attacked them as communist propaganda. It turned to Islam – as the US National Security Agency had suggested in 1958 – as the 'antidote to communism'. The 'Association to Combat Communism', founded in 1962, exploited Islam as an ideological tool against the Left. This trend continued throughout the 1960s, encouraged by money from Saudi Arabia, where an organization known as the 'Union of the World of Islam' had been founded to combat nationalism and communism. Turkey's provincial lower middle classes also used Islam to mobilize support for their cause in response to such internal developments as rapid industrialization and the growth of monopolies that undermined local crafts and commerce.

The Justice Party had come to power in 1965 and had to deal with these new forces. Its leader, Süleyman Demirel, symbolized the new face of capitalism intimately associated with the US. He had spent a year in the United States as an Eisenhower fellow and was then employed by a US multinational construction company engaged in Turkey. He and his policies were therefore an easy target for attacks from the Left and the religious Right, which described him as a freemason. By the late sixties, Demirel's position had become virtually untenable. The Cyprus question remained unresolved, with Turkish-Cypriots besieged in their enclaves or emigrating to Britain and Australia. Students and workers became more militant, and anti-Americanism increased along with US involvement in Vietnam, the pro-Washington 'Colonels' coup' in Greece in April 1967, and the Arab–Israeli war of June 1967. The last two events consolidated US hegemony in the eastern Mediterranean and weakened Turkey's role in the region.

The struggle between labour and capital became bitter, especially after students and workers in Paris almost succeeded in carrying out a revolution. These events were influential in Turkey; they encouraged the Left but showed the government the potential threats to its power. In 1967, some unions had already broken away from the pro-government and 'non-political' confederation (Türk-İş) and formed their own confederation (DİSK), which they described as 'revolutionary'. Türk-İş had been unofficially affiliated with the Justice Party, which enabled the government and employers to control the workers. Government and employers were alarmed by the workers' militancy and their growing strength at the expense of the docile Türk-İş. When they saw that they were losing control of the unions, they decided to act and regain control before it was too late.

POLITICAL FRAGMENTATION

As well as Leftist militancy, the government also had to confront a political Right that was fragmenting under the impact of socio-economic developments. Small enterprises throughout Anatolia owned by the traditional middle classes were unable to survive the competition of the large cosmopolitan corporations situated in the Istanbul-Marmara region. They felt that Demirel had betrayed them and given his support to the large holding companies. This resulted in their defection from the Justice Party after the 1969 election, thus weakening its electoral support. They began to turn to such small Rightist parties as Colonel Alparslan Türkeş's neo-fascist Nationalist Action Party (NAP), or the Reliance Party formed by Professor Turhan Feyzioğlu who left the RPP in protest at its left-of-centre programme, or the National Order Party (NOP) founded by Professor Necmettin Erbakan (1926–), or the Democratic Party formed by JP dissidents. Türkeş was an ultra-nationalist who claimed to be opposed to both monopoly capitalism and communism; Feyzioğlu was simply right of centre and had little to offer that was different from Demirel; Erbakan used 'Islamic' discourse to criticize the monopolies as lackeys of the Christian/Jewish West. Türkeş and Erbakan's parties acquired electoral strength only in the 1990s; until then they were not an electoral threat to the JP, but useful allies in coalition governments of the 1970s. As for the Reliance Party, it proved to be ephemeral and dissolved itself in the 1970s. But for the moment, the fragmentation of the Right became the major factor of political instability.

By the early 1970s, the situation in Turkey had become explosive. Student and working-class militancy, social and economic changes, growing political conflict, and the world situation proved to be a dangerous mix. There was a 'revolution of rising expectations' – expectations that were not being met for the majority of the people. There was widespread unemployment, aggravated by the end of the 'German economic miracle' that had siphoned off workers throughout the sixties. Population grew rapidly without the job market or the educational system capable of absorbing the younger population. Overcrowded schools and universities were ideal for recruiting militants for the Left and the Right, and these youths played a crucial role in creating the political instability that led to military intervention on 12 March 1971.

Demirel had attempted to control the situation in the assembly by having the 'national remainder system' of the 1961 electoral law abolished in March 1968. This provision had permitted the Workers' Party 14 seats in the 1965 assembly, and its representatives had played a very important role in the ranks of the opposition. The amendment had changed that and in 1969, the WPT won only 2 seats. The party's leader, Mehmet Ali Aybar (1910–95), had warned the assembly that 'if this law passes, unrest in the country will rise to another level ... you will be responsible for whatever befalls our democracy'. The Left, no longer having an outlet for expressing discontent in the assembly, vented their frustrations in the street, though the Workers' Party itself did not encourage subversion or violence. The Left was convinced that Demirel had shut off the parliamentary road to reform and power; the only way forward was via a military coup, made in partnership with radical officers who were sympathetic to the idea of a 'National Democratic Revolution'. This group became even more militant and espoused the ideas of Maoism and the Latin American urban guerrillas.

Demirel, having undermined the parliamentary Left, set out to destroy the political trade unions, led by DİSK, and to strengthen Türk-İş. The law the government wanted to amend would eliminate a union unless it represented at least one-third of the workers in a factory. That provision was expected to destroy DİSK. Workers – not only DİSK members – came out in protest against the law on 15/16 June 1970 and paralysed the Istanbul-Marmara region; the authorities shut down ferry services across the Sea of Marmara to prevent the protest from spilling over into European Istanbul. The Right described the protest as 'a dress rehearsal for revolution', and observers predicted that the military would intervene as civilians were unable to maintain law and order. Demirel had often complained that he found it impossible to govern with such a liberal and permissive constitution, suggesting that it had to be amended and made more authoritarian.

The generals were aware of the Left's contact with radical officers. The National Intelligence Organization and military intelligence, both created in 1963, knew of the conspiracies in the military from their moles. The press reported purges of officers in 1970 when 56 generals and 516 colonels were retired. There was a threat of intervention from officers outside the 'chain of command', and the senior generals decided to forestall it and appease the radicals by carrying out a reform programme of their own.

At the beginning of 1971, Turkey was in a state of turmoil. Leftist student militants robbed banks, kidnapped US servicemen, and attacked American targets. The Gray Wolves, neo-fascist militants linked to NAP, attacked professors who were critical of the government. There was constant strike activity and more workdays were lost between 1 January and the military intervention of 12 March 1971 than during any previous year. The Islamists became more aggressive and openly rejected Atatürk and Kemalism, infuriating the armed forces.

On 8 March, Demirel, unable to control the situation, lost the support of his party's group. This triggered the military intervention, for the generals rationalized that Demirel had to go now since even his party no longer supported him. Therefore on 12 March, five senior generals – the chiefs of general staff and the commanders of the army, navy, and air force – presented a memorandum to President Cevdet Sunay and the speakers of the two chambers. They demanded the government's resignation and the formation of a strong, credible cabinet, capable of implementing the reforms envisaged by the constitution. Demirel reluctantly resigned and his resignation cleared the way for an 'above-party' government that could pass the anti-democratic measures considered necessary to govern Turkey in turbulent times.

THE MEMORANDUM REGIME AND AFTER, 1971–1980

The coup of 12 March was thought by many to have been made by radical-reformist officers who supported the 1961 Constitution. The memorandum held the Demirel government responsible for Turkey's 'anarchy, fratricidal strife, and social and economic unrest', and called for a government – formed within the framework of democratic principles and inspired by Kemalist ideas – that would implement the reformist laws envisaged by the constitution.

But priority was to be given 'to the restoration of law and order' and that meant crushing the Left. The Workers' Party was proscribed on the same day as the memorandum was issued, its leaders accused of carrying out communist propaganda and supporting Kurdish separatism. All youth organizations affiliated to the Dev-Genç (the acronym for the Federation of the Revolutionary Youth of Turkey) were closed down. Offices of such groups as the 'Ideas Clubs' in the universities, and branches of the Union of Teachers, and DİSK were searched by the police. Meanwhile, 'Idealist Hearths', NAP's youth wing, acted as vigilantes against leftists. The principal aim of this attack on the Left was to intimidate the workers and curb union militancy.

After Demirel's resignation, the new junta was undecided as to how they should exercise the power they had just seized. The Greek colonels' experience deterred them from taking over directly, and so they decided to act through an above-party civilian government and a conservative assembly. In Professor Nihat Erim, who described the liberal 1961 Constitution as a luxury for Turkey, they found a politician who would be acceptable to both the JP and the RPP. Professor Erim (1912–80), though a Republican in the 1940s, was able to work comfortably with the Democrats and later the Justice Party. He was an ambitious man and he was quite willing to collaborate with the military, though it cost him his life when the 'Revolutionary Left' assassinated him in 1980.

Erim formed a cabinet of managers and technocrats, designed to carry out the reforms proposed by the generals. His ministers came from the World Bank (Atilla Karaosmanoğlu), from OYAK (Özer Derbil), from the Turkish Petroleum Company (İhsan Topaloğlu), and the SPO (Şinasi Orel). There were also notorious anti-reformist ministers, but they were supported in the assembly. The Erim cabinet was unlikely to carry out democratic reform! First and foremost, he had to deal with outbreaks of terrorism by the so-called 'Turkish People's Liberation Army' (TPLA). It was said by some that behind the terrorists were dissident military officers, while others claimed that terrorism was the work of provocateurs from Turkey's intelligence service, agents who had infiltrated the Left, just as the FBI in America had infiltrated the Weathermen and the Black Panthers.

The state responded by declaring martial law in eleven of Turkey's 67 provinces and unleashing brutal repression. Urban

Turkey, including Istanbul and Ankara, and the south-east, the centre of Kurdish nationalism, were placed under martial law. Political life was totally paralyzed; all meetings and seminars of professional associations and unions were prohibited; two news-papers were suspended and bookshops were ordered not to sell publications proscribed by the authorities. Publications of the neo-fascist Right continued to circulate freely. Two prominent jour-nalists, Çetin Altan, an ex-Workers' Party deputy, and İlhan Selçuk, a radical Kemalist, were taken into custody and tortured; this was the first sign of an impending crackdown on intellectuals. On 3 May, all strikes and lockouts were declared illegal, much to the relief of the Employers' Unions.

The abduction on 17 May of Ephraim Elrom, Israel's consul in Istanbul, aggravated the repression. The military regime was provoked and responded by imposing draconian measures against the Left, and power was placed in the hands of martial law author-ities. Hundreds were taken into custody, including such famous authors as Yaşar Kemal and Fakir Baykurt. Torture became routine; rather than to extract information, it was designed to break the will of political prisoners so that they would give up politics. Repression failed to save Elrom; it might even have hastened his murder on the night of 21/22 May, when the authorities ordered a house-to-house search in Istanbul. Political repression under martial law became the order of the day for the next two years.

The government amended the 1961 Constitution, which the Right blamed for the country's problems. Virtually every insti-tution of state and society was modified: the trade unions, the press, radio and television, the universities, the Council of State, the Constitutional Court, the assembly, the Senate and the Court of Appeal. The liberal rights and freedoms guaranteed by the 1961 Constitution were curbed so that – in Professor Erim's words – the amended constitution guaranteed 'that there is no going back to the period before 12 March'. The democratization of the sixties had proved too costly and the liberal constitution too great a luxury for a country that wanted to make rapid progress along the capitalist path.

The amendments were made without public debate and were supported by all parties. Only Mehmed Ali Aybar, who had been expelled from the Workers' Party before 12 March, became an

Independent deputy and protested in the assembly: 'The proposed amendments of the Constitution are against the basic principle of our current democratic constitution; their aim is to proscribe socialism and for that reason cannot be reconciled with the contemporary understanding of a democratic regime.' Erim agreed: the constitution was closed to socialism but not to social democracy.

The assembly and the Senate passed 35 amended articles and introduced nine new provisional ones. The Turkish state was no longer a 'social state'; it had given up all pretence of establishing any kind of social justice. When there was the possibility of carrying out genuine reform, Demirel created a governmental crisis by withdrawing JP ministers from the cabinet. He was looking ahead. The military regime was transitional and would restore power to the parties by holding elections that he intended to win. Therefore it was important to retain the party's popular base and not support reforms that would benefit only the major corporations. Eleven reformist ministers, who had fought to reform the economy, finally understood that reform was dead when Demirel's former minister of finance was appointed to the cabinet in December 1971. They resigned in protest and Erim was forced to follow.

Erim's second cabinet (11 December 1971–17 April 1972) became dependent on Demirel's support and was unable to pass any significant reformist legislation. Apart from the constitutional amendments, Erim had accomplished little except a ban on opium cultivation, a decision made under severe pressure from the US; the decision was reversed in 1973 when party politics were restored. The next two cabinets, led by Ferit Melen and Naim Talu, were essentially caretaker ministries, whose function was to prepare the country for elections in October 1973. During this period, the social and economic problems remained unresolved and Turkey remained under martial law. But with the promise of elections, the mood of the country began to change. Since 1950, Turkish voters have taken elections very seriously as a way of expressing their hopes and discontent. But before the next election, the parties in parliament had to elect President Cevdet, Sunay's successor. Since 1960, the presidency had mediated civilian–military relations and the president had always been a military man, chosen by the generals. His election by the two chambers was considered a formality. In March 1973, when Sunay's term ended, the generals expected parliament to elect General Faruk Gürler, Commander of the Land Forces. Gürler had retired and was appointed senator from the presidential quota so that he could become a candidate for the presidency. But Demirel and Ecevit, leaders of the two largest parties in parliament, refused to collaborate. After much wrangling, the generals told the politicians to elect their own president, provided that he was acceptable to the armed forces. Finally, on 6 April 1973, parliament elected retired Admiral Fahri Korutürk as Turkey's sixth president. He was a military man and independent of the parties, but was known to be cosmopolitan and liberal, a senator who had opposed the creation of State Security Courts. His election was seen as a rebuff for the military.

THE GENERAL ELECTION OF 1973

By the summer of 1973, the stage had been set for a general election. The state had been strengthened against the forces of civil society. Machinery for crushing dissidents was in place, whether in universities or factories. But as a response to these changes, the Left gathered around the RPP, which had become a social demo-cratic party under the leadership of Bülent Ecevit (1925–). Social democracy had become an important ideology in the seventies, and was partly responsible for the military intervention which was to take place on 12 September 1980.

The RPP's social democracy partially filled the gap left by the dissolution of the Workers' Party in July 1971. Republicans had moved 'left-of-center' in the mid-1960s and the right wing of the party had left after the election of 1969. The military coup of 1971 divided the party even more over the question of whether to support the military regime or not. İsmet İnönü, the party's chairman, had come out on the side of Erim; Ecevit, the general secretary, had opposed Erim and resigned. Ecevit's political future at that point looked bleak, but he became more populist and asked the party to abandon its elitism, summed up in the old slogan: 'for the people in spite of the people'. His populism began to pay off and he won the support of party organizations in the provinces. Alarmed by this trend, İnönü called an extra-ordinary party congress in May 1972 and confronted Ecevit. İnönü, certain of defeating his rival, asked the party to choose between himself and Ecevit. Much to everyone's surprise, the party voted for Ecevit and İnönü resigned as the party's chairman on 7 May. He had occupied that office since November 1938 when Atatürk died. The following week the congress elected Ecevit as the new chairman of the now social democratic RPP.

The 1973 election aroused great expectations throughout the country. It was impossible to predict how the parties, especially the RPP, would fare. Demirel and the Justice Party seemed best placed to win, for he had maintained control over his party and showed its strength during military rule. The RPP under Ecevit was still untried and İnönü's resignation from the party in November 1972 seemed to weaken it further.

The small parties of the Right – the Democratic Party, the Nationalist Action Party, the Reliance Party, the Republican Reliance Party after its mergers with the Republican Party in July 1972 – were not considered a threat. The new National Salvation Party (NSP), formed in October 1972 by Islamists as successor to the National Order Party which was dissolved in May 1971, was an unknown quantity.

In 1973, the NSP projected a more serious image than had its predecessor, emphasizing its opposition to the growth of monopolies and dependence on foreign capital. Necmettin Erbakan (1926–) called for heavy industry and an economy based on Islamic values such as interest-free banking. The political Islamists wanted to cultivate an image of 'Islamic socialism' (though they never used those words!) for this was more likely to appeal to the voters than 'Islamic fundamentalism'. Its propaganda was so successful that the NSP became the third party after the RPP and the JP in 1973. Thereafter the challenge of political Islam and the rising counter-elite had to be taken more seriously.

The election results were most revealing; the RPP victory had been a surprise, but the Right had fragmented more seriously than predicted. The JP vote had diminished from 46.5 per cent in 1969 to 29.8 per cent, to the benefit of the Democratic Party and the NSP; they won 11.9 and 11.8 per cent of the vote respectively in their very first election. The Reliance Party vote was reduced and the NAP made a modest gain of 0.4 per cent.

The RPP victory surprised most people, but the party failed to win sufficient votes and assembly seats to govern on its own; Ecevit won 33.3 per cent of the vote and 185 seats and needed 226 to form the cabinet. Nevertheless, the party fortunes were on the rise; not since 1961 had it been so successful. The new social democratic identity had helped and the RPP won its votes in the progressive, industrial belt of Turkey and not in its traditional stronghold of backward, east and central Anatolia. The party was attractive to urban migrants, who saw social democracy as the ideology of the future.

The rightist parties, which had garnered over 60 per cent of the vote, failed to agree on a government. Therefore Ecevit was asked to form the government. He offered to form the government with the secular parties of the Right – the JP and the DP – whose leaders turned down his offer. Ecevit then invited NSP's Necmettin Erbakan, who accepted the offer. Both parties were committed to protecting 'the little man' from the monopolies, and to economic development with social justice. They both claimed to believe in democracy and fundamental rights and freedoms. They agreed to paper over their differences on cultural values for the moment. For example, the Republicans wanted to emulate the example of social democratic Europe, and the Islamists were wary of it!

COALITION GOVERNMENT: RPP–NSP

In the end, the RPP–NSP coalition was formed due to political opportunism – and it collapsed for the same reason. Both leaders had to establish their legitimacy and leading the government was the best way to do so, especially for Erbakan whose NOP had been banned in 1971. Nevertheless it took three months of hard bargaining before the coalition was finally announced in January 1974.

The coalition presented a moderate programme that alarmed neither the business community nor the generals – although the Right opposed the government's proposals for a general amnesty for political prisoners, the restoration of rights lost by the unions, and to heal the wounds left by the military regime. The Right denounced the programme as an invitation to anarchy at a time when unemployment was rising as a result of economic depression in the West.

The formation of the Ecevit-led coalition was marked by political violence instigated by 'the Grey Wolves'. Political terrorism had become a staple of Turkish life, intensifying throughout the seventies until it became the pretext for the military coup in September 1980. Before the 1971 coup, leftist terrorism had been designed to ignite revolution; the aim of rightist terrorism was to demoralize the country and create a climate of uncertainty in which military law and order would be welcomed by the masses. In opposition, Demirel was both provocative and intimidating. He often referred to Bülent Ecevit as 'Büllende', an allusion to the Chilean President Allende, who had been killed during the CIA-backed military coup of 1973, suggesting that Ecevit might share Allende's fate!

After receiving a vote of confidence on 7 February 1974, the coalition began to carry out its campaign promises. Poppy cultivation was restored, and an amended amnesty bill was passed, resulting in the release of hundreds of political prisoners. Ecevit's growing popularity caused tension in the coalition, especially after he ordered the army to intervene in response to a coup d'état in Cyprus against President Makarios. On 15 July, the National Guard of Cyprus, acting on orders from the junta in Athens, over-threw the government and seized power. When Britain refused to intervene jointly with Turkey, Ankara decided to intervene unilat-erally, as one of the guarantors of the 1960 Treaty. Turkish troops landed on the island on 26 July and launched a second offensive on 14 August, capturing 40 per cent of the island. There was now a de facto partition of Cyprus. Relations between Greece and Turkey were already tense because of a dispute over territorial waters in the Aegean Sea. Relations deteriorated even more as a result of the Cyprus issue; even now, the search for a diplomatic solution has yet to be found, despite regular negotiations.

In Turkey, Ecevit became an instant hero and tensions between him and Erbakan became so intense that Ecevit decided to resign on 18 September, convinced that a fresh election would bring his party to power. But there were no elections because the parties of the Right refused to sanction them, knowing that they would be committing political suicide if they did so. Ecevit's crisis created a situation during which there was no government for 241 days. A caretaker government failed to obtain a vote of confidence and

Demirel was finally able to form a rightist coalition, known as 'the Nationalist Front', on 31 March 1975.

The Nationalist Front was composed of the Justice, Salvation, Reliance and Nationalist Action parties and was supported in the assembly by independents who had defected from the Democratic Party. The strong presence of the NAP, with its leader Türkeş as deputy prime minister, gave the coalition a neo-fascist complexion. The slogan 'Demirel in Parliament, Türkeş in the Street' was popularized by the activities of the Grey Wolves, who began to terrorize the social democrats in order to undermine their electoral strength. The extreme left-wing forces, organized in such factions as the 'Revolutionary Left' (Dev-Sol) and the Revolutionary Path (Dev-Yol), responded and added to the confusion.

The formation of the Demirel coalition ended the possibility of an early general election, and the coalition partners used the opportunity to colonize the state apparatus. The Justice Party controlled the media; NAP and NSP took over education, recruiting their militants from the schools and universities they now controlled, and control of the ministry of customs enabled them to import arms for their movement. The militants of the Right considered themselves as part of the state now that their leaders were in a governing coalition which gave them protection and the ability to terrorize their political opponents. They not only attacked RPP meetings (even in Ecevit's presence), but also the Alevis, a Shia sect in Anatolia, as well as the Kurds, because they supported the Republicans who were secular and not ultra-nationalist.

Despite the violence, the RPP's position improved in the Senate election on 12 October 1975 and the party's vote increased to almost 44 per cent, in comparison with 35.4 per cent in 1973. The JP's share also increased from 30 to 40 per cent, while the smaller parties of the Right declined. By the mid-1970s a two-party system seemed to be gaining momentum. Under these conditions the splinter parties wanted to avoid an early general election and were determined to continue the Nationalist Front coalition, even as they struggled to strengthen their parties before the election. Political violence continued into 1976; Demirel proposed declaring martial law but was rejected by his Islamist partners who feared the secularist military. It was an open secret that the NAP was guilty of fomenting the violence, but no action could be taken as its leader was the deputy prime minister.

There was fear of some sort of fascism under Türkeş because of his party's role in the violence during the 19 May Youth Day cele- brations of 1976. Even Demirel was alarmed and decided to agree to an election in order to free himself from the hold of his extremist partners. The constitution required that the election be held by October 1977, but in April, the JP and the RPP voted to bring the date forward to 5 June 1977.

The tempo of political violence increased once elections were announced and reached its climax during the May Day celebra- tions of 1977. The workers had organized a huge rally against 'the rising tide of fascism' and everything went off peacefully until shots rang out and a panic was created that led to 34 people being trampled to death and hundreds wounded. People were convinced that the May Day massacre had been orchestrated by rightist forces within the state to intimidate voters. But five weeks later, when the election was held, the voters were not intimidated. The turnout was higher than in 1973 – 72.4 per cent as against 66.8 per cent – and the RPP won 41.4 per cent against 36.9 for the JP. The Islamist vote declined, and only the neo-fascist NAP increased its assembly seats from 3 to 13; violence and state power had been effective!

This time, Ecevit fell short by 13 of the 226 seats required to form a Republican government. He formed a minority government, but failed to win a vote of confidence; on 21 July 1977, Demirel again formed the second Nationalist Front, even though the business community, led by TÜSİAD, proposed a JP–RPP coalition. The two major parties acted in the interests of their leaders rather than on behalf of the 'national consensus' of the business community. Although the business community was becoming more powerful and articulate, it was still not able to dictate politics to the parties. Elections had failed to provide stability, and political life became even more polarized and political violence continued unabated. The Second Front coalition, marred by ideological contradictions, fell apart after the local election of 11 December 1977, when Demirel failed to obtain a vote of confidence. In the JP, moderates resigned because the party had become captive by extremists. The following week, Ecevit formed a coalition with independents who had resigned from the JP and conservatives from the Reliance Party. Such a coalition was not designed to carry out reforms and it soon undermined RPP's electoral support; forming a coalition with conservatives proved to be a major political error on Ecevit's part, almost as great as his resignation in 1974.

Apart from his failure to institute reform, Ecevit also failed to restore law and order; there were 30 political murders during the first 15 days of 1978. In July, when the police failed to cope, Ecevit called in the gendarmerie, the first sign that martial law was on the way. The Right began to assassinate prominent intellectuals, the most dramatic killing being that of Abdi İpekçi on 1 February 1978. One of the most prominent liberal journalists committed to democracy, he was also a close friend of Prime Minister Ecevit, who had himself begun his career in journalism. As usual, very few rightists were detained. When İpekci's assassin was finally arrested, he turned out to be Mehmed Ali Ağca, who before long acquired universal notoriety as the Turk who made an attempt on Pope John Paul II's life in Rome in April 1981, after escaping from a Turkish military prison.

Because it was secular and supported the RPP, the Grey Wolves now targeted the Alevi community, a fringe Shia sect in Anatolia. They were attacked in Malatya (April 1978), Sıvas (September), and Bingöl (October), the violence being designed to destroy them economically. In the assembly, the opposition began calling for the imposition of martial law, which Ecevit was reluctant to implement, hoping to control the situation with a stricter application of existing laws. But the Alevi pogrom in Kahramanmaraş, a small town in central Anatolia, on 22 December, altered his plans. There were many deaths and hundreds were wounded when the Grey Wolves went on the rampage, shouting 'no funerals for communists and Alevis'. Air force jets and an armoured unit were sent to restore the peace and on Christmas Day, Ecevit was forced to order martial law in 13 Anatolian provinces. His failure to end terrorism was a crucial reason for the loss of support among voters. But even under martial law, terrorism continued, the opposition claiming that Ecevit was placing restrictions on the generals so that they were unable to deal with the terrorists. Nevertheless the generals now controlled the Kurdish-populated areas in eastern Anatolia and were able to ban May Day celebrations in 1979. These measures eroded support for Ecevit even more, so that when partial Senate and some by-elections were held on 14 October, the RPP's vote declined, while that of the JP increased in both these elections. Again there was a high turnout of 73 per cent; despite everything the voters still had faith in the ballot box. Following his defeat, Ecevit resigned on 16 October. Since the country found another Front coalition repugnant, Demirel formed a minority government on 12 November, rejecting the bourgeoisie's appeals for a 'grand coalition' with Ecevit. With the support of the Right, Demirel received a vote of confidence on 25 November 1979.

TURKEY'S RENEWED STRATEGIC IMPORTANCE

The strategic importance of Turkey changed dramatically after the 1978/9 Islamic revolution in Iran and the Soviet intervention in Afghanistan in December 1979. The West needed a stable regime in Turkey, something the political parties had been unable to provide it with; perhaps the generals could. By December 1979, the generals began discussing the timing and nature of their next military intervention. First of all, they agreed to tell the politicians to put their house in order. Had they wanted to end terrorism and bloodshed, they ought to have intervened long before September 1980, but they seemed more concerned about the consequences in Iran and the outbreak of a 'second Cold War' with the Soviet Union. As early as April 1979, *The Guardian*'s Brussels correspondent wrote: 'Not surprisingly Turkey ... is now seen as a zone of crucial strategic significance not only for the southern flank [of NATO] but for the West as a whole'. But Turkey, in her current state of political turmoil, was incapable of assuming her new responsibilities. In January 1980, when the terms of the new US–Turkish Defence and Cooperation Treaty were being finalized, Demirel refused to allow the use of Turkish bases by any future Rapid Deployment Force or to facilitate Greece's return to the NATO political structure, unless Turkey's rights in the Aegean were recognized. Washington concluded that, under Demirel, Turkey could not play the regional role that was being assigned her: it seems that only the military could.

The generals made unilateral concessions to Greece regarding Aegean airspace, without even informing the foreign ministry, and in March, the signing of the Defence and Cooperation Treaty anchored Turkey to the West; Ecevit's attempt to have a 'multi-dimensional' foreign policy was abandoned. Demirel also gave the generals full authority to crush terrorism which, they said, came only from the Left, for the Grey Wolves were considered allies of the state in its struggle against the communists. But the generals failed to put a stop to the violence that often took as many as 20 lives a day. The unending violence prepared the ground for military intervention, and many welcomed the generals' coup as salvation from the anarchy and chaos that gripped the country.

MOUNTING ECONOMIC GLOOM

As well as terrorism, the economy also required a regime of strict discipline and social peace that only the military could provide. Throughout the seventies, all the coalitions had neglected the economy, until Ecevit was forced to attend to it in 1978/9. During this time, successive governments had to cope with a worldwide economic downturn, the oil-price shock of 1974, the US embargo of 5 February 1975, and European sanctions that followed on the heels of the Cyprus intervention. The cost of military occupation of northern Cyprus and subsidies to the Turkish-Cypriot government were an added burden to the economy. With an eye to elections, the parties had pursued a populist policy and provided subsidies with public money to all sectors, to encourage high employment and economic growth. They borrowed money to finance the budgetary deficits. In the end, Ecevit had to turn to the International Monetary Fund (IMF) and accept its harsh terms as the price of the economic bailout. But the IMF and TÜSİAD wanted even more concessions than Ecevit was willing to make so that the austerity programme could be implemented. Finally Ecevit curbed consumption at home in order to encourage exports and all this undermined his support in the October 1979 Senate elections, forcing him to resign.

Thanks to US support, the economy showed signs of recovery following the revolution in Iran. The Demirel minority government implemented the IMF's programme under Turgut Özal (1927–93) who was appointed his economic adviser. Özal was a technocrat who saw politics as an impediment to the implementation of economic measures he introduced on 24 January 1980. The Turkish lira was devalued by 30 per cent and prices of virtually every commodity – oil and oil products, cement, sugar, paper and coal, cigarettes and alcohol – rose sharply in an attempt to cut consumption. The aim was to create a new economy based on exports rather than internal consumption. Turkey was thrown open to the capitalist world and globalization.

Özal's economic programme was the beginning of a transformation which would cause much social and economic turmoil. Özal asked the generals for a five-year respite from party politics for the success of his recipe, and that is precisely what the military coup of 12 September 1980 gave him. The generals planned to build new foundations for the political system in order to provide long-term stability by de-politicizing Turkish society; the restructuring of 1971 had proved insufficient. The country was tired of the antics of politicians and was ready to accept a military takeover. Demirel could not stop the terrorism because he needed the NAP to prop up his minority government, and the Islamists had to be appeased for the same reason. The generals were ready to intervene and the date for the coup was set as 11 July. But Ecevit's failure to bring down Demirel with a censure motion postponed the coup; and the generals did not want to be seen as doing something which Ecevit had just failed to do. Erbakan's support had saved Demirel in June. But in August, Ecevit and Erbakan agreed to introduce a motion of censure against Demirel's (and the generals') foreign policy and, on 5 September, Hayrettin Erkmen, Demirel's foreign minister, was forced to resign. The next day, a 'Save Jerusalem' rally in Konya angered the generals, as the secular state was openly insulted by this. There were other motions of censure against Demirel in the pipeline, but they could not be implemented because of a lack of quorum on 9 and 10 September. Political life had been paralysed. On 12 September, the generals intervened and, to the relief of the country, seized power.

SUGGESTED FURTHER READING

Feroz Ahmad, *The Turkish Experiment in Democracy, 1950–1975* (Hurst, London, and Westview Press, Boulder, Colorado, 1977).

Margret Kruhenbuhl, *Political Kidnappings in Turkey, 1971–1972* (Rand, Santa Monica, California, 1977).

Jane Cousins, *Turkey: Torture and Political Persecution* (Pluto Press, London, 1973).

George Harris, *Turkey: Coping with Crisis* (Westview Press, Boulder, Colorado, 1985).

Roger Nye, 'Civil–Military Confrontation in Turkey: the 1973 Presidential Election', *International Journal of Middle East Studies*, vol. 8, no. 2, April 1977, pp. 209–28.

William Hale, *Turkish Politics and the Military* (Routledge, London and New York, 1994).

7

The Military, the Parties, and Globalization, 1980–2003

RESTRUCTURING THE POLITICAL SYSTEM

Few people were aware of the intentions of the generals when they captured power; they claimed that they had intervened in order to save the state and its people from social division, economic breakdown, and the anarchy and violence for which the parties and politicians were responsible. They promised to restore the authority of the state in an impartial manner. To do that, the generals set up the National Security Council (NSC) headed by Kenan Evren, who was chief of staff, and composed of army, navy, air force, and gendarmerie commanders. The NSC was merely a front for other senior officers of the armed forces, who were divided as to the course of action they should take. As is often the case, there were moderates and hardliners, the latter in charge of martial law and restoration of law and order. General Necdet Uruğ, commander of the First Army and martial law, was a hardliner who was able to impose his will on his fiefdom. But these factional differences never emerged into the open because the generals abided by the well-established hierarchical principle: they all agreed to be committed to Kemalism which, since the death of Atatürk in 1938, still carried the symbolic significance of avowed loyalty to the original ideals of the republic. The hardliners won the internal debate and the NUC agreed to reconstruct the entire

political system on new foundations by composing a new constitution, disqualifying former politicians and introducing new ones,
and even establishing the military's own political party to contest
elections. Their main intention was to dismantle once and for all
the liberal regime introduced by the 1961 Constitution.

The NSC began by suspending the constitution, dissolving
parliament, closing down the parties and detaining their leaders.
Professional associations, such as those of lawyers and doctors,
were suspended, including the trade unions; strikes were declared
illegal and striking workers were ordered back to work. Employers
applauded these measures as a step towards restoring the economy.
Military officers replaced provincial officials, mayors, and
governors whose political affiliations were suspect.

On 16 September, head of state General Kenan Evren
announced the junta's plan to de-politicize society, so as to render
any future military intervention unnecessary. He promised radical
changes in virtually all areas of Turkish life, but left foreign policy
and the economy – then in the process of being restructured by the
programme of 24 January 1980 – untouched. The new cabinet, led
by retired Admiral Bülent Ulusu, was announced on 21 September:
most of the ministers were bureaucrats, professors and retired
officers, and Turgut Özal, who had been charged with economic
restructuring by Demirel, was retained. Özal had worked in the
World Bank and was known to financial circles in the West and
within the business community in Turkey. He was trusted by the
junta to run the economy. The regime also adopted a pro-Western
foreign and military policy, which was judged crucial in
Washington after the revolution in Iran and Soviet intervention in
Afghanistan. On US prompting, the Ulusu government lifted the
Turkish veto against the return of Greece to NATO's military
command without a *quid pro quo*; Greece had left the military
command following Turkey's intervention in Cyprus in 1974.

The junta gave priority to restructuring political life. They began
by crushing all aspects of 'the Left' – extremists, social democrats,
unionists, and even members of the Peace Association who
included the very elite of Turkish society. The extreme Right,
aligned with NAP, was also crushed, though the junta embraced its
ideology, designating it as the 'Turkish–Islamic synthesis'. For the
time being, 'combating terrorism' became the junta's principal

task. Arrests followed and thousands were taken into custody; torture became widespread and systematic, besmirching the reputation of the regime in the West. But the junta, relying on US support and its strategic importance, was undeterred and brutal repression continued.

Having established a semblance of law and order, the following year, in October 1981, the NSC appointed a consultative committee to write a new constitution. Meanwhile, a law was passed abolishing all political parties and confiscating their assets. In November, the 'Higher Education Law' placed education into the hands of so-called 'nationalist-conservatives' and liberal faculty members were dismissed from the universities. In January 1982, the calendar for restoring political life was unveiled after the NSC had made amendments to the draft constitution and presented it to the people in a referendum. If the people accepted the constitution, elections would be held in late 1983 under the new political parties and elections law.

A public debate followed Evren's declaration and the intelligentsia began to anticipate a return to normal political life. Alarmed by that trend, the generals issued a law on 12 February 1982, forbidding former politicians from engaging in public political debate. Arrests followed and Bülent Ecevit, the former prime minister, was put on trial and imprisoned. This was a clear warning that the country was still under martial law.

Presented to the public on 17 July, the draft constitution centralized power in the office of the president. He could dissolve parliament and call a general election if parliament was paralysed, rule by decree, and virtually appoint the constitutional court. A presidential council, the NSC in new guise, advised him. Other provisions would curb freedom of the press and the unions. This was to be a 'democracy without freedoms'! The political provisions of the draft constitution were tightened even further following public discussions. On 19 October, the junta strengthened presidential powers by allowing him to veto legislation and constitutional amendments, which would then be put to a referendum. The president was also to be given the power to select military judges and high-ranking officials, to appoint the chief of staff (in consultation with the prime minister he appointed), and to convene and preside over NSC meetings. If the new constitution was approved by the people on 7 November, General Evren would automatically become president for the next seven years, and the other four generals of the NSC would be his advisers! Finally, the new constitution would rule out legal action against orders and decisions signed by the president. New laws would disqualify all members of the 1980 parliament from political activity for five years and all party leaders for ten, and new parties could not be formed if most of their members came from the old ones. The intention was to introduce new and 'clean' politicians into the system – but that proved impossible to accomplish.

When the draft constitution drew criticism, the junta banned all discussion of the document, although Evren was permitted to disseminate propaganda on its behalf. Voters understood that only by voting 'Yes' for a constitution they disliked, would civilian rule be restored. Therefore they voted overwhelmingly in favour of it – 91.37 per cent of the valid vote – though the generals interpreted the referendum as a vote of confidence in the regime! Thus Kenan Evren became Turkey's 7th president on 19 November 1982, convinced that the people loved him as another Atatürk – whom he tried hard to emulate.

THE ESTABLISHMENT OF NEW POLITICAL PARTIES

Having legitimized the constitution, the generals set about finding politicians who would be loyal to their philosophy. On 12 November, President Evren announced elections in October 1983, if all went well. They set about forming a 'state party' and the hardliners won this battle when retired general Turgut Sunalp was chosen to head this party instead of the moderate, Prime Minister Bülent Ulusu. The new parties law came into effect on 24 April 1983 and the NSC lifted the ban on politics the next day. New politicians could be vetoed by the NSC for any reason and the new parties were obliged to accept the legacy of what has come to be known as the '12 September regime'.

Of the new parties founded in the spring of 1983, only three proved to be politically viable. One was the social democratic party, or SODEP, founded by Professor Erdal İnönü, the son of İsmet İnönü. Its support came from former Republican voters and the Left. The second party was called the Great Turkey Party, which was Süleyman Demirel's Justice Party under proxy leadership. The generals shut down the Great Turkey Party and vetoed SODEP's candidates to prevent the party from contesting the election. Had these two parties been allowed to survive, a stable two-party system might have been restored. But the generals wanted to establish new politics and politicians, and these parties represented the old. The third party was founded by Turgut Özal and was called the Motherland Party, or ANAP by its Turkish acronym. Özal claimed that his party was neither Left nor Right, but represented all the political tendencies in existence before the 1980 coup. General Sunalp headed the 'state party', the Nationalist Democracy Party (NDP), while Necdet Calp, İsmet İnönü's former private secretary, led the Populist Party, which was intended to fill the political vacuum left by the dissolved RPP. The generals calculated that Sunalp and Calp would become the new politicians committed to the 12 September philosophy and Özal would lead a party of no political consequence; after all, he was merely a failed politician who had stood as an Islamist candidate on the MSP ticket in 1977 and had not been elected. Had he been elected, he too would have been disqualified by the generals, but US support and intervention saved him from veto.

The election campaign opened on 16 October, and meetings held by both Sunalp's and Necdet Calp's parties failed to stir any public interest, for both men were uninspiring leaders. Voters simply did not trust a military man – or a former high bureaucrat such as Necdet Calp – to lead the country back to democracy. Sunalp had declared that his first commitment was to the state, then democracy, then to the party. In contrast, Özal was the only candidate who projected a liberal, anti-statist image and promised a swift return to democracy. Voters had forgotten Özal's role in the 'Bankers' scandal' of 1982 in which thousands had lost their savings, and which had resulted in his forced resignation. But the generals did not expect Özal to win and even wanted his party to merge with that of General Sunalp!

THE GENERAL ELECTION OF 1983

Despite – or perhaps because of – the generals' open support, Sunalp lost and Özal won the election on 6 November. Özal's

Motherland Party (ANAP) won 45.15 per cent of the vote, while Calp's Populist Party won 30.46 per cent and Sunalp's National Democracy Party came third with only 23.27 per cent of the votes cast. Having imposed a monetary fine of about US$25 for those not voting, there was a record turnout of almost 93 per cent. However, in spite of his victory Özal's position was barely legitimized, simply because the two genuine parties – SODEP and the Great Turkey Party – had not been allowed to contest the election. Consequently, the municipal elections the following year turned out to be the proving ground for ANAP. Özal took very seriously the challenge posed by SODEP and the newly-formed True Path Party which replaced the Great Turkey Party and exploited the advantages of patronage, in order to win. Patronage became the hallmark of his administration, especially the system of 'discretionary funds' established for the purpose of strengthening the executive against the legislature. These 'funds' became a valuable source of money outside the budget and beyond the control of the assembly or the finance ministry.

Özal won the municipal election but his vote declined from 45 to 41 per cent. Votes for the National Democrats and the Populists plummeted to below 10 per cent, marking their demise. The centre-left SODEP and the centre-right TPP became the opposition though they still lacked representation in the assembly, having to wait until 1987 before this was remedied. For the moment, Özal ruled without serious opposition in the assembly. He was a pragmatist who bragged that his government was essentially non-ideological: ANAP was not a continuation of the dissolved parties but contained their best elements and ideas. It was conservative like the JP, traditionalist like the Islamists, nationalist like the neo-fascists, and left-of-centre like the RPP because it believed in social justice. In reality, ANAP was conservative, undemocratic and wedded to the values of globalization and the free market. Liberals who questioned the party's leadership and its policies were forced to leave.

Turgut Özal concentrated on the economy and left the generals to maintain law and order. He had asked for five years of 'social peace' – that is to say, no strikes or protests – and the generals were providing that. The social democrats were divided between SODEP and the recently formed Democratic Left Party (DLP), and only the True Path Party provided any sort of challenge. ANAP had become a family affair with Turgut's brothers, Korkut and Yusuf, and his wife Semra, playing active roles. They recruited young men with experience of the US 'Reagan revolution' which they wanted to emulate in Turkey.

Just as conservatives in the US said they spoke for 'the silent majority', so Özal claimed to speak for the 'central pillar' of Turkish society, the *ortadirek*. His promise of a bright prosperous future for Turkey and the removal of many restrictions on the economy and society caught the imagination of the people. Turkey, he promised, would 'skip an era' and become a major power because his would be the government that 'got things done'! By 1986, however, Özal was again challenged by former party leaders banned by the generals but who were now guiding the leading parties: the True Path Party fronted for Süleyman Demirel; the Democratic Left for Bülent Ecevit; the Welfare Party for Necmettin Erbakan; and the Nationalist Labour Party for Alparslan Türkeş. The Populist Party and SODEP had merged and become the Social Democratic Populist Party (SHP), the principal party of the Left. The Right seemed more divided than ever with nine parties; for the moment, only the Motherland and the True Path Parties mattered.

FORMER POLITICAL LEADERS RE-EMERGE

One of the principal issues of Turkish politics in 1986 was the removal of the ban on former politicians. Demirel was gaining in popularity among the liberal Right and eroding ANAP's electoral support. The business community began to hedge its bets and financed the campaigns of both parties! Reacting to public pressure to restore the political rights of his rivals, Özal decided to put the question to a referendum and, although he campaigned vigorously for a 'No' vote, on 6 September 1987 the people voted to restore political rights. The banned political leaders were now back in business, finally reversing one of the most radical measures of the generals. To counter this, Özal decided to bring forward the general election before Demirel had time to get organized. When this was held on 29 November 1987, ANAP won 36.29 per cent of the vote which translated into 64.9 per cent or 292 seats in the assembly thanks to Özal's amended election law. In 1983, 45.1 per cent of the vote had given only 211 seats! Demirel described the new Özal government as 'the election-law cabinet' and the ministry lost its legitimacy in the eyes of the people. Özal had also lost much of his glitter and realized that it would be difficult to win any future election after seeing the results of the local elections in March 1988. In the four years since 1983, ANAP'S popularity had slipped from 45 to 22 per cent despite the patronage it had enjoyed. In August 1988, Özal tried to call another early general election for November but the measure was defeated in a referendum and Özal's prestige took another blow. He had done nothing to further the democratic process and all the laws passed by the junta – the trade unions law, the higher education law, the law on elections and political parties, the press law, the penal code law, and the law governing the running of Turkey's radio and television – remained on the books. Furthermore, corruption associated with the 'Özal dynasty' had damaged his reputation. Özal therefore decided to enter the running for president when President Kenan Evren's term expired in November 1989. His party had the votes in the assembly and that is what mattered. Özal was duly elected Turkey's eighth president by his party on 31 October – opposition deputies boycotting the session – and assumed office on 9 November, the second civilian president of the Republic. Within ANAP, the so-called 'Holy Alliance' of Islamists and Nationalists calculated that they would now be able to gain control of the party with Özal out of the way.

Özal's presidency (1989–93) was marked by political instability. Yıldırım Akbulut, the new prime minister, a puppet of the president, was not respected in the country. The opposition announced that they would remove Özal from the presidency as soon as they won the next general election. In light of the growing Kurdish insurgeny in south-eastern Turkey, there was talk of another military intervention; the Islamists became more vocal, and there were political assassinations in the capital and Istanbul in early 1990. In March the business lobby called for an early poll under a new elections law in order to restore political stability; however, the arrival of ex-president Kenan Evren in Ankara to confer with the chief of staff, raised political tensions. On 9 April, the government responded to the situation by passing an 'anti-terrorism law', which gave the army and police extra-ordinary powers. Late in July, the National Security Council had these emergency powers extended for a further four months in the eight provinces in the south-east.

Within weeks, Iraq's invasion of Kuwait on 2 August 1990 transformed Turkey's situation dramatically and the political crisis was forgotten for the time being. Turkey was in the midst of an international crisis that redefined her place in the world, especially after the fall of the Berlin Wall the previous year. Her strategic importance had faded with the end of the Soviet threat, but with the Gulf Crisis and the emergence of new Turkic states in Central Asia, Ankara gained a new significance. Özal bypassed the cabinet and supported President Bush's policy, gambling that Turkey would come out a winner, thereby garnering the goodwill of America and Europe. Ankara shut down the oil pipeline from Iraq to the Mediterranean on 7 August, and agreed to permit foreign troops to be based in Turkey. But chief of staff, General Torumtay, disagreeing with the way Özal was conducting policy without any consultation, resigned on 3 December. The soldier had advised a cautious policy that Özal had described as 'cowardly and timid'; nevertheless Torumtay's resignation reined in Özal and forced him to be more guarded and less adventurous. It seemed as though Özal was looking ahead to the partition of Iraq, and the formation of a Kurdish state that would join Turkey in a federation. He wanted to occupy Mosul and Kirkuk in Iraq and asked Torumtay how many troops would be lost in the invasion. Given a figure of thirty or forty thousand, he gave up the idea of invasion!

The Gulf Crisis exploded into war on 16 January 1991, ending with a cease-fire on 28 February. The influx of Iraqi–Kurdish refugees into Turkey aggravated the Kurdish insurgency and the economic situation. As a result, ANAP's standing in the country declined even further in favour of Demirel's True Path Party. ANAP hoped to strengthen its position by electing Mesut Yılmaz as its replacement leader for Özal, defeating the nationalist–religious faction. Yılmaz was 43 years old and a graduate of the Faculty of Political Science in Ankara. In contrast to Yıldırım Akbulut, he was modern, cosmopolitan, pragmatic and spoke a foreign language, German. He seemed to represent a leader who might revive the party's declining fortunes. Now Prime Minister Yılmaz decided that the party had better chance of success if elections were held before the economy declined even further. The assembly therefore voted to hold elections on 20 October 1991.

But the elections did not turn out well for Yılmaz: Demirel's TPP won the majority with 178 seats, while ANAP won only 115, and Erdal İnönü's social democrats, 88 seats. Necmettin Erbakan's Welfare Party won 62 seats, but only because the Islamists had formed an electoral alliance with the neo-fascists, an alliance that proved to be ephemeral. ANAP, without Özal, had survived, and Demirel, the principal leader of the Right since the sixties, had assumed his rightful place. Although there were hardly any ideological differences between ANAP and TPP, the two centre-right parties, there was no question of a merger, which would have permitted a strong government. With too many vested interests at stake and too much to lose on ANAP's part to contemplate a merger, Yılmaz preferred to be in opposition. Therefore Demirel formed a coalition with the social democrats in November 1991, a coalition he had refused to form with Ecevit in the 1970s! The Demirel–İnönü cabinet was supported by 266 seats in the Assembly and 48% of the popular vote. In theory, the government was strong and capable of providing stability and solutions to Turkey's problems. The principal problem requiring attention was the economy.

ECONOMIC PROBLEMS RETURN TO THE FORE

Turkey's economic development had gone through some radical phases since the fifties. After a decade of an unplanned economy during that decade, the country had quite successfully practised 'import substitution industrialization' in the sixties and seventies and had succeeded in creating an internal market for its goods, but these goods were never competitive and found no export market. In order to become competitive, the unions had to be disciplined and wages had to be cut. All this had proved impossible to accomplish under party politics and the coalition government of the 1970s. Consequently, one of the tasks for the military regimes of the eighties was to end party politics and establish a basis for economic development under the influence of 'global market forces' or globalization. Turkey had to become more productive and pay lower wages to its workers so as to be competitive.

The government was told to make a number of crucial changes in preparation to enter the global market. These included state withdrawal from production, in which it had played a vital role since the 1930s, in order to focus on building the country's infrastructure, its roads, communications systems and dams, to meet its energy needs. Other imperatives included the privatization of state economic enterprises, and the private sector and foreign capital were to be given the primary role in production. Also, the state had to abandon protectionism because protected industries, anti-statists argued, were weak and inefficient and provided consumers with expensive and inferior quality goods. Quality goods could be exported, thus attracting the much needed foreign exchange.

One of the results of these policies was that income distribution, always skewed, became much worse and undermined the middle and lower classes, while the rich prospered. According to the World Bank, Turkey was one among seven countries with the worst records for income disparity. According to Turkish economists, between 1980 and 1986, thirty trillion liras had been transferred from wages and salaries to the private sector. The SPO calculated that in ten years, the share of wages in Turkey's GNP declined from 36 per cent in 1977 to 18 per cent in 1987.

Despite the pain felt by the majority of the population (for there was no safety net), the economic policies of the 1980s produced remarkable results. Inflation fell and foreign exchange and imported consumer goods became available. The mood of the country was upbeat and optimistic after the depressing years of the late 1970s. The press spoke of an 'export miracle' because export earnings had increased from US $2.3 billion in 1979 to US $11.7 billion in 1988. This 'miracle' was aided by the Iran–Iraq war (1980–88) when Turkish goods were in great demand by both belligerents, and for a period, Turkish exports to the Middle East overtook those to Europe, Turkey's principal market. Corruption was endemic during these years, especially with regard to the so-called 'phantom exports' reported by companies so as to obtain export subsidies from the state.

Export subsidies benefited the large holding companies in western Turkey at the expense of smaller enterprise in Anatolia, although consolidation amongst these smaller enterprises became a feature, marking the rise of conglomerates strong enough to compete with the capitalist ventures of Istanbul and the Marmara region. These companies were known as the 'Anatolian Tigers' and they became the supporters of Erbakan's Welfare Party, which acted in opposition to the companies united in TÜSİAD. The Anatolian Tigers formed their own association known as MÜSİAD, standing for the 'Association of Independent Industrialists and Businessmen', although it was no secret that the 'M' in the acronym was the code word for 'Muslim', 'Independent' being intended to deceive the secularists. Meanwhile, such well-established conglomerates as Koç and Sabancı had grown and achieved what was described as 'global reach', due to investment in the Balkans, Russia, and the Turkic republics after the collapse of the Soviet Union, even though Turkey itself needed capital investment. In the summer of 1992, President Özal held a conference to launch economic cooperation among states of the Black Sea region. The idea was a good one, although Turkey lacked the resources to play the kind of role that Özal aspired to. This was the age of 'economic Darwinism' – survival of the fittest while the small and the weak were eliminated or swallowed up in mergers. At home, the state encouraged this trend, but it was unable to act abroad because of its economic weakness.

Turkey had become a strategic asset in the 'second cold war' after the revolution in Iran (1978–9) and Soviet intervention in Afghanistan (1978). The victory of Andreas Papandreou's socialist party in Greece in 1981 – ending nearly 50 years of conservative hegemony – increased the value of Turkey to US policy makers. Özal declared that it was his policies that had enabled Turkey (in his words) to 'turn the corner' and 'skip an epoch', and that Turkey was on the way to becoming 'the Japan of West Asia'. But all this was an illusion, for investments in industry actually declined in relation to those in the service sector, making tourism – a fickle industry at best – a major source of foreign exchange. People who became wealthy were rentiers not entrepreneurs. The so-called export miracle had been financed through a massive foreign debt, whose service costs became a nightmare for the government. Turkey expected to be able to pay off her debts by 1995, but in the end could not do so; even by 2002, she had not paid them off, and the Ankara Chamber of Commerce calculated that over the past two decades, the country had paid such vast sums in interest payments that its economic future was threatened.

TURKEY'S CHANGING SOCIAL AND POLITICAL LANDSCAPE

Nevertheless, Turkey's society and economy were transformed under Özal. Turkey had become a consumer society, serving about ten per cent of the urban population who were articulate enough to make demands on the state and have these demands satisfied. Everything was available to the new rich, even though advertising in the media – especially television – brought consumer goods into the homes of the less affluent as well! Cars, especially imported cars, became a status symbol, as did works of art, antiques and rare books. But the vast majority, living on wages and salaries, were barely able to survive, given the constantly rising cost of living. Employment patterns were also changing: university graduates no longer wanted to work for state concerns where salaries were low, but in the private sector, preferably for foreign companies, where salaries were high and the future promising. Universities were privatized to serve this new clientele and to produce the business managers which the private sector constantly needed. English was now the lingua franca of this class and positions were even advertised in the Turkish press in English, a language foreign to the majority.

Turgut Özal died on 17 April 1993, soon after his return from an exhausting tour of the Turkic republics of the former Soviet Union. He was succeeded as president by Süleyman Demirel, who was elected by parliament on 16 May. Demirel believed that he would retain control over the True Path Party if he handed it over to Mrs Tansu Çiller (1946–), whom he had promoted within the party. She was not the obvious choice, for she was a relatively young and inexperienced newcomer to the party and there were more seasoned men who had stronger claims to leadership. But Çiller had the advantage of being younger, female, attractive, and well educated in comparison with her rivals. Not only was she an economist, but she was also fluent in English and German, had a cosmopolitan outlook and was well acquainted with the West. Around the world, voters seemed to prefer young, dynamic leaders and Turkey was no exception. A youthful Mesut Yılmaz had taken over ANAP from Özal, and İnönü's SHP went in the same direction when he retired and elected a younger leader in September 1993. It made good political sense to elect a woman as TPP's leader, thereby strengthening the party's position in the forthcoming election. She would counter the qualities of her rivals, especially among female voters, who made up over half the electorate. The open support that the business community gave Çiller could not be ignored either. Moreover her success was expected to enhance Turkey's image in the West as a forward-looking Muslim country from an Islamic world that seemed to be looking to the past for inspiration.

Çiller came to public notice in the late eighties as one of the critics of Turgut Özal's economic policies. The support she enjoyed in the business community enabled her to enter Süleyman Demirel's circle as a consultant on economic matters. She was elected from Istanbul and entered parliament in 1990. Demirel appointed her minister of state in charge of economic affairs. Before entering politics, she had taught economics at Bosphorus University in Istanbul, having earned degrees in America at the Universities of New Hampshire and Connecticut. Thus at the party's convention, she defeated her male rivals and became the party's leader and the first woman prime minister of Turkey.

Çiller's coalition with the social democrats won a vote of confidence on 25 June 1993, and she took charge of the country's destiny. Being the junior partners, the social democrats' political position in the country had begun to erode among voters as SHP supported the policies of a right-wing leader. The social democratic programme was too timid to attempt to challenge the system and yet too daring to be accepted by the conservatives in the business community. The programme, premised on a fast rate of growth, was incapable of dealing with the economic crisis of the nineties. There was therefore no obstacle to Çiller's programme. Her success depended on her ability to find answers to Turkey's many problems: the economy, entry into the European Union and a solution to end the Kurdish question. Turkey was being held to ransom since August 1984, when the PKK – the Workers' Party of Kurdistan – launched its insurrection. This war was estimated to cost US $7 billion a year! If the conservatives failed to find a solution, the Islamists were standing in the wings to challenge them.

THE KURDISH QUESTION

The Kurdish question in its modern form had emerged in the 1960s, when the 'peoples of the east' demanded greater cultural freedom and questioned the state's policy of assimilation. Their demands were related to the backwardness of the region, which had largely been ignored by Ankara, especially during the period of multi-party politics. The market economy favoured by the Democrats had benefited large landowners, tribal sheiks, and the rich peasants. Landlessness increased during these years as peasants could no longer afford to cultivate their plots and therefore sold them and became labourers. A survey conducted in 1984, the year the insurrection began, revealed that 45 per cent of peasant families in the province of Diyarbakır and 47 in Urfa had no land. The private sector concentrated industrial production in western Anatolia, close to the ports for shipment to world markets. As a result, there was high unemployment in the east and south-east and the people, Kurds and Turks, lived in conditions that were often described as feudal.

In the 1960s, the Kurdish intelligentsia hoped that it would be able to make gains by working through the Workers' Party of Turkey and the left-of-centre RPP. But the political elite in Turkey, especially in the military, refused to promote a political solution, convinced that the armed forces could crush any challenge to the state, a challenge that was described as 'separatism' and fragmentation of the state. Ever since the aborted Treaty of Sèvres in 1920, Turks had lived under the 'Sèvres complex': they feared that the Western world had not forgotten its defeat at the hands of the Nationalists and that they were now trying to reimpose terms – in the form of a Kurdish state and Armenian irredentism – that it had failed to impose in 1920.

Initially, the elite saw the Kurdish insurrection as a minor internal matter that could be dealt with by military means. In the eighties, the generals took a harder line and in 1983 passed a law forbidding the use of any language other than Turkish. This law was applied only to the Kurds, who were not allowed to give 'Kurdish' names to their children, and the army often brutalized and humiliated them in the east. Özal had tried to deal with this problem politically but made no headway: he repealed the language law and even went so far as to claim that he was half Kurdish, but to no avail. Ironically, there were many Kurdish members of parliament, especially from the social democratic party; the Kurdish party they had formed had not been allowed to contest the general election and so they had joined the social democrats in order to enter parliament.

The situation changed dramatically in 1991, after the Gulf War and the defeat of Saddam Hussein. Northern Iraq was liberated and Iraqi Kurds were given control of the region and protected by the Western powers. The PKK acquired modern weapons in northern Iraq, and began to act more like an army than guerrilla bands. Its fighters were able to retreat into territory under the control of Iraqi Kurds, forcing the Turkish army to make regular incursions into Iraqi territory in order to destroy PKK bases. They also had the unofficial support of such neighbouring countries as Iran, Syria and Greece, who made use of the Kurds to embarrass Ankara. In the 1980s, the PKK had claimed to be a Marxist organization, but after the fall of the Soviet Union, it began to adopt Islamic discourse. The conflict was also internationalized and foreign non-governmental organizations (NGOs) began to monitor the conflict, accusing Turkish armed forces of violating the human rights of the Kurdish population.

While politicians tried to soften the conflict, the army and the extreme Right escalated it. In 1992, Prime Minister Demirel went so far as to declare that they recognized the 'Kurdish reality', a fact that governments had tended to deny. In Washington, in December 1994, Turkey's ambassador, responding to an editorial in the *Washington Post*, noted that the Kurds were only one of 26 different ethnic groups living in Turkey. They were not a minority, but were co-owners of the country. 'Diversity in the Turkish population is similar to that found in the United States'. This statement suggested that sections of officialdom in Turkey were coming round to an inclusive definition of nationalism/patriotism, abandoning the exclusive nationalism of the extreme Right. Two weeks later, the press quoted Premier Tansu Çiller as proposing that Atatürk's famous aphorism, 'Happy is he who calls himself a Turk', be altered to 'Happy is he who calls himself a citizen of Turkey'.

But such ideas had no affect on the military campaign and the conflict in the east, which was a drain on the economy and cost thousands of lives each year, and intensified in the years after 1992. It seems that money was being made out of the continuation of this conflict and the war profiteers did not want it to end. The army sent about one-quarter of a million troops and mobilized so-called village guards from amongst Kurdish tribes, who were paid to fight the PKK, thus providing them with money and 'employment'. Villages were evacuated and destroyed so that the PKK, not finding local support, would become 'a fish out of water'. An estimated two million refugees from such villages sought shelter in the cities throughout Anatolia. Those more fortunate fled to Western Europe, where they formed a vocal lobby for the PKK and agitated on its behalf, internationalizing the conflict.

The declaration of a unilateral cease-fire by Abdullah Öcalan, the PKK's leader, in March 1993, was seen as a sign of weakness by the generals, who thought they could now destroy the insurgency by stepping up their operations. They launched major incursions into northern Iraq in January 1994 and March 1995, but to no avail. The insurgency continued to cost thousands of lives each year, as well as isolating Turkey from the West. Nor were moderate Kurdish politicians allowed to become part of the political process by forming political parties, competing in elections, and putting forward their case in parliament. The People's Labour Party was banned by the constitutional court in August 1993, as were its successors, who were finally succeeded by HADEP (People's Democracy Party) in May 1994. Members of parliament belonging to these parties were imprisoned for 'separatist activities', closing the door to a political solution. Throughout the 1990s, European support for the Kurds continued to grow, with an estimated half a million displaced Kurds throughout Europe. In June 1998, a Kurdish rally in Dortmund was addressed by a former Danish prime minister, a former Greek minister, as well as the Green Party. So while the PKK had been weakened militarily, it had gained in diplomatic strength.

Ankara forced the Syrian government to expel Abdullah Öcalan and the PKK from Syria in October 1998 and finally captured him in Nairobi, Kenya in February 1999. He was tried and sentenced to death on 29 June 1999. The sentence was not carried out because Ankara awaited the outcome of a review of the sentence by the European Court of Justice. By now the Kurdish cause had been taken up by the European Union, which insisted that Ankara abolish the death penalty and grant Kurds the right to have education and broadcasting in Kurdish before Turkey would be considered for accession talks for membership to the EU. In the year 2002, these two issues divided the coalition government and threatened its very survival.

The war against the PKK also exposed the unofficial alliance between elements of the state and the criminal element, or 'mafia', known in Turkey as the 'deep state'. This relationship, though an open secret often referred to in the press, came out into the open as a result of an automobile accident in November 1996, known as the Susurluk incident. In July, a journalist had said in an interview that he wished the state would give up being a gang of criminals and abide by the rule of law. He was vindicated when a Mercedes crashed into a tractor on the Balıkesir–Istanbul road, resulting in the deaths of three of the four passengers. Those killed included Abdullah Çatlı, a neo-fascist militant involved in the murder of leftists in the 1970s, and now a criminal working with the state, his girlfriend, and Hüseyin Kocadağ, deputy chief of police for Istanbul and involved in state security matters. The surviving man, though injured, was Sedat Bucak, a Kurdish tribal chief and a member of Tansu Çiller's TPP, involved in the village guard movement against the PKK. The collusion between state officials, criminals and neo-fascists had begun in the seventies, when the military entered into an alliance to crush the Left. Such an alliance became unnecessary after the 1980 coup, but was revived during the Özal administration when criminals infiltrated the state mechanism and bought officials with money generated by 'phantom exports' and smuggling. This alliance was later used against the PKK and other 'enemies of state', and that is why their crimes went unpunished.

The incident aroused great anger in the country and was seen as another turning-point in Turkey's politics. But there was no serious outcome because too many politicians and officers had been involved over the years. Nevertheless, the public were now aware of the complicity between the state and criminals, an activity that continued despite the revelations. Turkey seemed to have more urgent matters to attend to, perhaps the most urgent being relations with the EU.

TURKEY AND THE EEC

Turkey joined the Western world, led by Washington, after the Second World War. The Truman Doctrine, the Marshall Plan, and NATO cemented the relationship and secured Turkey's position within Western security arrangements. In the fifties, as the European Economic Community took shape, Ankara followed Greece and applied for association with the EEC, wanting to become part of the economic system. After the Johnson Letter of 1964, Turkey became lukewarm to the US connection and began to see itself more as a part of Europe; Europe had become a major market for Turkish products and the supplier of capital goods. The ties became stronger as Turkish workers migrated to Europe, comprising about three million people or about five per cent of Turkey's population. Ankara signed the Association Agreement with the EEC in 1963. But in July 1980, when Turkey was asked to apply for full membership at the same time as Greece, Premier Süleyman Demirel put off the application in order to appease anti-EEC Islamists and win their support for his weak minority government. Greece joined the EEC the following year, while Turkey missed the boat. Since then, Turkey's attempts to join the EEC – later the European Union (EU) – have ended in failure and disappointment. But the customs union agreement that came into effect on 1 January 1996 marked Turkey's entry into the world of globalization, with almost total dependence on so-called 'market forces'. With the customs union, Turkey had given up its best bargaining card; the EU was now able to demand conditions before Ankara was allowed to negotiate a timetable for full membership.

TURKEY'S POLITICAL MALAISE

The roots of Turkey's political malaise, and its failure to resolve many related problems, are to be found in the political regime created after the coup d'état of 12 September 1980. By disqualifying former politicians and creating new institutions, the generals succeeded in de-politicizing the entire system. By the time the political rights of former politicians – Demirel, Ecevit, Erbakan and Türkeş – were restored with the 1987 referendum, the entire political architecture of the country had been altered. The centre-left and the centre-right had been fractured and non-systemic parties like the Islamists and the neo-fascists were able to play a critical role. During these years, Turkey had become part of the globalized world, accepted by both centre-left and centre-right, with the result that the social democratic parties were only that in name. There was no longer any significant difference between the parties save for the rhetoric; that was the end of ideology. And this is why social democrats under various leaders could co-habit with the True Path Party throughout the 1990s.

When Turgut Özal died in April 1993, Demirel's decision to become the next president proved disastrous for his party. Under Tansu Çiller's leadership, the party declined rapidly, leading to the Welfare Party winning the general election of 24 December 1995 with 21.38 per cent of the vote and 158 seats. Çiller is said to have even considered going to war with Iran to boost her vote! True Path's vote declined to 19.18 per cent and 135 seats, and ANAP's to 19.65 and 133. The centre-right parties had won almost 40 per cent of the vote and 268 seats, and could have formed a stable government had they united; but that was out of the question given the rivalry between the leaders. The social democrats also won over 25 per cent of the vote – the DLP won 14.64 and the RPP 10.71 – but they too could not unite because of rivalry between the leaders. The other parties failed to clear the 10 per cent hurdle required to enter parliament.

Again a coalition government proved difficult to form. The Islamists failed to do so; so did Çiller, though she tried to unite the centre-right under her leadership. In fact, TPP split as a result of her leadership and dissidents formed the Democrat Turkey party. While politicians were squabbling and bargaining, the press reported that people in the south-eastern province of Hakkari were struggling to feed themselves from rubbish heaps. Because of the war against the PKK, poverty had reached unbearable proportions.

NEW POLITICAL COALITIONS

Finally in March 1996, after much unsuccessful horse-trading, Mesut Yılmaz formed the 'Mother-Path' coalition between ANAP and the TPP, supported by Ecevit's Democratic Left. The new coalition had a rotating premiership on the Israeli model, with Yılmaz as PM in 1996 and Çiller in 1997. Immediately, Erbakan began to harass Tansu Çiller with threats to investigate alleged corruption. Anticipating an early election and pandering to his electorate, Erbakan also made statements provocative to the secularists, praising Iran's Islamic revolution and promising to lead a revolution that he said would be painful but unavoidable. He called for an Islamic version of NATO, an Islamic common market and an Islamic equivalent of UNESCO, before establishing an Islamic Union.

The 'Mother-Path' coalition was too unstable to accomplish anything. When an IMF team arrived in Ankara in late May 1996, it warned the government of an impending financial crisis because of the huge budget deficit. Tensions within the cabinet forced Mesut Yılmaz to resign on 6 June. The government had lasted 90 days; it had taken 60 days before it was formed. Few people were surprised, and most agreed that Erbakan would have to be included in the next coalition or the country would have to go to an early general election. Business circles also accepted the fact of Islamist participation, but they hoped that the next coalition would lead Turkey to an election under a new electoral law. Political instability had led to economic instability and that had to end; otherwise observers once more predicted military intervention and an early conclusion to the experiment in democracy. The results of a survey conducted by Anadolu University suggested that people were losing confidence in politicians, the local administration, the private sector, the universities, the IMF and the media; only confidence in the military increased.

Three days after Yılmaz's resignation, the Welfare Party asked parliament to investigate how Tansu Çiller had accumulated so much wealth in so short a time. Çiller had campaigned on the platform that she was the salvation for a secular Turkey threatened by the rising tide of 'fundamentalism', and that she would never form an alliance with the Islamists. But she succumbed to Erbakan's blackmail and agreed to form a coalition, providing he froze the investigation against her. Erbakan, ever the opportunist, agreed and a 'Welfare-Path' coalition, with Erbakan as prime minister, was announced on 29 June 1996.

Erbakan's ministry came under pressure from secularist forces from the very beginning. Most of the press, monopolized by Turkey's media moguls, was hostile. Erbakan was criticized about his visit to Iran and other Muslim countries in August, even when he was following in the footsteps of other prime ministers who had visited these countries regularly to further economic relations. The monthly National Security Council meetings, dominated by the generals, were an embarrassment to Erbakan as he was forced to accept policies – the growing relations with Israel, for example – that were distasteful. The press excoriated him for the rebuff he had received when he visited Libya in October when Colonel Muammer Qadhafi had criticized Turkey's Kurdish policy. Feelings were running so high that the press spoke of the possibility of military intervention and even Mesut Yılmaz acknowledged rumours of a coup. Yet Libya was an important market for Turkey's contractors and their spokesman noted that members of his association wanted new projects in Libya despite the unpaid debt and the political wrangling following Erbakan's visit: 'We don't want to lose a market worth billions.'

CONTINUING POLITICAL INSTABILITY AND ITS EFFECTS ON THE ECONOMY

The economy, already in poor shape, suffered as a result of the political instability. There was a flight of capital, and foreign capital in particular was not being invested in the country. Economists calculated that US $70 billion of Turkish capital had left the country to be invested in the West; US $45 billion was thought to be in Switzerland. Compared to September 1995, foreign investment had declined by 63 per cent, or US $67 million, in the same period in 1996. The Central Bank predicted that the economy would face higher deficits in 1996 amid increased uncertainty about the government. The current account deficit was expected to rise to US $6–7 billion in 1996 compared to US $2.3 billion in 1995; the public sector borrowing was expected to reach 9–10 per cent of GNP as compared to 6.5 per cent in 1995. By the end of the year, the Turkish lira had depreciated 65 per cent against the US dollar compared to 35 per cent in 1995. The dollar declined to 107,500 liras compared to 59,500 in 1995, and the decline continued throughout the next four years into the new millennium, when the lira sank to 1,700,000 liras.

Erbakan tried to improve relations with the generals at his party's congress, where he was greeted by military music. He denied that he was attempting to steer Muslim and secular Turkey away from the West and declared that Turkey was merely carrying out its own individual foreign policy. He even visited Anıtkabir, Atatürk's Mausoleum, something he had failed to do while in opposition, since Islamists had bitter disdain for the secular, anti-Islamic policies of the founder of the republic. The press noted that the government had increased the subsidy for the ballet and the opera by 129 per cent, cultural activities which Islamists had frowned upon as foreign and alien to Turkish culture. Visits made by Erbakan to various countries, especially the relationship with Iran, had annoyed Washington, and Erbakan wanted to appease the US. Consequently, in December 1996, he sent his minister of state to Washington 'in order to make ourselves better understood by our friend, America'. Fehim Adak was expected to discuss important issues, working to increase cooperation and to reassure the suspicions of US policy makers.

Erbakan's efforts to appease the secularists and the US were bound to fail, given the vast gap between the now moderate leadership of the Welfare Party and its militant rank and file, upon whom the party's success in elections depended. The leadership was becoming moderate and centrist because of the gains the Anatolian bourgeoisie – the 'Anatolian tigers' – had made since the 1980s; the 'tigers' wanted to share in the benefits of globalization, and these were forthcoming only if the party was in power. The rank and file, on the other hand, had only suffered economic loss during these years and remained radical in their demands. Erbakan continued to pay lip service to radicalism and was happy to talk of an Islamic common market and NATO, and a Developing Countries D-8 to counter the influence of the Western group of wealthy nations known as the G-7.

In February 1997, the Welfare Party mayor of Sincan, a village on the outskirts of Ankara, organized 'Jerusalem Day', to call for the liberation of the city from Israel. The Iranian ambassador was invited and, making anti-secular statements, he called for the establishment of Islamic law in Turkey, while the crowd demonstrated in support of Hamas and Hizbullah, two Islamist groups waging armed struggle against Israel. Secularist forces in Turkey were infuriated and appalled by the rally so close to the capital, and the generals responded by sending tanks through Sincan as a warning. The mayor was arrested, the Iranian ambassador declared a *persona non grata*, and an investigation launched against the Welfare Party. The Welfare Party had provided the generals with a pretext to curb the Islamic movement and they did so, with what is described as a soft or 'post-modern coup'.

SECULARISTS AND ISLAMISTS

The National Security Council, presided over by Erbakan, met on 28 February 1997. Political Islam was declared to be more dangerous than Kurdish nationalism and Erbakan was humiliated into accepting a twenty-point programme. The programme was designed to undermine the influence of political Islam by purging its supporters from the state apparatus and curbing the schools for prayer leaders and preachers, schools whose expansion the generals had legislated for after September 1980 in order to counter the influence of 'leftist ideologies'. A law extending secular education from 5 to 8 years was passed in August, and its aim was to weaken the hold of political Islam on Turkey's lower and lower middle class youth. The measure sparked angry demonstrations throughout Turkey, because it was blocking employment opportunities for an entire deprived section of population.

Premier Erbakan's position had become untenable and he resigned on 18 June 1997, hoping that President Demirel would appoint Tansu Çiller as prime minister and that the Welfare-Path coalition would continue. But Demirel appointed Mesut Yılmaz instead and an investigation was opened against the Welfare Party. The Islamists realize that their party would be dissolved, so in December 1997, they formed a new party, the Virtue Party (VP – Fazilet Partisi) with Recai Kutan as its leader; in January, the Constitutional Court banned the Welfare Party, confiscated its property and banned Erbakan and the party's principal leaders from politics for five years. Each time the Islamist party was dissolved, its successor claimed to be more moderate and less Islamist. By May 1998, Kutan seemed to be abandoning the hardline Islamism of Erbakan and no longer spoke of leaving NATO or of introducing Islamic banking. He also went to Anıtkabir to pay his respects to Atatürk, a demonstration that the Islamists were willing to join the mainstream of political life.

Nevertheless, the Virtue Party was dissolved by the constitutional court in June 2001. It was described as a hotbed of fundamentalism, especially for the role it had played in promoting the headscarf in its campaign against the secular state. In July, Erbakan's supporters formed Saadet, or the Felicity Party, while in August, the reformists in the Virtue Party formed the Justice and Development Party, or AK Parti, which they claimed was secular. But its leader was Recep Tayyip Erdoğan (1949–), the former mayor of Istanbul who had been imprisoned for inciting religious hatred and violation of secularism. He soon became the most popular leader, and polls showed that his party would win the next election.

The Yılmaz-led coalition, with the Democratic Left and the Democrat Turkey Party, lasted until November 1998. Yılmaz resigned on a censure motion brought by the opposition that charged him with corruption as well as links with the 'mafia'. In July, the coalition had already agreed that the election should be held on 25 April 1999. But Ecevit, one of the few politicians not tarred with the brush of corruption, was able to form his coalition with independents on 11 January 1999, with the task of leading the country to elections. The capture of Abdullah Öcalan, the PKK leader, in Kenya on 15 February, changed the mood of the country and improved the chances of nationalists in the coming election.

The nationalistic mood in Turkey explains why the Democratic Left and the Nationalist Action Party acquired the most votes in the general election in April 1999. The results were regarded as a political earthquake – the DLP and NAP emerging as winners while ANAP, TPP and CHP had collapsed. Turkey had moved to the extreme right. Though the Islamist vote had fallen from 19 per cent in 1995 to 15.94%, they had done very well in municipal elections, capturing the major cities of Turkey. The pro-Kurdish party, HADEP, had failed the at national level, but won control of the cities in south-eastern Turkey – Diyarbakır, Batman, Bingöl, Hakkari, Siirt, Şrnak – with large Kurdish populations. Results suggested that there would be a polarization of the conflict with NAP in government.

Ecevit had reinvented himself into an ardent nationalist and abandoned his leftism, while NAP had always flouted its extreme nationalism. His electoral success did not reflect the success of the Left, for Ecevit no longer spoke of changing the system as he had in the 1970s; nor did he associate himself with the leftward trend in Europe. The centre-right – ANAP and the True Path Parties – had collapsed, because voters were tired of the corruption and bickering between the parties and their leaders and preferred to vote Islamist, or in 1999, nationalist right. The voters' anger against Çiller and Yılmaz was responsible for NAP's success.

It was no surprise that when the next coalition was formed, it was composed of the DLP (supposedly centre-left), ANAP (centre-right) and NAP (extreme right). The principal concern of government was the economy and Ecevit noted on 30 May, that 'our economy is facing a serious problem. Political uncertainty, the world crisis, and foreign debt payments totalling US $30 billion have caused the Turkish economy to enter a bottleneck. We must rapidly revive the economy.' The prognosis looked good, as the coalition promised stability and a willingness to work together. The business community supported the government, while the generals were left to build up the military. They had plans to invest in an arms industry (Israel was expected to supply the technology), investing US $150 billion over the next ten years to make Turkey the most important regional military power. Turkey would have AWACS and 561 helicopters, giving it the strongest fleet in the region. When he was asked about his country's arms purchases, Baki İlkin, Turkey's ambassador to the US, replied: 'We are restructuring the army so that it has more mobility and rapid action units. We are surrounded by a lot of crises, in the Balkans, Kosovo, internal troubles in Georgia, The Caucasus, and we are following developments in Iraq.' Commenting on his country's political situation, Hüsamettin Cindoruk, a seasoned politician, noted that 'Turkey had failed to emerge from the status of a military republic'.

The devastating earthquakes of 17 August and 12 November 1999 put a damper on Turkey's economic plans. So dismal was the state's response to this tragedy that people believed the earthquakes were a turning-point in the country's political life. Civil society had responded energetically and had become self-reliant and assertive, while the state had weakened. But that proved not to be the case and the state soon reasserted itself, although the government's performance in rectifying the damage done by the earthquakes remained poor. Perhaps the improved Turkish–Greek relationship that resulted from 'earthquake diplomacy' was a positive outcome, establishing a friendship between the two foreign ministers. But the real issues between the two governments – the Aegean dispute and Cyprus – remained unresolved.

The three-party coalition seemed to be working well, though they could not agree on amending the constitution in order to give Demirel a second term as president when his term ended on 5 May 2000. But the parties agreed to elect Ahmet Necdet Sezer, president of the Constitutional Court, as Turkey's 10th president. He was a liberal, who wanted to see the 1982 constitution amended so as to permit free speech on such issues as Kurdish rights and political Islam. He was independent-minded and often took positions that did not please the parties that had elected him. In February 2001, these qualities led to a spat with the prime minister, which triggered the most serious economic and political crisis in republican history.

THE INCREASING IMPORTANCE OF EU ENTRY

Entry into the European Union had become the mission of government. In October 1999, a Union commission had recommended that Turkey be considered as a candidate, providing it met the so-called Copenhagen criteria, which included economic reform, human rights and the protection of minorities, i.e. the Kurds. The coalition also accepted the IMF's bitter prescription that asked for a 25 per cent inflation rate and a reduction in military expenditure, in order to cut the budget deficit. The three partners had agreed to await the European Court's review of the Öcalan trial before proceeding on the death sentence. NAP's leader, Devlet Bahçeli, seemed to have come round to Ecevit's way of thinking, despite dissent in his party and the demand for Öcalan's execution. But the murder of Ahmet Taner Kışlalı, an academic-journalist, on 21 October, was interpreted as a blow against democratization and rapprochement with Europe. There had been similar murders and the killers were still at large.

Meeting the EU's conditions for accession divided the coalition, despite the compromises of the leaders. A strong government would have carried out the reforms, not because the EU called for them, but because the reforms would make Turkey into a democratic society, bring it in line with the modern world and establish social peace. But Turkey lacked such a government. She had already made important economic concessions when she joined the customs union in 1996, without any of the substantial benefits that came with membership; that is why membership was so crucial. Polls suggested that around 60–70 per cent of the population favoured joining the EU, but felt pessimistic about the attitude of Europe towards Muslim Turkey. Would a 'Christian club' ever allow a Muslim country to become a member? The military's response was mixed: a retired general declared that EU membership was against Turkey's history and contradicted the Kemalist revolution, while Chief of Staff General Kıvrıkoğlu declared that 'joining the EU was a geopolitical necessity'. The generals were opposed to the EU demand that the military be brought under civil control, as in Europe. PM Ecevit therefore rejected TÜSİAD's proposal to abolish or diminish the role of the generals in the National Security Council. Big business was in favour of joining and TÜSİAD, its political lobby, insisted that Turkey needed companies that could compete in the global market, and proposed mergers between banks and companies.

The coalition had already lasted for 21 months, the longest and most stable government of the last five years, when a storm broke unexpectedly and created the worst economic crisis in the republic's history. On Monday, 19 February 2001, PM Ecevit got into a row with President Sezer, when the latter rebuked him for turning a blind eye on corruption in the cabinet and for obstructing investigations. Corruption had been widespread in the coalition and Ecevit, himself incorruptible, had tolerated corrupt ministers. The prime minister stormed out of the meeting, declaring that 'This is a serious crisis'. His words triggered a run on the financial markets and stocks plunged 7 per cent in a matter of minutes as investors feared that the coalition would fall. Interest rates rose as high as 3000 per cent and the Central Bank lost around US $5 billion – one-fifth of its foreign reserves – as investors dumped liras for dollars and euros. This was the result of deregulations, which allowed investors to take out their investments and run for safer markets. Turkey's financial situation had been weak for some time, and Ecevit's words merely triggered a storm that was about to break.

The IMF again stepped in, having already provided Ankara with US $11.4 billion in loans in November 2000, and Kemal Derviş, a vice-president at the World Bank, was sent to supervise economic and financial reforms as minister of the economy. The government agreed to privatize such state-owned assets as Turkish Airlines, the state petrol station chain, the oil-refining company, the electricity company, the national oil and gas pipeline company, Vakıfbank, the government-owned savings bank and the state spirits and tobacco monopoly. All this privatization was expected to raise about US $10 billion, if buyers could be found.

The ongoing economic crisis, the stabilization programme launched in January 2000 and the IMF prescription had already had severe consequences for society at large. The general situation was aggravated now by this new crisis. People were dying for lack of medicines as pharmaceutical companies stopped exports to Turkey. There was massive unemployment as plants shut down, and small businesses were squeezed out as a result of the reforms, which were marked by tight credit, slow production to bring down inflation and higher taxes.

Some NAP ministers obstructed the implementation of economic reform and the World Bank had to apply pressure to get things moving. The National Security Council, alarmed by the situation, discussed the possibility of a social explosion if the economy continued to deteriorate. Already there were demonstrations against the extravagance of the rich, and chants of such slogans as 'the plunderers are here, where are the workers?' and 'the bosses are here, where are the workers?' There were rumours that the coalition would not survive the crisis and there would be an interim government to prepare for fresh elections. As a result, on 16 July, Ecevit warned that speculation about an interim government of technocrats was undermining confidence in democracy and shaking the markets' confidence in the coalition's ability to carry out the IMF reforms. Next day, Enis Öksüz, MHP's minister of transport and communications, who had opposed Kemal Derviş and IMF reforms, resigned.

There was no short-term cure for Turkey's economic ills and the people continued to protest and suffer. Markets had fallen to a new low and the US dollar had risen to a new high of 1,500,000 liras. While the minimum wage was 100 million liras, unions calculated that the poverty line had risen to 797 million liras for a family of four, forcing workers to live in poverty. In November, workers from all over Turkey marched to Ankara to protest 'unemployment, poverty, corruption and war'. Outside the PM's residence, a mother of three set herself on fire, screaming 'I am starving to death'. In November, when the government issued a report on the state of the economy, 14,875 workplaces had closed down in the first eight months of the year, resulting in a million unemployed. Families were falling apart and crime had increased. The report also showed that the gap between rich and poor had increased and there was no safety net in place to protect the poor and the unemployed.

The attacks on the Twin Towers in New York and the Pentagon, on 11 September 2001, suddenly enhanced Turkey's role in President Bush's 'war against terrorism'. The Turkish government joined the war wholeheartedly, and was rewarded with more loans from Washington. Turkey was to receive an additional US $13 billion urgently, to help its recovery programme. Ankara opened its airspace and bases to US transport, and Ecevit declared that 'the fact that the US found the evidence against Bin Laden persuasive, persuades us also'. The government agreed to send 90 members of its special forces to Afghanistan, Foreign Minister İsmail Cem declaring that: 'this is not only the US's war; it is Turkey's war as well ... This is not a war against Islam; terrorism has no religion ... or geography'. Ecevit asked that 'friendly and allied countries recognize Turkey's importance and take Turkey's needs into consideration' when the time came for loan requests.

Meanwhile the coalition was making an effort to carry out reforms in order to satisfy the EU. Parliament adopted a package of 34 constitutional amendments to liberalize society; but there was no agreement on such critical issues as abolishing the death penalty, giving the Kurdish people the right to broadcast and have education in Kurdish or to limit the generals' power in the political life of the country. While Mesut Yılmaz and the liberals in the coalition supported these issues, Devlet Bahçeli and the NAP (and many generals) were opposed. Liberals argued that Turkey had no alternative but the EU; Bahçeli and the extreme right opposed the

EU, arguing that demands for 'the abolition of the death penalty, education and broadcasting in Kurdish were a plot against the unity of Turkey, sponsored by the 'so-called pro-EU lobby in Turkey and EU officials'. Bahçeli was concerned about the votes of the lower middle classes in Anatolia, who were hurt by the process of globalization and who voted for such parties as the NAP and the Islamists. He wanted to guarantee their votes in the coming election.

The political and economic situation was adversely affected when the 77-year old Ecevit was suddenly taken ill and hospitalized on 4 May 2002. His illness created a crisis, brought on by speculation as to whether he would step down and who would succeed him; the stock market responded by a sharp decline. He was hospitalized again on 17 May, but refused to resign as he believed that his resignation would lead to the break-up of the coalition and early elections, and a political crisis at a time when the country was focused on the economy and accession to the EU. The coalition was paralysed. The three parties knew that an early election might mean that they would not clear the 10 per cent hurdle and would be left out of the next parliament. Polls showed that the new party, the Justice and Development Party, led by Recep Tayyip Erdoğan, the former Islamist mayor of Istanbul, was considered the favourite in an early election. The only bright spot came in June, when the Turkish [soccer] team reached the semi-final of the World Cup tournament before being defeated by the eventual winners, Brazil.

Devlet Bahçeli's call, on 7 July, for an early election to be held on 3 November brought the political crisis to a head. The next day, Deputy PM Hüsamettin Özkan, and three others all belonging to the DLP, resigned. More resignations of ministers and legislators followed, until Ecevit announced that he would step down if the coalition no longer enjoyed a majority in parliament. When Foreign Minister İsmail Cem resigned from the cabinet and the party, there was talk of a new political party, led by İsmail Cem, Kemal Derviş and Hüsamettin Özkan, which would govern the country with the support of centre-right parties (ANAP and TPP). The new party would marginalize the extreme nationalists and carry out the reforms necessary to satisfy the EU before the Copenhagen summit on 12 December 2002. However, on 16 August, Ecevit, having failed to resign, agreed to lead the country to an early election. The DLP dissidents had failed in their political manoeuvre to capture power and establish a totally pro-EU, IMF coalition. They had also burned their boats when they resigned and had no choice but to form a new party to contest the election.

The New Turkey Party was formed on 22 July, with former foreign minister İsmail Cem as its leader. Kemal Derviş, the most significant member of the troika failed to commit himself, leaving the new party weak and colourless. When he resigned in August, he joined the RPP after attempting to bring about a union of the centre-left, even including elements from the centre-right. He wanted to create a political movement – 'Contemporary social democracy' he called it – capable of coming to power on its own at the next election and forming a strong government that could carry out the reforms necessary to end the political and economic crises that had plagued Turkey throughout the 1990s. When he failed to form such a movement, Derviş realized that the NTP would fail, as all new parties in Turkey tend to. He therefore joined the only centre-left party, the RPP, which was likely to succeed. Surveys showed that the party under Deniz Baykal was receiving only about 6 per cent of the vote, while the AK party was in the 20 per cent range. Baykal had failed to enter parliament in 1999 and it was doubtful that he would do so in 2002. But once Derviş joined the RPP, the establishment's media promoted Derviş and the RPP endlessly and the party's ratings began to increase. By early September the polls showed that the RPP had moved up from 6.9 to 14.3 per cent, thanks to the 'Kemal Derviş factor'. Meanwhile, the AK Party's vote had risen to almost 25 per cent. Confronted with this reality, on 18 September, TÜSİAD's chair Tuncay Özilhan, speaking for the business community, stated his preference for a CHP-AKP coalition, especially if Kemal Derviş was in charge of the economy. This was the hope of the bourgeoisie: that the election of 3 November would produce a two-party coalition so that the RPP would control any 'extremist, Islamist' tendencies of its AK Party partners.

The election results on 4 November therefore produced a surprise when the AK Party emerged as the winner with over 34 per cent of the votes and 363 seats, more than the number required to form the government. The RPP had won 19 per cent of the votes and had 180 seats and became the only opposition. All the other parties had failed to clear the 10 per cent barrier and therefore had no representation in parliament. It seemed that the voters had humiliated and eliminated the former party leaders – Bülent Ecevit, Devlet Bahçeli, Necmettin Erbakan, Mesut Yılmaz, and Tansu Çiller. Even the newly-founded 'Young Party' of the business tycoon, Cem Uzan, won only 7.2 per cent of the vote. Professional advertisers had run his campaign and given the voters musical concerts and free food, as well as much publicity in the Uzan-owned media.

What accounted for the success of the AK Party and its leader Recep Tayyip Erdoğan? If the polls were right, the voters wanted a new leader and not a new party and Erdoğan fitted the bill. He was a new kind of leader who did not come out of the system as did most of his rivals. He came out of the rough-and-tumble district of Istanbul called Kasımpaşa, from a humble background, lacked a modern education, and did not speak a foreign language. But he had proved himself as mayor of Istanbul and as a politician who could get things done – and is said to have become a US dollar millionaire in the process. He was the symbol of the party and not its sole leader, and he was being persecuted and prosecuted by the establishment.

Although the AK Party had its roots in political Islam, most of its leaders had moved to the centre and declared their party to be secular democratic and conservative Muslim democrats rather like the Christian democrats in Europe. Surveys showed that the party's support was 51 per cent rural and 49 per cent urban, and largely male. Housewives (17 per cent) tended to vote AKP while urban working women tended not to. The AK Party was not a continuation of the former parties of political Islam, whereas the recently formed Felicity (Saadet) Party was. The voters marginalized the FP, giving it only 2.5 per cent of the vote even although Necmettin Erbakan, the foremost leader of Turkish political Islam, had campaigned vigorously for the FP and was himself defeated when he ran as an independent. The AKP had come to represent the counter-elite that had emerged in Anatolia; it had finally come to power. That is why the Istanbul daily, *Sabah*, described the election as 'the Anatolian revolution'.

But the party still relied on Islamist support though only a minority (22 per cent) still called for the Sharia while 43 per cent opposed it. Overall the fear of the Sharia had declined to just one per cent of the population. AKP took 27 per cent of its vote from the FP's base and 22 per cent from other parties. The party had a broad social base and it would be incorrect to call it the party of 'political Islam'; nor had it won a 'protest vote'. Voters, alarmed by the ongoing economic crisis, massive unemployment and rising prices, placed their hopes in a leader who had managed to govern Istanbul efficiently; they believed he could do the same throughout Turkey.

Since Recep Tayyip Erdoğan could not become a member of parliament or the prime minister because of his prison sentence, Abdullah Gül was appointed prime minister on 16 November. He was regarded as caretaker prime minister until the constitution is amended, allowing Erdoğan to take his place.

Abdullah Gül was born in Kayseri in 1950. He has a Ph.D. in economics from Istanbul University and has studied in England. He taught economics and worked for the Islamic Development Bank in Saudi Arabia before entering politics in the Welfare Party in 1991. In August 2001, he was one of the founder members of the AKP. He is a man of some experience, perhaps more so than the charismatic Erdoğan.

The Gül government faced a number of interconnected challenges: the new UN (Kofi Annan) plan for the reunification of Cyprus, which has added pressure to find a settlement for the island's problem; the question of EU accession, which will now be taken up in December 2004, after Ankara's human rights record has been reviewed, before a date is given for further talks; negotiations with the IMF and Turkey's huge debt; the problem of the economy at home and related unemployment and poverty; human rights and torture; the headscarf issue and the generals' warning; the possibility of a US war with Iraq in which Ankara, under great pressure from Washington, finally agreed to deploy US troops in order to open a northern front against Baghdad. These monumental challenges are waiting to be met. The government has begun cautiously. They know that while they control parliament and the cabinet, they do not control the state, that is to say the armed forces and the entire bureaucracy.

There is also the danger that this two-party formula might create a political situation which existed in the 1950s: 'a majoritarian democracy' in which the Democrats claimed that they could do as they wished because they held such an overwhelming majority in parliament. This led to undemocratic behaviour on the part of the DP, with military intervention in May 1960. But the AKP seems to have learned from past experience and should therefore behave responsibly towards the opposition as well as the secular population, which is now in the majority. Moreover, 45 per cent of the electorate is not even represented because of the 10 per cent electoral barrage and that makes the government's position less legitimate.

Prime Minister Gül seemed to be aware of the situation. In his first statement to the press he declared: 'We have no secret agenda. I will take care to ensure transparency and accountability ... We are not going to spring any surprises ... We are not elitist. We are children of the people, people who come from the middle class and poor segments of society. Our priority is to give them some relief. We will work hard. First of all, we will deal with the State Security Courts and the detention period.'

But Abdullah Gül was regarded as the caretaker prime minister, waiting until the constitution had been amended in order to permit Erdoğan to be elected to parliament and become prime minister and party leader. The world was already treating Erdoğan as though he was at least the co-leader. He made statements and went on visits around the world where he was treated as the true leader. He visited Athens, Copenhagen, New York, Washington, Moscow, and Davos and he was given the red-carpet treatment in all these places. The constitutional amendment was passed in January 2003 and Erdoğan was elected to parliament on 9 March in the Siirt by-election. Abdullah Gül resigned on 11 March and President Sezer appointed Erdoğan as the new PM.

Meanwhile on 1 March, Turkey's establishment experienced a trauma resulting from parliament's defeat of the government's motion to permit the deployment in Anatolia of 62,000 US troops intended to open a northern front in the war against Iraq. Some one hundred MPs from the governing party voted against the motion in collaboration with the opposition. The vote was a major surprise because one month earlier, on 6 February, parliament had agreed to allow US forces to modernize their bases and transport heavy equipment to northern Iraq via Turkey. Virtually everyone was convinced – the media, big business, the generals, the politicians – that Turkey would be an active member of the US led coalition. The 'rewards' were thought to be considerable: US financial aid and soft loans worth billions of dollars necessary to get a crisis-ridden economy on its feet and influence in post-war Iraq, as well as construction sub-contracts to rebuild a war-torn Iraq. The government's defeat showed that the governing party was deeply divided. In electing the AKP, the voters had swept aside much of the old political establishment and opened the door to a new generation of leaders from the Anatolian heartland. Unlike earlier party governments, the AKP was not a tightly-controlled political party doing the bidding of its leader and manipulated by the elites. It was responsive to popular opinion and the anti-war demonstration had been significant in directing the negative vote. As some Turks noted, the concept of democracy had changed as a result.

Despite attempts to repair relations with Washington, Turkey had little success. The Assembly agreed to open Turkey's airspace to the US and there were discussions about sending Turkish troops to Iraq. But, suspicion among Turks prevailed that hawks in the Bush administration were out to punish Turkey for not letting US troops use it as a rear base in the war against Iraq. There was also a deeper explanation for the distrust. The interest of both countries had diverged since the end of the Cold War. Ankara was apprehensive about US support for Kurdish self-rule in northern Iraq because that would fan separatist sentiment among Kurds in Turkey. The Süleymaniye incident on 4 July 2003 seemed to confirm Turkey's fears. US forces in northern Iraq seized 11 members of Turkey's special forces, blindfolding and humiliating them. Ankara protested to Washington and the Turkish officers were released. But the damage had been done to Turkish–US relations and even the pro-Pentagon generals were alienated by what was described as 'US arrogance'.

Even before the Süleymaniye Incident, the government had won the military's support to prepare Turkey for accession talks with the EU. On 30 May, PM Erdoğan again stressed his government's determination to pursue the road to the EU for that was 'our debt to our people and our country'. The deputy chief of staff, General Yasar Buyukanit, also reaffirmed the military's support for the EU, saying that 'it was Atatürk's path and we cannot be against the EU'. Two days earlier, the National Security Council had agreed to amend laws that violated human rights and to permit Kurdish-language broad-casts on private channels, thereby meeting some of the EU's demands. Business organizations came out in support of the government and placed a full-page advertisement in the press stating: 'We support the 6th harmonization packet [of reform] and all the steps Turkey is taking for EU membership'. When the foreign minister addressed the Royal Institute of International Affairs in London in early July, he declared that Turkey would carry out a program of 'determined and sustained reforms' to meet the Copenhagen criteria set out by the EU. Later in July, he addressed the Washington Institute of Near East Policy, the conservative think-tank, his talk titled 'The US–Turkish Relationship: Prospects and Perils'. He noted that under his party's rule, the old elites were no longer in power and those outside Turkey faced a new country. Reform was transforming the political land-scape which was now more democratic. Joining the EU was at the top of the government's agenda and the NSC would be reformed in the seventh reform packet and thereby meet other EU objections. As for Turkish–US relations, they would thrive as they were based on such common values as democracy, freedom, and a market economy; in fact, Turkey's relationships with the US and the EU complemented each other.

The Assembly passed the 7th reform packet on 31 July, with the support of the opposition and TÜSİAD. The structure of the NSC was altered: the secretary general lost some of his powers, he was to be appointed by the PM and his appointment approved by the president; the council would meet bi-monthly instead of every month, and its role would be purely advisory; and the military budget was opened to civil scrutiny. The EU was happy with the passage of the packet though, as with other reforms, it wanted to see how the laws were implemented before deciding on Turkey's accession. Had the wings of the powerful military establishment been clipped by these reforms? While most agreed that they had, some noted that the military still retained control of the intelli-gence establishment, and therefore of the so-called 'deep state', a state within the state which was out of the control of its political masters and responsible to no higher authority. When PM Erdoğan was asked about the role of the military, he replied, rather ambi-giously, that on paper there was now no difference compared with NATO and EU standards.

Relations with Washington remained strained and on 7 November, Ankara shelved its decision to send troops to Iraq after the Iraqi administration vetoed having Turkish troops on its soil. The Kurdish north was opposed, as was the Shia south. Even within the Sunni triangle, the mayor of Falluja declared that Turkish troops would be seen as occupiers. Under these circumstances, Washington welcomed Ankara's decision, preferring to rely even more on its Kurdish allies.

The suicide bombs in Istanbul on 15 November that targeted two synagogues, the British consulate, and a British bank, brought Turkey closer to Europe as a front against terrorism. Britain's Foreign Secretary Jack Straw and German Chancellor Gerhard Schroeder spoke of integrating Turkey rapidly into the EU as Turks described the attack as the country's 11 September. Ankara was more determined to open accession talks with the EU and play the role of a bridge between Europe and the Middle East, a role that Europe, especially Britain, had wanted Turkey to play since beginning of the Cold War.

The state visit of Syria's President Bashir Asad to Turkey was therefore politically significant. Before his arrival on 6 January 2004, Asad had assured Turkish journalists that he wanted to put the problems of the past behind them – a reference to Turkey's annexation of Iskendurun/Hatay in 1939 – and described the Turkish-Syrian border as a border of friendship. Turkey's membership of the EU, he said, would also benefit Syria, bringing Europe to its border. Moreover, neither Syria nor Turkey wanted to see the break-up of Iraq and neither favoured a Kurdish state.

The campaign for accession talks with the EU continued to gather momentum throughout the year. The generals agreed to work with the Annan plan to reunify Cyprus, and Erdoğan also accepted all its conditions on 30 January. Kofi Annan was given a free hand to carry out a referendum on both sides of the island so that it could join the EU on 1 May.

Erdoğan's visit to the US at the end of January papered over some of the cracks in US–Turkish relations. The relationship, explained the foreign minister, was no longer just strategic but based on human rights and democratization. In Turkey, that raised the question as to whether Ankara would play the role of a 'moderate Islamic' state in the region and be the model for a democratic 'Greater Middle East'. That was the role many thought Washington had assigned to

Ankara so as to establish US hegemony in the Islamic world. But the generals – and the intelligentsia – rejected the notion of 'moderate Islam' for Turkey; the country could not be Islamic and secular at the same time. Erdoğan agreed and stated that Turkey was a secular and social state and there could be no Islamic state within a secular state. The discussion on President Bush's 'Greater Middle East project' and Turkey's role within it continued.

The local election of 28 March 2004 strengthened the position of the governing party and weakened that of the opposition. Its vote increased in round figures from 34 to 43 per cent and that of the RPP declined from 19 to 15 per cent. Even before the election, the media had discussed the problem of government without opposition; the problem was now even more acute. But analysts raised important questions about who really ruled Turkey; whether elections necessarily gave power to the winner, or whether the government actually controlled the state. These were questions that PM Erdoğan had always understood, declaring early in his premiership that although his party was in government, it did not control the state apparatus. The Justice and Development Party had been trying to gain control of the state, and seemed as though it might be doing so little by little.

In the referendums on Cyprus on 24 April, the Turkish community voted (65 per cent) for unity while the Greeks voted against (76 per cent). That improved Ankara's position vis-à-vis the EU, but the government continued to pass legislation to meet EU criteria. On 26 September, Parliament completed sweeping reforms of the country's penal code bringing it in line with those of the EU. About 350 articles of the code were amended, said to be its most radical rewriting in recent times. There were heavy penalties for torture and 'honour killings', stronger sanctions against corruption, as well as fewer restrictions on the freedom of expression. The debate over the law to criminalize adultery had created serious doubts in Europe about Turkey's determination to preserve its secularity. Despite popular support, the measure was dropped in order to meet EU objections. In October, the EU Commission stated that Turkey had successfully crossed the first set of hurdles to membership, having sufficiently fulfilled the political criteria, and recommended that accession negotiations be opened. Finally, on 17 December, the EU accepted Turkey's membership conditionally and set the date for accession talks to be opened in October 2005.

The media hailed the EU decision as a great success for the government and PM Erdoğan's position was strengthened. Many wondered whether he would now practice 'majoritarian democracy' and attempt to amend the constitution; would he implement changes and move towards a semi-presidential system, have parliament appoint judges to the Constitutional Court, open the Supreme Military Council to judicial oversight, and abolish the headscarf ban in public institutions?

But Erdoğan and his party have probably learned the lesson of the 1950s when the Democrat Party enjoyed a strong majority and ruled without opposition. Therefore, the government is likely to focus its attention on getting accessions talks started. The road to the EU is going to be long and arduous. Not only will the new laws have to be implemented to the EU's satisfaction; more importantly, the economy will have to be drastically reformed. The real problem with Turkey joining the EU is not its religious and cultural differences, but its economic weakness. Turkey is not only one of the poorest countries among the applicants, it is also the largest. It has a national income of $2,790 compared to the UK's $28,530, and, with a population of 70 million, would become the second largest EU member after Germany. Writing in the *Guardian* on 5 October 2004, Richard Adams noted: 'Nor may it be assumed that the economy will be transformed just by entry into the EU. In fact entry could easily lead to recession, unemployment and instability and an ill-timed entry could be disastrous for the country'.

SUGGESTED FURTHER READING

Metin Heper, Ayşe Öncü and Heinz Kramer (eds.), *Turkey and the West* (I.B. Taurus, London and New York, 1993).

Tosun Arıcanlı and Dani Rodrik (eds.), *The Political Economy of Turkey: Debt, Adjustment and Sustainability* (MacMillan, London, 1990).

Jenny White, *Islamist Mobilization in Turkey* (University of Washington Press, Seattle, 2002).

Ayata, Sencer and Ayşe Güneş-Ayata, 'Religious communities, Secularism, and Security in Turkey', in *New Frontiers in Middle East Security*, Lenore Martin (ed.) (Palgrave, New York, 2001), pp. 107–26.

Ayata, Ayşe Güneş- and Sencer Ayata, 'Ethnicity and Security Problems in Turkey', in *New Frontiers in Middle East Security*, Lenore Martin (ed.) (Palgrave, New York, 2001), pp. 127–50.

Postscript:
Turkey 2005–2013

From the beginning of 2005, the Justice and Development Party's (JDP) principal concern was not merely to win the 2007 general election, but to increase its majority in parliament sufficiently so as to write the new constitution alone. The continuing weakness of the opposition gave the party greater confidence. The main opposition, the Republican People's Party (RPP), continued to stagnate under the leadership of Deniz Baykal. On 5 January 2005, the press discussed division within the RPP and an impending challenge to Baykal's leadership. In fact, the challenge came from Mustafa Sarıgül, the dynamic, young mayor of Şişli, an up-market district of Istanbul. But such was Turkey's political culture that nothing came of the challenge. The RPP had become Baykal's party and he was re-elected unopposed at the party's congress on 20 November to lead the party in the 2007 election. The opposition continued to limp along, only criticizing JDP policies without offering a viable alternative.

If there was an opposition to JDP rule it came from urban women protesting the attack on their rights. On 8 March, they demonstrated in Istanbul but were brutally repressed by the police. Nor had the military been silenced yet. On 25 April 2005, the daily newspaper, *Radikal* reported that Chief of Staff General Hilmi Özkök, had commented on the situation claiming that Islamic reaction was continuing under the very eyes of the state, while the

Workers' Party of Kurdistan, the PKK, was exploiting European Union demands on Turkey. The EU, he said, did not understand the value of Turkey, that the unitary state was absolute and could not be divided. Nor was there any crisis with the United States despite the breakdown over Iraq in 2003.

In the French referendum on the EU on 29 May 2005 the voters voted No – 55 per cent to 45 – against the constitution, putting back the EU project and Turkey's chances of accession. But Ankara tried to put a bright face on the decision and Foreign Minister Abdullah Gül said that the referendum was no obstacle for Turkey to start negotiations, and Prime Minister Recep Tayyip Erdoğan supported the statement. In fact, the referendum only succeeded in strengthening the government's determination to improve relations with the United States.

Erdoğan went to Washington in June. After his meeting with President Obama the Turkish press commented that the 'strategic partnership' was still shaky as Washington was reluctant to become involved in the Kurdish conflict. It refused to agree to persistent Turkish requests to destroy PKK bases in northern Iraq. But in New York, Erdoğan received the medal of honour from the Anti-Defamation League. That was seen as compensation for the still-weak relationship with Washington; Ankara had won the support of the Jewish lobby so critical in Washington politics. Gündüz Aktan, a former ambassador to the US, described the visit as the beginning of a 'new era with America'. Moreover, on 11 June the *New York Times* wrote that Erdoğan, nervous about European prospects was turning increasingly to the US. The paper quoted a Turkish businessman who said: 'Don't count on the European Union. Look to the US; they're our real friends'.

Leaving aside foreign relations, the real drama at home was the growing tension between the government and the military. The government, exploiting EU criteria about the need to bring the military under civilian control, was trying to limit the power of the generals, however much they denied it. General Hilmi Özkök stated publicly in *Cumhuriyet* on 8 June that the army's powers had been limited in the fight against terrorism. He appealed for total collaboration between the people, the administration, civil society and the Turkish Armed Forces. He wanted the army to be given greater powers to deal with the PKK, which had just launched another bombing campaign killing and wounding a number of soldiers and civilians. The next day, Cemil Çiçek, the Justice Minister, denied any differences and said that 'the soldiers and government were a single voice and one fist'. The government and the army, he said, were on the same side as far as terrorism was concerned and there was no shortage of dialogue. The laws were sufficient to deal with any situation but would be changed if necessary. 'We don't want any pressure from the EU, we want cooperation', he stated.

For the moment relations with the army were put on hold and Erdoğan turned his attention the to Kurdish issue. In August he came to Diyarbakır, a Kurdish town in southeast Turkey, where he declared that the Kurdish problem would be solved democratically: 'Though Turkey has a Kurdish problem we have the confidence to face it with democratic courage'. On 11 August, *Milliyet* noted that the prime minister had opened a new page by admitting that there was, in fact, a Kurdish question. The next day, Erdoğan admitted that the state had made mistakes in the past. But 'the Kurdish question is everyone's problem, first and foremost it is my problem. It doesn't suit big states not to accept the mistakes of the past. The solution is more democracy, more civil law, and more welfare'. The press noted that in Diyarbakır the prime minister spoke to an empty square surrounded by security befitting President Bush!

Erdoğan's speech in Diyarbakır had won him praise from diplomats in Ankara and European Union politicians said that they supported his initiative. However, French President Jacques Chirac and Angela Merkel, Germany's conservative leader, raised some serious doubts about forthcoming talks. They accused Ankara of failing to act 'in the spirit' of a country hoping to join the EU. Sure enough, in early September, talks with the EU were stalled. On 2 September, Erdoğan declared that Turkey would not make any more concessions, accusing EU governments of pandering to public opinion.

In October, Chirac aggravated the situation by declaring that Turkey would have to undergo a 'major cultural revolution' if she were to realize her forty-year-old dream of joining the EU. Turkey had already undertaken major reforms such as abolishing the death penalty, opening her market to European goods, and giving linguistic rights to the Kurds. But the EU demanded more changes such as greater civilian control over the military, the release of political prisoners, the recognition of Cyprus as well as the opening up of Turkish ports and airports to Cypriot shipping and aircraft, the speeding up of judicial reforms, and proof that human rights were on a par with those in the EU. That was the situation at the end of 2005 and that is how it remained for some years to come.

If Europe was sympathetic to JDP's Kurdish initiative the opposition at home remained hostile. The centre-right parties – True Path and Nationalist Action – denounced the prime minister's efforts and said that only traitors had come out in support. The RPP's Baykal stated that Erdoğan had confused the Kurdish question with the question of terror. But following a wave of attacks on Aegean tourist resorts and military targets, the PKK, responding to Erdoğan's initiative, declared a one-month ceasefire.

Erdoğan's initiative was not well received by the generals either. Commander of the First Army, Hurşit Tolon, who was retiring in August, sent a stern message to the prime minister. He believed that when Erdoğan spoke of democracy and made concessions to the EU and the PKK he was abandoning the position of the Kemalists who had founded the Republic in 1923, and Commander Tolon did not want to do this. At the National Security Council meeting on 23 August, Erdoğan backed down and seemed to agree that the 'Kurdish problem' was open to misinterpretation. He said that they had to win over the Kurdish people. Turkey was faced with the problem of witnessing events in Iraq where a constitution was making Kurdish and Arabic official languages and Islam was being considered as a source of law. Despite further attempts to solve this problem, there was no major breakthrough for the next seven years.

Ever since the JDP came to power in 2002, fears were expressed of 'creeping Islamization'. There were reports that the Ankara JDP-led municipality had a programme of changing the names of streets named after secular and progressive historical figures. The latest example was removing Abdullah Cevdet's name and replacing it with that of Professor Yusuf Halaçoğlu, a defender of the official thesis against the Armenian claim of 'genocide'. Islamists hated Abdullah Cevdet (1869–1932) and his contemporary Mehmet Akif (1873–1936) branded him an apostate. Cevdet had defended the Latin alphabet, the civil code and the idea of secularism. Later the Islamist even alleged that he had called for importing virile men from Europe to reinvigorate the Turkish race, an allegation that was totally unfounded. In 1910, he had translated Reinhart Dozy's history of Islam but the book was proscribed and copies were thrown into the sea.

The generals were alarmed by such activity and the Chief of Staff, Yaşar Büyükanıt, warned that 'the bell was tolling for Turkey'. The first threat to Turkey was reaction (*ırtıca*) and the second, partition i.e. the PKK. The call to remove the pictures of Atatürk from state offices, he warned in *Milliyet* on 27 October 2005, were voices that should awaken Turkey.

JDP rule was also a struggle for the universities between staunchly secular state institutions and a government with roots in political Islam. The victim in this war was the president of the university in Van in eastern Turkey. Professor Yücel Aşkin was arrested on a corruption charge and became the first Turk holding this academic title to be put in prison. While the prosecutors charged him with corruption, the independent board that appointed university presidents said he was a victim of a conspiracy by Islamic mystical orders in Van. When the police searched Aşkin's home, the president of the Higher Education Council (YÖK) described it as 'an action against the freedom of the university'. Once the government had captured YÖK it was able to appoint its candidates as rectors of numerous universities.

By the beginning of 2006, there were rumours that there might be an end to political stability if PM Erdoğan decided to run for the presidency. Would he make the same mistake that Turgut Özal and Süleyman Demirel had made when they had opted for the presidency and destroyed their parties in the 1990s? If Erdoğan chose to run for presidency in May 2007 and then the elections took place on schedule in November 2007, the JDP would suffer greatly. Many voted for the JDP just because the party was led by Erdoğan. Without him the party would find it hard to attract as much support and would probably not remain the leading party, opening the way for coalitions. That was the principal discussion throughout 2006.

By January 2007, a poll showed that the majority of voters were against Erdoğan becoming Turkey's president. But the office acquired significance for the JDP as Ahmet Necdet Sezer, the current president, vetoed a bill passed by the Assembly. Sezer returned the law, which regulated the appointment of rectors to fifteen new universities, for reconsideration. But on 12 January the Assembly adopted the law without making any amendments. Acquiring the presidency for the party therefore became a priority.

When Erdoğan refused the presidential candidacy, speculation of Abdullah Gül's candidacy increased and he became the JDP's candidate for president. But on 27 April the Assembly failed to elect Gül because of a lack of the required 367 quorum. Abdullah Gül received 357 votes, the highest number gained by any presidential candidate until that day. But the opposition RPP claimed that the vote was invalid and took the issue to the Constitutional Court to make the decision official. On 1 May, the Constitutional Court approved the RPP's petition to invalidate the presidential election rounds, citing the requirement to have a quorum of 367 deputies to elect a president in parliament. The Court therefore cancelled the first round held on 27 April. On the same day the prime minister announced that an early election would be held on 22 July.

Another institution suddenly cast a shadow on the political scene: the military. This was surprising given all the legal changes made by the JDP government to comply with the EU's Copenhagen criteria. The 29 March issue of *Nokta,* a weekly magazine, ran a story based on the diaries of a retired admiral, that retired generals were planning a coup. This came to be known as the Ergenekon conspiracy. Some weeks later, on 27 April, the general staff issued an e-warning on its website emphasizing that the presidential election process should focus on laicism. Therefore the Turkish Armed Forces could not stay out of it. The following day, the government issued a counter-warning, perhaps the first of its kind in the history of the republic, reminding the general staff that it was affiliated to the prime minister's office.

The election campaign held the nation's attention and on 22 July the JDP won by a landslide with 47 per cent of the vote. The victory had broken the political deadlock and the rightwing Nationalist Action Party (NAP) declared that its deputies would attend the presidential election rounds thereby ending the problem of a quorum. However, the RPP declared that it would boycott the presidency if Abdullah Gül were elected president.

On 28 August 2007, Abdullah Gül was elected president and as head of state became the commander-in-chief of Turkey in peace-time. Throughout the campaign he assured the army that there was no need to worry about secularism just because his wife wore a headscarf. He told reporters that Turkey was governed by laws and that the constitution guaranteed basic human rights, including the right to dress as one pleased. When, on 16 August, journalists questioned General Büyükanıt on Gül's presidential bid, the chief of staff preferred to remain silent. He said: 'They claim that the stock exchange indexes fall when I speak...' But political observers wondered what had been said at the Dolmabahçe Palace meeting between the general and Erdoğan on 4 May 2007. The two men refused to say what was discussed and to this day no one knows what the two spoke of during the two-and-a-half hour meeting. But to end speculation, on 20 August the prime minister asked the army to stay out of politics. '... Let it stay in its place. Our institutions conduct their duties in line with what is set out in the Constitution.'

Before the general election, Professor Yılmaz Esmer of Istanbul's Bahçeşehir University carried out a survey of political and social attitudes among the electorate. He found that while voters did not want Islam to regulate social and political life they regarded religiosity as an important attribute in a president. The results confirmed the general belief that religion was a critical element separating the two parties, the JDP and the RPP. 59 per cent of the JDP electorate regarded religious books as more important than scientific inventions in order to understand the universe; while 84 per cent of the RPP supporters said that science was more important. Nevertheless, despite the emphasis on religion, 85 per cent said that unemployment was their foremost concern. Unemployment and the economic situation of the country were the first two factors affecting voter preferences. The economy had been doing well and the business community therefore supported the JDP party and its presidential candidate.

Abdullah Gül's election was seen by many as the beginning of a new era marked by an Islamist taking over the citadel of secularism. On the eve of the presidential vote the general staff declared that Turkey was under attack by forces of evil. On the armed forces website, Chief of Staff Büyükanıt wrote that: 'our nation has been watching the behaviour of centres of evil, who systematically try to corrode the secular nature of the Republic of Turkey. Nefarious plans emerge in different forms every day.' But, as a sign of protest, the generals could do little more than boycott the president's swearing-in ceremony.

In his inaugural speech, President Gül was careful to give a conciliatory message to everyone. He began his speech with a reference to Atatürk, the founder of modern Turkey, a message to the 'secular camp' and finished with reference to God – 'May Allah not embarrass us.' But he emphasized that secularism 'guarantees the freedom of religion and conscience', rhetoric often used by religious parties to justify wearing a headscarf as a fundamental right and freedom of religion.

With his position strengthened by the election victory and Gül's election, PM Erdoğan went on the offensive. On 19 January 2008 he warned the judiciary against interference in the controversy surrounding the wearing of the Islamic political symbol, the headscarf, in universities. A week earlier, while on a visit to Spain, he had stated that the use of the headscarf as a political symbol was not an offence. The chief public prosecutor joined the debate and said that wearing a headscarf in school went against the unitary structure of the state. He then denounced as 'unconstitutional' the government's proposal to ease the headscarf ban. Erdoğan responded that no one should see himself as superior to the executive or the legislature. As there was a separation of powers in Turkey, he said, every branch of government should know its boundaries. With the attack on the judiciary, observers of the political scene wondered how the struggle over the headscarf would end.

What became known as the Ergenekon conspiracy was first mentioned by the weekly newspaper *Nokta* in March 2007. But the court ordered the arrest of 13 officers only on 28 January 2008. General Büyükanıt criticized the attempt to link the 'Ergenekon gang' with the Turkish Armed Forces. There had been attempts in the past to link the military with such bodies. But the Army was not a criminal organization and those who were guilty in the armed forces would be punished.

During the next few years, arrests of officers, retired and serving, as well as journalists and academics said to be involved in the Ergenekon conspiracy to carry out a coup d'état, followed (see chronology). Such people were detained and no bail was given while their trials were pending, although they were unlikely to violate their bail. Indictments that ran into hundreds of pages were published and even put online. Few people tried to make any sense of them except for one scholar-journalist by the name of Gareth Jenkins, a British journalist residing in Istanbul. In 2009, he analysed the first two indictments. His monograph, *Between Fact and Fantasy: Turkey's Ergenekon Investigation*, published by Johns Hopkins University-SAIS, caused a stir in Turkey among those who read English. But it was never published in a Turkish translation.

The Ergenekon investigation has continued into the present. On 11 March 2009, the second indictment of 1,909 pages covering the sixth, seventh and eighth wave of arrests was sent to the Istanbul High Court. A life sentence was requested for two generals while the prosecutors accused 14 others of attempting to annul parliament through the use of violence. The indictment also accused a businessman, Sinan Aygün, and journalists Mustafa Balbay and Tuncay Özcan. On 14 April there were 29 arrests in the twelfth wave, including university professors and rectors.

The fear of a military intervention seemed odd to many observers; in the past, the military had intervened only when progress of the system was blocked politically by either the Left or the Right and only a military intervention could reopen it. Thus after the 1960 intervention the junta, supported by law professors, found the 1924 constitution out-of-date for the 1960s. They wrote a liberal constitution for the multi-party period that moved Turkey from a commercial to an industrial economy. In 1971, the military destroyed the threat from a revolutionary trade union movement – known by its Turkish acronym DISK – that the governing Justice Party could not cope with democratically and which threatened the developing, capitalist economy. In 1980, the junta intervened to clear political obstacles – political parties and unions for example – that stood in the way of Turkey's path to globalization. At the beginning of the twenty-first century there was no such threat to the system. The EU had necessitated the making of the military subordinate to civil authority as a condition for Turkey to join the EU. Perhaps the governing party saw the threat of an alleged military conspiracy as a drastic measure to bring the generals to heel.

In January 2008, General Yaşar Büyükanıt, commented on and criticized the 'Ergenekon operation' and the arrest of officers accused of provoking armed rebellion against the government. He also stood firm on the army's opposition to the government's plan to allow women in universities to wear the turban, a headscarf worn as a political statement by Islamist women.

Secular-minded journalists observed that the so-called National View or *Milli Görüş*, the Islamist ideology of Necmettin Erbakan's parties, was gradually taking over the JDP. The aim was to transform Turkey into a more conservative and religious country. The way to do that was to capture all ministries, especially the Ministry of Education, by appointing like-minded officials. For example, the appointment of Yunus Söylet as the rector of Istanbul University on 30 December 2008 led to student protests. Yunus Söylet was the prime minister's family doctor with close ties to his party. Even TUBITAK, the Scientific and Research ouncil of Turkey was governed by an administration opposed to the idea of evolution. Thus in 2009, declared by UNESCO as the 'Year of Darwin' because of his 200th anniversary, Darwin and the story of evolution were removed as the cover story and replaced with the cover on 'global climate change'! On 16 March 2009, the *New York Times* and other journals around the world reported on the Darwin scandal, emphasizing the growing influence of religion on secular institutions.

On 1 January 2009, PM Erdoğan began his diplomatic offensive against Israel, visiting Syria, Jordan, Egypt, and Saudi Arabia in order to try and stop Israeli attacks on Gaza. He accused Israel of causing a human tragedy while President Gül declared on 4 January that what Israel had done in Gaza was nothing but an atrocity. On 16 January, Erdoğan proposed that Israel should be barred from the United Nations while she ignored the body's call to stop fighting in Gaza. These were political gestures aimed at the Middle East but meaningless while Washington stood behind Tel Aviv!

Relations with Israel suffered a further blow when on 29 January, PM Erdoğan walked out of a session criticizing President Shimon Peres. Before walking out, vowing never to return to Davos, he said: 'Mr Peres, you are older than I am. Your voice is too loud. I know why that it is because you suffer from a guilty conscience. When it comes to killing, you know very well how to kill. I know very well how you hit and killed children on the beaches.'

Meanwhile the offensive against the military continued; on 8 January the press described the tenth wave of Ergenekon arrests as a 'tsunami'. The arrests included high-profile jurists denounced by Muammer Aydın, the head of the Istanbul Bar Association. Turkey's Judges and Prosecutors Association also criticized the government over its handling of the Ergenekon investigation saying the situation recalled 'the eras of Hitler and Mussolini'.

On 25 January, at President Gül's lunch for members of the executive and legislative branches, Sabih Kanadoğlu, the honorary chief judge of the Supreme Court, was equally blunt. He said that the lunch was against the principle of the separation of powers and the investigation was an indirect attack in the independence of the judiciary.

But a modicum of judicial independence remained; on 29 January the constitutional court cancelled legislation that mandated the prime minister to oversee the wiretapping activities run by the country's security forces. Legal experts and analysts hailed the decision, saying the ruling would help to base wiretapping activities on court orders.

While RPP, the principal opposition party, said that the entire Ergenekon investigation had a purely political motive, Devlet Bahçeli, leader of the NAP, supported the investigation. He stated that Ergenekon cast a shadow over Turkish democracy and the fight against criminal organizations was a national duty. In Brussels, EU ministers demanded clarification on the Ergenekon arrests from Foreign Minister Ali Babacan. He took refuge behind the judiciary, which was totally independent in Turkey, declaring that the case was in their hands. He added: 'There is no need to worry. If there is a crime, it will be revealed'.

The press of 23 January 2009 reported on the eleventh wave of the investigation with operations taking place in 16 provinces. There were arrests of trade unionists, journalists, and army and police officers. Retired General Tuncer Kılınç, who had been arrested earlier that year, said he had no idea why he had been detained and questioned. He claimed that the main reason was to tarnish the image of the armed forces and was an act of revenge by those who felt they had been wronged in the past.

In February, the attack on the freedom of the media began in earnest. On 19 February, the treasury imposed a half-billion-dollar levy on the Doğan Media Group, allegedly for tax evasion. The press noted that the government had brought its war against the media to a new level. The next day, the Society of Turkish Journalists denounced the 'unfair' tax imposed on the Doğan Group as a dangerous way to silence the media. The Associated Press saw the huge fine as a struggle between Aydın Doğan, one of Turkey's richest men and a staunch secularist, and Prime Minister Erdoğan, the leader of 'an Islamic-oriented government'. In an interview with the AP Doğan said: 'He wants to turn us into other media groups that support him ... but we are not like them'. Even Washington weighed in: the Human Rights Report for 2008, publicized by Secretary of State Hillary Clinton, criticized the JDP government for putting pressure on both the judiciary and the media. 'Freedoms in Turkey are being curtailed while torture is on the rise', wrote *Cumhuriyet* and *Hürriyet* of 26 and 27 February respectively.

In early March, the media showed concern about the government's indirect tools of censorship against its critics. On 4 March, the prime minister admitted that his government used wiretaps; but he said that any private group with the means to do so was able to use technology to put anyone under surveillance!

In 2009, the situation for the JDP was not going well. According to *Milliyet* on 17 March, unemployment had climbed to 13.6 per cent and with one in every four youths unemployed the country's social structure could be harmed. Export figures were down by over 25 per cent while import figures were up by almost 40 per cent. Capacity utilization in industry had dropped to its lowest levels in recent history. One in every four small- and medium-sized enterprises had closed down while three in every four had scaled down their businesses and laid off almost 75 per cent of their workers. In the local election of 29 March, the JDP lost 8 per cent of its support compared to the 2007 general election. That gave hope to the opposition parties. Despite everything, Erdoğan's support was still 15 points higher than his closest rival and he was able to declare that he had won a vote of confidence. The RPP, despite its loss, decided that a change of leadership was not needed! It would soldier on under Deniz Baykal who had never won an election.

But things were also looking up for Turkey in the region. During President Obama's two-day state visit on 6 April he supported Turkey's accession to the EU so that the West would be closer to the Islamic world. Ever since the Davos incident of January 2009, Turkey was being recognized in the Middle East as a key player, especially by 'the Arab street'. Its growing soft power, the popularity of its TV soap operas among the viewing public in the regions, also played a role. In recognition of these developments Al-Jazeera invited a number of Turkey's scholars and journalists to its fourth annual forum in Doha in March. *Cumhuriyet* of 28 April wrote that Israel was alarmed especially when it learned of a Turkish–Syrian joint military exercise, which it saw as a new sign of tripartite alliance between Turkey, Syria and Lebanon.

The political situation in Turkey was beginning to change around 2009. When the JDP came to power in 2002, the party described itself as conservative-democratic, suggesting that it was abandoning its Islamist roots. That divided Turkey's liberals. Many liberals, described as neo-liberals, supported the JDP because it promised to break the hold of the armed forces and Kemalist ideology and create a liberal society. Such liberals also supported the JDP's efforts to enter the European Union. But in November 2005, JDP's attitude towards the EU underwent a change when the European Court of Human Rights upheld the ban of the headscarf on Turkey's university campuses. Nor did many liberals like the governing party's patriarchal attitudes towards gender equality and freedom for women. In fact, Turkey seemed to be declining in this area: the UN's index for gender empowerment showed that Turkey had dropped from 63 in the world in 2002 to number 90 in 2008. Liberals did not approve of the government's position on censorship though they could do little about it. They were alienated by the arrest of such journalists as Nedim Şener in June 2009 for violating secrecy laws in his book on the murder of the Armenian journalist, Hrant Dink.

At the same time, the government kept taking away the military's authority. On 26 June 2009, the generals suffered another blow when parliament passed legislation that prevented military courts from prosecuting civilians and allowed civilian courts to prosecute officers who committed crimes within their jurisdiction. President Gül sanctioned the law on 5 July. The neo-liberals saw the law as a leap forward for Turkish democracy but secularists felt that the force that could defend the country from Islamization had been further weakened.

One of the major problems facing Turkey was the Kurdish question which had cost the country tens of thousands of lives since the beginning of the PKK rebellion in 1984. PM Erdoğan had already admitted that Turkey had a 'Kurdish problem'. On 23 July 2009, the press announced that the prime minister was launching the 'Kurdish initiative' in order to solve this problem. It was a brave step to take and it would require much discussion with Kurdish parties in the years to come.

But the idea of the initiative was not shared by the rightwing NAP whose leader, Devlet Bahçeli, denounced Erdoğan's initiative as a plan to destroy Turkey. That led to the rise of ultra-Turkish nationalism and resulted in growing violence between the two communities. In December, the Constitutional Court ordered the closure of the Democratic Society Party for its links with the outlawed PKK. But the banned party reinvented itself and on 14 December emerged as the Peace and Democracy Party (BDP).

PM Erdoğan promised to go on no matter what. On 12 October 2009, Deniz Baykal said he was willing to discuss the initiative with the prime minister. But Erdoğan refused to meet Baykal because of the latter's stipulation of a live broadcast of the meeting. The PM later accused the two opposition parties of cowardice on the Kurdish issue. 'Mothers did not cry during the War of Independence. But they cried in Dersim, Sıvas, Çorum, and Maraş' when there were massacres of minorities. It was not just the Kurds. The Greek Orthodox Patriarch, Bartholomew, complained about the closure of the Halkı seminary saying that: 'We are without oxygen, the Patriarchate is dying'. While that remained an issue, the government announced that the Armenian, Akdamar Church in Van would be open for worship in September 2010.

Ahmet Davutoğlu replaced Abdullah Gül as foreign minister on 9 May 2009 but only unveiled his policy of 'strategic depth' in January 2010. In his vision Turkey must be the centre of the world. 'We must have a message for the world. We are in the position of doing justice to this region. There is no other country in the world that has the same location as us. We must be active in these five, six regions simultaneously ... Turkey's diplomacy can only be compared with that of five or six countries in the world.' However, his policy soon ran into trouble when the 'Arab spring' exploded around Turkey, especially the rebellion in Syria in 2011 and 2012. Only in late December 2009 during his visit to Damascus had Erdoğan described Syria as the 'door to the Middle East'. President Assad had described Erdoğan as his brother and asked that he be the mediator between Syria and Israel. Relations with Israel, already bad, worsened when Turkey's ambassador was humiliated by Israel's deputy foreign minister who kept him waiting, seated him in a lower chair, and finally refused to shake hands for the photographers. On 13 January 2010, there was even talk that Ankara would recall its ambassador.

The relations with the armed forces took another blow when on 20 January the neo-liberal daily, *Taraf*, published a story about how, in 2003, Çetin Doğan, the commander of the First Army and other senior commanders had planned a coup called 'Sledgehammer' or *Balyoz*. Their goal was to overthrow the JDP government by creating chaos in society, bombing mosques and museums, and making it appear that Greek air forces had shot down a Turkish aircraft. The following day, the General Staff denied the existence of any such fantastic plan. The retired General Doğan swore on his honour on live television that there was no coup plan called 'Operation Sledgehammer' and it was just a 'malicious fabrication'. However, in this climate, on 4 February the protocol that had permitted the armed forces to intervene in order to maintain internal security was annulled. That was another victory for the government over the military.

On 22 February, the press reported that there were arrests of both retired and active military officers for alleged connections with 'Operation Sledgehammer'. More arrests were reported on 26 February; 'Sledgehammer' was to become a new trial of the military and like 'Ergenekon', would continue for some years. But sceptics about this affair asked why anyone plotting such a coup would leave behind a 5,000-page document about their plan? Others saw the hand of the Gülen movement, allies of the JDP, which had penetrated such institutions as the police and the intelligence network and were wiretapping officers and having them arrested. Fethullah Gülen was said to be directing the entire operation from his self-imposed exile in Pennsylvania.

The weakness of the opposition parties had been a blessing for the JDP ever since it came to power in 2002. This was especially true for the RPP while Deniz Baykal was the leader of the party.

He had become leader in 1992, and soon succeeded in making the party 'his party', as was Turkey's political culture. Even though he led his party to defeat time and again, he was re-elected at the RPP's general congress. Only the alleged sex scandal captured on a hidden camera forced him to resign in May 2010 after a reign of 17 years. The party was finally given the opportunity to renew itself and play the role of an opposition party.

Though Baykal had resigned, his party organization remained intact and they wanted him back. But Kemal Kılıçdaroğlu succeeded in winning the support of the provincial organizations and was elected at the convention on 22 May 2010. He was seen as a transitional lame duck leader, a puppet in Baykal's hands. He therefore had the difficult task of somehow renewing the party.

Kılıçdaroğlu has not been able to do that so far. The RPP has not been able to put forward a new programme that appeals to the voter. Instead it has been reactive, responding to Erdoğan's initiatives. When the JDP said it faced both ways, Kılıçdaroğlu responded by declaring that Turkey's direction should be towards the EU and the West, along the path to modern values. If Erdoğan talked about the 'Kurdish initiative', Kılıçdaroğlu said that should be the 'Eastern or Southeastern issue'.

Such arguments had little or no appeal for the majority of voters. As most surveys showed they were more concerned about bread and butter issues. Unemployment was a major problem in which the press reported a rapid rise, the rate of increase was estimated to be five times higher than the global average. The rate of unemployment reached 13 per cent, marking a 3.6 per cent increase. *Cumhuriyet* and *Radikal* of 16 September 2009, quoting *The Economist*, reported that Turkey ranked fifth in the world in terms of its high unemployment rate. Even the government had revised its economic estimates. It reduced the growth rate from 4 per cent to 3.6 per cent for 2009. According to its medium-term economic programme the economy was expected to shrink 6 per cent in 2009 and the government was expecting 3.5 per cent growth in 2010. The budget deficit, earlier estimated as $10 billion, was expected to become $62.8 billion. *Hürriyet* and *Milliyet* of 17 September 2009 also noted that the rate of unemployment was predicted to be 14.8 per cent at the end of the year. The RPP which had a number of talented economists within its ranks did not seem to want to use them in preparing its programme; that would have made sense to the voter if the party proposed solutions to the country's economic problems.

Soon after Kılıçdaroğlu became the leader of the RPP there were signs that the fragmented centre-left might be coming together. In June 2010, Bülent Ecevit's widow, Rahşan, decided to dissolve her Democratic Left People's Party (DLPP) and support the RPP so as to bring about unity on the left. Earlier in June 2009, Rahşan, the first chair of the Democratic Left Party, had resigned from the DLP and said that she would not return to the party until its leadership decided to return to the line of Bülent Ecevit. In October, when that did not happen, she founded the DLPP which became 'her party' from the very beginning. But by dissolving the DLPP and supporting Kılıçdaroğlu she was bringing Bülent Ecevit supporters to the RPP.

In October 2010, as Turkey's parties canvassed for the election of 2011, the issues continued to be over secularism, the head-scarf, tax on alcoholic beverages, and the dangers of 'creeping Islamization'. The opposition seemed to have forgotten about bread and butter issues, the economy, the high cost of living, and the growing unemployment, especially the urban young. Voters wanted to hear about these issues and what the opposition would do to solve them. Naturally, PM Erdoğan was delighted when he was able to control the agenda.

After Kılıçdaroğlu became the party leader and led the party into the 2011 election he continued to criticize the government, though rarely on the economy. The Israeli raid on the *Mavi Marmara* on 31 May strengthened Erdoğan both internally and in the Middle East. The Turkish vessel was sailing with peace activists to take aid to the Gaza strip and break the Israel blockade. Hostility towards Israel increased and Erdoğan declared that Turkey's new target was a Middle East union. But that was just rhetorical talk for there was no Middle East union on the horizon; in fact the region was more divided than usual.

Internally, the Ergenekon so-called conspiracy was in its third year of arrests and indictments with no end in sight. At the same time some people in the country were becoming richer. The number of lira millionaires rose from 23,000 in 2009 to 29,000 in 2010. As a sign of a growing 'spending class', on 27 July 2009

Radikal reported that 94 more shopping malls were planned just for Istanbul by the end of 2010. Despite the 'Kurdish initiative' the problem remained unresolved, the prime minister accusing the Kurdish Peace and Democracy Party (PDP) of supporting the PKK and terrorism on 15 June 2010.

The passage of a bill on 17 June about changing the system of choosing a president again prompted serious debate on Erdoğan's future candidacy for the post. The bill gave the people the right to select a president directly with their votes and allowed the prime minister to run for office without being obliged to resign from his current post. People speculated whether Abdullah Gül would become party leader in the event of Erdoğan assuming the presidency. They also knew that if Erdoğan were elected president then there would be competition for the JDP's leadership and, following earlier examples – Turgut Özal's Motherland Party and Süleyman Demirel's True Path Party – the JDP would fall apart.

Tension between the government and the generals had been growing as a result of the coup allegation and the arrest of retired generals as well as those on active duty. The government tightened its grip on the armed forces when, in August, it interfered in the promotions among military ranks in the Supreme Military Council or *Yüksek Askeri Şurası* where the generals had had autonomy. For the first time the military was forced to bow to government pressures in establishing its upper echelons. This was an unprecedented development for the country, given its well-established traditions as far as its military culture is concerned. The government and the army reached an agreement on appointments of the country's top commanders. General Işık Koşaner became the new chief of staff while General Erdal Ceylanoğlu was appointed as the new commander of the Land Forces. Military influence had clearly declined.

The referendum of 12 September 2010 on constitutional reform was seen as a forerunner of the general election of 2011. The JDP secured 58 per cent of the yes-vote, a 6 per cent increase in its votes since the 2009 local elections. Though the amendments had passed by 58 per cent, 42 per cent of the voters, over 32 million people, said no to the JDP. Critics of the referendum said that its intention was to establish political control over the judicial branch of government. That would pave the way for the excessive concentration of power in the executive branch, essentially doing away with the separation of powers.

In the general election of 12 June 2011, Kılıçdaroğlu claimed that the RPP was the only party to increase its seats; all other parties had won fewer seats than before. But the JDP won 49.83 per cent of the votes, while the RPP won only 25.94 per cent; the NAP won 12.99 per cent and the independents 6.58 per cent. With these figures, the JDP won 326 seats at the 550-seat parliament, the RPP had 135 seats, the NAP 53 seats and the independents, namely members of the Kurdish PDP, had 36 seats. With these results there was no threat of coalitions though the governing party did not have the required 367 seats to be able to pass a JDP-shaped constitution in parliament; it would have to work with the RPP while a new constitution was being drafted. But on most issues the prime minister would claim his 50 per cent of the vote to push through other legislation. Let's not forget that the 50 per cent mark had been reached in Turkey only in three earlier elections: in 1950 and 1954 by Menderes' Democrat Party, and in 1965 by Demirel's Justice Party. Thus Erdoğan became the fourth man to break the 50-percent mark.

The JDP benefitted from the 10 per cent threshold required for a party to enter parliament, disenfranchising millions of voters who voted for those smaller parties who received less than the required 10 per cent of the vote, giving their votes and seats to the JDP. For example, in the 2002 election the JDP won only 34 per cent of the votes but garnered 66 per cent of the seats in parliament. All parties other than the RPP failed to clear the threshold! Thus 16 parties which between them won 45 per cent of the total vote were kept out of parliament and 14 million voters had no voice. Again in the 2007 election, the JDP won 46 per cent of the vote but had 62 per cent of the seats. Despite almost 50 per cent of the vote the JDP did not win the 367 seats in the 550-seat parliament to enjoy an overall majority. It would have to work closely with the opposition while the new constitution was being drafted.

The new parliament met on 28 June boycotted by the RPP because two of its elected members – Mustafa Balbay and Mehmet Haberal – had not been released from jail. Despite the political tension, Erdoğan was in a more confident mood after his third electoral victory. Unlike Mohammad Mursi in Egypt he waited until his third élection triumph before he began to implement a more populist democratic Islamic agenda. A victim of Turkish political culture he seemed to believe, like his predecessors beginning with Prime Minister Menderes in the 1950s, in 'majoritarian democracy' in which he who wins the election is able to impose his agenda on the rest of society.

The resignation of the chief of staff and the commanders of the land, sea, and air forces on 29 July allowed Erdoğan to extend his authority over the armed forces. On 31 July, he appointed General Necdet Özel as his chief of staff, an officer who had good relations with the government. On 7 August, the government and the generals agreed on the need to amend Article 35 of the Turkish Armed Forces Law that had provided the justification for military intervention. Even the RPP agreed that the change was necessary. At the same time the government raised the military budget to a new high and Turkey's defence spending was to be $5 billion in 2011, an all-time record likely to appease the generals.

The generals, in turn wanted to appease the governing party. General Özel proposed that on 30 August President Gül receive the Victory Day greetings instead of the chief of staff. The previous day, the general staff had removed from its website the 2007 memorandum criticizing the nomination of Abdullah Gül as president, a symbolic gesture before Victory Day which was seen as a sign of continuing 'normalization' in civilian–military relations.

If the JDP was resolving the civil–military relationship to its satisfaction, the Kurdish issue continued to be a headache, though the 'initiative' had been launched in 2007. There were rumours that the government was secretly talking to the PKK and its de facto leader Abdullah Öcalan who was in jail on the island of İmralı. But on 9 June 2011, Erdoğan denied such rumours most indignantly. He said that Devlet Bahçeli, the NAP leader, was making such slanders. He said Bahçeli had prevented the PKK leader from being hanged after his arrest in 1999; if the JDP had been in the coalition at the time they would either have supported hanging Öcalan or left the coalition. However, on 14 September 2011 a tape recording of secret talks between Turkish officials and Kurdish militants was leaked. These talks, it was said, were carried out with direct instructions from the prime minister. Next day Cemil Çiçek, a senior JDP minister, said that an alleged meeting between

Turkey's intelligence chief, Hakan Fidan, and senior members of an outlawed terror organization was nothing different from what Britain and Spain had done in the past. Now that such talks were out in the open, on 21 September President Gül called on the PKK to lay down their arms. A few days later, Erdoğan took a tougher position and declared that talks with the PKK were over until they laid down their arms. The PKK responded on 25 September by attacking a military post in Siirt killing six soldiers!

By January 2012, Erdoğan had become more conciliatory stating that he stood behind the idea of negotiations with political representatives of the outlawed PKK. But military measures would continue. Meanwhile the Kurdish PDP began to rehabilitate Öcalan. On 21 May 2012 one of its leaders, Pervin Buldan, declared that Kurds respected Öcalan and had never viewed him as a criminal but as a leader. Despite such differences, talks between the two sides continued. On 24 January 2013, Prime Minister Erdoğan talked about the peace process with the JDP's Kurdish deputies, euphemistically described as 'party deputies from the east'. The NAP vowed to resist peace talks with the PKK while the RPP remained divided. Kurdish MPs were allowed to send delegations to see Abdullah Öcalan in prison and on 18 February his brother, Mehmet, visited him. On 25 February, through intermediaries, Öcalan called for the finalization of the peace process within two to three weeks. On 9 March, Erdoğan responded by asking the PKK to lay down their arms and conduct discussions in parliament. A few days later, on 13 March, the PKK made a gesture and released eight Turkish hostages as part of the peace process. The government expected a PKK ceasefire before the Nevruz celebration on 21 March. Abdullah Öcalan was expected to make his 'historic call' for peace on the same day. Öcalan's Nevruz message was seen by the government to be in the spirit of the peace process. On 22 March, the PKK in northern Iraq were ordered to halt all actions and the PDP declared the 99 per cent of the Kurdish armed campaign was over.

The government's negotiations with the Kurds had gone on secretly and the RPP called upon the government to share with the opposition what was going on. But secret negotiations continued. A PDP delegation visited Öcalan on 3 April and stated on 15 April that the PKK's withdrawal might be concluded by the autumn.

PKK guerrillas began to leave their bases in Anatolia for northern Iraq, the first group arriving on 14 May. During the negotiations the Turkish government seems to have consulted the British about how the Good Friday talks with the IRA had been conducted; these talks seem to have become the model for talks with the PKK with the hope that they would yield a peace agreement after 30 years of conflict. But peace is still not on the horizon and the secret negotiations have continued.

While the government conducted these negotiations, it also continued to implement its programme in other areas as well. It has succeeded in establishing party control over much of the state apparatus: the armed forces, the judiciary, and the education system. The governing party's control over the legislature enabled it to pass virtually any law it saw fit. As a result social scientists saw that Turkey was becoming more conservative though not more religious. But the government-enforced conservative social transformation of society contradicted the concept of liberal democracy. Women, in particular, were becoming the victims of this growing social conservatism.

The opposition parties were too weak and without programmes to challenge the JDP. They seemed only to respond to JDP initiatives without offering alternatives that appealed to the electorate. In the cities, especially Istanbul, people, particularly young people, were becoming restless, antagonized by the government's policies designed to create a conservative consumer society. On 30 May, a group of people, not affiliated to any party, occupied Gezi Park in the heart of the modern city. They wanted to protect the only green space around Taksim in the centre of Istanbul. There were rumours that this small park in the heart of modern Istanbul was going to be transformed into yet another shopping mall. The police, as was their practice, responded by firing tear-gas canisters in order to disperse the crowd but only succeeded in injuring some demonstrators.

By 2 June, the protest in Gezi Park and Taksim square intensified and thousands chanted anti-government slogans, making the ongoing demonstration the biggest challenge to Erdoğan's ten-year rule. Taksim turned into a war zone with violent clashes between the riot police and demonstrators outraged at the heavy-handed response of authorities to what began as an environmental protest.

The prime minister was on a visit to North Africa when the demonstrations began. But in Rabat on 3 June he was defiant against the demonstrators. He repeated his accusations against the main opposition and blamed 'extreme groups' for the ongoing protests. In Ankara on the same day, President Gül, when asked about the demonstrations, declared that democracy was not just about elections. He added that the message had been received by the authorities; hours later the police withdrew from Taksim square. When asked about President Abdullah Gül's remarks that 'the message had been received' and whatever is necessary would be done, Erdoğan replied that he 'couldn't know' about the message Gül had received!

On 4 June, Bülent Arınç, standing in for Erdoğan as his deputy prime minister, also gave a conciliatory message. He offered to meet the leader of the protest so as to ease tensions and even offered a partial apology for the brutal police crackdown. He said: 'Our citizens showed their legitimate, logical and righteous reaction at Gezi Park'.

When the prime minister returned to Istanbul on the night of 6–7 June he was greeted by a 10,000 'rent-a-crowd' brought to the airport by the party faithful. Erdoğan delivered a fiery speech and declared that: 'These protests that are bordering on illegality must come to an end as of now'. On 8 June, the prime minister decided that he would hold rallies in Ankara and Istanbul in order to show the popular support he could garner. The rally in Ankara was held on 5 June, and in Istanbul the next day. But such JDP rallies only only alienated the demonstrators further, showing that the prime minister was in no mood to compromise.

The demonstrations that began in Istanbul continued throughout the month and spread to Izmir and Ankara, and to virtually every other and town in Turkey. Police violence became worse with the use of not only pepper gas, and water cannons using chemicalized water, but also with plastic bullets.

It is not yet clear what the political consequences of 'Gezi Park' will be. Polls taken during the month of demonstrations suggest that the JDP has lost six points. But the gains made by the opposition parties are insufficient to bring them to power in the next election. But one thing seems certain. The JDP has lost the support of the so-called 'neo-liberals' who supported the party since it came to power in 2002. One such 'neo-liberal', the journalist Cengiz Çandar, gave his reasons for why he had supported Erdoğan and why he was coming out in opposition to him.

On 18 June, while the demonstrations and police violence was in full swing, he wrote that he supported Erdoğan because the oppressed had supported him; because he was bringing the army under civilian control and thus promoting democracy; because he had taken the road to the EU, thus consolidating democracy; and because he wanted to resolve the Kurdish question.

Why was Erdoğan now losing Cengiz Çandar's pen? Because Erdoğan had permitted police terror in Istanbul, and the rest of Turkey between 31 May and 16 June, especially during the night of 17 June. Pepper-gas canisters were thrown into the Divan Hotel (where demonstrators had taken refuge from the police); doctors who came to help the injured were handcuffed; on İstiklal Avenue, a woman bared her chest to the police; a woman in the red dress who stood before the water cannon will be remembered more than any one else. That is what was etched in Çandar's memory when he wrote the article.

We will only know if what has come to be known as the 'Gezi Park Resistance' has had a long-term impact on Turkey's politics. Will voters turn against the JDP in the municipal election of 2014 and the general election of 2015 and bring the opposition to power? The results of these elections will depend also on how the RPP, the principal opposition party, can reinvent itself in the months to come.

SUGGESTED FURTHER READING

R.Q Mecham, 'From the Ashes of Virtue, a Promise of Light: the Transformation of Political Islam in Turkey', in *Third World Quarterly*, 25/2, 2004, pp.339–58.

Chronology of the Ottoman Empire and Modern Turkey

THE OTTOMAN EMPIRE, 1260–1923

1071   Battle of Manzikert opens the way to Turkic invasions of Anatolia.
1096   The first crusade.
1207   Seljuks capture Antalya from the Byzantines.
1219   Mongols begin the conquest of Anatolia; they conquer Iran and establish the Ilhanid dynasty, ruling from 1256 to 1336.
1261–1300 Foundation of gazi principalities of Menteşe, Aydın, Saruhan, Karesi and Ottoman in western Anatolia.

1. Osman Gazi, c.1290–1324

2. Orhan Gazi, 1324–1362

1326   Bursa conquered, becoming the first capital of the Ottoman state.
1331   İznik (Nicae) conquered.
1336   Fall of the Mongol Empire in Iran.
1345   Ottomans annex the beylik of Karesi, opening the road to Europe.
1354   Occupation of Gallipoli and Ankara.
1361   Conquest of Adrianople (Edirne), the second Ottoman capital.

3. Sultan Murad I, 1362–1389

1363–1365 Expansion into Thrace and southern Bulgaria.
1371–1373 Victory at Chermanon over Byzantium; Ottoman suzerainty recognized over the Balkans.

1385   Sofia conquered.

1387   Antalya conquered from the Hamid Emirate.

1389   (15 June) Battle of Kosovo and defeat of Balkan coalition.

4. Bayezid I, Yıldırım (the Thunderbolt), 1389–1402

1396   Battle of Nicopolis, marking the defeat of the crusaders.

1402   Battle of Ankara and destruction of Bayezid's empire by Timur.

1402–1413 Interregnum: civil war among Bayezid's sons with the victory of Mehmed I.

5. Mehmed I, 1413–1421

Consolidated Ottoman power after the civil war.

6. Murad II, 1421–1451

1423–1430 Ottoman–Venetian struggle for Salonica.

1425   İzmir annexed and western Anatolia reconquered.

1439   Serbia annexed.

1444   Battle of Varna; Ottomans regain control of the Balkans.

1448   Second battle of Kosovo.

7. Mehmed II, Fatih (the Conqueror), 1451–1481

1453   Conquest of Constantinople.

1459   Morea conquered.

1461   Greek empire of Trabzon conquered.

1463–1479 War with Venice.

1468   Karaman conquered.

1475   Conquest of Genoese colonies in the Crimea.

8. Bayezid II, 1481–1512

1485–1491 War with the Mamluks of Egypt.

1493   Jews expelled from Spain; set up a printing press in Istanbul and then Salonica.

1499–1503 Wars against Venice.

9. Yavuz Sultan Selim I, 1512–1520

1514   Defeat of the Safavid ruler, Shah İsmail at Chaldiran.

1516   Eastern Anatolia and Syria annexed.

1517   Conquer of Egypt; the Sharif of Mecca accepts Ottoman sovereignty.

10. Sultan Süleyman I (The Law Giver/the Magnificent), 1520–1566

1521   Conquest of Belgrade and Rhodes (1522).

1526   Battle of Mohacs; Hungary becomes an Ottoman vassal.

1529   First siege of Vienna.

1534   Conquest of Tabriz and Baghdad from the Safavids.

1537–1540	War against Venice.
1538	Naval Battle of Dui in India against the Portuguese.
1541	Hungary annexed.
1553–1555	War with the Safavids.
1565	Siege of Malta.

11. Selim II, 1566–1574

1567	Armenian community sets up printing press.
1569	Capitulation privileges granted to France to improve trade.
1570	Capture of Tunis and Cyprus.
1571	Ottoman naval defeat at the Battle of Lepanto.
1573	Peace with Venice and the Holy Roman Empire.

12. Murad III, 1574–1595

1578–1590	Annexation of Azerbaijan.
1580	Capitulations granted to England.
1584–1592	Devaluation and growing population pressure lead to inflation and social turmoil. Janissary revolt in Istanbul (1589); revolts continue into 1592.
1593	War against the Hapsburgs.

13. Mehmed III, 1595–1603

| 1596ff | Celali rebellions in Anatolia; continue until mid-seventeenth century. |
| 1603–1639 | Wars with Iran. |

14. Ahmad I, 1603–1617

1606	Peace with Austria.
1609	Attempts to suppress Celali rebellions in Anatolia.
1612	Dutch capitulations.
1618	Peace with Iran; Ottomans lose Azerbaijan.

15. Osman II, 1618–1622

| 1621 | Invasion of Poland. |
| 1622 | Osman assassinated. |

16. Mustafa I, 1622–1623

17. Murad IV, 1623–1640

1623	End of fratricide; Prince İbrahim remains the only surviving Ottoman prince. For the sake of dynastic succession, he is not killed but isolated in the Palace and allowed to lead a life of debauchery.
1624–1628	Rebellion in Istanbul and Anatolia.
1627	Ottoman Greeks set up printing press.
1637	Cossacks capture Azov on the Black Sea.
1624–1639	War with Iran and fall of Baghdad.
1638	Ottomans recapture Baghdad from Safavids.

18. İbrahim I, 1640–1648

1640	Azov recaptured.
1645–1669	Wars with Venice.
1648	İbrahim assassinated.

19. Mehmed IV, 1648–1687

1648–1651	Regency under Mehmed's mother, Valide Sultan Kösem.
1649–1655	Anarchy in Istanbul; Janissaries control Istanbul, and landed notables Anatolia. Venice continues blockade of the Dardanelles.
1656–1659	Age of the Grand Vizier begins under Köprülü Mehmed, who restores order in the empire.
1661–1676	Grand Vizierate of Köprülü Fazıl Ahmed Pasha.
1663	War against Austria.
1669	Peace with Venice.
1672–1676	War with Poland and Treaty of Zuravno.
1676–1683	Grand Vizierate of Kara Mustafa.
1677–1681	Struggle with Russia for the Ukraine.
1683	Second siege of Vienna.
1684	Austria, Poland and Venice form Holy League against Ottomans.
1686	Fall of Buda; Russia joins the alliance; Venetians invade the Morea.
1687	Second battle of Mohacs; military rebels depose Mehmed IV.

20. Suleyman II, 1687–1691

1688	Austria captures Belgrade.
1689	Austrians advance to Kosovo; Russians in the Crimea.
1689–1691	Grand vizierate of Köprülü Fazıl Mustafa. Carries out reforms and recaptures Belgrade from Austria in 1690.

21. Mustafa II, 1695–1703

1695	Fall of Azov to Russia.
1696	Ottoman counter-attack in Hungary.
1697	Ottoman defeat at Zenta.
1698–1702	Grand Vizierate of Köprülü Hüseyin.
1699	Treaty of Carlowitz; marks a turning-point in relations between Ottomans and Hapsburgs. Ottomans now forced on the defensive and begin to take European threat seriously.
1700	Peace with Russia.
1703	Military rebellion: Mustafa II deposed.

22. Ahmed III, 1703–1730 (Tulip Period)

1709	Ottomans grant asylum to Charles XII of Sweden.
1711	Peter I (the Great) of Russia defeated at Battle of Pruth; but rebellions in the provinces of Egypt and Syria.

1713	Treaty with Russia: Ottomans recover Azov.
1714–1718	War with Venice and Austria (1716), leading to fall of Belgrade.
1718–1730	Grand vizierate of Damad İbrahim Pasha.
1718	Peace of Passarowitz with Austria and Venice; Ottomans forced to cede parts of Serbia and Wallachia while recovering Morea from Venice.
1723–1727	War with Iran.
1727	Hungarian convert, İbrahim Müteferrika sets up first printing press. Because of opposition from the conservatives, the press is shut down in 1743 and reopened in 1784.
1729	Count Alexander de Bonneval, a French officer, invited to Istanbul to modernize the engineer and bombardier corps of the Ottoman army.
1730	Patrona Halil rebellion: Ahmad III deposed, ending Tulip Period.

23. Mahmud I, 1730–1754

1730–1736	War with Iran and loss of Azerbaijan.
1736–1739	War with Russia and Austria.
1739	Peace Treaty with Austria and Russia: Belgrade recovered.
1740	Ottoman–Swedish alliance against Russia.
1743–1746	War with Iran.

24. Osman III, 1754–1757

25. Mustafa III, 1757–1774

1768–1774	War with Russia.
1768	Baron de Tott arrives to modernize the army (see 1729).
1773	Rebellion in Egypt.

26. Abdülhamid I 1774–1789

1774	Treaty of Küçük Kaynarca: crushing defeat for the Ottomans at the hands of Russia; Crimea and northern coast of Black Sea become independent. Catherine the Great obtains right to protect Orthodox Church in Istanbul. This treaty marks beginning of the Eastern Question. Sultan recognized as Caliph of all Muslims, a claim confirmed under subsequent treaties.
1783	Russia annexes the Crimean Khanate.
1784	Printing press reopened.
1787–	War with Russia.
1788	Sweden declares war on Russia.

27. Selim III, 1789–1807

1789	Revolution in France.
1792	Treaty of Jassy.

1798–1801	Napoleon's army invades Egypt and occupies Ottoman province with ease; for first time since crusades of the eleventh century, heartlands of Islam invaded by a Christian power.
1801	Beginning of revolt in Serbia, which becomes autonomous in 1815.
1804	Russian annexation of Armenia and northern Azerbaijan.
1805	Mehmed Ali begins rule in Egypt as Ottoman governor and establishes a dynasty that lasts until 1952.
1807	Selim killed by reactionaries and his reform programme crushed by Janissary revolt.

28. Mustafa IV, 1807–1808

29. Mahmud II, 1808–1839

1808	Document of Alliance signed between Porte and provincial notables.
1812	Treaty of Bucharest.
1821	Beginning of Greek War of Independence.
1826	Mahmud destroys Janissaries after their failure to crush the Greek insurrection, which exposes weakness of the Janissary army. Mahmud now carries out reforms to establish a new system.
1829	Great Powers establish Kingdom of Greece.
1832	Mehmed Ali of Egypt defeats Ottomans at battle of Konya.
1833	Treaty of Hünkar-İskelesi with Russia, marking zenith of Russian power in Istanbul.
1838	Anglo-Ottoman Trade Convention establishes free trade regime in the empire.
1839	Battle of Nezib.

30. Abdülmecid I, 1839–1861

1839	Reform programme known as *Tanzimat* launched with Imperial Rescript of Gülhane.
1853–1856	Crimean War between the Ottomans, England and France, and Russia.
1856	Treaty of Paris. The Porte forced to move into 'the European political, cultural and economic orbit'. The Porte launches reform charter, the Imperial Reform Edict.
1858	Land Code establishing private ownership in the empire.

31. Abdülaziz, 1861–1876

1868	The Ottomans, taking the Red Cross as a model, establish the 'Red Crescent Society'.
1869	Galatasaray Lycée opens in Istanbul.
1870	Bulgarian Church created by the Porte, independent of authority of Greek Orthodox Church.

1875	6 *October*: The Sublime Porte declares bankruptcy.
1876	Abdülaziz forced to abdicate and commits suicide. International conference held by ambassadors of Great Powers to discuss reform in the Ottoman Empire. First constitution announced 23 December 1876.

32. Abdülhamid II, 1876–1909

1876	*31 August*: Abdülhamid succeeds Murad V, who is declared insane.
1877	*19 March*: Parliament convened.
	24 March: Russia declares war to support rebellions in the Balkans that began in 1875.
1878	*February*: Constitution shelved.
	3 March: Treaty of San Stefano ending war with Russia signed, forcing Porte to make major concessions.
	June: Congress of Berlin revises the Treaty of San Stafano in Porte's favour.
1881	Formation of Ottoman Public Debt Administration to regulate Ottoman finances.
1885	Bulgaria occupies eastern Rumelia.
1896–1897	Insurrection in Crete; successful war against Greece.
1898	Kaiser Wilhelm II's state visit begins on 18 October; he proclaims himself a friend of the Muslim people.
1908	Military mutiny and the restoration of the Constitution on 24 July.
1909	Abortive counter-revolution of 13 April designed to destroy the CUP, and Armenian massacres in Adana carried out to instigate European intervention. Abdülhamid deposed.

33. Mehmed V (Mehmed Reşad), 1909–1918

1911	War with Italy in Libya.
1912	Conservative military intervention against CUP leads to its downfall.
1912–1913	Balkan Wars and Ottoman defeats.
1913	Unionists seize power on 23 January.
1914	In April, the Porte sends troops and distributes arms to the Armenian community in Bitlis province to protect it from assaults by local Kurdish tribes.
	In July, the Chamber votes for 40,000 pounds for the salaries and expenses of the two European Inspectors-General of the 'Armenian' provinces and their staff to carry out reform.
	2 August: Secret treaty with Germany after beginning of war in Europe.
1915	Throughout the year, Gallipoli campaign and Russian invasion of eastern Anatolia threatens existence of the

Ottoman Empire.
Secret agreements signed between England, France and Russia to partition the Ottoman Empire after the war.

1916   *June*: Arab revolt in the Hijaz; British advance into Palestine and Iraq.

1917   Revolution in Russia in March and November eases pressure on Ottomans.

1918   *28 October*: Ottomans sign armistice with England.

34. Mehmed VI (Vahdettin), 1918–1922

1919   *28 March*: Italians land at Antalya, pre-empting Greeks.
           14 May: Greek army invades İzmir.
           19 May: Mustafa Kemal lands in Samsun, marking beginning of war of liberation.
           28 June: Balıkesir congress to organize resistance; followed by other regional congresses, Erzurum (23 July) and Sıvas (4 September). In Erzurum and Sıvas, delegates agree that Anatolia belongs to Turks and Kurds.

1920   *18 March*: Istanbul parliament meets for last time and adjourns *sine die* after protesting British actions.
           23 April: Grand National Assembly opens in Ankara, electing Mustafa Kemal as president.
           10 August: Treaty of Sèvres partitioning Asia Minor; treaty rejected by Nationalists is never enforced.

1921   *21 January*: National Assembly passes Law of Fundamental Organization, marking formation of a new state.
           16 March: Nationalists signed Treaty of Friendship with Soviet Union.

1922   *9 September*: Nationalists re-enter İzmir, marking defeat of Greek army.
           1 November: National Assembly abolishes the sultanate but retains the caliphate; Vahdettin, the last sultan, flees on a British warship.

THE REPUBLIC OF TURKEY, 1923–2002

1923   *8 April*: Mustafa Kemal announces formation of People's Party; 'Republican' is added later and it becomes the RPP.
           24 July: Treaty of Lausanne signed, recognizing the state of Turkey.
           13 October: Ankara is declared capital of the new Turkey.
           29 October: Republic of Turkey proclaimed and Mustafa Kemal elected president.

1924   *3 March*: Caliphate abolished and Ottoman family exiled.

This is a setback for conservative opposition; state begins to control organized Islam.

17 November: Opposition to Mustafa Kemal forms Progressive Republican Party.

1925   *11 February*: Kurdish tribes led by Sheikh Said rebel against Republican regime.

3 June: Progressive Republican Party dissolved and opposition crushed, enabling Mustafa Kemal to launch his radical reform programme to secularize state and society.

25 November: Fez banned and 'Hat Law' passed.

30 November: Dervish Orders proscribed.

17 December: Soviet–Turkish Treaty of Friendship (renewed in 1935).

1926   *17 February*: Secular civil code introduced giving equal civil rights to women; criminal code follows on 1 March.

1927   *28 October*: First republican census gives a population of 13.6 million.

1928   *9 April*: Reference to Islam as 'religion of the state' removed from constitution.

9 August: Roman alphabet adopted, thereby severing the republic culturally and intellectually from its Ottoman past.

1930   *3 April*: Women given the vote in local elections.

12 August: Mustafa Kemal allows the founding of Free Republican Party but has it dissolved on 17 November when it attracts popular support.

23 December: Islamic demonstration in Menemen, western Turkey, leads to the murder of an officer and forces the regime to rethink its ideology.

1931   *10–18 May*: At the RPP's convention, the 'six arrows' – Republicanism, Nationalism, Populism, Laicism (state control over religion), Statism and Revolutionism/ Reformism – adopted as regime's ideological platform.

1932   *19 February*: People's Houses founded to educate and spread regime's ideology around the country.

18 July: Turkey joins League of Nations and rejoins the West.

26 September: First Language Congress launched so as to make Turkish principal language of the new nation.

1933   *30 January*: Hitler comes to power in Germany.

9 February: Balkan Entente between Turkey, Greece, Yugoslavia and Rumania signed.

1934   *9 February*: Turkey, Rumania, Yugoslavia and Greece sign the Balkan Pact.

16 June: Iran's Shah Reza Pahlevi's state visit to Turkey.

26 June: Law requiring all citizens of Turkey to take last names.

26 November: Grand National Assembly (GNA) bestows the name Atatürk ('Father Turk') upon Mustafa Kemal and abolishes all Ottoman titles of honour and rank such as Pasha, Bey, Hanım and Gazi.

5 December: Turkish women given right to vote and hold office.

1935   *25 January*: Aya Sofya mosque in Istanbul restored as a museum.

3 October: Mussolini's Italy invades Abyssinia; Turkey more fearful of Italian designs on western Anatolia.

7 November: Treaty of Friendship and Non-Aggression with USSR renewed for 10 years.

1 December: Non-Aggression Pact signed with Iran, Iraq and Afghanistan.

1936   *8 June*: New Labour law passed forbidding strikes and lock-outs and introducing compulsory arbitration.

18 July: Civil war in Spain; Turkey supports Republicans.

20 July: Montreux Convention signed, permitting Turkey to militarize the straits.

25 October: Rome–Berlin Axis signed.

25 November: Anti-Comintern Pact signed between Germany and Japan.

1937   *5 January*: Article 2 of Constitution amended to read: The Turkish State is Republican, Nationalist, Populist, Statist, Secular and Revolutionary.

March–September: uprising by Kurdish tribes crushed.

8 July: Turkey signs Saadabad Pact of Friendship with Afghanistan, Iran and Iraq.

1 November: Atatürk appoints Celal Bayar as prime minister, replacing İsmet İnönü, seen as move against statists in RPP.

1938   *5 July*: Turkey begins to occupy *sancak* of Alexandretta, France having virtually conceded it separate status in May 1937. It becomes a part of Turkey in June 1939 following Franco-Turkish agreement.

10 November: Atatürk dies after prolonged illness.

11 November: İsmet İnönü voted in unanimously as president.

26 December: At the Extra-Ordinary Congress of the RPP, Atatürk is proclaimed party's 'founder and eternal leader' and İnönü the 'permanent National Chief'.

28 December: İnönü introduces his policy of reconciliation, with opposition to Atatürk and Kemalism.

1939   *12 January*: Tevfik Rüştü Aras, Atatürk's foreign minister since March 1925 and a known Anglophile, is appointed to London.

18 January: National Defence Law gives government broad powers to regulate economy.

26 March: In general election, many staunch Kemalists left out while a number of old opposition elected.

8 May: Ankara signs trade agreement with Germany.

12 May: England and Turkey sign joint declaration of friendship and mutual assistance in case of aggression or war in the Mediterranean region.

29 May: İnönü permits formation of Independent Group which would act as opposition in the assembly.

26 June: Turkey and France sign non-aggression pact; France agrees to return Alexandretta (Hatay) to Turkey; Turkey annexes Hatay on 20 June.

23 August: German–Soviet Pact signed; for Turkey, pact marks end of any possibility of tripartite guarantee against threat of fascist aggression.

1 September: Germany invades Poland and begins World War II. Turkish foreign minister goes to Moscow for talks but receives no guarantees. Turkey declares her neutrality when Britain and France declare war on Germany.

17 October: The Turkish government believed that Moscow sought to change the Montreux convention of 1936, leading to suspicion in Ankara of Moscow's motives.

19 October: Anglo–French–Turkish Fifteen Year Mutual Assistance and Alliance signed in Ankara.

1 November: President İnönü declares Turkey will remain neutral while maintaining her friendship with Britain and Soviet Union.

1940   *18 January*: Another 'National Defence Law' passed to prevent hoarding and profiteering.

1940   *2 November*: Fascist Italy attacks Greece. Turkey's support becomes even more vital to Britain. Meanwhile, Hitler tries to buy off Stalin by concessions at Turkey's expense.

1941   *28 February*: Hitler writes to İnönü, reminding him that Turkey's interests lie with the 'new order' Hitler is creating in Europe; letter received well in Ankara.

25 March: Turco–Soviet Mutual Declaration of Neutrality.

18 June: Non-aggression pact with Germany after Germans occupy Balkans.

21 June: Germany invades Russia, easing fears of a German invasion of Anatolia and encouraging pan-Turkist activities.

26 June: Law passed allowing call to prayer (*ezan*) be made in Turkish not Arabic; law is repealed on 16 June 1950.

9 October: Turco–German Trade agreement, marking rapprochement with Berlin. Later in month, Turkish generals tour Russian front as German guests.

7 December: Japan bombs US Pacific fleet at Pearl Harbor

and US joins war. Hitler declares war on United States of America on 11 December.

1942   *11 November*: Encouraged by German victories, government enacts so-called Wealth Tax (*Varlık Vergisi*) that discriminates against Turkey's non-Muslim minorities.

1943   *2 February*: German army surrenders at Stalingrad after long siege, marking turning-point in war and Turkey's domestic and foreign policy.

1944   *15 May*: Wealth Tax law annulled.

18 May: Government begins to prosecute anti-Soviet Turkists to demonstrate its change of policy.

1945   *7 May*: Germany surrenders.

7 June: Demand for political liberalization from member of RPP. On same day, Moscow proposes modification of Turco–Soviet border and joint defence of the straits as condition for renewing 1925 Treaty which expired in November.

7 July: Businessman Nuri Demirağ founds National Development Party.

6 September: US Congress delegation arrives in Turkey to pressure government to liberalize its economic policies.

21 September: Adnan Menderes and Refik Koraltan expelled from RPP.

1 November: President İnönü calls for formation of a serious opposition party.

3 December: Having resigned as a deputy on 28 September, Celal Bayar resigns from RPP in order to form a new party, the Democrat Party.

4 December: Offices of newspaper *Tan*, which has criticized government, destroyed by a crowd organized by state officials; incident takes place while Istanbul is under martial law.

1946   *7 January*: Democrat Party formed by Celal Bayar, Adnan Menderes, Refik Koraltan and Fuad Köprülü.

5–7 April: The US battleship *Missouri* visits Istanbul, a symbol of US support for Turkey against Soviet pressure.

5 June: Law permitting direct elections instead of two-tier elections passed.

21 July: Early general election, held before the DP could organize and under pressure from state apparatus, ends in RPP victory.

22 August: Turkey rejects Soviet offer of joint defence of the straits.

4 December: Martial law is extended for further six months.

1947   *12 March*: Truman Doctrine – US promises support for Turkey and Greece against Soviet subversion. Turkey enters cold war.

12 July: İnönü declares himself a non-partisan president and supports legitimacy of the DP; hardline Prime Minister Recep Peker forced to resign on 9 September.

1949   *1 August*: As cold war continues, president informs Congress it is important for Middle East that Turkey be fully armed.

1950   *9 March*: Turkey and Iran recognize Israel.

14 May: Democrat Party wins overwhelming electoral victory in general election and Adnan Menderes forms new government on 22 May.

25 July: Democrats decide to send troops to Korea.

1952   *21 February*: Turkey and Greece join NATO.

3 March: General Eisenhower, NATO's commander, arrives in Turkey.

1953   *29 May*: 500th anniversary of conquest of Constantinople is celebrated for first time, marking a turn towards neo-Ottomanism' and increasing tension with Greece over Cyprus.

1954   *2 May*: General election – Democrat Party wins a crushing victory, which seems to confirm its popularity and therefore increases autocratic tendencies of leadership.

20 August: Mammoth demonstration in Athens in support of independence of Cyprus from Britain and union with Greece. On 28 May, PM Menderes declares that Greece will never acquire Cyprus.

1955   *24 February*: Baghdad Pact signed between Iraq and Turkey; later joined by Iran, Pakistan and Britain. The Democrats believe that Turkey is playing a pivotal role in the region on behalf of the West.

6/7 September: Anti-Greek violence in Istanbul and İzmir sponsored by government to show public sentiment on Cyprus issue; events get out of hand and prove an embarrassment to government.

1956   *31 October*: Suez war – Israel, Britain and France attack Egypt. In Hungary, uprising against Soviet domination.

1957   *27 October*: Democrats win general election but their majority declines sharply because of the falling economy and PM Menderes's increasingly undemocratic behaviour.

1958   *26 May*: Nine army officers put on trial accused of conspiracy against government; the first sign of political dissent in armed forces.

14 July: Military coup in Iraq leads to overthrow of monarchy and end of Baghdad Pact, which is soon to be called the Central Treaty Organization, or CENTO.

20 July: US marines land in Beirut using Incirlik in Turkey as base.

23 August: Government devalues Turkish lira by 321%,

introduces the IMF's stability programme and receives US $359 million in loans.

1959   *17 February*: PM Menderes survives plane crash in London where he attends conference on Cyprus; his survival seen as a miracle and heightens his charisma.

19 February: London Agreement between Turkey, Greece and Britain is signed, leading to formation of Republic of Cyprus in 1960.

31 July: Turkey applies for associate membership of the European Community.

1960   *28 April*: Martial law declared in response to student demonstrations in Ankara and Istanbul. Army enters political arena and government puts an end to all political activity.

27 May: Military coup overthrows DP government and rules through junta called National Unity Committee (NUC). DP is closed down on 29 September and its members put on trial for violating constitution.

13 November: Fourteen radical members of NUC who oppose restoration of political power to civilians are purged.

1961   *28 February*: Justice Party formed and ten other parties follow in preparation for restoration of political life on 25 March.

11 July: New, liberal constitution accepted by NUC after referendum of 9 July.

17 September: Adnan Menderes and two of his ministers are hanged; soldiers execute Menderes in order to destroy his charisma!

28 October: General election leads to series of unstable coalition governments until 1965, when Justice Party wins the majority and forms cabinet.

1962   *23 February*: Junior officers dissatisfied with outcome of post-1960 regime, carry out a coup but it is aborted.

1963   *20/21 May*: Talat Aydemir's second coup foiled; this time he is hanged.

1964   *4 June*: President Johnson's letter to PM İnönü warns him not to depend on NATO if Turkey intervenes in Cyprus and has a confrontation with Moscow. Inter-communal violence in Cyprus paralyses terms of 1959 London Agreement; also marks beginning of anti-Americanism in Turkey, especially after it becomes public on 13 January 1966.

1965   *30 June*: Süleyman Demirel, who became leader of JP on 28 November 1964, describes left-of-centre policy adopted by RPP as 'road to communism'. Polarization between Left and Right sharpened.

10 October: Justice Party wins general election, ending period of coalition governments.

1966   *20 December*: PM Kosygin of Soviet Union pays state visit to

Turkey, acknowledging working relations that have developed since 1965.

1967　　20/21 April: Colonels in Greece seize power, overthrowing democratic government; US no longer has to rely on Turkey's bases.

5 June: The Six-Day War between Israel and Arabs ends in an overwhelming Israeli victory.

29 November: War between Turkey and Greece averted after Greek forces withdraw from Turkish villages on Cyprus when faced with threat of Turkish intervention.

1968　　29 May: In France, General de Gaulle dissolves parliament in order to deal with student demonstrations that have paralysed Paris since 13 May. French example influences leftist students in Turkey, who become more militant: they begin to demonstrate against NATO and Turkey's alliance with US.

15 July: Demonstration against US 6th Fleet's visit to Turkey's ports continues throughout the month and often becomes violent.

20 August: Soviet Union occupies Czechoslovakia to put an end to 'Prague Spring'; Soviet action splits the Left in Turkey.

1969　　14 January: US ambassador Robert Komer's car set on fire by students at Middle East Technical University in Ankara, a sign of increasing violence. On the right, Colonel Alparslan Türkeş's neo-Fascist party training so-called 'komandos'.

16 February: 'Bloody Sunday' in Istanbul when demonstration against US 6th Fleet is attacked by rightist militants, assisted by police; two youths killed and about two hundred wounded. Youth violence continues until military intervention on 12 March 1971.

1970　　26 January: Necmettin Erbakan, Independent MP for Konya, founds National Order Party, first party in Turkey committed to political Islam, representing Anatolia's lower middle class, who are suffering because of the rise of large corporations and monopolies in western Turkey.

15/16 June: Massive and bloody workers' demonstration in Istanbul region leads to declaration of martial law.

28 August: The lira is devalued by sixty-six per cent, reflecting the country's economic crisis.

28 December: National Security Council under President Sunay meets to discuss memorandum presented by General Muhsim Batur, Commander of Air Force, warning of unrest in armed forces.

1971　　12 March: Commanders present memorandum to PM Demirel and force him to resign; they take over the reins of government. Turkey ruled by 'above-party' cabinets until election of 1973.

27 April: Martial law declared in eleven provinces and a reign of terror follows, especially against the Left.

1972 14 May: İsmet İnönü resigns as RPP's leader after thirty-three years and Bülent Ecevit elected in his place, representing historic change that would revive the fortunes of the party.

1973 6 April: Retired Admiral Fahri Korutürk elected 6th president after political parties refuse to elect military's candidate.

14 October: In the general election, no party wins an overall majority; after much bargaining, a coalition agreed between Ecevit's RPP and Erbakan's National Salvation Party, and formed on 25 January 1974. Islamists share political power for first time.

1974 15 July: Greek National Guard carries out coup against Archbishop Makarios, triggering Turkish intervention as one of guarantor powers. Turkish army expands its control over the island during second military operation in August.

17 September: Ecevit tenders his resignation, counting on his popularity to win election and form RPP government. Rightist parties refuse to sanction early general election and form their own coalition.

1975 13 February: In Cyprus, Turkish Cypriots proclaim statehood.

31 March: First Nationalist Front coalition with Demirel as PM of centre-right, supported by Islamist MSP and neo-fascist MHP; youth violence increases with coalition partners protecting rightist militants.

5/6/75 5 June: First Nationalist Front coalition collapses.

1977 5 June: Ecevit's RPP emerges as first party for general election, but with insufficient majority to form successful government alone. His minority fails to obtain vote of confidence on 3 July and Ecevit resigns.

21 July: Demirel forms second Nationalist Front government, composed of centre-right, Islamists and neo-fascists.

31 December: Coalition falls as a result of internal contradictions and squabbling between parties.

1978 17 January: Ecevit forms an unstable coalition with Independents, marred by rampant corruption among Independent ministers; country continues to be plagued with youth violence and instability.

2 October: The neo-fascist Nationalist Action Party calls for proclamation of martial law, i.e. military intervention to deal with violence.

9 October: In Ankara, 7 Members of the Workers' Party shot; press constantly report assassinations of liberal academics and perpetrators rarely caught.

25 December: Press describes attacks on Alevi community by neo-fascist gangs in the province of Kahramanmaraş as civil war; fifteen people die and martial law declared in thirteen provinces.

1979   *10 January*: Shah of Iran flees the country in revolution and Ayatullah Khomeini arrives in February to consolidate Islamic revolution. Need for a stable Turkey, which politicians could not provide, becomes more critical for the West.

14 October: PM Ecevit, whose political position weakens as a result of violence and attacks from the Right, loses support in Senate and by-elections and resigns; Demirel forms a minority JP government.

1980   *2 January*: Generals call for national unity among parties and issue a guarded warning.

24 January: Government introduces a radical deflationary economic programme, devaluing lira by 33 per cent. Programme is designed to bring Turkey in line with trend towards globalization and be enacted under an authoritarian regime.

19 July: Former PM Nihat Erim, who led a military-backed cabinet in March 1971, assassinated – one of many murders taking place in the country.

12 September: Generals seize power, complaining of anarchy reigning in the country and the need to strengthen state; they establish National Security Council and proclaim martial law.

21 September: Cabinet announced with retired admiral as PM; political life comes to an end and some party leaders detained, later to be arrested, tried and imprisoned.

1981   *29 June*: Generals set up constituent assembly to write new, authoritarian constitution to replace liberal constitution of 1961.

1982   *7 November*: New constitution put to referendum and accepted by 91.3 per cent of the ballot.

19 November: Kenan Evren becomes 7th president of Republic.

1983   *3 March*: Constituent Assembly passes new political parties law and sends it to generals for approval. In May, 'new parties' begin to emerge and some are banned by generals because they are judged to be reincarnation of old parties.

6 November: Turgut Özal's Motherland Party wins general election and presents his government on 13 December; continuing economic policies set in motion on 24 January 1980; Özal continues to rely on martial law to maintain law and order.

15 November: Turkish Republic of Northern Cyprus established; only recognized by Turkey.

1987   *6 September*: Referendum allows banned party leaders to participate in politics again and Demirel and Ecevit take charge, formed by their proxies.

29 November: Özal calls early general election before his rivals have time to organize; wins with smaller majority and forms his new cabinet on 21 December.

1989   *26 March*: Özal's party suffers major defeat in local elections because of corruption and economic policies' unpopularity with both voters and private sector.

17 August: Chief of General Staff, Necip Torumtay, virtually declares war on Workers' Party of Kurdistan (PKK), which had launched its insurrection in 1984.

31 October: Turgut Özal elected 8th president of Turkey, after General Evren's term expired; Yıldırım Akbulut replaces him as PM. He lacks Özal's authority and fortunes of party decline hereafter.

18 December: Commission of European Community rejects Turkey's application to EC.

1990   *2 August*: Iraq invades Kuwait and triggers international crisis. Led by Özal, Turkey joins President Bush's coalition though UN sanctions against Iraq have a disastrous effect on Turkey's economy. Özal nevertheless tries to find Turkey's place in post-cold war world.

1991   *April*: Iraqi Kurds flee into Turkey to escape Saddam Hussein's forces after their rebellion collapses, causing major refugee problem in Turkey. Using Turkish bases, US, France, and Britain declare a no-fly zone over northern Iraq.

11 April: Parliament passes law to combat terrorism; considered undemocratic, it gives government very broad powers of coercion.

15 June: Mesut Yılmaz elected leader of Motherland Party and forms new cabinet on 23 June; he is expected to give party youthful and modern image.

20 October: In general election, Süleyman Demirel's centre-right True Path Party wins and he forms coalition with centre-left Social Democrats rather than centre-right Motherland Party.

7 December: PM Demirel makes important statement that 'Turkey recognizes the Kurdish reality'; his hope is to find political solution to continuing Kurdish rebellion, said to be costing Turkey about US $7 billion and hundreds of lives each year.

1993   *17 April*: President Turgut Özal dies of heart attack at age of 66.

16 May: Parliament elects Süleyman Demirel as Turkey's ninth president; leaving his party without strong leader!

13 June: Tansu Çiller elected leader of True Path Party and PM – first woman to lead Turkey, heading coalition with the Social Democrats.

27 November: Turkey and Israel sign memorandum that includes cooperation in intelligence gathering on Syrian-sponsored terror groups, marking the beginning of broader relationship.

1994   *26 March*: Coming third, the Welfare Party, the party of political Islam makes a breakthrough in local elections, its candidates becoming mayors of Istanbul and Ankara.

5 April: True Path–Social Democrat coalition introduces new 'stability packet' in which lira is devalued by 38 per cent with price increases of 100 per cent. Economy going through another crisis. During 1994, inflation rises by a record 148 per cent.

14 July: Parliament decides to investigate how PM Çiller acquired her wealth, suggesting impropriety; this causes tensions in coalition.

1995   *1 January*: Istanbul daily, *Milliyet*, quotes PM Çiller as paraphrasing the famous Kemalist statement, 'Happy is he who can say he is a Turk' to 'Happy is he who can say he is a citizen of Turkey'. Çiller's words reflect changing character of identity in Turkey.

18 February: Social Democrat parties – RPP and Social Democratic People's Party – unite under umbrella of RPP.

20 March: Turkish army sends 35,000 troops into northern Iraq to destroy PKK bases, escalating conflict with PKK.

23 July: Parliament passes amendments to 15 articles of constitution, designed to make political life more democratic.

20 September: Coalition collapses, leading to early election on 24 December.

24 December: Welfare Party, representing political Islam, wins with 21.38 per cent of vote and 158 seats, insufficient to form government; political crisis follows.

1996   *1 January*: Customs union agreement signed with the EU on 6 March comes into effect, marking major transformation in Turkey's economic policy and another step towards globalization.

6 March: Motherland–True Path Party coalition (Mother–Path) is formed after weeks of negotiations between parties; but is unstable given hostility between its two leaders, Motherland's Mesut Yılmaz and TPP's Çiller.

6 June: Mesut Yılmaz resigns, again opening way for Necmettin Erbakan, leader of Islamist party, who calls for parliamentary investigation of Çiller's wealth.

29 June: Erbakan and Çiller announce formation of coalition between Welfare Party and TPP (Welfare–Path) after both leaders agree to shelve investigations of corruption against each other!

3 November: An automobile accident, known as 'Susurluk incident', shakes establishment, revealing extent of governmental corruption and role played by so-called 'deep state' in Turkey's political life.

1997 *28 February*: National Security Council, dominated by generals, advises Erbakan-led coalition to clamp down on Islamist activity, especially the wearing of headscarves in universities, a decision which comes known as the '28 February Process'.

18 June: Despite efforts to seem moderate, Erbakan decides to resign, hoping to be replaced by Tansu Çiller as PM and for coalition to continue. But President Demirel appoints Motherland's Mesut Yılmaz to form new coalition, which Yılmaz does with Bülent Ecevit's Democratic left party.

1998 *16 January*: Constitutional court orders dissolution of Welfare Party for violating principle of secularism, and bans Necmettin Erbakan from party's leadership for five years. In anticipation, Islamists had already formed Virtue Party (Fazilet Partisi) on 17 December 1997.

21 April: In continuing offensive against political Islam, Recep Tayyip Erdoğan, Mayor of Istanbul and member of Virtue Party, is sentenced to 10 months' imprisonment for a speech made in 1997, exploiting Islam and inciting religious hatred.

26 November: PM Mesut Yılmaz resigns amid charges of mafia connections.

1999 *11 January*: Democratic Left Party's leader, Bülent Ecevit forms new cabinet to lead the country to an early general election, to be held in April.

15 February: Abdullah Öcalan, leader of Workers' Party of Kurdistan (PKK), is captured in Nairobi and brought back to Turkey, a triumph for Ecevit and an opportunity for government to 'declare victory' over Kurdish rebels; sentenced to death on 29 June, but reprieved due to abolition of death penalty in 2002.

18 April: General election is won by Ecevit's social democrats and Nationalist Action Party of extreme right, while centre-right parties collapse.

2 May: New parliament erupts in fury when Islamist MP, Merve Kavakçı enters chamber to take oath of office wearing a navy blue headscarf, the symbol of political Islam; she is later deprived of her parliamentary seat because she omitted to inform ministry of interior that she is also a US citizen.

3 May: Bülent Ecevit is reappointed PM and on 28 May, presents his coalition with NAP and Motherland Party, a coalition that proves to be surprisingly durable, given its ideological contradictions!

17 August: Massive earthquake in north-western Turkey undermines people's confidence in state because of its failure to provide relief to millions of victims.

13 October: European Union Commission recommends that Turkey be considered as candidate for EU; but would have to meet Copenhagen criteria, which include human rights, the protection of minorities and economic reform. A tall order!

2000

17 January: Dramatic shootout in Istanbul, in which important leaders of Hizbullah movement are shot and captured, leading to nationwide operation against Hizbullah, a body rumoured to be supported by 'deep state' to combat its enemies. Office of General Staff denies press claims that Turkey's armed forces have in any way supported Hizbullah activities against PKK.

5 May: Ahmet Necdet Sezer, president of Constitutional Court, replaces Demirel as president of Turkey; described as a liberal reformist who supports Turkey's membership of EU.

2001

19 February: Turkey experiences an economic crisis of major proportions as a result of PM Ecevit's spat with President Sezer over corruption. Stock market plunges, interest rates rise and Central Bank loses one-fifth of its foreign reserves as investors dump liras for dollars and euros.

1 March: Kemal Derviş from the World Bank is made minister in charge of the economy, an appointment expected to give confidence to foreign investors; he introduces important reforms to bring Turkey's economy in line with global trends.

21 June: Constitutional court dissolves Virtue Party, describing it as centre of Islamic fundamentalism.

21 July: Political Islamists form Felicity (*Saadet*) Party as successor to Virtue Party.

14 August: Moderates from Virtue Party, led by Recep Tayyip Erdoğan, found Justice and Development Party (*Adalet ve Kalkınma Partisi*), claiming to be secular 'Muslim democrats', not successors to former Virtue Party.

11 September: The events of 9/11 in New York, Washington and Pennsylvania, and President Bush's 'war against terrorism' suddenly make Turkey a 'strategic asset', worthy of IMF financial loans. In February 2002, IMF agrees to lend Turkey US $16 billion over next three years with US $9 billion to be made available immediately.

2002

4 May: PM Ecevit hospitalized; his illness creates political crisis, brought on by speculation as to whether he will step down or who should succeed him; stock market is adversely affected.

10 May: Kemal Derviş reported as saying that early general election would end uncertainty about Turkey's political future; his words mark the beginning of political manoeuvring that leads to early general election on 3 November.

29 May: TÜSİAD places full-page ads in press and calls for urgent reforms: abolition of death penalty, education and broadcasting in Kurdish and bipartisan policy towards EU.

7 July: Fearing that his party might be replaced in coalition by True Path Party, NAP's leader and Deputy PM Devlet Bahçeli calls for election on 3 November. While Ecevit and Bahçeli oppose an early election, Derviş and Turkey's big capitalists believe elections would put an end to prevailing uncertainty. Following resignations from Democratic Left Party, coalition loses its majority and on 16 July, Ecevit agrees to lead country to elections in November.

3 August: Parliament passes the 'democratic packet' of new laws, designed to meet EU requirements, which is seen as major step on road to EU and critical measure to end economic crisis.

10 August: Kemal Derviş resigns from government. Having failed to create a new centre by uniting some parties of centre-left and centre-right, on 21 August, Derviş joins RPP, so destroying any chance the newly founded New Turkey Party might have had of getting into parliament.

3 November: General election brings Justice and Development Party to power with 34.3 per cent of ballot and 363 seats, allowing it to form party government for first time since 1987. The RPP, with 19.4 per cent and 178 seats, becomes the opposition, with no other parties managing to clear the 10 per cent electoral barrier.

16 November: President Sezer appoints AKP's Abdullah Gül to form government and his cabinet is approved by the president on 18 November; he presents his programme and receives vote of confidence on 28 November.

19/24 December: Parliament passes the constitutional amendment permits Recep Tayyip Erdoğan to stand for election, enter parliament, and become prime minister.

2003   *26 January*: Large-scale anti-war demonstrations in Turkey; an estimated 85 to 90 per cent of Turkey's population oppose the coming war.

1 March: Parliament votes against the motion to deploy 62,000 US troops in Turkey and open the northern front in Iraq; US–Turkish relations are thrown into confusion.

9 March: Recep Tayyip Erdoğan elected to parliament; PM Gül resigns on 11 March and Erdoğan appointed as new prime minister.

19 March: President Bush's ultimatum to Saddam Hussein expires and the US-led coalition begins bombing of Baghdad.

20 March: Ankara agrees to open Turkey's airspace to US aircraft but relations with Washington have been undermined; the neo-conservatives in the Pentagon are determined to punish Turkey and the generals.

9 April: US forces seize control of Baghdad.

22 May: The generals agree to support the government's plan to join the EU.

28 May: The National Security Council agrees to amend the anti-terror law and grant Kurdish-language broadcasting so as to meet EU criteria on human rights. The business community supports the government. A former Kurdish MP describes the reforms that follow as the end of the 80-year ban on the Kurds and the recognition of the 'Kurdish reality'.

4 July: US troops in northern Iraq seize 11 Turkish soldiers, torturing and humiliating them. The Turks are released after protests from Ankara but Turkish–US relations suffer a major setback. The US action is seen as punishment for the negative vote of 20 March and the end of the 'strategic alliance'.

22 July: Foreign Minister Abdullah Gül visits the US, seeking to reinvigorate a troubled friendship.

29 July: The Assembly passes new 'reform packets' to meet EU demands. The main goal is to rein in the generals and 'civilianize' the NSC. On 11 September, Foreign Minister Gül claims that the reformed NSC now meets all the EU's objections.

7 November: The US informs Ankara that it does not need Turkish troops in Iraq; thus end negotiations that began in July.

15 November: Suicide bombings in Istanbul destroy two synagogues, the British consulate, and the building of the British bank, BHSB. The day is described as 'Turkey's 11 September', making Turkey a victim of 'Islamic terrorism'.

2004

6 January: Bashir Asad, the President of Syria, arrives in Ankara. Both sides want to repair relations and Ankara wants to get closer to the European position.

23 January: At the NSC meeting it is reported that Turkey has decided to work with the UN Annan plan to reunify Cyprus and solve the long-festering crisis.

31 January: As a result of PM Erdoğan's visit to the US, Foreign Minister Gül declares that Turkey has established a new relationship with America: It is no longer a strategic partnership bound by military ties, but based on human rights and democracy. The press wonders whether Turkey, with its 'moderate Islam' is being dragged into America's 'Greater Middle East project' to spread democracy.

22 March: Responding to the debate as to whether Turkey is a 'moderate Muslim state', as Washington claims, Prime Minister Erdoğan and the generals declare that Turkey is secular and would remain secular; there could be no Islamic state within a secular Turkey.

28 March: The local elections are a triumph for the governing Justice and Development Party (JDP); its vote increases from 34 to 43 per cent while that of the opposition declines from 19 to 15 per cent.

24 April: In the referendum in Cyprus, 65 per cent of the Turkish population votes 'yes' for reunification while 76 per cent of the Greek population votes 'no'. The result opens the way to EU accession talks.

27 September: Turkey drops the law criminalizing adultery to meet an EU requirement for women's rights. The governing party is still divided over such questions between 'Islamists' and secularists and the pro-EU faction has won.

6 October: The EU Commission report notes that Turkey has sufficiently fulfilled the political criteria and recommends that accession negotiations be opened.

17 December: The EU accepts Turkey's membership conditionally and accession talks begin on 3 October 2005 provided certain conditions are met.

18 December: Human Rights Association (IHD) President Yusuf Alatas says that while human rights in Turkey had improved, compared to EU standards the progress made was inadequate.

2005

7 January: The press reports on a divided opposition RPP with a leadership contest between its leader, Deniz Baykal and Mayor of Şişli Mustafa Sarıgül. Speaker Bülent Arınç calls for the abolition of the headscarf ban, especially in universities. This sparks a debate throughout Turkey.

8 March: On the occasion of International Women's Day, there are anti-JDP demonstrations in Istanbul that are brutally repressed by the police.

21 April: The daily newspaper *Radikal* reports Chief of Staff General Hilmi Özkök as saying that: 'Islamic reaction was continuing under the very eyes of the state'.

29 May: In the French referendum, the voters reject the EU constitution. But Foreign Minister Abdullah Gül says that there is no obstacle for Turkey to start the EU talks.

6 June: After the meeting between President Bush and Prime Minister Erdoğan in Washington the press disagree with the prime minister and write that the US–Turkey 'Strategic Partnership' remains shaky because the US had refused to do anything about the PKK guerrilla bases in northern Iraq.

11 June: Prime Minister Erdoğan receives a medal of honour from the Anti-Defamation League; he hopes to repair the damaged relations with the US by winning the support of the Jewish lobby. The *New York Times* writes that Turkey, nervous about EU prospects, is turning to the US.

19 July: *The Guardian* in London reports that a survey found that only just over a third of Europeans backed Turkey's membership.

6 August: The press reports that Chief of Staff Hilmi Özkök said that the army's powers had been curtailed by the government in the fight against Kurdish terrorism.

10 August: Justice Minister Cemil Çiçek says that the government and the army are on the same side as far as the fight against terrorism is concerned.

11 August: In a meeting with intellectuals, Erdoğan says that the Kurdish problem could be solved only with democracy. The press notes that the prime minister has opened a new page by admitting that there is a Kurdish question.

12 August: In Kurdish Diyarbakır, before a small crowd, Erdoğan admits that the state had made mistakes and that the Kurdish problem is everyone's problem.

16 August: The opposition criticizes Erdoğan's remarks. RPP's Deniz Baykal says that Erdoğan is confusing the Kurdish question with the question of terror.

17 August: *Radikal* writes that the process of monopolization is going on within the economy and Koç Holding seems to be winning.

20 August: The PKK announces a one-month truce. General Hurşit Tolon, ex-commander of the First Army, also denounces Erdoğan for his comments on the Kurdish question.

23 August: At the National Security Council meeting, the generals ask the prime minister what he meant by the Kurdish question. Erdoğan backs down and agrees that what he said could be open to misinterpretation. He admits that he had wanted to win over the Kurdish people.

26 August: *Hürriyet* reports that the Doğuş Group's Garanti Bank is selling its General Electric shares which are worth $1.8 billion. The sale shows a growing confidence in Turkey both economically and politically.

30 August: At the 'Victory Day' celebrations, General Yaşar Büyükanıt, commander of the Land Forces, warns the country that 'they' want to reduce Turkey to the state of Palestine.

1 September: A case opens against the author, Orhan Pamuk, accused of 'insulting Turkishness' for making false statements about the Armenian massacres.

3 September: According to *The Times*, Erdoğan is furious at the stalled EU talks. He says that Turkey would not make any more concessions and accuses EU governments of pandering to public opinion.

13 September: The Pamuk decision is criticized by the EU; it is unacceptable that Turkey practises such restrictions on free speech.

20 September: Ministers from EU member states fail to approve a declaration that would allow talks on Turkish accession to begin next month. Turkey has to formally recognize Cyprus before it can join the EU.

24 September: A conference on the Armenian question opens in Istanbul. It is described in the press as a 'turning point' because hitherto the subject had been taboo.

27 September: General Büyükanıt declares that the first threat to Turkey is reaction and the second, partition.

2 October: Erdoğan declares that if the EU shows political maturity then it will become a global power, otherwise it will end up as a Christian club.

4 October: President Jacques Chirac of France declares that Turkey would have to undergo a 'major cultural revolution' if it was to join the EU.

7 October: Hrant Dink, the Armenian journalist, is sentenced to six months in prison for 'insulting Turkishness'. 'So much for the freedom of expression', writes the press the following day.

10 October: Turkey's universities become the new battleground between a staunchly secular state establishment and a government with roots in political Islam.

29 October: At his Republic Day reception, President Sezer invites all the university rectors to show his support for them. Chief of Staff Hilmi Özkök is reported to have said that the patience of the military is being tested by all the provocation.

16 November: Prime Minister Erdoğan declares that the last word on the headscarf issue does not belong to the European court of Human Rights – which had supported the ban – but to the Muslim clerics, the *ulema*.

16 November: In Copenhagen, Prime Minister Erdoğan leaves a press conference, criticizing Denmark for permitting cartoons of the prophet Muhammad to be published in the press and for not expelling the Kurdish journalist from the press conference.

20 November: Deniz Baykal is again re-elected as leader of the RPP at its 31st congress.

2 December: Erdoğan is at odds with the generals who had expelled military personnel accused of Islamic fundamentalism.

7 December: Responding to a conference in New Zealand on the Kurdish question, Erdoğan says that in Turkey there were Turks, Kurds, Laz, Circassians, Georgians, Abkhazians and whatever else came to mind. What binds together all these ethnic elements is the bond of their religion. That is because Turkey is 99 per cent Muslim.

7 December: JDP's deputy, Resul Torun asks General Hilmi Özkök to remove the military division from the grounds of parliament, declaring that Ankara seemed more like a 'military' than a 'civilian capital'.

8 December: The General Staff release a statement describing Resul Torun's article as shocking. It condemns any effort to remove 'the military from the bosom of the nation', adding that the people of Turkey understood what kind of aims people who suggested such things had.

14 December: A change in regulations allows graduates from religious schools (the *imam-hatip* schools) to enter any university after completing the necessary courses in the open high school system. Improving the lot of such graduates was one of the main campaign promises of the JDP.

2006

18 May: *The Times* reports that the EU would suspend membership talks unless the JDP government stops back-sliding on reforms needed to meet European standards. The EU's most immediate priority is to have Turkey open its ports and airports to boats and planes from Cyprus.

14 June: Baskın Oran & Elçin Aktoprak write that while the rise of the Muslim bourgeoisie began under the Welfare Party, it began to mature under the JDP. Supporters of the party go to pop concerts and wear designer clothes; in short the JDP is becoming the party of Muslims undergoing change.

15 June: The EU decide that the law did not allow the wearing of the turban, considered by some as an Islamic requirement. After this the secular–Islamist quarrel begins. The JDP's patriarchal attitude towards women does not change, explaining the violence against women.

5 July: *Milliyet* discusses the appointment of Professor İbrahim Özdemir as the director of the Ministry of National Education. He is a self-proclaimed member of the Nurcu Order determined to Islamize education.

22 November: A survey conducted by Turkey's Economic and Social Studies Foundation finds that although the interest in Islam is growing, interest in the sharia is dropping. Those who describe themselves as Muslims account for 44.6 per cent but those wanting the sharia account for only 9 per cent. For most, the biggest problem is unemployment.

29 December: A survey on the family finds that 58.4 per cent describe themselves as happy, 10.9 per cent as very happy, 26 per cent in the middle, 4 per cent as unhappy and 0.7 per cent as very unhappy.

2007

11 January: A poll shows that a majority is against Erdoğan becoming President.

13 January: Parliament adopts a law, previously vetoed by President Sezer, on the appointment of rectors to 15 new universities.

20 January: Journalist and activist, Hrant Dink, editor of the Armenian paper *Agos*, is murdered by an ultra-nationalist.

27 *April*: Abdullah Gül, the JDP candidate, fails to be elected because of a lack of the required 367 quorum. He receives 357 votes and the vote is declared invalid by the opposition RPP, who then take the issue to the Constitutional Court. The General Staff issue an e-warning on its website emphasizing that the presidential election process is also its concern.

28 *April*: The government issue a counter-warning reminding the General Staff that it is affiliated to the prime ministry.

1 *May*: The Constitutional Court approves the RPP's petition to invalidate the presidential election. Prime Minister Erdoğan responds by announcing an early general election for 22 July.

4 *May*: For two and a half hours, Erdoğan meets Chief of Staff Yaşar Büyükanıt in his Dolmabahçe office. The conversation has remained a secret to this day.

22 *July*: The JDP win a landslide victory in the general election with 47 per cent of the vote. With the support of the Nationalist Action Party (NAP), the JDP now have the required 367 quorum and Abdullah Gül can be elected president.

18 *August*: General Büyükanıt refuses to comment on Gül's presidential bid but, on 22 August, denies any deal with Abdullah Gül. The prime minister asks the military to stay out of politics.

28 *August*: Abdullah Gül is elected president, head of state and the commander-in-chief of Turkey in peacetime.

29 *August*: The generals boycott President Gül's swearing-in ceremony.

5 *November*: Prime Minister Erdoğan meets President George W. Bush during his visit to the United States. The US is said to be providing real-time intelligence on the PKK camps in northern Iraq, crucial for eliminating the PKK in Turkey.

2008

19 *January*: Erdoğan criticizes the judiciary for involving itself in the headscarf issue. He says that nobody is superior to the executive or the legislative branches of government. There is a separation of powers in Turkey and the legislative, executive and judicial branches should not interfere with one other, 'everyone should know their boundaries.'

22 *January*: The JDP-dominated Assembly begins its attack on the judiciary.

23 *January*: The TV channel ATV cancels its serial of 'Sinekli Bakkal' because of the negative image of the imam character who is portrayed as a cruel bigot, resembling Fethullah Gülen, the controversial Islamic leader, living in America.

28 *January*: There are more arrests in the ongoing 'Ergenekon conspiracy'.

4 *March*: Columnist Cüneyt Ülsever writes about how the government is taking Turkey in a conservative direction by appointing Islamists in the ministry of education which would shape the future of Turkey's students.

31 July: The Constitutional Court decides to impose a financial penalty on the JDP rather than declare it illegal for violating secularism.

3 December: The military expels five officers for allegedly having Islamist ties.

13 December: RPP leader Deniz Baykal is criticized for making statements in favour of the headscarf.

25 December: JDP's Culture Minister Ertuğrul Günay opens Turkey's first Alevi Institute in Ankara and apologizes to the Alevis for the discrimination and suffering of the past.

30 December: Yunus Soylet, who has close ties to the JDP and is Erdoğan's family doctor, is appointed rector of Istanbul University. Students demonstrate against the appointment.

2009

1 January: Erdoğan leaves for a visit to Syria, Jordan, Egypt and Saudi Arabia in a bid to stop the Israeli attack in Gaza.

8 January: In the tenth wave of the Ergenekon inquiry there are 37 arrests, including those of high-profile jurists. The opposition parties denounce the investigation as a political ploy.

12 January: Commenting on Ergenekon and the arrest of judges, Erdoğan says that nobody is above the law and that Turkey is ridding itself of its shackles.

12 January: Turkey's Judges and Prosecutors Association harshly criticizes the government over its handling of the controversial Ergenekon case, saying the situation recalled 'the eras of Hitler and Mussolini'.

16 January: The EU asks for clarification on Ergenekon from Foreign Minister Ali Babacan. He replies that the case is in the hands of the judiciary. 'The judiciary is completely independent in Turkey', he states.

23 January: In the eleventh wave of Ergenekon, there are operations in 16 provinces with 30 arrests, including those of 20 army and police officers. Retired General Tuncer Kılınç says that the main reason is to tarnish the image of the armed forces.

26 January: Sabih Kanadoğlu, the honorary chief judge of the Supreme Court, declares that the judiciary is no longer independent.

29 January: The constitutional court cancels legislation giving the prime minister a mandate to oversee the wiretapping activities run by security forces.

30 January: After criticizing Israel's Prime Minister Shimon Peres, Erdoğan walks out, vowing never to return to Davos. The event marks the beginning of declining relations with Israel.

8 February: The press reports that retired General Hurşit Tolon, in prison for the past seven months, has been released for a lack of evidence.

19 February: *Milliyet* reports that a meeting in Istanbul of Hamas and 200 Sunni leaders calls for a 'Third Jihad Front' against Israel. Erdoğan is praised at the meeting.

19 February: The Treasury imposes a half-billion-dollar levy against the Doğan Media Group and industrial empire. The press describe it as the government waging war against the media to a new level. The next day, the Turkish Journalists' Association says that the freedom of the press is under attack.

26 February: The US Human Rights Report for 2008 criticizes Turkey, stating that 'Freedoms in Turkey are being curtailed while torture is on the rise'.

4 March: Erdoğan admits in an interview that governments carry out wiretaps.

9 March: In the state run Ulu Mosque in Diyarbakır the sermon is read in Kurdish for the first time. This is part of the government's policy to promote Kurdish rights as well as Islamic brotherhood.

10 March: The Scientific and Technological Research Council of Turkey (TUBITAK) remove Charles Darwin as the cover story of its magazine on the occasion of the 200th anniversary of his birth. The Turkish and the international press see that as the growing influence of Islam on secular institutions.

11 March: The prosecutor's office publish the second indictment of the Ergenekon case. It is 1,909 pages long and covers only the sixth, seventh and eighth waves of arrests.

17 March: *Milliyet* reports that unemployment has risen to 13.6 per cent, with 25 per cent youth unemployment. This is seen as a threat to the social order.

31 March: In the local elections, JDP's vote declines by eight points but is still 15 per cent more than the RPP.

6 April: President Obama arrives in Ankara for a two-day visit. US investments are expected to flow into Turkey after the visit. He calls for better Turkey-Armenia relations.

9 April: Prime Minister Erdoğan announces that May Day will be a national holiday.

14 April: There are 29 arrests, including five professors, in the twelfth wave of the Ergenekon probe.

15 April: In a speech at the War Academy Chief of Staff General İlker Başbuğ says that he will address civil-military relations but he does not mention the Ergenekon investigation.

21 April: Deputy Prime Minister Çiçek says that in talks with Armenia the interests of Azerbaijan will not be sacrificed.

25 April: Haşim Kılıç, President of the Constitutional Court, says that the authority of the majority is not unlimited.

1 May: May Day is celebrated as Labour & Solidarity Day.

9 May: In Ankara, Finnish Foreign Minister Alexander Stubb says that the freedom of the press is the key to the EU.

11 May: Judge Mustafa Birden declares that: 'Attempts by political powers to take the judiciary under control may lead to chaos. The judiciary must be independent, and politics must be made in line with the basic principles of law'.

14 May: The RPP decides to focus its attention on the Islamist charity, 'Lighthouse', and the JDP. It is said to have collected 900 billion euros in Germany and is being investigated for fraud.

5 June: Bülent Ecevit's widow, Rahşan Ecevit, resigns from the Democratic Left Party because the party has abandoned Ecevit's line. Such is the state of Turkey's social democracy.

21 June: The media is divided over the authenticity of a document published by *Taraf* which claimed that officers had plans to topple the JDP government. In *Radikal* on 23 June the military prosecutor says such a document has not been prepared by the General Staff.

26 June: During the midnight session, the JDP-majority parliament passes an amendment that paves the way for the trial of military personnel, including the chief of General Staff, by civilian courts. The amendment shows the decline of military influence under JDP rule.

20 July: The prosecutors submit a third 1500-page indictment in the Ergenekon case.

23 July: Erdoğan declares that his government has launched the 'Kurdish initiative' so as to bring about peace.

25 July: In a meeting where the appointment of judges is discussed. Kadır Özbek, the board's president, declares: 'I want them (the government) to leave justice to the judiciary, and want them to know that the only interlocutor of the judiciary in the board is the justice minister...'

6 August: Russia's President Putin arrives in Ankara.

30 August: The Armed Forces celebrate Victory Day with the slogan 'A Powerful Army, A Powerful Turkey'.

8 September: Speaking on the occasion of the new judicial year, Judge Hasan Gerçeker accuses the government of forming a party judiciary. He says that the new draft judiciary reform will undermine the independence of courts and politicize the judiciary: 'We must exert efforts to establish an independent and unbiased judiciary, not an adherent one.'

9 September: A tax fine of 3,755 billion liras, the biggest in Turkey's history, is given to the Doğan group for tax evasion. The EU warns that the fine could impact the Progress Report and TÜSİAD notes that 'the current practices caused concern that tax administration was open to political influence.'

17 September: During President Assad's visit, there is talk of the beginning of a new era with Damascus, marked by the end of visas between the two countries.

25 September: At the UN, Erdoğan criticizes the world leaders for turning a blind eye to the crisis in Gaza.

30 September: Güler Sabancı, chairperson of Sabancı Holding says: 'Turkey, with strong capital and a healthy financial sector, has left behind the difficult days of 2009. 2010 will be better.'

4 October: A fish restaurant run by the JDP municipality stops serving alcohol. There are protests when a JDP-run restaurant does the same in the Moda district.

5 October: President Gül urges academics to stay away from politics. In response, Professor Cemal Taluğ, the president of Ankara University, says all governments expect universities to think along their political lines.

6 October: *Radikal* writes that in UNDP's Human Development Index, Turkey has slipped three places in 2009, but specifically the role of women in society has earned the worst mark. Turkey is ranked 101 out of 109.

9 October: Lawyers of Ergenekon suspects say that the meeting of judges and prosecutors in the Ergenekon case over a fast-breaking dinner has irrevocably shaken their confidence in justice.

11 October: Turkey cancels an annual joint air force drill scheduled for this week because it opposes Israeli participation. The Israeli military says that this is the latest sign of deteriorating relations between the two countries.

14 October: In its annual progress report the EU criticizes Turkey for its campaign against the Doğan Media Group.

24 October: Rahşan Ecevit founds the Democratic Left People's Party.

29 October: Responding to Tehran's comment that Turkey has turned its face to the East, Erdoğan replies that Turkey faces both East and West.

6 November: The EU asks Ankara to reconsider the visit of Sudanese President Omar Hassan al-Bashir, wanted by the International Criminal Court for war crimes.

18 November: The Justice Ministry announces that 113,270 people have been wiretapped over the last three years. The number includes 12,988 who were told that no crime had been detected in their wiretap!

25 November: Erdoğan meets Muammar Gaddafi with a delegation of 200 businessmen. Gaddafi agrees to pay Libya's debt to Turkish companies and visa requirements are lifted between the two countries.

25 November: *Vatan* quotes a full-page article from the *Financial Times* on 'Turkey's Ottoman vision'. Turkey is re-engaging with countries, extending from the Balkans to Baghdad, once ruled by the Ottomans. The most important weapon in this neo-Ottomanism is not religion but trade.

26 November: The US State Department says that Turkey is an important model for the region in terms of its very vital democratic institutions.

30 November: The World Association of Newspapers and News Publishers express grave concern at the mounting judicial actions and intimidations facing journalists and independent media in Turkey.

7 December: Erdoğan meets President Obama in Washington to discuss various issues.

9 December: The European Court of Human Rights find Turkey guilty of violating the European Human Rights Convention and sentence it to pay a fine of 297,000 euros.

10 December: The resignation of Nabi Şensoy, a veteran diplomat and ambassador to Washington, suggests a growing rift between the JDP government and the diplomatic service.

11 December: The Constitutional Court order the closure of the pro-Kurdish Democratic Society Party for its links with the PKK.

11 December: Yusuf Ziya Özcan, president of the Higher Education Board of YÖK says that the religious schools – İman-Hatip schools – can be treated as high schools so that their students can enter university.

14 December: Members of the banned Kurdish Democratic Society Party unveil the Peace and Democracy Party or BDP.

16 December: The case of Dev-Yol (a militant leftist group), which began 29 years earlier, ends with 39 members being given life sentences. A total of 1,243 were put on trial.

24 December: Erdoğan, visiting Syria, announces that a total of 51 agreements have been signed between the two countries. President Bashar al-Assad, says that he does not want mediation from the French President Nicolas Sarkozy as proposed by Israel. He says, 'Erdoğan's mediation was impartial. I want my brother Erdoğan as mediator!'

2010

2 January: With the increase in taxes on fuel, the price of most commodities rise and inflation accelerates to 6.5 per cent cancelling out the government's earlier wage increase.

7 January: Turkey and Syria agree to build a 'friendship bridge' on a shared river.

8 January: *Vatan* report that the number of Turks with a bank balance of one million liras has risen to over 30,000.

12 January: PM Erdoğan denies that Turkey is moving towards a civilian dictatorship or 'civil fascism'.

20 January: *Taraf* publishes a 5,000 page coup plot called 'Sledgehammer' (*Balyoz*) which was prepared between 2002 and 2003 by retired General Çetin Doğan, commander of the First Army. Like 'Ergenekon', 'Sledgehammer' leads to arrests and an ongoing trial. The next day, the Armed Forces deny allegations of such a plot.

4 February: The Interior Ministry announce that the protocol allowing the Armed Forces to intervene in order to maintain domestic security has been annulled.

11 February: Chief of Staff İlker Başbuğ says that the allegations against Turkey's soldiers are demoralizing the army.

14 February: During his visit to Qatar, PM Erdoğan increases Turkey's economic ties with the Gulf state.

22 February: Before leaving for Spain, Erdoğan says: 'We are determined to take any step even a referendum on judicial reform'.

24 February: In response to the arrest of officers on the 22 February, the EU Commission voices concern about the 'serious allegations' of coup plotting levelled against dozens of senior military figures in Turkey.

26 February: There are 18 further arrests of officers. This is described as 'Phase 2 of Sledgehammer'. PM Erdoğan criticizes the judiciary for exceeding its powers.

1 March: The Harvard economist Professor Dani Rodrik launches a blog to defend General Çetin Doğan, his father-in-law.

5 March: The clash between the government and the judiciary over judicial independence becomes inflamed in the wake of the government's announcement that it will push for constitutional amendments involving a judicial reform package.

16 March: PM Erdoğan says that he will not go to Washington because the House of Representatives' Foreign Affairs Committee has adopted a resolution affirming Armenian allegations of genocide in the Ottoman Empire in 1915. Foreign Minister Ahmet Davutoğlu will go in his place.

19 March: Another 33 people are indicted in the 'Sledgehammer' plot.

31 March: President Gül's appointments to the Supreme Court draw criticism from the judges. 'The move is a clear indicator of the determination to seize the judiciary,' says Emine Ülker Tarhan, chairwoman of the Union of Judges and Prosecutors.

8 April: In Diyarbakır the court sentences a member of parliament to three years in prison on charges of creating propaganda for the terrorist organization, the PKK. On the same day, parliament passes a bill allowing campaigning in Kurdish.

12 April: The judiciary accuses the JDP government of threatening its independence with its constitutional reform package.

17 April: The Gaza Islamic University confers an honorary doctorate on Prime Minister Erdoğan. He says that he has received many honorary doctorates but that this one has a different meaning!

19 April: Erdoğan says that the presidential system might be submitted to a referendum after the general elections in 2011. This marks the beginning of the ongoing political discussion on the presidential system.

24 April: President Obama avoids using the word 'genocide' while discussing the events of 1915 and the Armenian question.

2 May: Parliament discusses the JDP's constitutional bill in the second round of voting.

5 May: Parliament passes a fiercely criticized constitutional reform article to overhaul the board that appoints judges. The change increases the number of people on the board from 7 to 21 and gives the president and Parliament the power to appoint some of its members.

7 May: RPP's leader, Deniz Baykal is said to have been caught on a 'sex tape'. This leads to his resignation on 10 May but with his organization in the party still intact. He is succeeded by Kemal Kılıçdaroğlu.

12 May: Opposition parties vow to challenge the reform package even after the president has signed it.

13 May: President Dmitri Medvedev arrives on a state visit to Turkey, a visit seen as a turning point in the relationship with Russia.

14 May: The RPP applies to the Constitutional Court to annul the reform package.

31 May: Israeli troops board the Turkish ship, the *Mavi Marmara*, as it sails for Gaza. The raid embitters already bad relations between the two countries.

11 June: PM Erdoğan delivers a speech at the inauguration of the Turkish – Arab Co-operation Forum in Istanbul. He declares that there is a deep-rooted relationship between Turks and Arabs, and that Turks cannot live without Arabs. But Turkey is not drifting away from the West either.

17 June: A parliamentary commission approves a draft law regulating procedures for presidential elections, allowing the prime minister [i.e. Erdoğan] to run for the office without being obliged to resign from his current post.

18 June: Retired ambassadors accuse Erdoğan of ignorance stating that: '[F]oreign policy is a long-term and serious job. It's a serious pursuit that requires knowledge, foresight and calm analytical abilities.'

1 July: According to *Milliyet*, Turkey's economy grew 11.7 per cent in the first quarter of 2010, becoming the top economy in Europe and the fifth in the world.

1 July: Kemal Kılıçdaroğlu, the new RPP leader says his party would 'support girls wearing headscarves going to universities.' This is the new RPP.

5 July: Israel rejects Erdoğan's demand for an apology for the *Mavi Marmara* incident.

20 July: Foreign Minister Ahmed Davutoğlu meets the Hamas leader Khalid Meshaal in Damascus.

23 July: The court orders arrest warrants for 23 people in the 'Sledgehammer' case, including retired generals who had already been released.

4 August: Journalists note that the Supreme Military Council (or YAŞ) faced a grave crisis given all the arrests. There is a power struggle between the government and the army and the government is winning.

20 August: PM Erdoğan files a case against General Saldıray Berk, commander of the Third Army, who is alleged to have asked villagers in Erzincan province: 'Do you know that the prime minister has stolen the country?'

31 August: Former Police chief Hanefi Avcı testifies about his book *'Devotee' Residents of the Golden Horn: Yesterday the State, Today a Religious Congregation*. The book claimed that the police force and other departments of state had been infiltrated by the religious Fethullah Gülen community.

12 September: The JDP secures 58 per cent of the 'Yes' vote in the referendum, Erdoğan's sixth victory in eight years.

17 September: PM Erdoğan visits the tomb of Adnan Menderes, executed after the military coup of 27 May 1960. He begins to see himself as the successor of Menderes and Turgut Özal.

22 September: *Habertürk* report that police in a park told couples not to hold hands and checked their identity cards. On the same day *Vatan* reports that three art galleries in Beyoğlu, the most westernized district of Istanbul, were attacked by men with tear gas, sticks, and bottles. They shouted Islamic slogans and 'you cannot drink alcohol here'. These incidents are seen as a sign of 'creeping Islamization'.

9 October: In Ankara, Alevis protest against mandatory religious classes in the country's public education system.

10 October: Two journalists, Ertuğrul Mavioğlu and Ahmet Şık go on trial for their book, a guide to the Ergenekon case.

11 October: Members of Turkey's Supreme Board of Judges and Prosecutors resign in protest against the Justice Ministry's blocking of its work on summer appointments.

13 October: President Gül decides to hold a Republic Day reception. On 29 October this will also be open to women wearing headscarves.

21 October: The index of Reporters Without Borders rank Turkey 138th among 175 countries, just above Ethiopia and Russia, and 16 spots lower than the previous year. On 10 November, Erdoğan says that freedom of the press cannot be limitless and that criminal convictions of a number of Turkish journalists is a judicial, rather than a political, concern.

28 October: *Milliyet* reports that a special consumption tax on alcoholic beverages has increased by 30 per cent.

5 November: During a meeting Erdoğan is asked how women will be able to work if they all have three children, as he proposes. He replies: 'You cannot increase employment by not having children.'

21 November: *Hürriyet* citing *The Economist* reports that the 100 richest Turks have $227 billion between them.

29 November: Diplomatic cables released by WikiLeaks to German news magazine *Der Spiegel* show that American diplomats have doubts about Erdoğan's dependability as a partner.

4 December: The violent dispersal by police of several student protests heading towards Dolmabahçe Palace draws a harsh response from the RPP leader. Students protesting the prime minister's meeting with university rectors are violently beaten by police forces who also deploy pepper gas to subdue the demonstration.

14 December: Intimidated by government pressure, the Doğan group decide to withdraw from the media sector.

15 December: Student protests against the government continue despite police violence and threats of jail.

21 December: Turkey and Syria renew diplomatic pledges during a ministerial meeting in Ankara.

2011

2 January: The municipality of Kars decide to destroy a monument described by Erdoğan as 'freakish'. The sculpture was put up by the JDP municipality as a 'Peace and Friendship monument' to mend relations with the Armenian community.

7 January: A letter written by Hayati Asıltürk in 2007 and addressed to Erdoğan complain that he is an unemployed engineer who has looked for work for three years. The letter is seen as a criticism of the government and of the prime minister personally. The court sentences Asıltürk to ten months in prison, commuted to a fine of 6,000 liras.

9 January: When on 5 January, the serial on Suleiman the Magnificent is aired, conservatives find it controversial because of the way the sultan is portrayed. Deputy Prime Minister Bülent Arınç intervenes and says: 'Those who try to humiliate the important people of our history by portraying them inaccurately should face retribution. What is necessary will be done'.

10 January: President Gül says that Turkey is in dire need of judicial reform.

12 January: The president of TÜSİAD, Turkey's leading business association, says that the 10 per cent election barrier should be lowered so that smaller parties can be represented in parliament.

15 & 16 January: The Alevi congress convenes in Ankara and complains that the fundamental problem for the Alevis was that they are not given the same rights as those enjoyed by other religious communities.

24 January: A school teacher is told not to talk about Darwin's theory of evolution. This sparks a debate over whether education in Turkey is becoming more religious.

25 January: The foreign ministry is reorganized, with new regulations passed in 2010 that create new positions, 'consular and specialization', changing educational criteria for civil service exams.

27 January: The opposition RPP says that the JDP is trying to weaken the Constitutional Court, the Supreme Court of Appeals, and the Council of State, thereby establishing a 'fascist judiciary'.

30 January: A report is released from Cairo of anti-government revolt, i.e. the 'Arab spring'. According to the press of 31 January, Erdoğan phones President Obama about the situation.

1 February: Haşim Kılıç, President of the Constitutional Court, criticizes members of the judiciary who oppose the government on reform.

2 February: PM Erdoğan declares that Hosni Mubarak of Egypt should go.

10 February: Egypt's Muslim Brotherhood envoy, Ashraf Abdel Ghaffar, arrives in Turkey to confer with the JDP.

13 February: President Gül approves the new, controversial law to reform the judiciary.

14 February: Police raid the HQ of Oda TV, a fierce critic of government policies. The next day, US Ambassador Francis Ricciardone says that a free press is vital for democracy. He says that he does not understand how Turkish journalists can be detained while at the same time talks about freedom of speech are being given.

18 February: PM Erdoğan defends freedom of the press in Turkey and describes the US ambassador as a novice.

27 February: Necmettin Erbakan, the founder of political Islamic parties in Turkey, dies at the age of 84.

March 9: The EU parliament adopts a resolution concerning the deterioration of press freedom in Turkey.

30 March: Commenting on the controversial removal of Prosecutor Zekeriya Öz from the Ergenekon case, Erdoğan says that it is an issue for the judiciary, not the executive branch: 'Turkey is a democratic, secular state of law. I cannot intervene with the judiciary, and the judiciary cannot intervene with my job'.

1 April: A week earlier, Ahmet Şık's unpublished book, *The Imam's Army*, is seized by the police, but downloaded thousands of times. It tells the story of how Fethullah Gülen's people had infiltrated the ranks of the police and the judiciary.

4 April: Because of income distribution, 20 per cent of the population is able to survive only on state aid.

14 April: According to a case filed by the Ankara Public Prosecutor's Office, more than 100 students from Turkey's leading universities face one to ten years in prison for illegally protesting and resisting arrest.

17 April: Erdoğan announces his party's manifesto for the parliamentary election of 12 June. He promises to build two new cities in Istanbul, one on the European side and the other on the Asian side.

21 April: Minister of State Egemen Bağış says that the European Union needs Turkey more than Turkey needs the European Union.

24 April: In the demonstration against the Assad regime in Syria, Turkey joins the US and the EU in calling on Assad to stop the killing.

1 May: Unions are allowed to celebrate May Day in Taksim Square.

2 May: Osama bin Laden is killed by US Special Forces in Pakistan.

4 May: Erdoğan tells Maummar Gaddafi to step down for the sake of Libya's future.

6 May: EU Enlargement Commissioner, Stefan Fule, says that Turkey should amend its criminal code and anti-terror legislation to ensure full respect for freedom of expression and the media.

7 June: In an interview, Foreign Minister Davutoğlu reaffirms that Turkey 'looks to the Syrian government as legitimate and has no plans to contact any Syrian opposition groups.'

9 June: Taunting the NAP leader, Devlet Bahçeli, Erdoğan declares that he would have hanged PKK's chief, Öcalan, had he been in the ruling coalition in 2002 or he would have left it.

12 June: In the general election, four parties are represented in the new parliament: the JDP, the RPP, the NAP, and the Kurdish BDP. The JDP wins around 50 per cent of the vote but only 326 seats and strengthens their mandate. The opposition parties are divided, the NAP criticizing the other two parties rather than the JDP.

23 June: The court refuses to release two detained in the Ergenekon case – the journalist Mustafa Balbay and the academic Mehmet Haberal – despite the fact that they had been elected MPs on the RPP ticket.

28 June: Parliament convenes but the RPP refuses to take the oath in the new parliament while its elected members are in jail.

14 July: The Kurdish Democratic Society Congress declares 'democratic autonomy' during its extraordinary congress in Diyarbakır, thus raising a new demand. Ethnic polarization in Turkey is on the increase.

19 July: For the first time in Turkey, a high court accepts a defendant's request to make his case in Kurdish.

22 July: There are clashes in the Zeytinburnu district of Istanbul between opponents and supporters of the PKK.

29 July: Days before the Supreme Military Council, the Chief of Staff, and Commanders of the Land, Air, and Naval Forces resign. This gives the prime minister an opportunity to extend his authority over the military.

31 July: General Necdet Özel, the new Chief of Staff, is known for having good relations with the JDP government.

7 August: The government and the military agree on the need to amend Article 35 of the Turkish Armed Forces Law that had provided the justification for military intervention. Even the RPP agree to the changes.

23 August: Foreign Minister Davutoğlu says that Turkey supports Libya's National Transitional Council after the fall of Gaddafi. Turkish firms also look for quick returns.

26 August: Two arrested journalists, Ahmet Şık and Nedim Şener, are accused of aiding and abetting the alleged 'Ergenekon terrorists'.

30 August: President Gül and not the Chief of Staff receive greetings on Victory Day, marking the new standard in defining civil–military relations. The JDP see this as the normalization of relations.

1 September: The pro-Kurdish BDP says it will end its boycott on 1 October when parliament meets.

8 September: Turkish–Israeli relations are formally downgraded.

14 September: A tape of the secret talks between the government and the PKK are leaked to the press.

21 September: Ankara cuts all ties with Damascus.

22 September: Five high-ranking officers are arrested by an Istanbul court as part of the ongoing 'Sledgehammer' trial. There are now 54 generals and admirals in prison facing charges related to three separate ongoing coup-plot cases.

28 September: Cartoonist Bahadır Baruter is put on trial for drawing a cartoon in which he renounced God, thereby 'insulting the religious values of a part of the population'.

15 October: After her five-day visit to Turkey, Gabriela Knau, the UN special reporter speaks about the independence of judges and prosecutors and states that she was 'most concerned at the lack of respect for fundamental procedural guarantees, notably at the restrictions to the right to defence' in cases of terror-related charges handled by special-authority courts.

16 October: Family and Social Policy Minister Fatma Şahin says that the government plans for a minimum per capita income of $4 a day by 2023 in order to relieve poverty in Turkey.

18 October: *Vatan* reports that the man who insulted the prime minister on Facebook could serve two years in jail.

19 October: Turkey launches military attacks against PKK targets in Iraq.

21 October: Six suspects are released in the 'Lighthouse' fraud case where Islamists in Germany collected millions of euros for charity and then embezzled them.

1 November: Twenty-three suspects, including a university professor, Buşra Ersanlı and publisher, Ragıp Zarakoğlu are arrested in the probe into the Kurdish Communities Union or KCU (KCK in Turkish).

6 November: PM Erdoğan states that Turkey will not allow the creation of a parallel state as envisaged by the KCU.

15 November: Fifty-seven academics resign from the Turkish Academy of Sciences (TÜBA) in protest of a statutory decree that annulled the institution's autonomous member selection process while allegedly bringing it under tighter government control.

23 November: PM Erdoğan apologizes for the Dersim killings of 1937–39 when thousands of Kurdish tribesmen were killed. This is seen by the RPP as another attack on the Atatürk period.

22 December: Turkey freezes relations with France over the 'genocide' issue, recalls its ambassador and suspends all economic, political, and military meetings.

30 December: The International Press Institute names Turkey as an 'enemy of press freedom'.

2012   *2 January*: The civilian national Intelligence Organization (MİT in Turkish) takes over military intelligence.

3 January: Nine more are detained in Ergenekon searches in Ankara.

6 January: The former Chief of Staff, General İlker Başbuğ, is arrested, accused of plotting to overthrow the JDP government.

10 January: General Hurşit Tolon is arrested on 'serious suspicion of a criminal act', as part of the Ergenekon case.

18 January: The Kurdish BDP hints at federalism for Turkey.

21 January: The Council of Europe again criticizes the judiciary in Turkey.

27 January: Erdoğan rejects mounting Western criticism over a record number of imprisoned journalists in Turkey. He argues the outside world is not aware that they are involved in subversive and violent activities.

2 February: Accusing Kemal Kilicdaroğlu of wanting to raise an 'atheist generation', Erdoğan says that they wanted to raise a 'religious generation'.

10 February: By agreeing to host NATO'S Radar System in Malatya, Ankara draws criticism from Iran and Russia.

15 February: Kurds take to the streets to mark the 13th anniversary of the capture of PKK's leader Abdullah Öcalan.

17 February: Parliament passes a bill to save National Intelligence Organization (MİT) officials from a judicial probe as the government defends secret talks between MİT and the outlawed PKK.

4 March: RPP leader Kılıçdaroğlu says that his party is not anti-religious, a perception he claims was being created by the ruling party as propaganda.

7 March: Erdoğan says that there are only six journalists in prison; the other 99 'were made to look like journalists'!

11 March: The new education bill passes through commission. After four years of primary education children will be permitted to opt out in favour of 'home education'. Critics say that this will encourage child labour and undermine the education for girls.

19 March: The prosecutor asks for five years in jail for two students who threw eggs at EU Minister Egemen Bağı in December 2011.

24 March: PM Erdoğan gives a speech to military officers during his first visit to the Academy since coming to power.

2 April: Turkey hosts a 'Friends of Syria' conference in Istanbul so as to put pressure on Damascus.

12 April: General Çevik Bir, former Deputy Chief of Staff, is detained as part of the probe of the so-called 'post-modern coup' of 28 February 1997.

13 April: Erdoğan goes to Saudi Arabia to discuss the crisis in Syria.

15 April: Erdoğan declares the era of military coups in Turkey is over.

1 May: The Council of State annuls the government's decree to limit 19 May celebrations marking the beginning of the War of Independence.

3 May: On World Press Freedom Day, International Press Institute (IPI) and the Turkish Journalist Association warn against the worsening situation around media freedom in Turkey.

5 May: President Gül replaces the Chief of Staff as the host for Victory Day celebrations on August 30, further curbing the military's profile.

9 May: PM Erdoğan urges generals to sue journalist Bekir Coşkun because he described generals as 'tamed dogs'.

10 May: Six active duty and five retired officers are imprisoned as part of the latest wave of the investigation of the 28 February 1997 'post-modern' coup.

16 May: The commission agrees to hear the accounts of former politicians like Süleyman Demirel, Deniz Baykal, and Hüsamettin Cindoruk about the US role in the coup of 12 September 1980.

17 May: The clause that bans visitors from wearing beards, religious robes, türbans, headscarves or religious caps in officers' clubs and other social facilities is removed.

21 May: The BDP declares that Abdullah Öcalan was a leader and not a criminal. This is the beginning of their struggle to rehabilitate him.

27 May: The RPP declares that members of the Constitutional Court had ceased to be judges after judicial reform. Therefore the RPP's application to scrap the controversial new education is not surprising.

29 May: Six retired generals are arrested because of the 'so-called post-modern coup' of 28 February 1997.

3 June: The EU finds PM Erdoğan's description of abortion puzzling. He says: 'every abortion is an Uludere, every abortion is a murder.' Uludere was an incident when smugglers were killed in a bombing raid, mistaken for the PKK.

10 June: Former President Süleyman Demirel defends the February 28 process and says that whatever happened in 1997 was done within the boundary of the law and the constitution.

22 June: A Turkish fighter is shot down by Syria, suggesting that Syria has an air defence capability.

30 July: After an Istanbul Court refuses to release some 65 suspects, including RPP deputies Mehmet Haberal and Mustafa Balbay, the RPP describes Silivri prison, where the Ergenekon was being tried, as a concentration camp.

4 August: The Supreme Military Council (YAŞ) retires 40 generals who are currently under arrest in ongoing trials.

13 August: PM Erdoğan attacks journalists who criticized Foreign Minister Davutoğlu for visiting Myanmar and not focusing on Syria. Erdoğan calls upon the media bosses to dismiss them.

15 August: The defence offers its final arguments in the 'Sledgehammer' case. The CDs that almost everyone agrees are fakes and are the principal part of the prosecution's case are not investigated.

30 September: The court finds 330 military officials guilty of attempting to stage a coup.

9 October: NATO agrees to defend Turkey against Syria.

19 October: Ankara calls on the major powers to intervene in Syria. Davutoğlu says that Turkey will not act alone or without UN authorization.

18 November: The British journalist Gareth Jenkins speaks in the US Congress on the Ergenekon case and the situation in Turkey. He concludes that there is absolutely no proof of the existence of an organization called Ergenekon and that the 5,800-page indictment is full of holes.

28 November: The government lifts the ban on headscarves in the public sphere. School children would also not be required to wear a uniform, a reform criticized by the Education Union.

3 December: The private TV channel, CNBCe, is fined for an episode in which God is taking orders from the devil.

9 December: A soap opera that Erdoğan thinks maligns Sultan Süleyman the Magnificent could lead to a law banning the misrepresentation of historical figures. The JDP proposes such a law.

2013

24 January: PM Erdoğan talks about the peace process with party deputies from the east. The NAP vows to resist peace talks with the PKK. Even the RPP is divided. BDP deputies had already been allowed to visit Öcalan in prison and the second visit is to follow. The JDP also says that Öcalan has changed.

25 January: For the first time, a female lawyer enters court wearing a headscarf.

26 January: The first NATO Patriot battery becomes operational in Turkey under a Dutch unit.

28 January: PM Erdoğan, in Qatar, discusses regional issues, especially Syria.

2 February: A prosecutor demands a sentence of up to 50 years in prison for a former police intelligence chief, Hanefi Avcı, in the ongoing Revolutionary Headquarters probe. In July, he is given 15 years.

3 February: Erdoğan says that EU membership is no longer a must for Turkey.

6 February: The JDP outlines a proposal for a major overhaul of the judiciary, describing it as a reform and not a coup.

12 February: Erdoğan wins 20,000 liras in compensation from the main opposition party leader, Kemal Kılıçdaroğlu, for the latter's use of the word 'traitor' to describe the prime minster in a speech.

13 February: More retired generals are questioned in the 28 February 1997 probe. On the 16 February it is reported that 72 retired generals are behind bars.

18 February: Mehmet Öcalan is to visit his brother Abdullah again, having last visited him on 14 January.

24 February: Chancellor Angela Merkel arrives in Turkey for a two-day visit.

25 February: Through intermediaries Abdullah Öcalan from his island prison calls for the finalization of the peace process in two to three weeks.

27 February: Four retired generals and a colonel who is on active duty are detained and taken to the Ankara Courthouse, in the latest wave of the 28 February 1997 'post-modern' coup investigation.

2 March: The Republican People's Party's (CHP) İzmir deputy and journalist Mustafa Balbay marks his fourth year in jail.

3 March: The fourth judicial package sparks controversy when it arrives in Parliament.

9 March: Erdoğan asks the PKK to lay down its arms and conduct politics in Parliament.

13 March: Reporters Without Borders says that radical reform is needed to end judicial harassment of journalists in Turkey.

13 March: The PKK releases eight Turkish hostages as part of the peace process. The government expects a PKK cease-fire before the Nevruz celebration on 21 March. Abdullah Öcalan is to make his 'historic call' for peace on the same day.

21 March: The PM's adviser, Yalçin Akdoğan says that Öcalan's message matches the spirit of the peace process.

22 March: The PKK in northern Iraq is ordered to halt all actions. The BDP declares that 99 per cent of the Kurdish armed campaign is over. The RPP calls upon the government to unveil negotiations with the PKK.

27 March: Israel apologizes to Turkey for the *Mavi Marmara* incident after Foreign Secretary John Kerry's visits.

3 April: BDP deputies visit Öcalan in prison to discuss the peace process.

8 April: Abdullah Öcalan reiterates his thesis on the creation of a 'Kurdish Democratic Confederation'. It will comprise the Kurds of Iran, Iraq, Syria and Turkey.

10 April: Female deputies are allowed to wear trousers, jackets and suits in Parliament's General Assembly after a change to the legislature's internal regulations.

11 April: Turkey is given UK's know-how about how Good Friday negotiations were conducted with the IRA.

11 April: The fourth judicial package passes into law with critical last-minute changes. President Gül approves the package on 29 April.

15 April: The BDP says that the PKK's withdrawal will be complete by the autumn.

25 April: The PKK will begin to withdraw from Turkey on 8 May. All these are seen as steps towards solving the Kurdish issue.

26 April: PM Erdoğan promises to introduce new measures against the consumption of alcohol. He says that this should not be considered as an obstacle to particular lifestyles of secularism.

28 April: The RPP leader describes the peace process as the first step towards a Greater Kurdistan.

6 May: PM Erdoğan dismisses the Islamist call to reopen Aya Sophia for prayers.

8 May: The RPP begins rallies to spread its 'Democracy Manifesto'.

10 May: Child marriage is still an issue in Turkey.

13 May: PM Erdoğan says that Reyhanlı blasts on the Syrian-Turkish are intended to drag Turkey into a 'bloody swamp' in Syria.

14 May: The first group of withdrawing PKK militants arrive in northern Iraq.

14 May: During his US visit, the Pentagon is to give PM Erdoğan a briefing on Syria.

15 May: The EU socialists tell the RPP leader that Turkey needs a modern and progressive RPP; it is no longer in harmony with today.

16 May: PM Erdoğan has talks with President Obama, focusing on Syria. He delays his trip to Gaza after his talk with Obama.

19 May: Deputy PM Bülent Arınç, who joins Erdoğan's delegation, pays a 'humane visit' to Fethullah Gülen.

24 May: Parliament adopts the alcohol restrictions law, banning sale between 10pm and 6am. Erdoğan cites Article 58 of the Constitution which covers the protection of youth: 'A state will naturally protect its youth, its people from bad habits. Shall we promote it?'

25 May: The company, Diageo, which bought Mey İçki and became the owner of Turkey's biggest rakı brand 'Yeni Rakı' warns that restriction on alcohol would damage Turkey's image.

24 May: PM Erdoğan sues Kılıçdaroğlu for one million lira for comparing him to the Syria's Bashar al-Assad.

28 May: The 'Gezi Park' protests are sparked over attempts to demolish the trees in the only green space in Istanbul. It is, in reality, a protest against the government's plan to construct another shopping mall. PM Erdoğan refuses to back down, saying that the 'decision had been made.'

28 May: The RPP calls for the election barrier to be reduced from 10 to 3 per cent. Two days later, the JDP parliament refuses even to discuss reducing the election threshold.

29 May: Some 324 retired and active-duty officers on trial are sentenced to prison terms ranging from between 13 and 20 years in the Balyoz case. The Ergenekon case is trying 275 suspects, of whom 67 are still under arrest.

30 May: The police fire tear-gas canisters at the Gezi Park demonstrators injuring and hospitalizing many.

2 June: Protesters chant anti-government slogans as the demonstrations in Taksim Square and then throughout Turkey intensify. Violent clashes take place between riot police and tens of thousands of demonstrators.

3 June: On his tour of North Africa, Erdoğan remains defiant against the demonstrations taking place in Istanbul. But in Ankara President Gül, responding to the demonstrations, says that democracy is not just about elections and that a message had been received by authorities. Hours later the police withdraw from Taksim Square.

4 June: Active Deputy PM Bülent Arınç offers to meet protest leaders in a bid to ease tensions. He offers a partial apology and says that 'Our citizens showed their legitimate, logical and righteous reaction at Gezi Park'.

6/7 June: Erdoğan is greeted by a 10,000 'rent-a-crowd' when he arrives at Istanbul airport. He delivers a fiery speech saying, 'These protests that are bordering on illegality must come to an end as of now'.

15 June: Erdoğan holds a mass rally in Ankara. The rally in Istanbul takes place the next day. The decision is taken on 8 June. Meanwhile demonstrations against the JDP government continue throughout Turkey.

Glossary

Ağa	Commander of the janissaries; also title for landlords, especially in eastern Anatolia and region dominated by Kurdish tribes.
Alaylı	Officer who rose through the ranks in the army of Abdülhamid II.
Alevi	Heterodox offshoot of the Shia movement in Turkey, people who venerate Hazret Ali, the son-in-law of the Prophet Muhammad and the fourth caliph.
Ayan	Landed, provincial notables in the Ottoman Empire.
Celali	Mercenaries and peasants who rebelled against the Ottoman state in the late sixteenth and early seventeenth centuries.
Cemaat	Congregation or community of Muslims.
Dev-Genc	Turkish acronym for the Federation of the Revolutionary Youth of Turkey.
Devşirme	Method of collecting Christian youths in the Ottoman Empire for service to the Palace or as soldiers.
Dev-Sol and Dev-Yol	Turkish acronyms for the 'Revolutionary Left' and 'Revolutionary Path' organizations.
Divan	The government of the Ottoman Empire presided over by the grand vizier.
Ezan	The Muslim call to prayer.
Fetva	A legal opinion delivered by the religious head in the Ottoman Empire, legitimizing actions of the sultan.
Gazi	Title adopted by early Ottoman leader, meaning that they were Muslims fighting for Islam.
Halk	Term for the 'people'.

Harem	The private quarters of a household where access was restricted usually to family members.
İrade	Sultan's or governmental decree; also 'will' as in 'national will' or *milli irade*.
Janissaries	Elite infantry usually recruited through the *devşirme* system.
Jihad	Holy war; but also the individual Muslim's struggle against evil and temptation.
Kadı	A Muslim judge.
Kaza	Administrative unit governed by a *kadı*.
Kanun	Law passed by the sultan as opposed to a Sharia law. But a *kanun* was not to violate the Sharia.
Kul	Servitors, usually recrited through the *devşirme*.
Laiklik	The state's control of religion as opposed to secularism which implies the separation of state and religion.
Medrese	School or college where the *ülema* were trained in Islamic knowledge. In the late Ottoman Empire *Mekteps* were established to teach secular subjects.
Meşveret	The principle of consultation in Islam and therefore said to constitute a proto-democratic practice.
Mektepli	An officer who had been trained in the secular academy as opposed to the *alaylı* who had risen through the ranks.
Millet, Milli, Milliyetçi	Term applied to a religious community but over time came to mean 'nation' (*millet*), 'national' (*milli*) and 'nationalist' (*milliyetçi*).
Milletvekili	Term for member of the assembly in Turkey, elected as 'representative of the nation' and not of his constituency.
Milli irade	'National will' or the 'will of the people'.
Muhtesib	Officer in charge of regulating the market in Ottoman times.
Mufti	Religious official who issued the *fetva*.
Reis-ul kuttub	Official in charge of foreign affairs in the period after 1826; precursor of the foreign minister.
Ser'asker'	Commander of the army who replaced in 1826 the *ağa* of the janissaries when the janissaries were destroyed.
Sharia	Islamic law derived from the Quran and the traditions and practices of the Prophet Muhammad, as well as the juridical commentaries of the ulema.
Shiism	The minority denomination in Islam, the majority being Sunnism. They were the followers of Ali, the fourth caliph.
Sipahis	Ottoman cavalry provided by holders of timars to serve in the sultan's campaigns.
Şeyhülislam	Head of the *ülema* who after 1826 became part of the sultan's administration.
Timar	A prebend granted by the sultan in return for military service.

Tanzimat	The period of reform, 1839–1876.
Ülema	Doctors of Islamic jurisprudence, the body whose task it was to see that the sultan did not violate the Sharia.
Vakf	Pious foundation or endowment.
Valide sultan	Mother of the reigning sultan who exercised considerable influence on the government in the late sixteenth and seventeenth centuries.
Vatan	Country or father/motherland as a source of loyalty and patriotism.

Index

Note: page numbers in *italics* refer to maps

X

JUV
FIC

Reuter, Bjarne B.

Buster's world

e. 1

$12.95

DATE			
MAY	1990		

Blackstone Branch

4904 S. Lake Park Ave.

Chicago, Illinois 60615

Buster's World

Buster's World

★ BJARNE REUTER ★

translated by
Anthea Bell

E. P. DUTTON   NEW YORK

Frontispiece by Paul O. Zelinsky

Library of Congress Cataloging-in-Publication Data

Reuter, Bjarne B.
  Buster's world.

  Translation of: Busters verden.
  Summary: Buster's magic tricks get him in and out
of trouble.
  [1. Magic tricks—Fiction]   I. Title.
  ISBN 0–525–44475–0
PZ7.R3259Bu   1989   [Fic]   89–11919
                                             CIP
                                             AC

First published in the United States 1989 by E. P. Dutton,
a division of Penguin Books USA Inc.

Originally entitled *Busters Verden* and published in 1980
by Branner og Korch, Copenhagen, Denmark.

Designer: Alice Lee Groton
Printed in U.S.A.   First American Edition
ISBN 0–525–44475–0   10 9 8 7 6 5 4 3 2 1

Contents

The Power of Buster's Biceps

The whole thing started when they discovered that he'd brought a dish towel to school instead of a regular towel.

It was down in the locker room, after gym. He had already messed up two penalty kicks during soccer, hitting Mr. Olsen, the gym teacher, in the pit of the stomach so hard that his whistle went flying through the air.

"Hey, look at that jerk fooling around with a dish towel!" yelled Hans, and that set the warm bodies of all the other boys in motion. They jumped up and down, shaking and laughing.

"A dish towel, that's what it is, a dish towel!" scoffed Eric, parading past Buster mockingly with his own towel twisted into a damp rope.

"Our towels were all in the wash," shouted

1

Buster, and then he ignored his classmates, just as he did when they laughed at his brown rubber-soled shoes and his cutoff corduroy pants.

"What'll you give me for Buster's moldy old underpants?" shouted Hans, holding up the grayish garment by his fingertips.

Wild yells of delight echoed back and forth, rebounding from the hard tiled walls onto the shivering gooseflesh of the boys' bare bodies.

"Give those back, you big, fat, slimy pig!" spat Buster, making a grab for his underpants.

"Hey, look at him, look at him!" shouted Eric, slapping Buster's bottom with his towel. Within two minutes, all Buster's clothes had been tied up in a bundle that went flying from boy to boy. While their owner ran after first one boy and then another, the rest of them went on getting dressed, so that his own nakedness became more and more embarrassing.

"Give my things back!" he shouted. "I'm freezing."

"Look at his wobbly weenie!" called Jens, grinning gleefully as he retreated into a corner.

"You just shut up, Jens!" said Buster furiously. "Wait till I get my hands on you—I'll pull your thing out root and all!"

The other boys roared with laughter.

"Going to do the gorilla act, Buster?" shouted Eric above the other voices. "Do the gorilla act and you can have your clothes back."

"Yes, yes!" yelled the others.

"Promise, Eric?" asked Buster, his eyes large and wide as he looked up at tall, thin Eric, who was holding the bundle of clothes high above his head.

"With the rubber teeth and everything!" shouted Hans, getting all excited.

"Nothing doing!" said Buster. "No rubber teeth—it takes me two days to get that stuff out."

He turned his back on them.

Eric threw the bundle to Hans. "Too bad— you'll just have to go into class with a bare pink bottom, then," he sighed.

Buster got out the erasers for his rubber teeth.

He hunched his back. His arms looked ten centimeters longer. He bent his legs at the knees. Before they knew it, he had pushed his damp hair up like a brush and quickly fitted

3

two erasers into his mouth, in front of his own teeth and between his upper and lower lips. The transformation took place so quickly that although most of his classmates had already seen it a dozen times, it still surprised them. There before them stood a real live gorilla, growling with suppressed anger, steam rising from its bright red body. It wasn't crazy Buster standing there anymore.

To start with, the gorilla just walked around, head bent, arms swinging. Audibly gnashing its teeth, it swayed from side to side, apparently paying no attention to the giggling audience. But then all hell broke loose. With a deafening yell, the ape went for Verner, who howled with genuine fright and tried to escape into the showers as the monster grabbed his hair.

The chase began: The monster with its huge, long arms was everywhere, now scratching a face, now shaking two other boys off its back; no one dared come too close, yet no one wanted to be too far away from the weird creature either.

But just as the ape decided it would be a good idea to stand on a rolled-up mat and bellow, "Me King Kong, me just like old Olsen!" Mr. Olsen himself came into the locker room.

Unfortunately, the ape, or rather Buster, had his back to Mr. Olsen and carried on just as before, although all the others quickly quieted down.

"Me hairy ape, me got big hairy chest, me got the biggest weenie in the school, me Great Ape Olsen, me . . . me . . ."

Mr. Olsen and Buster looked at each other. Buster straightened up.

"Here we go again." Olsen shook his head wearily. "Take those erasers out of your mouth and put your clothes on. The rest of you can go."

Mr. Olsen locked up the apparatus room while the others ran upstairs, shouting. Buster spat the erasers out. Mr. Olsen watched him in silence. Then it came. "When and if you're through with that, come upstairs and close the door behind you. And you can mop the shower floor dry."

"But last time I—"

"So you did, Buster Oregon Mortensen, so you did—and what sort of an animal act were you putting on last time? Let me think. . . ."

Mr. Olsen gazed at the ceiling, lost in thought.

"A hyena," muttered Buster.

"So you were, Buster, a hyena, so you were—don't forget the floor, all right?" And Mr. Olsen went off.

Buster put his jeans on. He fished out the socks he had rolled up and tucked inside his wooden clogs. He smiled. They were terrific socks. Red, yellow, green, blue, and black stripes, with a karate symbol on each stripe. They were brand new. Bought yesterday. He was really supposed to have had a new pair of pants, because the old pair stopped somewhere between his knees and his ankles. But since a new pair would cost nearly a hundred and fifty Danish kroner, and his father had just bought a new magic trick, Buster got the bright idea of buying long socks instead.

"Buster," his father had said, "you're a genius." Buster had smiled.

"We'd like the best pair of socks you've got for this young man," his father had said when they went into the shop, feeling rather awkward.

"What's a genius?" Buster had asked afterward.

"A genius, son, is someone who'd rather have a pair of multicolored socks than a pair of pants that's just one color, thus saving more than a hundred kroner."

Then they had gone straight home to Hope Street, where his father had showed Buster his latest trick. He brought bright yellow balls out of his mouth, twenty-seven of them in all.

"As performed by the Great Osman from Osmania!" his father had announced, throwing the leopard skin from his old Strong Man act over his shoulders. . . .

Buster sighed and inspected his own muscles. If he clenched his fist, he could feel the pull at his elbow. If he moved his little finger, the muscles in his upper arm rippled.

"Buster the Great!" growled Buster, standing in front of the mirror with his upper arm tensed. "If the ceiling wasn't in the way, my colossal biceps would go up and up and up to the art room on the top floor," he muttered to himself. He climbed up on the bench, slinging his Hawaiian shirt around his shoulders.

"Ladies and gentlemen, you are now about to see Buster Oregon Mortensen shake four stories of a Copenhagen school with the power of his right biceps—step up, step up, hear the terrified children beg for mercy."

He was abruptly interrupted by the school bell ringing. Last lesson. Danish, with Mrs. Hansen, their class teacher, whom they all called by her first name, Rosa, sometimes adding Doza, which more or less rhymed, for fun. Better get the rest of his clothes on, quick. Darn, there went his money rolling all over the floor. As he picked it up, he recited his mother's shopping list: "Potatoes, half a pound of chopped meat (veal and pork), three tomatoes, an elephant (a large bottle of ale), ten cigarettes (Cecil brand), half a liter of light cream (not whipping cream, remember, and make sure it's fresh)."

He could hear the others clattering around in the classrooms overhead. Buster stood perfectly still and gazed into the mirror. His hair stood out in all directions. His large, round, pale blue eyes stared straight back at him. Then his reflection grinned. Either his mouth had stretched—maybe there'd been razor blades on his harmonica when he was little— or he had missed out on his fair share of teeth. Every other tooth seemed to be missing. However, those teeth he did have were large and square.

"Doza Rosa, here I come. . . . Doza Rosa Lazy-Daisy . . ."

* * *

After school he went downstairs behind Hans and Eric, who were going to play with Eric's walkie-talkie radio set. Buster was just about to point out that they needed a third person for their game when he suddenly saw his little sister, Ingeborg, standing all by herself in the playground. It was pouring rain out, and she was soaked. He put his satchel over his head and went down the steps to her.

"What are you doing here, standing out in the rain staring at nothing?"

Ingeborg looked down at the ground, where the raindrops were bouncing merrily. Eric and Hans, now some way off, disappeared on their bikes.

"It's that stupid Lars," she muttered.

"What Lars? Where is he?"

"Outside the school gates. He's been after me all day. First he kept calling me Limping Lizzie. Then he came and hit me."

Buster looked at his watch. He bent down and picked up a stone.

"Here, take this, Ingeborg. I don't have time to walk you home. I've got to go shopping."

"What am I supposed to do with a stone?"

"Throw it at him."

Ingeborg took the stone and went off toward the school gates. Buster watched her go. Even though she had a built-up shoe, you could still see that one leg was six centimeters shorter than the other. And now this rain . . . "Ingeborg, wait a minute. . . ." He ran after her. "Where is he?"

She pointed to the playing field, where several children were standing around.

Buster took the stone. "Okay, now call him," whispered Buster, and ducked behind the outdoor toilets.

"Call him? What shall I say?"

"Just shout, 'Come here, Lousy Lars!' "

Ingeborg stared straight ahead of her. Then she called, "Come here, Lousy Lars!"

Buster nodded and got the stone ready. "Is he coming, Ingeborg?"

"I think so. Can't you hear his moped?"

The stone in Buster's hand suddenly seemed very heavy. "Moped? You don't mean this Lars is one of those big fifteen year olds?"

"The kids say he's sixteen," said Ingeborg.

★ ★ ★

Buster was in Toilet Stall Number One, which was lucky. It had a door you could lock. Outside, he heard four slaps.

"And now get lost, Limping Lizzie!" said a harsh voice.

Two minutes later a moped sputtered away, and Buster came out.

"Ingeborg," he said, emerging into the drizzle, "do you know where Lousy Lars lives?"

Ingeborg sniffed and nodded.

"Then I'll show you a magic trick this evening, when it's dark." Buster nodded importantly, and put his arm around Ingeborg's shoulders.

They went toward Frederikssund Road. It was the month when the lilac blossoms smell so wonderful that just half their fragrance would really be enough. . . . But Buster did not discover that until later.

The Sleeping City

Gradually the rain stopped. The soft, fresh summer wind wafted in to Buster and Ingeborg through the attic window. They had just gotten into bed.

Their little room with its sloping walls was above the living room. It was not really meant to be lived in at all, which was why it contained only two rickety dining room chairs (painted different shades of horrible pink) and a monstrous worm-eaten bed that was too small for a grown-up but too good to be thrown away. The fourth piece of furniture stood beside the bed. It was a small white chest of drawers with one drawer that didn't open unless you knew its secret. This was Ingeborg's private drawer, and she was the only person who knew what she kept in it. How-

12

ever, Buster had once gotten her to reveal that it contained, among other things, a very beautiful old music box that played a soft tune when you opened the lid, while a little ballerina pirouetted on one leg in front of a mirror.

Buster and Ingeborg had shared this attic bedroom ever since they were four and three. In winter they lay with their heads under the slope of the wall, and then, when the snow was thawing, they could hear it slip off the roof. In summer, however, they lay with their heads at the other end of the bed, so that they could look up into the dark blue sky, which, now that the rain had stopped, stretched high and clear above them and was thickly sprinkled with twinkling stars.

"Why don't you take your socks off?" whispered Ingeborg, without taking her eyes off the window.

"Why are you whispering?" Buster asked.

"Because the stars are so beautiful," she said. "Aren't you all sweaty with your socks on?"

"No. Anyway, they've got karate symbols on them. See that big star above the three little ones?"

Ingeborg nodded. "I feel kind of scared

when I look at the dark sky. Do you, Buster?"

"The sky's a hole," said Buster. "A big hole."

"A hole in what?"

"What do you mean, in what? The sky's just a hole."

"So what are the stars?"

"The stars . . . well, they're kind of . . . kind of like bubbles in water."

They lay there for some time, until they heard their father turn off the radio news. Their mother had gone to bed long ago. She had to be up early in the morning.

"Dad and Mr. Larsen have mended their old accordions," said Ingeborg. "They were saying that when it gets warm enough they'll go around the streets playing and singing again, like when they were young."

Mr. Larsen was their neighbor. He was a disabled pensioner, at least sixty years old. His wife, Mrs. Larsen, was always in bed. You hardly ever saw her out in the street. Sometimes she was taken away in an ambulance, but she always came home again a few days later. Buster often sat talking with her in the afternoon. The light is at its loveliest then, Mrs. Larsen told him. In winter it's delicate and blue, but in summer it's full and yellow.

Mrs. Larsen always wore a hand-knitted pale pink jacket, tied at the neck with two strings that had little fuzzy balls at the ends. Buster thought Mrs. Larsen's eyes and teeth looked too big for her. But she knew a great many fairy tales and other stories; it was as if she could paint stories in the air with her long, white fingers. He also suspected her of having given Ingeborg the secret music box. Why it had to be Ingeborg who got it was a mystery to Buster. Ingeborg had never done anything but sit there blowing a plastic whistle she had gotten out of a Cracker Jack box. As if that counted for anything. He, Buster, on the other hand, did conjuring tricks for Mrs. Larsen. Once he even managed to make all her pill bottles disappear into a hat without her noticing.

"The pills are all gone," he had said. "Conjured away!"

"Dear me, Mr. Oregon," whispered Mrs. Larsen, "are they really? That's terrible! I can't do without my pills."

"Buster Oregon Mortensen can make anything disappear by magic," announced Buster, in an impressive singsong voice. He had put his pointed magic hat on specially for Mrs.

Larsen that day. "Now I say the secret magic spell, and meanwhile you can look for one of those candies, the ones with nice fillings, and then I'll magic you all better, Mrs. Larsen."

The candy had tasted very good. But even though Mrs. Larsen said she felt much, much better, she had still stayed in bed.

Buster looked at Ingeborg.

"If Dad and Mr. Larsen do go around singing and playing this summer, I want to go too," he said firmly. "I'll be the one who collects the money."

"Do you think I could come as well?" said Ingeborg.

"Well, you never know. . . . We'll see," said Buster, getting up and balancing on the bed so that he could look over the rooftops. And he could see a long way. Over Bellahøj and Utterslev Park. The city lay far, far away, sleeping like a giant scrap heap. Ingeborg propped her head between her arms. Her long hair smelled of shampoo. It began growing up high on her forehead, so that she had a smooth, domed brow, which gave her face a demure and wise expression.

Buster looked at her. "You look like an angel," he said.

Ingeborg giggled. "That's because my hair's grown so long. Or it's because you've been looking at all those stars."

"Perhaps you *are* an angel," Buster went on, sticking to his point, and he sat down on the bed again. "Without knowing it."

"Oh, do shut up. I couldn't be, not with these legs."

No, too bad, that's true, thought Buster, but he didn't say so.

"I did once know a girl who really was an angel, though," he began after a bit.

Ingeborg lay back expectantly and pulled the covers up.

"And for ages, you see, she just lived at home, and went to school, and went shopping for her mother, and she was perfectly normal, like ordinary people."

"Did she have wings?"

"Oh, let me finish, will you—no, of course she didn't have wings. She had legs and arms and . . . no, wait, I forgot to tell you that part of the story. She only had one arm. That's important. Just the one. But she still went to school, the same as you and me. . . ."

"Did she get teased because of her arm?"

"Everyone always gets teased about something, Ingeborg. Yes, they used to say, 'Hi there, one-armed bandit!' and 'Give us a hug, Sophie!' because Sophie was the girl's name, and some of them used to ask her, 'Do you clap with your feet?' And other people asked, 'Can you walk on your hands?' And—"

"Yes, all right, so then what happened?"

"Well, one day when she was at home, just hanging up the dish towel—and it was evening, an evening like this—she was standing outside on the balcony, you see, a big balcony with flowers on it, and stone statues, and she was all by herself—and then suddenly she noticed. It was as if the stars and the hole in the sky, the deep, deep hole in the sky, were beginning to pull her their way. And she got a tickly feeling in her stomach. And then she flew."

"Flew?"

"Yes, she flew far away. She'd turned into an angel. And from that day on nobody ever teased her about her arm again."

Ingeborg turned around and looked at him, hard. "Then she did get wings."

"No, she definitely didn't. She did not get wings. She flew all by herself."

"With just one arm?"

"Well, of course she flew with just one arm, Ingeborg. That's why they didn't tease her anymore, don't you get it?"

Ingeborg wrinkled her nose. Buster turned his back to her. He felt tired. They could hear a plane in the distance.

"Buster," said Ingeborg, "how come you put all that sugar into Lars' gas tank?"

Buster cleared his throat. "Well, it was mainly because . . ."

"Can't he ride his moped anymore now?"

There was a suppressed chuckle from Buster.

"I mean, will he have to take it to the garage?"

"Take it to the garage?" said Buster. "He can take the stupid thing straight to the dump!" Buster was enjoying himself immensely.

Ingeborg smiled and pulled the covers right up to her nose. "Well, it serves Lars right," she said to herself.

* * *

Buster went to sleep soon afterward, but Ingeborg lay awake looking up at the dark sky. And when her father began to play his old accordion downstairs, very quietly, it was a long time before she could get to sleep.

She had put a little sprig of lilac in a glass on the white chest of drawers. Every time Buster breathed out, his breath set the flowers in motion. And every time he breathed in, he breathed the scent of the lilac.

Ingeborg smiled and closed the attic window.

3

Some Conjuring Tricks

Sleepily, Ingeborg made her way downstairs to the living room. Her mother was sitting at the dining table in her blue bathrobe. She seemed tired. Her head was bent forward, as if she were intent on the plastic tablecloth. She held a cigarette in the hand supporting her forehead. The color of her own pale hair showed under her chestnut tint, and her part looked like a cowpath.

"We're out of cornflakes," she murmured. "Help yourself to coffee, but keep quiet." She yawned, looking as if she had a bad taste in her mouth. "He's still asleep," she added.

Ingeborg went cautiously over to the bedroom door and peeped in. Her father was lying across the bed, fully dressed. His breathing sounded like a horse snorting.

She heard the shuffle of her mother's slippers behind her.

"Pretty sight, isn't he, Ingeborg? Take a good look—that's where the last of the household money went. Ten large ales and half a liter of spirits. I give up!" Her mother shuffled back to her chair. "But otherwise everything's just fine!"

Ingeborg poured herself a cup of coffee. "Don't we have any money left at all?"

"A little. Fifty kroner. I hid it in the kitchen canister. You mustn't show him where it is. You know what he's like when he's this way, but you mustn't show him where it is."

Ingeborg shook her head.

"Is Buster up yet?" her mother asked.

"He's putting on his conjuring things."

"His conjuring things?"

"Yes, he says he wants to surprise the class. He's got his red shirt on—you know, the one Mr. Larsen gave him—and the belt with the seven secret signs. I think he's planning to do the trick with the strips of colored paper—you know the one, where he pulls all those strips of paper out of his mouth."

Her mother nodded, smiling. "I think I know someone rather like him!"

Just then Buster came downstairs. Sure

enough, he was wearing his conjuring outfit.

"And here before you," he announced, "the great Buster Oregon . . ."

"Ssh, you'll wake Dad," hissed Ingeborg, giggling.

Buster sat down.

"What on earth's the matter with your mouth?" His mother pointed at his lips.

"Strips of paper," mumbled Buster. "Inside."

His mother put her cigarette out and examined him closely. "Just when is this performance to take place?"

"Second lesson. That's our class's free period."

"So will you be sitting all through math with your mouth full of paper? In those clothes?"

Buster shook his head. "I'm going to wear a sweater over the magic shirt. I want it to be a surprise."

Their mother stood up, went into the kitchen, and handed them their sandwiches to take to school.

"Are you going to the dairy about that delivery job this afternoon, Buster?"

"Yes," said Buster.

"You really feel sure you can manage it?"

"Of course I can."

Ingeborg got up. It was time to go. Buster

23

wriggled into a sweater. Soon afterward they were on their way.

Buster was late for math, as usual, because he still had two problems to do. Today, however, not even multiplication could get him down. Today he was going to show all these boneheads what Buster Oregon Mortensen was really like.

And it did look as if his plan was going to work. He sat right through math, rigid and silent with expectation, although he was rather uncomfortable in the thick sweater, with his mouth full of strips of paper.

The free period came at last, and Buster felt himself squirming with excitement. But instead of their own class teacher Rosa, Viggi came to substitute for her, carrying some skinny bats and balls. Two minutes later the whole class was on its way to the playing field for a long-ball game. So much for Buster Oregon Mortensen and his talents.

He went slowly down the stairs. His gums were beginning to bother him. Then he spotted two little boys standing outside room 18, staring into space.

"Well, well," he said condescendingly, "and what have we here? Got kicked out of class, did you?"

The two dunces grinned proudly. They knew that weirdo Buster Mortensen. He once hoisted a homemade flag up the flagpole on his birthday. The flag said, in red letters, Happy Birthday Buster Oregon Mortensen!

"Like to see the hardest conjuring trick in the world?" he whispered. The little boys nodded eagerly, and in a flash the thick sweater had been discarded and lay in the corner, and Buster's bright red magic shirt was lighting up the dark corridor. "Ha-ha!" shouted Buster three times, putting his pointed hat on his head.

"Now, ladies and gentlemen, watch my fingers carefully, keep looking very hard, see for yourselves there's nothing funny going on. I am now about to pull out all my brightly colored intestines before your very eyes! That's right, I'm going to pull them up and out through my own mouth—yes, you will now see seventeen and a half meters of my insides emerge through my slavering jaws! Watch out, here comes the first bunch!"

A red paper strip came into view between Buster's lips.

The little boys stared in amazement.

Buster pulled and pulled. The strip got longer and longer.

"Oh, my tummy, my tummy!" groaned the conjuror most impressively, failing to see the figure that had stationed itself behind him, hands clasped behind its back. Buster took the alarm in the little boys' eyes for the effect of his terrifying performance. Not until he had pulled two meters of red paper out of his mouth, moaning as he pulled, did he notice the principal, who just stood there staring at him, rocking slightly on his feet.

Buster tried to stuff the strip back in again. The principal looked icily at his pointed hat.

"What are you doing, Buster Mortensen?"

"Pulling out his guts," one of the little dunces began to explain.

Buster tried a tiny smile.

"Aren't you supposed to be in a class?"

Buster nodded, finding it difficult to express himself more clearly while he had a long red strip hanging out of his mouth.

"Come up to my office." The principal turned his back on Buster and strode away.

* * *

Buster had been up to the principal's office twice before. The first time was when he and Eric had installed a microphone behind the sofa in the teachers' room and linked it up to a loudspeaker in the bicycle shed. Quite a number of children had paid good money to hear Mr. Christensen the art teacher telling Mrs. Hartmann about the boil on his behind. The second time was when he put a worm in Rosa's briefcase.

The principal stood with his back to Buster, acting as if Buster weren't there. Buster knew this was one of the principal's tricks. The principal liked to make people feel small and insignificant, and then he could deal with them more easily.

Even though Buster knew this, he still had the feeling that he was getting smaller and smaller as he stood in front of the big desk. Up here in the office it was very quiet. The other children in their classrooms seemed very far away. Perhaps the principal had had his office soundproofed. Buster didn't know. In any case, he had his work cut out for him, hiding the long red strip under his magic shirt. He couldn't tear the strip, because then he could never use it again.

The principal turned around, looking grave. Something like a thunderstorm appeared to be brewing in his face.

Buster thought it might be a good idea to take off his pointed hat.

"And perhaps you could remove that strip of

27

paper from your mouth too," said the principal very quietly.

Buster pulled out a meter of red paper, which he carefully wound up.

The principal looked at him. "If you have any more paper in your mouth, wouldn't it be sensible to take it all out while you're at it?"

Buster put a finger down his throat and fished out two meters of green paper. Next came three meters of orange paper and two meters of blue paper. The principal's jaw dropped. He hardly noticed when his secretary put her head around the door to say there was coffee in the thermos. Altogether, Buster pulled seventeen meters eighty-six centimeters of colored paper out of his mouth, and it was roughly five minutes before the last meter emerged.

The telephone on the big shiny desk rang.

"Yes, Schlutter speaking," barked the principal, never taking his eyes off Buster. "Oh, good morning—the Education Department there? Yes, yes . . . the same to you, and yes, it's about the extension. . . ."

Here the principal stopped, for at that moment a white egg was coming out of Buster's mouth.

"Er . . . yes, yes, please forgive the interruption, it was just . . . oh, good Lord!"

The principal waved Buster out of his office as a second egg appeared. Buster left, holding the egg in his mouth. But as he went into the room outside the office, he remembered his pointed hat and turned back for it.

The principal was now sitting with his back to the door, talking into the telephone. Buster didn't want to disturb him, but on the other hand he hadn't had a chance to do his best trick yet, the one where he put a nylon stocking over his head and it looked as if he were sticking ten knitting needles in his ears. He decided to practice it, so he would be ready when the principal finished his phone call. He whipped the nylon stocking onto his head, and he had three knitting needles halfway into his ears when the principal put the receiver down and turned around.

Buster smiled through the stocking in a friendly way, thinking this would be sure to pacify the principal. However, the principal, whose nerves were not strong, really became unglued at the sight of the smiling Buster. He bellowed like a bull calf in spring, and tripped and fell sideways over his office chair, which was on casters. It rolled him over to the sofa, where he knocked a vase of ten tulips on the floor. At this point the secretary, the coffee lady, and the remains of a part-time substitute came charging through the door.

"Get him out of here, get him out of here!" screeched the principal, and while the coffee lady went to fetch Buster's math teacher, the office staff gave notice.

So Buster ended up with Mr. Martinsen, the math teacher, in the little room where you found yourself if you were stupid or rude and things didn't go your way. Here he learned that the principal was an excellent old gentleman who had sacrificed his time and talent to the school all his life, and now it was Buster's fault he had a migraine headache. Not to mention the fact that the secretary had spilled coffee all over her new skirt.

Buster said he'd only been doing a few conjuring tricks.

"I'll teach you tricks, Buster Mortensen!" roared the math teacher, bringing his slide rule down on the desk so hard that the indicator fell out of it. "You can't add two and two either, can you? How do you see your future? Yes, well, of course you can't answer that one, can you, but you can stick knitting needles into your head and take strips of paper and eggs out of your mouth; you can do that all right. We have enough unemployed already. Isn't your father out of a job himself?"

"My father is a conjuror and street singer," muttered Buster.

"Exactly. There we have it, don't we? Heading the same way yourself, eh, Buster? Well, my young friend, if you don't pull yourself together pretty quick, you will certainly end up in . . . good Lord, I don't know *where* you'll end up. I don't suppose they could even use you to sweep the streets."

The math teacher said a great deal more, too, and by the time he let Buster go, Buster was feeling really lousy. What *was* going to become of him when he grew up? Well, thank goodness they couldn't use him to sweep the streets. That was something, anyway. He might as well go home now, although he was supposed to have two periods of General Knowledge. They were studying the Ice Age and drawing snowdrifts in Jutland. Imagine that: stuck there drawing snowdrifts in summer, when the sweet-smelling lilacs were out and the birds were scuffling about in the sand!

Buster knew a place on Brookwood Road that smelled as sweet as if the whole summer came from that spot. It was probably the scent of some bush or hedge or tree, but anyway it was wonderful. And that wasn't all. Just where the scent was strongest stood a big yellow house with white shutters. It looked strangely closed up, as if it were asleep. But one day, as he had been rather dreamily breathing in the wonderful odor, smelling hard, he had suddenly heard a window open. It was as if the sound fell down to him, and for a moment he had forgotten to inhale, because a girl with curly hair had appeared at an upstairs window. Luckily he had had his Hawaiian shirt on that day, so that the girl had noticed him right away. And she had spoken to him, even though she was at least twelve.

"What are you doing?" she asked.

"Smelling," said Buster, taking such a deep breath that his rib cage visibly expanded.

The girl laughed. "What are you smelling?"

"There's such a lovely scent here. Can't you smell it?"

The girl leaned well out of the window, breathing in deeply too. Buster saw that she was wearing a white dress.

"Yes, maybe," she said. "Perhaps."

Buster sort of hoped she would stay at the window, but then again he was not quite sure what to say to a girl like this, with curly hair and a white dress, in the middle of all the sweet fragrance. That was probably why he told her that the shirt had come straight from Hawaii and that he had been there himself and bought it there. It was a lie. The shirt had really been bought in Husum, and Buster had never in his life been further than Great Heddinge.

Later, whenever he thought of the girl, he was sorry he had shown off like that. His boastfulness could be why the girl never again appeared at the window when he came to the place where you could smell the wonderful scent.

And now he wondered whether to go for a little walk down Brookwood Road, just to get a whiff of the air there. But he had to go to the dairy. . . .

On the way to the dairy he made up a little song:

I like it in the summertime,
when flowers smell sweet I sing this rhyme,
but now my conjuring tricks must stop
because I'm going to the shop.
It's a shame.
Just go on growing, flowers, all the same.

4

Full Moon

"Ever done anything like this before? You don't look all that big to me."

"I'm small for my age," said Buster, removing his pointed hat.

"There's sometimes heavy stuff to be carried, you know."

The owner of the dairy was tall and fat and wore a white coat with red and blue marks from his ball-point pen on the breast pocket.

"I work out every evening, Mr. Jensen."

"Work out? What for?"

"So I'll get good strong muscles. My dad used to be the Great Osman, and he could lift a ball weighing more than two hundred kilograms."

Mr. Jensen looked at his wife, who was very fat too, but not much taller than Buster if he stood on tiptoe, which he had been doing ever since he entered the dairy.

"Do your parents know?" asked Mrs. Jensen. "We don't want any trouble."

"Oh, they know all about it," said Buster firmly.

"Then it's okay. You start at three on Friday. Have you ever ridden a delivery bike before?"

"Yes, often," Buster lied.

Mr. Jensen found a piece of paper. "What's your name?"

"Buster," said Buster.

"Yes, and what else? That's not your real name, is it?"

"Yes, it is. I'm Buster. Buster Oregon Mortensen."

"Buster what?"

"Oregon Mortensen," said Buster, speaking very slowly and very clearly this time.

"You a foreigner or something?" asked Mr. Jensen suspiciously.

"No," said Buster, smiling proudly, "but my grandfather was Oregon the Cannon King. I'm sure you've heard of him, Mr. Jensen."

"No," said Mr. Jensen. "Never."

"He used to perform in Husum, right opposite the community gardens, the ones called Bellevue."

"I know what the community gardens are called—we used to have a little plot there ourselves before we started this dairy," growled Mr. Jensen. But right then Mrs. Jensen came out from behind the counter. She was giving Buster a very strange look.

"Oh, I remember your grandfather very well," she said. "I was born right behind the Husum cinema."

"In a flimsy place with walls like cardboard," grunted Mr. Jensen.

"He was a tall, handsome man with a big black moustache."

"That's right," said Buster, beaming, "that's right. And he always wore his medals when he was shot into the air."

"I bet he made the medals himself," said Mr. Jensen crossly, pushing the oldest cartons of milk to the front so that they would be sold first.

"I first saw your grandfather at the Laredo Tivoli. Goodness, that must have been in the thirties! I was only about six, but my word, he looked fine, Oregon did! Tell me, is he dead, Buster?"

Buster nodded, looking sad.

"He jumped off the roof of the nursing home where they took him."

36

"Ah, dear me." Mrs. Jensen sighed.

"His last flight," quipped Mr. Jensen darkly, from the room behind the shop, where he had been able to hear this conversation. "Well, off you go now, lad. We've got better things to do than stand around chatting about you and your funny old grandpa."

Buster hurried to the door.

"Mrs. Jensen," he whispered, "shall I bring a picture of my grandfather on Friday?"

Mrs. Jensen nodded vigorously and waved good-bye in a way that made Buster feel like pulling strips of paper out of his mouth. He contented himself with just putting his pointed hat on. Then he went down Frederikssund Road to the marketplace.

He loved this time of day, when the shadows of buildings, trees, and parked cars grew long and began to wander. The day seemed striped now, as the light turned yellow and orange. Faces looked more satisfied, and sometimes, however loud the roar of the traffic, however fast and furiously people did their shopping, sending sharp, clattering sounds drifting out of the stores—sometimes there would be a sudden lull in all the noise. A strange silence, when all at once you could hear a little bird in the chestnut tree, or a flock of gulls wheeling above the park. Then people would raise their heads and look at one another, until suddenly the whole thing started up all over again. Buster loved the long, pleasant summer afternoons! Not that summer mornings were to be despised. It was just that they were so uncertain, so pale pink and delicate, like something that wasn't quite ready yet.

Buster got a move on. He wanted to get home and tell Ingeborg about his new job, not to mention the splendid bike with the delivery basket. He rushed down Hope Street, whirling around all the trees, until he reached the small gray building and the even smaller garden with all the dandelions and the red bench in it.

Ingeborg was sitting there, looking through a piece of colored glass.

"Abracadabra hocus-pocus—I got the job in the dairy!" shouted Buster, trying to vault the garden gate. Unfortunately, he didn't jump high enough and ended up landing on the sidewalk with a tremendous thud.

"You'd better not go upstairs," said Ingeborg, when he was on his feet again. "Dad's furious because I won't tell him where the rest of the household money is."

"Is he drunk?"

Ingeborg put the piece of glass in her pocket. "Worse. He's got a hangover."

"Poor Dad." Buster sighed, sitting down.

"Yes. Poor Buster, too," said Ingeborg calmly.

He looked at her.

She nodded gravely. "Lars is after you."

"Lars who?"

"Lars who has the moped, of course."

"But how does he know it was me?"

"From that kid in your class—Jens. He saw us when we went over there in the evening with the bag of sugar."

Buster adjusted his pointed hat. This called for serious thought.

"So I'm in trouble, right, Ingeborg?"

"Jens says Lars will strangle you when he gets his hands on you."

Buster stared into space. The street was quiet. Apart from a lawn mower, all he could hear was his own breathing.

"What are we going to do, Ingeborg?"

His little sister stretched her non-matching legs out in front of her. "Get Jens to change his mind and tell Lars it wasn't you."

Buster looked at her. Then he gave her a big

kiss on the cheek. "I tell you what, Ingeborg, you're a genius! We'll give Jens such a thumping his own mother won't know him."

"That won't work, Buster," said Ingeborg softly.

"What won't work?"

"Thumping Jens. He'll only get even with us. We have to think of something else."

"Think of what else?" said Buster unhappily. "Big horrible Lars is always hanging around this neighborhood. He could show up and strangle me any moment. We don't have much time for thinking." Buster felt his throat.

"Suppose we play a trick on Jens. You're so good at conjuring tricks, Buster, can't you think of something?"

"Conjuring tricks," muttered Buster, gloomily recalling the principal.

"Have you still got that arm?"

"What arm?"

"The one Dad gave you for your eighth birthday. The artificial arm."

"You don't want me to give Jens the artificial arm, do you, Ingeborg? Are you crazy?"

"No, of course not. But you know Jens. He always has to have everything other people have—and more if possible. There's just about nothing he hasn't got. Two bikes with sixteen gears, an electric train, a set of drums, four aquariums, walkie-talkie radios. You said so yourself."

Buster nodded. "Must be nice to be Jens," he sighed.

"For goodness' sake, what's the matter with you today?"

Buster told her about his day and how it had gone wrong.

"Okay," said Ingeborg, when he had finished, "but at least you've got something Jens doesn't have."

Buster just looked at her wearily, without much hope in his eyes.

"When the moon is full you have three arms."

* * *

In New York, a man was getting into a supercar that flew him up into the air; in Madrid a painter was cutting off his right ear because he had forgotten to buy olives; and in the Brønshøj district of Copenhagen, a boy named Buster was standing in his attic bedroom inspecting his three arms.

"That one hangs down a bit too far," he said.

Ingeborg showed him how to fix it.

"You think he'll fall for this?"

"Of course he will. But you could try it out on Mrs. Larsen first and see what she says."

The air in Mrs. Larsen's bedroom seemed very thick. The blinds were lowered halfway, and the red sun and brown curtains turned the room the color of syrup.

Mrs. Larsen was sitting up in bed with a magazine when Buster came quietly in. There was something forced about his smile, because he only took small, shallow breaths around Mrs. Larsen, to keep from inhaling her sickness too far into his own lungs.

"Hello, Buster," she said solemnly. "Do sit down—you look so serious! Has something happened?"

Buster had the third arm hidden behind his back. He sat down on the chair beside the bed. It was a green chair with a hard back that had three little buttercups painted on it. The flower in the middle had almost faded away.

He looked at Mrs. Larsen's smiling mouth. When she spoke you could hear little clicks. Ingeborg said they came from Mrs. Larsen's false teeth. He looked at her hands lying white and almost transparent on the striped bedspread, and he followed the lines of the veins on them, running this way and that like shadows in the long afternoons.

"Would you like a lemon drop?" asked Mrs. Larsen.

Buster didn't hear her. He was clearing his throat. "Mrs. Larsen," he said, "there's something I have to tell you."

"By all means," said Mrs. Larsen solemnly, "by all means, Buster. But you must straighten the pillow behind my back for me first—you know how old and weak I am."

Buster straightened the pillow with one of his real hands, which brought him so close to Mrs. Larsen that he had to smell her. He usually didn't do that except on Tuesdays and Fridays, when the nurse had been there to wash her. And although it was Wednesday, she didn't smell too bad after all.

Buster sat down again. He heard the grandfather clock in the living room take a deep breath and strike the half hour.

"I'm listening," said Mrs. Larsen.

"It's like this," Buster began. "Something very, very strange has happened."

Mrs. Larsen nodded, looking as if she feared the worst.

"Part of me has started to grow."

"Started to grow, Buster?"

"That's right. Not all of a sudden. Little by little. It got bigger and bigger, sort of slowly."

Mrs. Larsen was frowning now. Her mouth was drawn tight and looked quite stern.

"I don't dare show it to anyone but you, Mrs. Larsen," said Buster, staring straight ahead.

Mrs. Larsen cleared her throat and drummed her fingers on the bedspread.

"Well, so what part of you has been growing?" she asked. Buster felt there was a slightly nervous undertone to her voice.

He put all the three arms on the bedspread. "I've grown an extra arm, Mrs. Larsen—look!"

Mrs. Larsen stared at Buster for a moment, and then she glanced down at the three arms. Her nostrils began to quiver. Seconds later she was laughing her usual silent laugh, and Buster noticed, as he had many times before, that when Mrs. Larsen laughed like that, a very pretty young girl looked out of her eyes.

"Oh, Buster Oregon Mortensen!" she whispered, shaking her head slightly.

"It's very serious, you know," said Buster.

Mrs. Larsen nodded and bit her lip. "Yes, Buster. But when your mother comes home today, will you send her over to see me? I'd like a word with her."

Buster unscrewed the artificial arm. "Okay," he said. "And Mrs. Larsen, could you have a word with Dad too? He hit Ingeborg because she wouldn't tell him where the rest of the household money is."

"Do you think it would do any good, Buster?"

Buster shrugged his shoulders and shook his head.

Mrs. Larsen took his hand. One of his real hands. "Let's hope that the world will come around to appreciating its magicians again one of these days," she whispered.

Buster nodded. "Because if it doesn't, I'll end up . . . good Lord, I don't know where I'll end up."

* * *

When he got back home, his mother and father had begun to make supper. His father was acting the way he always did when he had a guilty conscience—being very nice to people. He picked Buster up and lifted him to the ceiling.

His mother, however, said that Mr. Martinsen, the math teacher, had phoned. Buster came down to the ground again.

"You just let me speak to that math teacher the next time he calls!" growled his father, winking at Buster.

His mother put a square piece of margarine in the frying pan.

"Oh, yes," she said, "that'll be a great help, I'm sure!"

Later, after supper, Buster went up to the bedroom. Ingeborg was standing there looking out of the attic window. The sky was already dark blue.

"You know what?" she said.

By now Buster was in a very good mood. He jumped up on the bed beside her, lifting her so that she was hanging half out of the attic.

"No, Ingeborg—what?"

"It's a full moon tonight. See that?"

"Full moon?"

"Yes, and when the moon is full, some people grow three arms."

5

No Cornflakes

It was a mild summer evening. Featherweight clouds hung beneath the twinkling stars, like a safety net as thin as silk.

Down on the road with all the big houses in Brønshøj, the blue neon lights were on. Dew had formed fast. The birds had stopped twittering and put their heads under their wings.

Buster walked slowly down Church Street, wondering how to broach the subject to Jens. When he got to Cliff Road he put his real arm under his denim jacket and stuffed the artificial one into the sleeve. The artificial arm looked really good. Here in the dark, it almost fooled its owner.

He stopped at Poplar Crescent, in front of the building where Jens lived. But he could hardly just march in without some kind of plan. He went across the grass, down to the lake, and sat on a damp bench. At that moment a duck came waddling out of the water.

"Quack, quack," said the duck.

"Quack, quack, quack," said Buster, through his nose.

The duck waddled right up to him and inspected him from head to toe.

Buster smiled. "I say, Jens," he said, "did you notice it's a full moon today?"

"Quack, quack!" said the duck.

"That's right, Jens," said Buster, nodding. "So listen. I came to tell you a secret. That is, I came to offer you a deal, because this evening—tonight—if you say certain magic words, you can get something nobody else has, except me, of course."

The duck waddled back to the water. "Okay, maybe you don't believe me," said Buster. "Well, take a look at this. . . ."

He stood up. He realized it was suddenly very dark all around him. What was that rustling in the bushes? Peering ahead of him, Buster thought he could see someone coming his way.

He started to run along the path when two figures suddenly appeared in front of him, a tall girl and an even taller boy. Buster stopped automatically. He had never seen the girl before, but when the boy stepped under the yellow park light, Buster recognized him at once.

"Lars!" he said, and felt his legs give slightly at the knees.

The girl, whose arms were bare, pulled at Lars. But Lars stared at Buster in surprise. Then he began to grin.

Buster thought he had better smile back, though it was rather difficult, particularly when Lars bent down, picked up a stout branch, and tried it out by whirling it through the air like a flail.

"Come on, Lars, let's go!" said the girl.

"Just a moment," said Lars, keeping his voice low, "just a moment. There's something I've got to settle with Buster here. Also known as Sugar Baby Buster."

Lars walked a little ways down the path and stopped in front of Buster.

"Evening, Buster. So where's your pointed hat?"

"At home, I think," mumbled Buster, wishing he had his running shoes on. It was very quiet at this time of night in Utterslev Park. Even the duck had paddled away by now, and the cars on Harewood Road were in a great hurry to get wherever they were going.

"And how's your sister, Little Limping Lizzie?" snarled Lars, hunching over as he came up to Buster, who was busy with his real arm under the jacket.

"Come on, Lars, I'm freezing!" called the girl, beginning to jump up and down.

"She's freezing," said Buster in friendly tones.

But Lars suddenly changed his tune. "And what's that got to do with you, you ugly little beast?" he shouted. "You disgusting, horrible little devil! Do you know what you did to my Puch, do you? Well, I'll tell you! It was a complete wreck after you got at it, fooling around with sugar like that!"

Buster swallowed a big lump in his throat.

"How in hell would a normal person think of a thing like that? Well, what about it, half-wit Buster? Only of course you're not normal, are you?"

Feeling at a loss, Buster shrugged his shoulders. Out on the lake, the duck said, "Quack!"

"Just what would make a person go pouring a kilo of sugar into another person's gas tank?"

Buster looked genuinely conscience-stricken.

"It was all we had," he whispered, resigned.

"What d'you mean, all you had?" Lars seized his collar. The artificial arm swung back and forth.

"Well, we didn't have any rolled oats, or salt and pepper, or cornflakes!" squeaked Buster.

"I'll give you cornflakes, you little so-and-so!" yelled Lars, hitting out.

The gnarled branch struck Buster above his hip. He staggered to one side. It hurt.

Lars made the branch whistle through the air like a whip. "You'll pay for it now, Buster! And you can go home and tell your club-footed sister that if she isn't a total cripple yet, she will be when I'm through with her. Get it?"

Buster was not quite sure whether he got it or not. He just closed his eyes as the second blow fell. It struck him on the shoulder above the plaster arm, which consequently dropped about twenty centimeters. The white hand dangled in front of his knee. It looked weird, and Buster was about to readjust it when his glance fell on Lars.

Lars was standing there with his mouth and eyes wide open. The branch had slipped from his hand. His lower lip began to tremble, and his whole body shook violently.

Buster realized that this was the moment for a few cries of pain. Therefore, he began to howl as he backed away from Lars.

But now the girl came running up. When she saw the length of the arm, and the branch lying on the path, she let out a scream and began to tug desperately at Lars, who simply clutched his head.

"I didn't hit him that hard!" he whimpered softly. "Not that hard . . ."

Buster let the arm drop a few more centimeters. It had the desired effect. The girl ran off into the dark, screaming.

"Buster!" cried Lars. "I'm sorry . . . your arm . . . but how . . . Oh, help! What are we going to do?"

By now he was sobbing loudly. Buster was near tears himself. It was all so sad. The screaming girl, the weeping Lars, the lonely duck out on the lake, not to mention the arm that was so much longer than normal. He gave it another two centimeters.

Horrified, Lars turned his back to him. He was now wailing so loudly that Buster had to resort to his best wolf howl to make himself heard above the noise.

"Buster!" cried Lars, turning around, utterly beside himself.

But at that moment Buster lost control of the plaster arm. It slipped out of his sleeve and fell to the path with a dull thud.

Dumbfounded, Lars stared at it. His expression changed, for now the arm did not look real at all.

Buster slowly picked it up and cautiously retreated. Not until he was safely around the corner of Church Street did the roar reach his ears.

"Buster!" bellowed Lars, so that the television aerials on the rooftops shook. "I'll skin you alive! I swear I'll skin you alive, Buster Mortensen. . . ."

6

Something the Size
of a Dray Horse

On the Friday Buster was going to start work
as a delivery boy, it began drizzling at noon.
By the time school was over and he was walking down Frederikssund Road, it was raining
so hard that the awnings above the shops were
full of water and sagged down low.

"You're lucky there's only one delivery, in
this weather!" Mrs. Jensen smiled and filled
the wire basket with eggs, butter, margarine,
and five bottles of mineral water. "Jensen's put
a crate of dark ale out in the yard—you're to
take that too," she said, going through the bill.

They were in the room behind the shop. It
smelled of sour milk. Buster winked at her
and took a big envelope out of his school
satchel.

"These are the pictures of my grandfather,"

he whispered. "You can look at them while I make my delivery."

Mrs. Jensen's hands trembled with eagerness. She could hardly wait. The pictures were yellowish brown, some of them so old that they seemed to be disappearing through the back of the paper. Of course Mrs. Jensen recognized the Great Oregon, standing there in good old Husum, in front of his impressive cannon. He looked very dashing in a white leotard, and Buster was able to supply the additional information that his moustache measured fifteen centimeters from tip to tip.

"And all those medals!" Mrs. Jensen sighed, enraptured.

"Er, yes," said Buster, for it was a fact that the Great Oregon had manufactured some of them himself.

Mrs. Jensen went on leafing through the photographs until she came to one that showed the Cannon King standing beside a short, fat man in a vest.

"That man," Buster eagerly explained, "the short one, he's Laredo the ringmaster. His real name was Wolfgang Rasmussen, but no one ever called him anything but Laredo. You can see a striped wagon in the background—that was my grandfather's. He had a dog called Quick who could walk on his front legs and quack like a duck. The dog died of cold in Jutland. In Fredericia, it was. But then my grandfather got a new dog—you can see him in one of the other pictures. Look, that's him. He wore a clown's hat on his head, but he never learned to walk on two legs."

"Did he die too?" asked Mrs. Jensen, with a little smile.

"Yes," Buster solemnly told her, "of constipation."

"Where?"

"In his guts, of course."

Mrs. Jensen gurgled with laughter. But then a faraway look came into her eyes.

"Just think, Buster," she said, "just think how long ago that was—why, it was in the thirties. I was only six or seven at the time. And there were all fields in between Brønshøj and Husum. Hard to believe now! My father was out of work—we'd come here from the country. My mother earned a little money sewing. My little sister Dagny and I had to share a doll between us. Molly, the doll's name was. My mother always said she wouldn't have people able to tell we were poor just by looking at us. So Dagny and I always wore wonderful dresses, while my mother and father . . . dear me, why am I telling you all this?" Mrs. Jensen sniffed and looked for a hanky in her pocket. Buster fished a rag out of his own back pocket, but as it had a horrible oily smell even at a distance, he stuffed it back in again.

Mrs. Jensen had now reached the last picture, which was more recent. "Why, that's you, Buster!" she cried. "What's that fine hat you're wearing?"

"It's my magic hat, Mrs. Jensen," said Buster, beaming. And so saying, he produced a long dagger and thrust it into his chest, after which he collapsed into an empty milk crate, giving a loud death rattle.

"Oh, dear, Buster!" exclaimed Mrs. Jensen. But Buster jumped up again, laughing, and explained that it was a trick dagger with a blade that disappeared into its handle.

"Like this, Mrs. Jensen," he said reassuringly and "stabbed" her in the chest four times.

At this moment Mr. Jensen appeared. "What does that little imp think he's up to?" he bellowed.

In alarm, Mrs. Jensen told Buster to hurry up. "And be sure you work the money out right—there's change in the wallet."

"In where?" called Buster, already on the way to his delivery bike in the yard.

"In the wallet—the thing for the money!" called Mrs. Jensen.

Buster nodded and waved. Then he turned to the loaded bicycle. It was a big bike, very high, even though Mr. Jensen had lowered the seat.

Buster got on cautiously. He could just touch the ground with the tips of his toes. The crate of dark ale was very heavy, and it was difficult to keep his balance. He started by tottering a little way with his toes on the ground, while the big handlebars swayed back and forth. The wheel in front of the basket seemed several kilometers away.

Finally he managed to sit on the seat. Now to make contact with the pedals, and then to get a little speed up to keep his balance. There! It worked.

"Whoopee!" he shouted. "I've done it! I'm cycling! I'm steering!"

Now, pedal toward the gate, swerve gently to the right, watch the clothespoles—good!

Now he could turn boldly into the bicycle lane, which luckily started by going downhill. Just suppose Eric or Jens saw him now!

Wouldn't they be surprised! Buster's amazing, they'd think, and Jens would go home this evening and tell his mother and father he wanted *two* delivery bikes.

Buster was chuckling to himself as he steered his way along Church Lane.

This was fantastic! He didn't mind the pouring rain one bit. He had no problem bringing the bike to a stop outside number 28, the house where he was going, either. He felt for the wallet—was it still there? Yes.

Buster nimbly picked up the wire basket and carried it briskly to the garden gate, which opened with a squeal. He kicked it shut with his heel and ran most of the way up the garden path. He couldn't leave a whole crate of dark ale standing in the street unattended for too long. Just as he reached the front steps, however, he heard a fierce growl that rooted him to the spot.

Something on four legs and about the size of a dray horse came prowling out of the back garden, baring its teeth. Buster clutched the wire basket. The monster had obviously taken a dislike to him.

At this moment the door of the house opened, and an elderly lady called, "Nero!

Nero! Leave the boy alone. He won't hurt you; he's delivering from the dairy—come here, Nero! Good dog!"

"You heard what the lady said!" whispered Buster as the monster climbed the steps.

The lady took it by the collar. Buster went up sideways, like a crab, keeping as far over as he could, and put the basket down at the top.

"Rather small for a delivery boy, aren't you?" asked the lady.

"Yes," muttered Buster, glancing at the dog, hoping it preferred its delivery boys considerably fatter.

"But I suppose they can't get anyone else these days." The lady sighed, shaking her head in a resigned way.

"That's it, they'll take anyone nowadays," agreed Buster politely, heading back down to fetch the bottles of dark ale. They were unexpectedly heavy. The last part of the journey, up the eight steps with the lady and the dog watching his tottering progress, was positive torture. His arms hung limp as spaghetti by the time the crate was finally resting on the doormat.

"Here, what's this?" asked the lady.

"Dark ale, I think," panted Buster.

"I can see that for myself. But it's not what I ordered. I ordered pale ale."

"Pale ale," muttered Buster.

"Yes, pale ale," said the lady, "but never mind. Have you got the bill with you?"

Buster fumbled in his pocket. "I'll have to look in that wallet thingamajig," he said.

The lady stared at him. Buster fished something crumpled out of his pocket. Thank goodness she had the correct money. Buster thanked her politely and was going to pat Nero on the head, but the mean beast snapped at his hand.

Then he waded out into the rain.

The bicycle seat was soaking wet, of course, but Buster didn't mind, because now the bike was easy to steer. He rode a circuit of honor around Holck Square and tooted his horn like the big ferryboat. He even allowed himself the luxury of putting his feet on the delivery basket as he coasted downhill.

Then, suddenly, he saw Ingeborg coming down from the church. She was wearing her red raincoat and her yellow rainhat.

Buster leaned over the handlebars. "Ingeborg!" he shouted at the top of his lungs.

Ingeborg stopped and waved her hat. It shone brightly in the gray rain.

"You look great!" She laughed as he coasted to a stop by the curb.

Buster nodded.

"Isn't it kind of hard to handle that bike?"

"Hard? You've no idea! I can tell you, it's like ten wild bulls from Barcelona!"

Ingeborg looked at him, full of admiration. "You must be terribly wet, aren't you, Buster?"

Buster giggled. "Soaked to my underpants! Where've you been, anyway?"

"Girl Scouts. There's a fair in the church garden on Sunday. Nanna and I are running the gift lottery. And there's going to be a real shooting gallery, and an outdoor refreshment area, and a band playing music."

"Sounds good," said Buster. "Do you think I can come too?"

"Maybe," said Ingeborg. "I can always ask Margaret—she's our troop leader. You know, Buster, I don't think what you did to Lars yesterday evening was a very good idea."

Buster felt his stomach churning.

"Because I saw Lars with Finn and Ivor," Ingeborg went on, "and he shouted that we'd better get our first aid box ready. Jens was with them, too."

Buster looked thoughtful. "Oh," he murmured. "Ah. Well, I'll have to get going, Ingeborg. I'm working, you know. See you."

He swung the bicycle around and pedaled

back to the dairy, where he parked it very neatly.

Mr. Jensen picked up the wallet without a word and counted the money twice. "You can take the garbage out," he grunted.

Buster carried the bucket out. It was as heavy as the crate of ale. Just as he was about to put the lid on the dumpster, his eye fell on something lying in the middle of the rubbish. A great big slingshot. Beautifully made, with brand-new elastic. He weighed it in his hand. Probably a weapon thrown away by some angry father because his son and heir had smashed a windowpane. Buster smiled. It was only drizzling now; in fact, the sun was shining. He pulled the elastic to test it, slanting the slingshot upward. High above Husum, there was a wonderful rainbow glowing in the sky.

Mrs. Jensen came outside with the pictures. "Thank you very much," she said.

"Did you see the rainbow?" He pointed up. "Over there, where my grandfather used to perform."

Mrs. Jensen nodded.

"That's the rainbow he got shot to!" called Buster, disappearing through the gate.

But no sooner was he out in Frederikssund Road than he dashed off toward Church Lane. A magnificent plan had formed in his mind.

He still owed stupid Jens some revenge, and revenge would be sweet.

He ran down the road until he was back at number 28. Then he bent down and picked up a suitable stone. He rattled the garden gate a couple of times. Less than twenty seconds later, just as he expected, Nero came racing out of the back garden. Hot breath, like drifting mist, poured from his open jaws.

I hope this old gate holds, thought Buster, taking two steps back as the monster jumped up, snapping at him. Nero's bloodshot eyes flashed angrily.

Buster glanced around.

"Okay, Nero, you nasty animal, see what nice little Buster's got for you," he whispered, and he fitted the stone into the slingshot, pulling the elastic as tight as it would go. Then he marched up to the barking dog. Nero was still snapping at him.

The stone hit the monster right between the eyes. Nero stopped barking and staggered back, rolling his eyes frighteningly. Then he ran into the garden, howling.

The dog is man's best friend, thought Buster, walking away. Maybe I ought to give the poor thing a bone when all this is over.

7

Mr. Jensen
and the Rainbow

It was evening. After supper, the children went up to their attic bedroom, and Buster got Ingeborg to tell him all about the church fair.

"There's going to be a folk dance group, and the minister will make a speech, and you can win prizes at the different stands, and you have to pay to get in."

"Couldn't you wangle your way in?" asked Buster, slyly. He was busy cleaning up the old six-sided concertina his father had given him for a christening present.

"No, you could not wangle your way in!" Ingeborg said. "The entrance money's for poor, sick, lonely people."

"I wouldn't mind doing a bit of conjuring and playing some music at this fair," said Buster, looking into space.

Ingeborg opened the attic window, sat by the chest of drawers, and got her hairbrush out. Then she loosened her long, fair hair. It fell down her back in a cascade.

"I said I wouldn't mind doing a bit of conjuring and playing some music at this fair," repeated Buster impatiently.

"Yes, I heard you," said Ingeborg, shaking her head, "but it's no good."

"Why not?"

"Because conjuring tricks aren't the right thing for a fair in the church garden."

Buster thought this over. "Well, then, at least I can play some music."

Ingeborg gathered her hair together at the nape of her neck. "When did you ever learn to play music?"

Buster was genuinely insulted. "Look here, Ingeborg Mortensen, have you forgotten that song I made up myself—words *and* music?"

"Oh, that."

"What do you mean, 'Oh, that'?"

Ingeborg shrugged her shoulders. Buster pulled out the little concertina and cleared his throat.

"Mother's asleep," snapped Ingeborg.

"I won't play loud. How did the first verse go?"

"Something like 'Here comes Buster Oregon . . .' "

"I don't mean that; you know I don't, Ingeborg. . . ."

"Oh, okay," giggled Ingeborg, lying down on the bed.

Buster sat there, fingering the concertina.

"Ssh!" said Ingeborg. "Now you've gone and waked Mother up."

Buster listened. He did not have to strain his ears very hard.

"I'm so tired, Emil," his mother was saying. "Do stop it. . . ."

"Oh, come on!" his father begged her.

"Stop it, Emil. Oh! Listen, I told you I'm tired. Emil! Oh, for goodness' sake!"

"Buster, play that concertina," said Ingeborg suddenly.

"My word, she's good and mad down there," muttered Buster. It sounded as if his mother and father were running around the room in circles.

"Let me go, Emil, let me go!"

"Come on, Kitty. . . ."

"Go on, play, Buster!" cried Ingeborg, shaking him.

"But why do you want me to play it all of a sudden?"

"Just play it, Buster, and sing—listen, I *do* want to hear that song, the one you made up yourself. Sing it."

"Well, if I can remember it."

Buster tried the buttons, unsuccessfully. Downstairs, his father sounded as if he were crying. Buster looked up and put the concertina down. Everything in the building had somehow grown very still.

Ingeborg went over and opened her secret drawer. The precious music box came into view. It was little and brown, about the size of a cigar box. And when she lifted the lid, a little white ballerina rose from the bottom of the box. The ballerina turned slowly, standing on one leg, in time to a pretty little tune.

Buster watched the ballerina, enchanted. He had never seen her before. She was so lifelike. So delicate. She was wearing a little ballet dress and ballet shoes. Her eyes were blue; her mouth was red. One leg was bent, and her slender arms met somewhere above her head. When the tune came to an end, the ballerina stopped too.

"Can she be wound up again?" whispered Buster, spellbound.

Ingeborg nodded without looking at him. "Yes, but we won't," she said.

"What happens to her when you close the lid?"

"She goes back into the box."

"Does she lie down?"

Ingeborg opened the drawer. "Nobody knows." She put the music box away again.

It was silent downstairs now. Buster undressed. He suddenly felt very gloomy. He didn't know why.

Luckily Ingeborg had a piece of news to cheer him up a bit before he went to sleep. "Oh, Dad promised we'd all go rowing in Frederiksberg Park tomorrow."

"Did he really?"

"Mmmm."

"What's the matter with you? And the fair's on Sunday!" Buster jumped up. "I can't sleep now—can you, Ingeborg?"

"Mmmm," she murmured.

He looked at her. Or just at her neck, to be precise. Why was she being so peculiar? As if she were sad about something. Going rowing tomorrow and then to the fair in the church garden the next day—that was terrific! Oh, perhaps it was the ballerina. Of course. Ingeborg would probably have liked to be a ballerina herself one day, only she couldn't, not with her lame foot.

Buster waved his arms in the air, crossly. Then he had an idea. "Hey, Ingeborg."

"What is it now?"

"Want to hear a story? A really true story?"

"It'll have to be a short one."

"Yes, of course it's a short one. Let's see. Right. Once upon a time there was a girl in Russia who had a stiff leg. Completely stiff, see? She couldn't even bend it. Well, so one day she told her mother she wanted to be a ballerina, but her mother said she couldn't possibly, but then the girl said . . ."

"Buster."

"What?"

"Do you think you could shut up now?"

"Yes, but the story . . ."

"I couldn't care less about the story."

"Okay, okay."

Buster lay down. It was quiet now. Very quiet. Not a sound anywhere in Brønshøj. You could probably hear a man in Malmö sprinkling salt on his midnight snack. It would obviously be very quiet in Malmö too. Buster couldn't help thinking of the lonely duck. And

70

the dog Nero. And sick Mrs. Larsen. And fat Mrs. Jensen. And silly Jens. But last of all he thought of the curly-haired girl from Brookwood Road.

Perhaps she would come to the church fair. Perhaps she'd bring the sweet scent from Brookwood Road with her.

Buster closed his eyes.

* * *

There was a big stage, illuminated by a huge spotlight. The minister stepped forward in his long black robe.

"Ladies and gentlemen," he called through a megaphone. "I now have the honor and the pleasure of announcing a show we have long been anxious to obtain for our program here in the church garden. A world-class performance . . . ladies and gentlemen, I now introduce . . . Buster Oregon Mortensen!"

There was loud applause. The curtain slid back, and a fanfare rang out through the old garden, where people were crowded close together to mark this special day.

Buster was wearing a gleaming black costume with a dragon breathing fire on his back and mysterious symbols on his chest. With an elegant gesture, he threw off his cloak. It in-

71

stantly turned into a delivery bike with a cross-eyed dog on it, panting heavily. Another wave of the magician's hand, and there stood a terrified little boy who bore an uncanny resemblance to Buster's classmate and enemy Jens.

"Abracadabra!" cried Buster, whereupon the dog ate the little boy, leaving nothing behind.

The people, who were not used to a performance from anyone except the minister, clapped like mad.

Buster bowed and wheeled a cannon into position. Mr. Jensen was inside the barrel, waiting impatiently for his entrance. Buster lit the fuse. Several seconds passed. Then there was a deafening bang, and with a great roar Mr. Jensen went shooting over the city rooftops, unfurling a rainbow behind him. It looked unbelievably beautiful. The applause was ecstatic, and while it was still going on the magician pulled a whole two and a half kilometers of paper out of his mouth.

At this the crowd went wild. Some of them began dancing around the flagpole, while others rang the church bells, making them peal out far and wide over the whole country.

* * *

Suddenly everything went dark. The silence came back. There was only a faint sound of church bells ringing in his ears. Buster staggered backward, farther and farther backward, until he was falling, falling down into a great hole that never, never came to an end. . . .

8

A Dragon
with Gooseflesh

The church fair began at exactly 1 P.M. on Sunday. The Reverend Mr. Kjaerulf came ceremoniously out on his big terrace. Smiling kindly, he folded his hands and cleared his throat into the little microphone, so loudly that people in Bellahøj thought something in Valby must have exploded. But after a Boy Scout, age about fifty, had adjusted the loudspeaker system, the minister was able to welcome everyone to the fair and then hand the microphone over to the chairman of the parish council, who bowed respectfully and tripped over the cable.

The garden was fantastically beautiful. Its lawn was perfect, with blades of grass arranged side by side like tidily cut stems. All these unspoiled beauties of nature made people walk around in a very reverent way, as if they were in the Garden of Eden.

However, other things were being offered here besides apples. Some ropes had been put up in the middle of the garden, marking off the big outdoor refreshment area, where you could buy cakes and hot chocolate from big-busted lady volunteers who hurried about in sturdy walking shoes.

All over the garden, in among the trees and bushes, there were stands where you could win, among other things, pots of geraniums, dolls, camel-skin hassocks, and sky-blue nylon teddy bears. And at the very end of the garden there were two shooting galleries, one for grown-ups and one for children. Both galleries backed up to the churchyard, probably because if a shot went wildly astray in that direction there wasn't too much damage it could do.

The grown-ups' shooting gallery had real targets and real air guns; if you scored three hits you won a paper flower for your buttonhole, assuming you had a buttonhole. Children, however, had to throw balls filled with sand through holes in a big sheet of plywood set up seven or eight meters away from the counter.

The band stood in the middle of the garden, playing a rousing tune. It sounded splendid and attracted lots of people.

Ingeborg was running a potted plant gift lottery with her friend Nanna. She did not have much to do, so she was able to keep an eye out for Buster. He had not been given permission to make his own contribution to the fair. Ingeborg's troop leader didn't think his conjuring tricks were a particularly good idea.

However, he had been given another job instead, down at the end of the garden where the shooting galleries were, although Ingeborg was not sure exactly what it was. Right now she was more concerned with the fact that Big Lars and his friend Ivor had just shown up. The two of them were wandering from stand to stand, grinning nastily. It was a good thing Buster did have a job. They wouldn't be able to get at him.

Lars and Ivor went off toward the far end of the garden. It made Ingeborg uneasy to see them headed that way. She left the potted plant stand to Nanna and followed the two big boys. They stopped when they came to the air guns.

Ingeborg looked for Buster in the children's shooting gallery, but all she saw was a Boy

Scout in a green uniform taking the money. Where could Buster be? She was about to move on when she suddenly spotted him. He was on his knees behind the sheet of plywood with the seven holes in it, putting his round head through whichever hole the children were to aim at. This seemed to be proving a profitable idea, for there were a lot of children standing around, eager to hit Buster's face. They were apparently quite good shots—judging by his nose, anyway. It was all red and swollen from the direct hits that had been scored.

"Hi, Ingeborg!" Buster called cheerfully, putting his whole head through one of the holes. Right then a child flung a ball of sand at his eyes so hard that it hurt Ingeborg to watch. The children, however, shouted with glee, so loudly that they drowned out the sound of the band. Buster tried to smile. Ingeborg shook her head. Then, to her horror, she saw Lars and Ivor walking toward the children's shooting gallery and the balls of sand. Of course they spotted Buster at once.

"Hey, look at that!" exclaimed the surprised Ivor. "Isn't that old ugly Buster putting his noggin through the hole?"

Buster didn't see the two boys help themselves to three balls apiece. He was telling Ingeborg he would soon have earned enough money to invite her to the outdoor refreshment area when Ivor's first ball struck the plywood above his head.

The stand rocked. Lars took a step back and flung his first ball too. It hit the wood ten centimeters below the hole where Buster was crouching. Then, once Buster had seen who was throwing balls so hard, Ivor let fly with his second, as if firing it from a tightly wound-up crossbow. A shout of delight came from the children standing around.

The ball hit Buster right on the nose. He scurried off to another hole, the one in the top corner of the plywood. But no sooner had he stuck his head out than Lars threw two balls in quick succession, hitting him square in the face. After Ivor's last shot had struck him on the forehead, Buster retired with a nosebleed.

"Oh no!" groaned the kids, and one of them, a boy of Buster's own age—it was Jens—shouted, "Namby-pamby Buster!" He had just paid for three balls, and now there was nothing to throw them at, because Buster was crawling off through the bushes toward Ingeborg's stand, to get some cotton from her.

"Lie down, you idiot!" she said crossly, holding her checked handkerchief to his nose. "Goodness, your face is all swollen!"

"I earned a lot of money, though," said Buster proudly. "Come over to the refreshment area and have some chocolate. It's on me."

"I've got to look after the stand. Maybe later. You'd better go and wash up. Here, take this cotton and put it up your nose."

Buster did as he was told and got up. He was feeling all right again now. Darn Jens. Never mind, his time would come. Buster smiled. Just you wait, little Jens! He passed the band, which was taking a break and drinking lemonade.

"Careful you don't get drunk on all that fizz!" he shouted cheerfully, nudging the little tuba player, who swallowed the wrong way. The entire band promised to thump him the first chance they got. They were about to start playing again. Buster didn't care. He was wearing his Hawaiian shirt; he had money in his back pocket. He also . . . and here he glanced surreptitiously around . . . he also had a cigarette butt in his other pocket. Perhaps he could . . .

He froze. His hands dropped. It was as if everyone else faded from view, as if the music disappeared, and so did the noise of the shooting galleries, the voices, the sound of spoons stirring coffee cups. He saw nothing but one person. Oh mama mia! The curly-haired girl from Brookwood Road. Here in the church garden. In her thin white dress. Her hair was longer than he had imagined it in his dreams, and her eyes . . . what could he say about her eyes? It was as if a special sort of light shone around her little head. But who was the tight-lipped old bag with her? You'd have to look hard to find a more sour face.

Buster hid. His hands were trembling, his legs were like jelly, but his mind was working perfectly.

The curly-haired girl was walking around looking at all the stands with a little smile. No, not walking; she was floating, like a hover-craft. Buster followed her, taking care to keep out of her line of vision. Now the sour old bag was talking to someone. Buster clutched the tree he was hiding behind. The curly-haired girl walked on. She reached the far end of the garden, passed the stands selling hand-embroidered tablecloths, and all of a sudden she was just five meters from the place where he was standing chewing the bark of an oak tree.

He pulled himself together. It was now or

never. He turned around as the girl passed the tree, meaning to go up to her with a jaunty smile on his face. Instead, he tripped over a tree root and landed on the ground about five centimeters behind her heels.

He was on his feet again in a moment, dusting himself off as best he could. She hadn't noticed; that was the main thing. Now to go after her.

He straightened up. She was over there, at the counter with whipped-cream cakes. Buster felt in his pocket. Yes, thank goodness, the money was still there. Quick as a flash, he undid the top button of his Hawaiian shirt to show his new tattoo, painted on by himself. It was a four-headed dragon. Then, his heart thumping, he went up to the counter. The girl was asking for a bag of meringues.

"Ahem." Buster cleared his throat, put the jaunty smile on his face, and squashed a whipped-cream cake with his arm.

The lady at the stand looked daggers at him. Luckily the girl didn't see him having to pay for the cake. The lady scooped its remains onto a paper plate.

Buster craned his neck. The girl had gone to sit in the outdoor refreshment area with her yellow meringues. Meringue dust flew in the air as she took a bite. He put the paper plate down. Then he raised his arm and looked at his elbow. Half the whipped-cream cake was sticking to it.

First he tried rolling up his sleeve, but that did no good. Then he asked if he could borrow a knife to scrape the cake off, but the lady told him to get lost before she did something to him. He came to a swift decision. It was quite warm, at least 18°C, so he took his shirt off. You could see the dragon even better when he had nothing on his top half.

"What on earth are you doing?" asked the lady behind the counter.

"Taking my shirt off." Buster smiled. "A little fresh air is very good for the nipples. You should try it yourself sometime."

As she picked up a large spoon, Buster retreated, ignoring some little kids who were staring at his bare chest.

Then he made his way over to the girl sitting on her bench, gazing off into space.

Next he had to find the right thing to say. But it was terribly difficult, now that he was here, within ten centimeters of the girl from Brookwood Road. Suddenly, however, she turned and looked at him. She stared at the dragon. Then she smiled.

"Did you paint that yourself?"

"Yup," said Buster proudly. "In front of the mirror. Like it?"

The girl pursed her lips thoughtfully.

"You live on Brookwood Road, don't you?" he continued, taking care to give a jaunty smile, the way he had seen the men do in the ads.

"How do you know?"

I've aroused her interest, thought Buster. "Oh, I often go that way when I'm at work," he said.

The girl looked at him curiously. "Why have you got cotton up your nose?"

This remark shook him. How could he have forgotten that stupid cotton?

"I . . . er . . . I sort of had a nosebleed. I was in a fight, see?"

"Are you the boy with the flowered shirt?"

Buster beamed. "Yes, that's me. It's a Hawaiian shirt. My name's Buster, by the way."

The girl laughed. "Mine's Joanna."

"Jo—anna," he whispered, enraptured.

She nodded kindly. "Aren't you cold?"

"Er—no, no, not at all."

"You've got gooseflesh all over, even the dragon."

"Do I? I hadn't noticed, but . . . er . . . well,

would you like a cup of chocolate? Hot chocolate?" Buster put his hand in his back pocket.

The curly-haired girl looked quickly in all directions, and then she giggled and nodded.

Buster jumped up to buy two cups of hot chocolate and one large and one small slice of whipped-cream cake. After his recent mishap, he couldn't afford two large slices.

He glanced over at her from where he stood by the counter. She was so pretty sitting there, looking straight ahead. Sitting there waiting for him! All at once he noticed the way the blood was rushing through his body.

"Hadn't you better put something on?" asked the volunteer lady pouring chocolate.

His glance fell on her moustache. He thought it wouldn't matter so much now if there were a few stains on the Hawaiian shirt. Also, he was really freezing.

So he put his shirt on.

"Here—the big piece of cake's for you," he said, pushing the cup and the plate over to Joanna.

"Thank you, Buster," she whispered, looking at him intently.

He started searching for the cigarette butt in his other pocket, but at that moment someone called her. In a cross, sharp voice.

"Wherever have you been, Joanna? Come here at once."

Buster looked up. It was the sour old bag.

The curly-haired girl stood up. "I'll have to go now," she said.

Buster's fingers crumbled the cigarette in his pocket.

"Good-bye—see you soon."

It was as if all the other sounds came back the moment she went away. People began walking around again under the trees, which were casting long shadows now.

Buster looked at the two cups and the two slices of cake. The big one and the little one.

"Hi," someone suddenly said.

He looked up. It was Ingeborg. She was smiling.

"Hi," he said wearily.

She sat down.

"Is that big piece of cake for me?" she asked, cocking her head to one side.

Buster stirred his chocolate. "You can have them both, Ingeborg."

9

Revenge on Jens

Buster was going down Rostgaard Road. He couldn't even enjoy the lilacs today, although the weather was doing all it could to cheer people up. He was thinking of the ambulance with the blue light that had taken Mrs. Larsen away very early in the morning, at dawn. In his mind, he heard the lowered voices in the hall, saw the worried faces as his mother said, "Good-bye and good luck." Mr. Larsen, as usual, had not said a word.

For some reason or other Ingeborg had stayed up in the bedroom. It wasn't at all like her. Mrs. Larsen had asked for her, also.

"She's asleep," Buster had fibbed, standing on the sidewalk and feeling the gravel under his bare toes.

Mr. Larsen had gotten into the back of the ambulance too.

"Off you go, now," his mother had told Buster, giving him a little slap on the bottom.

The driver had been about to shut the back door of the ambulance when Mrs. Larsen had called out, "Just a moment! Come here, Buster, will you?"

Buster had scrambled into the ambulance. Mrs. Larsen had tears in her eyes.

"Don't forget your magic . . . before we meet again," she had whispered. "You must never forget your magic, Buster, whatever happens. Whatever they do to you."

Buster had felt a lump in his throat.

Immediately after that the ambulance drove away. Without flashing its blue light. So it couldn't really be too serious, he thought.

He walked past the library and through the marketplace. The school bell was already ringing. It didn't usually ring until he stepped on the fourth paving stone of Riding School Hill. As if there were some mysterious connection between that paving stone and the bell.

He began to run, because arriving late would be particularly stupid today. This evening was Parents' Evening, and he had lessons today with Doza Rosa (who was quite all right, really) and Mr. Martinsen the math teacher (who was not all right at all).

Yes, he had a lot on his mind. Not to mention the job this afternoon.

Eric and Jens were standing outside the classroom. They grinned as they saw him coming up the steps.

"Why didn't you leave your head in that hole yesterday?" scoffed Jens. "Scared they'd knock your nose right into the back of your neck?"

At this point Rosa came along. Eric went into the classroom first.

"Ever been on a big man's bike?" Buster whispered to Jens.

"No, and I bet you haven't either," said Jens confidently, sitting down beside Amelia.

Buster told Jens about his new job at the dairy. "So if you want to try the bike, meet me at three this afternoon."

Jens just shrugged his shoulders. Rosa picked up the attendance book and went through the names.

Buster was sitting at the back, where he had a desk to himself. He always sat there. Then at least he wouldn't disturb the others, as Rosa said.

She was now collecting the poems they had written over the weekend. The poems were all supposed to be about summer. Some of the children had done theirs on a typewriter. It made them look really good.

Rosa read Maurice's poem out loud:

> When summer comes
> I go out bathing
> and I go eating plums
> and I go to the sea at Gilleleje
> to dig in the sand with a spade.

Maurice turned red in the face, but Rosa said it was a very good poem and that all the poems were going to be duplicated and put together in a little book, to be given to the parents that evening.

Buster had not had time to make up a poem. He had picked a white lilac instead. He put the blossom on the desk when Rosa came around for his poem.

"Hasn't done his homework again!" whispered Amelia.

Rosa stared at the flower. Buster didn't know whether he had better look sorry or smile, so he bit his lip.

Nicholas and Sarah were bent over laughing.

"Did you imagine this flower would appear in our collection of poems?" asked Rosa.

Buster looked down at his desk.

"He can't be in the poetry book, can he?"

called Jens from his place in front near the teacher's desk, and the others agreed. It might have seemed Buster didn't care about the poetry book one way or the other, but in fact he did. Under no circumstances did he want his parents going home without that collection of poems.

Rosa put the lilac in a plastic mug.

"While the rest of us go down and begin copying the poems, perhaps you can think of one of your own after all, Buster," she said.

Buster saw light at the end of the tunnel. Yes, of course he could. He could write about thirty poems if he had to.

"That's not fair," said Sarah. "The rest of us had to do it at home. Why's he allowed to sit here and write one, and you aren't even scolding him?"

Suggestions for ways to punish Buster positively hailed down on Rosa, who was looking hesitant.

"Okay, go ahead and scold me," said Buster.

"That's what you say now," said Sarah, "but it's still not fair."

"Put it down on his report," suggested Ollie, and ducked.

"Yes, and show it to his mother and father tonight!" cried Tina.

Rosa murmured something to the effect that she would come to her own decision.

"And it's no good sending Buster out of the room," insisted Sarah, "because he'll simply go home. He shouldn't be in a normal school at all."

"That will do!" said Rosa, cutting the argument short. "If you insist on making all this fuss, we'll never get anything copied."

There was dead silence in class.

"Buster is going to write his poem now, and that's that. The rest of you come downstairs with me. You can follow us when you're ready, Buster," said Rosa.

The class surged out. It was quiet in the room.

Buster looked at his chewed pencil lying on the graph paper he had torn out of his math exercise book. He couldn't write a poem about summer, though.

So he wrote:

Mrs. Larsen has gone to the hospital.
I went inside the ambulance myself.
I hope she isn't going to die.

All the others were downstairs in the duplicating room, pushing and shoving to be the first in line.

"That was very quick, Buster," said Rosa, taking the graph paper.

Buster looked away while she read it.

"What's he written?" asked Amelia.

"Read us Buster's poem!" called Jens.

Rosa looked at Buster, but she said nothing, and his poem was duplicated the same as all the others.

Last period was gym. They were going to play soccer outside.

"Look sharp and get changed!" called the gym teacher, blowing his whistle twice, so loudly that it curled your ears up.

They had to stand in a long line on the playing field, and the gym teacher told anyone who was slouching to stand up straight, and anyone who was fat to pull his stomach in. All he said to anyone who talked too much was "Shut up!" As usual in gym, the rules were different. You got reprimanded for swearing in math or language lessons, but as soon as you had your soccer shoes on, you could swear and say as many rude words as you liked.

"We can't stop to worry about details down here!" bellowed the gym teacher. "Now then, it's down to business the moment the whistle blows, and what the referee doesn't know won't hurt him—that's the way of the world, and it's not for slackers. Now warm up a bit, that's it, up with your knees—hop, hop, hop. . . . Kurt, I just don't believe it; what the hell do *you* think you're doing?"

Kurt was a fat boy from the same grade. He always went around on his own, and he was not in the least interested in gym or warming up.

"I'm hopping, like you said," explained Kurt.

"You call that hopping? You're just standing there shaking those rolls of fat. Come on, make an effort; you need it more than most."

The gym teacher showed them how. He was wearing a new red sweat suit.

Then Eric was chosen to pick one team and Willy to pick the other. The picking was done very quickly, because the boys knew exactly who could do what on the soccer field.

Finally Buster, Kurt, and a boy known as Sleuth-hound were left.

Eric pointed to Sleuth-hound.

Buster began running up and down in place, as if he were in great shape. He didn't want to be the last one left.

"Okay, we'll take Kurt," said Willy. "He'll fill the space between the goalposts nicely."

The gym teacher gave them the ball and blew the starting whistle. Buster, who hadn't been picked by anyone, simply trotted over to Eric's team, where he was told that he was a right defensive back. Alf was to be the goalie. Alf was all fired up and was wearing the local home team's colors. Buster was wearing khaki shorts and a T-shirt saying Kellogg's Cornflakes.

"Now we'll get 'em! They'll have to come to school with their heads bandaged tomorrow!" cried Alf, clenching his fists. Buster nodded and watched a man cleaning windows opposite the field.

After the game, which ended in an 11–4 win for Eric's team, the gym teacher showed them how to do a solo run properly and how to dribble around a defender.

"You, Kurt, come here," he said. "Now try to stop me."

Kurt stumped gloomily toward the gym teacher, who slipped easily and elegantly past him and kicked the ball in the goal.

"That's the way to do it!" he said triumphantly, but Eric remarked that getting past a big fat lump like Kurt was nothing to brag about. Even his grandmother could do that, he said.

"Okay, okay," said the gym teacher. "Come

on, Eric, you and—let's see, Buster—see if you can stop me."

The teacher raced twenty meters away from the goal and then ran toward Eric and Buster. Half a meter away from Eric he feinted, but Eric was ready for it, and flung himself at the gym teacher's legs so hard that for a moment it looked as if the teacher would fall headlong to the ground. The next moment, however, he got the ball under control again and managed to send it spinning between Buster's legs. Buster came to a swift decision. When the gym teacher shouted, "Madonna!" and swerved around him, Buster kicked his ankle so hard that for a split second the gym teacher was hanging horizontal in the air.

Naturally he was furious and took off after Buster, who ran across the soccer field, over the little path, over the school playground, and up the steps. Instead of going down to the locker room, however, Buster ran along the corridor, straight into the arms of Mr. Martinsen the math teacher, who of course hauled him down to the locker room after all. By now everyone else was showering. The gym teacher showed Mr. Martinsen his reddened ankle.

Mr. Martinsen nodded. "What next, I wonder?" he said darkly, and both teachers stalked out.

As for Buster, he got under the shower, feeling lonelier than ever. At least until Kurt came over to him and said, "I have a canoe down by the millstream."

* * *

Later on, when Buster was down at the dairy with Mrs. Jensen, he told her about his rotten day.

"Have a drink of buttermilk, my dear," said Mrs. Jensen comfortingly. Buster sighed and looked gloomily at the green carton of buttermilk.

"I think it's really chocolate milk I need," he said. Then he cycled off to Marigold Road with eggs, butter, and half a crate of mineral water.

When he came back, Mrs. Jensen had gone to the hairdresser's. Mr. Jensen was counting the day's receipts in the room behind the shop.

"At last," he grunted. "You were a very long time for such a small order."

Buster handed in the wallet with the money. Mr. Jensen looked at him. "You seem to be all down in the dumps. That's not like you."

"It's because of Mrs. Larsen," said Buster. "She's gone to the hospital again."

96

Mr. Jensen stroked his chin, then muttered something or other and went into the shop. "Would you like a lollipop?"

Buster looked up. Mr. Jensen was holding a big yellow lollipop.

"Thank you," he said.

"You mustn't think you'll get one every day. We won't make a habit of it. It's expensive enough having you deliver things anyway. And off goes my old lady to the hairdresser, spending good money to get her hair trimmed. Leaving me to manage on my own. As if I had ten arms! It's not as if my name was Rockefeller."

Buster looked up in surprise. "Did he have ten arms?"

"Oh, suck your lollipop."

Buster took the cellophane wrapping off. "Wasn't there another delivery for me to make, Mr. Jensen?"

"Yes, that's right," said Mr. Jensen. "I've packed the basket. Number 28 Church Lane— you've been there before."

Buster nodded and picked up the basket.

"Wait a minute . . . er . . . Buster," said Mr. Jensen, casting a glance at the shop. "Come here a moment, boy—that's it, put the basket down."

Mr. Jensen sat down on an empty ale crate. "You say you can do conjuring tricks, right? Well, watch this."

Mr. Jensen took a handkerchief out of his breast pocket. "Now, I'm putting a whole match here in the middle of the handkerchief. There. Now I'm folding the handkerchief up. There. Now, come here; can you feel that match?"

Buster nodded wearily.

"Good. Break it, then."

Buster broke it.

"Good—so now you're sure it's broken, aren't you? Well, take a look at this," said the dairyman, unfolding the handkerchief. A whole match fell out. "What do you say to that, eh? Didn't expect that, did you?"

Buster pulled on his earlobe. "I learned that trick from my father when I was four, Mr. Jensen," he said. "The broken match is hidden in the hem. Well, I'd better be going. See you soon."

* * *

When Buster reached Frederikssund Road, he didn't go straight to Holck Square. Instead, he looked around until he caught sight of Jens, approaching on the other side, as agreed.

"Hi, Jens!" he called.

Jens came over, looking bored. "Call that a big man's bike?" he asked scornfully.

"You can try it out, Jens—see if you can ride it. Just ride it to Church Lane and I'll run after you."

Jens spat out his chewing gum and got on the bike. At first he wobbled so much that Buster had to hold onto the carrier to keep the bike from tipping over. He didn't want Jens to lose interest at this stage of the game.

"Go on—ride it to number 28!" called Buster, panting along behind.

Jens stopped at the garden gate. "That was nothing," he said.

"Oh, well, riding the bike's not the most difficult part of this job," said Buster, looking up at the sky. "It's delivering the stuff to the customers and getting the right change that's really tricky. Well, I'll have to take the basket in myself now. I can't very well leave it to you, Jens."

"It can't be as hard as all that," remarked Jens.

"Some can do these things and some can't," said Buster, pausing by the garden gate, which he was careful not to touch.

"Give me the basket," said Jens.

"No, Jens, no," murmured Buster pityingly. "I really can't do that. I mean, suppose you didn't get the change right?"

"Give me that basket! Of course I'll get the change right. I'm better at arithmetic than you, anyway. Hand it over!"

"Okay, if you insist." Buster sighed, handing Jens the basket. Jens opened the garden gate. It swung aside with a squeal.

It was a quiet afternoon in Brønshøj. You could hear the distant hum of traffic on Frederikssund Road. Here, on the street lined with big houses, it sounded no louder than a wasp trapped in a matchbox. Even Jens was a charming sight as he walked up the quiet garden path to the house—until Nero picked up his scent, that is. For, as Buster had expected, the big dog had it in for any delivery boy now, and naturally he thought it was poor Jens who had hit him with the stone.

Buster shook his head sadly as he saw Jens fly a meter into the air, throw away the basket, and rush screeching around the front garden with the monster barking at his heels.

"Keep running till he tires out, Jens!" called Buster. But Jens didn't hear him. He seemed to be running for his life—which was not, perhaps, so far from the truth.

However, the old lady at last appeared at the top of the steps and called Nero. By now Jens looked like something that had been dragged along behind a bus. His own mother wouldn't have recognized him.

Buster realized he had better go put the things back in the basket. He handed it to the old lady, who had just steered Nero into the kitchen.

Behind him, what remained of Jens crawled out of the garden.

"Poor old Nero, it's very sad," sighed the old lady, looking at her bill. "He's not getting any younger. He isn't what he used to be. Why, just the other day his eyes had a kind of cross-eyed squint, as if he couldn't control them."

"Such a fine dog, too . . . what a shame," sighed Buster, a remark that earned him a tip of two kroner.

Later, as he was cycling back to the dairy and thinking of something that had once been a boy called Jens, he was in a much better mood. He decided that on Wednesday he would teach Mr. Jensen a few good conjuring tricks.

10

Parents' Evening

Buster's father was wearing his new black shirt, the one with Texas Boys written on the back in little yellow stitches. Unfortunately, the words couldn't be seen because he had his blue jacket on over the shirt. He had just shaved, and he had brushed his black hair back so that it had a bluish sheen on it just like Tarzan's. This was the first time he was going to Parents' Evening at school. Buster's mother was at home with a headache.

On the way to school, Buster's father showed Buster a brand-new trick that required such dexterity only the very best conjurors could do it.

"Now, watch my nose carefully, Buster," he said, stopping in the middle of the market-place. People were hurrying in all directions, but Buster, just out of the bath, his hair wet and his fingernails clean, stood watching, fascinated, as his father swept the palm of his right hand past his nose, instantly turning it into a clown's big red one.

Buster shouted with delight and hopped up and down, which made the heels of his new blue running shoes squeak, though his mother had stuffed cotton into their toes. His father had a huge smile on his face, and Buster thought nobody in the world could have whiter teeth. Then, with another sweep of the hand, the clown's nose was gone again, and there stood his father with the superior smile all conjurors can turn on at will.

"Seeing it's Monday today, and the girls' legs are beginning to tan, I'll teach you that trick," said his father, patting a couple of Buster's freckles. "Look, you hold the thing in the hollow of your hand, like this. As you've seen, the art of it is in the movement. Get that wrong and the whole trick's ruined. Give it a try."

Buster smiled. But the nose wouldn't do what he wanted, and the elegant sweep of his hand didn't quite come off either. However, his father wasn't giving up: Try again, he said . . . and again, from the beginning . . . and suddenly it worked. The nose was in place just where it should be. Sheer magic! Buster beamed like the sun.

"If you can remember the trick, I'll give it to you," his father said.

* * *

Up in the school corridor, Hans' parents were sitting talking to Sarah's parents. Chairs had been put outside the classroom.

Buster said hello to Hans, but avoided speaking to Sarah, who was standing by the window in her new clothes.

"Yes, we're thinking of taking Sarah out of this school," said Sarah's mother, picking a few bits of lint off her flowered skirt.

"Oh—don't you think she's learning enough here?" asked Hans' mother. She had her shopping bag on her knees.

"It's not that—we just don't care for the atmosphere," replied Sarah's mother. "It's really demoralizing, the way some of the children think school's a kind of youth center where you just go for fun. And nobody does anything about it. Far from it! Rosa Hansen seems to be very lax in her attitude. As for homework—well, the children simply don't do their homework at all if they don't have time."

Buster's father looked down at Buster. Buster smiled and shrugged his shoulders. Then, at last, it was their turn.

Mr. Martinsen and Rosa were sitting in the classroom. They had coffee cups in front of them and a pile of books between them. Rosa was deep in the attendance record.

"Ah, so this is Buster's father," said Mr. Martinsen rather stiffly, shaking hands with him.

Buster held his own hand out too, thus causing some confusion. Rosa colored as she shook Buster's hand. Then his dad got confused, because once he had shaken hands with Rosa, he offered Mr. Martinsen his hand again, and then Mr. Martinsen had to put his notebook down.

"Perhaps we could begin now," said Mr. Martinsen irritably, giving Rosa a meaningful look. After all, she was the class teacher.

She cleared her throat. "Yes, well, we planned to spend a little extra time discussing Buster," she began. Buster's father nodded appreciatively at his son, and Buster himself seemed pleasantly surprised. "Well, now, Buster's a delightful pupil to have in class . . . when he's here . . ."

Dad winked at Buster.

". . . but we feel that his schoolwork hasn't

been very good recently, and we also feel that his concentration in lessons leaves something to be desired. . . ."

"He can't seem to concentrate at all," interrupted Mr. Martinsen. "He sits there right through his lessons, looking out the window and drawing matchstick men on his desk."

"How can he look out the window and draw matchstick men on the desk at the same time?" asked Buster's father, genuinely surprised.

"I've no idea, Mr. Mortensen. But Buster is well below average in math; that's the point! For instance, he can't even understand the simplest equations with an unknown factor. He won't get anywhere that way."

"Mr. Martinsen says I won't even be able to sweep the streets," muttered Buster, looking down at the table.

"Why, do you have to be able to solve equations with an unknown factor before you can sweep the streets?" asked his father.

"Please stop reducing everything to the ludicrous, Mr. Mortensen!" said Mr. Martinsen. "It happens to be my duty to point out to you that Buster won't face facts, and no one gets far these days without a grasp of mathematics."

"Ah, well, you may be right there," murmured Buster's father.

"And from all I've heard, his language work isn't much better," Mr. Martinsen went on. "In fact, I don't know if he's good at anything at all."

Mr. Mortensen looked at Buster sadly. Then he said, "I think he's pretty good at yodeling."

Rosa began to giggle. Mr. Martinsen brought his fist down on the math book, or rather on one of the math books, since the method he used in class involved sixteen different textbooks.

"You seem to think it's funny, Rosa, but Buster's gym teacher would have been here too this evening—if he could have gone anywhere. However, as Buster Mortensen kicked his ankle during soccer today, he had to stay home. Do you know what I call that kind of thing, Mr. Mortensen? I call it physical violence!"

"Did you really kick the teacher's ankle, Buster?" asked his father, sounding very grieved.

"He said we were supposed to try to stop him," Buster explained.

"This kind of thing won't do!" said Mr. Martinsen angrily. "You must see that, Mr. Mortensen. Admittedly, as Rosa here says, he doesn't bother the others, but several parents have complained about him. They say he's a bad influence on their children. We can't blame anyone for wanting the best possible education for a child these days, now can we?"

"No, certainly not," murmured Dad.

"Well, you can be absolutely sure that every single day there's going to be something or other. . . ." But here the math teacher suddenly found himself unable to go on because, for reasons known only to himself, Buster had tried out the new conjuring trick, and now he was looking at Mr. Martinsen with a red clown's nose in the middle of his face.

Rosa had another attack of the giggles, but the math teacher merely pushed his chair back, as though he were fearful of something.

"And there you are—this is exactly what I mean!" he said. "Only the other day he was pulling string out of his mouth. Where does he learn these things?"

Buster conjured the nose away again.

"I taught him that one this evening," said his father.

Here, however, Rosa pulled herself together. "Well, it's very nice that Buster has such . . . er . . . interests, but you must agree, Mr. Mortensen, that an ability to perform conjuring tricks with his nose isn't adequate. We're telling you all this for Buster's own sake. I like Buster very much, but a pleasant nature just isn't enough—you have to know things too, if possible some of the things we teach here in school. Without that kind of knowledge, I'm afraid Buster will find himself rather at a loss one of these days."

"Hm, yes," murmured Buster's father.

"He doesn't even know his multiplication tables," said Mr. Martinsen, who was now standing at the teacher's desk, where he felt more secure. "The way things are going, the boy will never get a job."

"I've got a job," said Buster. "At the dairy down in town."

Rosa frowned. "A job? At your age? Don't you think he's too small for that, Mr. Mortensen?"

"If Buster says he can do it, then he can. Why would he be too small?"

"Well, only you can decide that," said Rosa. "But in any case, I think you might help Buster get his homework done on time."

Buster's father nodded. So did Buster.

Rosa smiled with relief and handed Mr. Mortensen a copy of the lovely collection of poems. It said *Price: 2 kroner* on the cover.

"The money's for class funds," she said with a nice smile.

Mr. Mortensen searched his pocket. He had no money with him. Under the table, Buster fished out his tip and put it in his father's hand.

"Thank you, Rosa," his father said, giving her the money and offering Mr. Martinsen his hand again. "Very interesting to meet you. Buster's told us a lot about you. We'll do our best. But you mustn't get too upset about all this. We artists are a dying race, you know. We can't seem to master electronic data processing and robots and equations with an unknown factor. Only the other day I was after a job in a café in Nørrebro. I can play music and sing, and my card tricks are among the best in the country. Do you know what the owner told me, Mr. Martinsen? He said he already had someone who could play the synthesizer, and in case you don't know what a synthesizer is, let me tell you it's a machine that can produce all possible kinds of sound, from Mantovani and his orchestra to a Dixieland banjo. Just by pressing a button."

The math teacher stared at him.

Buster and his father sat down on a bench in Brønshøj marketplace. After all, Mother was at home with a headache and just wanted to be left in peace; Ingeborg was at Scouts, so there was no reason to hurry home. They spent some time playing guessing games: Where were the people going? How old were they? And so on. But after a quarter of an hour, his father put his arm around Buster's shoulders and said, "There's something in it, you know. Working at school, I mean. You know there is, don't you, Buster?"

Buster nodded. His freckles had appeared rather early this year, and his hair was standing out in all directions because it hadn't been properly dried before they set out.

"Do you feel you'd rather not be going to school?"

Buster looked up in surprise. "I like it at school," he said.

Mr. Mortensen shook his head and smiled. It was nine o'clock but still quite light. He looked across at the restaurant where Mr. Larsen was waiting for him with the dice cup.

"Look, Buster," he said, "I'm going to stop to see Larsen for a while. You can find your way home by yourself."

Buster nodded. His father stood up, pulled his cuffs down from under the sleeves of his jacket, and then smoothed back the hair at his temples.

"But Dad, you haven't got any money."

His father laughed and held out his hands so that Buster could see they were empty. "Nothing here, nothing there, nothing there either!" He grinned, pointing to his forehead last of all.

Buster laughed.

"Remember, Buster, here before you stands the king of dice," his father whispered, winking. "I'll teach you a few good tricks with the dice sometime soon, but off you go home now. Be quiet, though; your mother's asleep."

His father sprinted across the road. Buster saw that he was wearing yellow socks and thought how great they looked with the black shirt.

But now what? He didn't want to go home. Ingeborg wouldn't be back till about ten. He looked around. There was a half moon in the sky above the church, with thin wisps of mist coming from its mouth.

"Hello, man in the moon, are you smoking?" called Buster, going around by the back of the marketplace and past the old school.

112

And suddenly he was there.

It must be the scent, yes, it must be the lovely scent that drew a person back to this place.

11

The Hospital

It was Saturday night. Buster was lying in bed, not quite awake yet. Why would he be awake in the middle of the night anyway? He turned to Ingeborg, but she wasn't there.

Hadn't she called out?

Somebody had called him. Far away. He thought of the sewer under the main street in Lyngby and of the trip on the millstream. And in the middle of it all he suddenly couldn't sort it out. The whole thing ran together. He had been on a canoe trip. A wonderful canoe trip. Up the millstream all the way to Brede. Kurt had shown him how cleverly he could skip stones, and Buster had called him the Longskipper. To return the favor, Kurt had called Buster the World's Greatest Sewer Yodeler. Because when they were taking the canoe under Lyngby's main road, they had to go through a long sewer pipe, and Buster yodeled so that the sound sang in the cars' tail pipes.

"How far can we get canoeing on the millstream?" Buster had asked.

"To the end of the world," Kurt Longskipper had answered.

"But I have to be home for dinner," Buster yelled and stuck his heels down in the stream's muddy water.

He opened his eyes. Somebody was calling again, and this time there was no doubt about it. It was his mother's voice, and the way she called got him out of bed quickly.

Ingeborg was sitting downstairs in her striped nightie, staring in the direction of the bookshelf, with her mouth shut tight. His father was standing by the window, with his back to her. For some strange reason, he kept running his fingers through his hair. He was wearing a sleeveless undershirt.

Buster couldn't figure it out. He looked at his mother. She had on her blue housedress. Her right hand lay on the telephone. What was happening?

Now she looked at him. It was as if that

115

look took a long time to reach her eyes, and then, when she spoke, her voice was more than tired.

"I'm glad you've come down, Buster," she said. "We must go now."

"You're not taking him, are you, Kitty?" his father said from over by the window, his voice low.

"Get dressed," said his mother, and went into the kitchen.

Drunk with sleep, Buster staggered up the stairs. As he was putting on his trousers, Ingeborg came and joined him.

"What's going on?" he asked, putting his forefinger through a hole in one trouser knee.

Ingeborg let herself drop on the bed.

"It's about Mrs. Larsen. Mom's tried to get hold of Mr. Larsen, but he's nowhere to be found. I think she's phoned every bar in the city."

Buster sat on the edge of the bed. "What about Mrs. Larsen?"

"She seems to have given them our telephone number because they don't have a phone themselves," mumbled Ingeborg, getting under the covers.

"Yes, but what's the matter with Mrs. Larsen?" insisted Buster.

Ingeborg turned her face to him. "They called and said we have to go to the hospital because Mrs. Larsen . . . well, Mom says she's in a kind of sleep now . . . and she might wake up once more before . . ." Her hands came up from under the bedspread and covered her eyes.

Buster stared straight ahead, his trousers still halfway up his thighs.

Ingeborg sighed. "You're supposed to go there with Mom and say good-bye to her."

"Good-bye," murmured Buster.

Ingeborg nodded and looked at the ceiling. "Mom can't get Dad to go with her. He says there's nothing he could do, and she doesn't want to go by herself."

"Aren't you coming too?"

Ingeborg shook her head.

Buster went over to the basket of dirty clothes and rummaged through it. He pulled out the Hawaiian shirt, which was all wrinkled and more than a little stained.

Ingeborg stood up on the bed to open the attic window. Fresh air blew into the little room.

Buster put the crumpled shirt on and went over to his sister. Far, far away a star twinkled down at them.

"It's funny, when you think of it," Ingeborg whispered. "Space going on and on and on and on . . ."

Buster nodded. "Space is a hole. A big black hole," he said firmly.

"Not a hole," Ingeborg continued, "not a hole. An endless space where everything goes on and on . . . so . . . so I think Mrs. Larsen will go on too . . . maybe somewhere else. . . . Well, it has to be like that, or else . . ."

Ingeborg turned around. Buster had gotten off the bed and was busy pinning his tin medals to the brightly colored shirt. Then he looked for his hat.

Ingeborg cleared her throat. "Buster, it would probably be a better idea to leave your pointed hat at home."

He was already holding it. "Think so?"

She nodded.

They could hear their mother's voice now, downstairs. "The taxi's here. Are you ready, Buster?"

The taxi honked its horn impatiently. Buster looked at the hat for a moment, but then he put it away and went downstairs.

It was beginning to get light when they arrived at Bishop's Hill Hospital. Buster stood at the big gate, breathing deeply, while his

118

mother paid the driver. The air was fresh, as if it were brand-new, and everything was quiet.

They went to the receptionist, who told them where to find the right ward.

Buster thought all the colors seemed as if they were mixed with too much white so early in the morning. As if you'd been looking straight at the sun. He almost had to run to keep up with his mother, walking ahead of him with her legs bare and her feet in wooden clogs. Creases fanned out on the back of her yellow cotton coat. For some reason or other, she had her transparent rain hood on. He noticed that her legs were already suntanned.

". . . Because the girls' legs are beginning to tan," his father had said. His mother stopped at a glass door and blew a few tendrils of chestnut hair off her forehead, but they fell back down again right away. Then she looked more closely at Buster and frowned.

"Why on earth did you put that wrinkled shirt on? Your green shirt was clean. . . . Oh, and those medals!"

Buster flapped his arms, like a penguin flapping its wings.

"And the shirt's filthy too—oh, Buster, for goodness' sake, can't you even . . ."

Suddenly his mother began to tremble all over, and then she bent down and hugged him. He felt her tears on his cheek. Her face was just opposite his, and she was sniffing. Buster thought she was calm enough now for him to take his old magic wand out of his pocket.

"I'm not sure that . . ." she began, but then she took his hand and went through the door.

On the first floor they were told that Mrs. Larsen had been moved to the second floor, where there was a single room empty.

Apart from a few clattering noises, it was all very quiet. Over at the desk sat a young nurse, who took off her glasses when she saw them coming. She said good morning to Buster's mother in a friendly voice. And although she wasn't the person who had phoned, she knew all about Mrs. Larsen.

"Are you family?" she asked, pulling two chairs out.

"We're neighbors," said Buster's mother, rolling her rain hood up in her lap. "Mr. Larsen's sometimes . . . I did try to reach him, but . . ."

"He's hanging around somewhere, drunk," said Buster.

The nurse looked at him with raised eyebrows. Then she put her ball-point pen down and stood up.

They went to the end of the long corridor. The nurse stopped in front of a gray door with the number 12 on it. She put her hand on the door handle and smiled at them.

"Mrs. Larsen died half an hour ago," she said quietly.

Buster felt his mother's hand clench his.

The door swung open. There was only one bed in the room, and a single greenish ceiling light was switched on. The curtains were drawn, but by now it was so light outside that sunbeams mingled with the cold green glow. Mrs. Larsen looked as if she were asleep. The bedspread was drawn up to her chin, so that only her motionless face could be seen.

"We should have brought a flower with us," whispered his mother, stroking Mrs. Larsen's cheek with her bent forefinger.

They've taken her teeth out, thought Buster. He kept waiting for Mrs. Larsen to open her eyes and ask him to do a conjuring trick, but she didn't.

Then he realized that his mother was watching him. She smiled. "Don't you want to say good-bye?" she whispered.

Buster went up to the bed. A bright sunbeam made its way through the white curtains and fell across Mrs. Larsen's face. And when Buster gave her a light kiss on the cheek, it felt quite warm.

. . .

When they were out in the hospital garden again, it was not Saturday night anymore, but Sunday morning. They headed back the same way they had come, and as they were about to go through the gate, Buster stopped.

"So that's what it's like," he said, looking into space.

"Yes," said his mother, "that's what it's like."

★ 12 ★

Buster Cheers Up

When Buster got to the dairy on Monday afternoon, Mr. and Mrs. Jensen could both tell that something was wrong. For one thing, Buster hung his head so much, and for another, he answered them only in monosyllables. However, what really let them know was the black band he had tied around his upper arm. In fact it was only an old scarf, but he had made it look like a mourning band.

"Has something happened?" asked Mrs. Jensen with concern.

Buster nodded and sighed. "Mrs. Larsen's dead," he said, "and nothing will help with that—not chocolate milk or lollipops or licorice sticks or green fizzy drinks."

Mrs. Jensen, realizing how serious this was, looked gloomily at her husband, who was wiping down the deep freeze cabinet.

"Oh, then I suppose a white chocolate frog wouldn't help either," she sighed.

Buster gave her a sidelong glance. "Well, I don't know. . . . A few chocolate frogs might cheer a person up a bit," he said miserably, looking down at the floor.

Mr. Jensen wrung out his cleaning cloth and threw it back in the bucket. "Nobody said anything about a few frogs. One frog, that's what my wife offered you."

"Oh, Arnold," said Mrs. Jensen crossly, "the boy's in mourning, so mind what you say. Here, Buster, one for each hand. This was all we needed!"

Buster sat down in the room behind the shop and stuffed the frogs into his mouth. Mrs. Jensen went up to the Jensens' living quarters.

Mr. Jensen came out to Buster. "Wasn't there some talk of showing me a conjuring trick?" he growled.

"All right," said Buster, "but only because the girls' legs are beginning to tan now, Mr. Jensen."

Mr. Jensen stared at him openmouthed. Buster produced a piece of rope from his pocket. At that moment, the phone rang. Mr. Jensen went into the shop, and when he came back he was carrying the wire basket.

"You can get ready to be off," he told Buster grumpily. "Might as well at least get some use out of you, right? Up you go and bring the bike around."

Buster went into the yard and wheeled the delivery bike around to the steps. Mr. Jensen came out with the basket, the wallet, and the money for change.

"Right, it's number 18 Brookwood Road, and be sure you go carefully—that crate of soft drinks is heavy."

But Buster was not listening.

Number 18 Brookwood Road.

Oh, good heavens, that was where . . . that was where . . .

He tore the cap off his head and shined the visor with his sleeve. It was like feeling forty-nine mourning blackbirds lift off from a runway inside him and fly away.

He cycled along Frederikssund Road, waving to a dog that had had the bright idea of peeing against the windows of the bank, and then he turned off and pedaled along Cliffholme Road. On a day like this, the road was swarming with children playing longball. Then down Fjenneslev Road—oh, goodness!—and there he was.

Well before he arrived, the lovely scent

came wafting out to meet him. The whole road was humming with summer. The trees and bushes seemed to grow and flourish more luxuriantly here than anywhere else, particularly around the yellow house with the number 18 on it.

He parked the bike and was about to pick up the basket when the sound reached him. It came floating out of an open window, over the hedge and into his ears. It was delicate and demure, but he wasn't sure if there might not be something supernatural about it, for what ordinary instrument could make such heavenly sounds? It was more like a piano than anything else, but the notes had something fine and bell-like about them—something mystical, or so it seemed to him. For it was as if those notes went deeper into him with every breath he took and then set such a whirlwind going inside him that he was left quite overwhelmed.

It was hard for him to lift the wire basket containing the eggs, margarine, and whipping cream, but it had to be done. So he picked it up, pushing the white garden gate open with his hips. Finding his way wasn't so easy, since the whole garden was a wilderness of plants and bushes growing in wonderful confusion. Perhaps the idea was for the house to disap-

126

pear entirely among all the greenery one day.

When he reached the door, he glanced at the window through which he heard the delicate notes. He stole over on tiptoe and leaned back against one of the shutters, breathing deeply.

Now and then a firm voice could be heard through the music. "Andante, andante, supple wrists, Joanna, supple wrists, that's it; now straighten your back. . . ."

Realization dawned. So it was *she* playing in there.

Buster bent down and ventured to look in. A sigh escaped him. For there was almost nothing to be seen in the big room—except the fantastic light that obviously fell into it from all sides, and where all the rays of light met, there sat Joanna in a wonderful dark red dress, playing an instrument like a piano with crooked legs. Her hair was piled on top of her head, and she looked extremely elegant. She was sitting up very straight, and when he looked more closely, he saw she had a pair of gold-rimmed glasses on the bridge of her little nose. Her face was indescribably beautiful, but it seemed to Buster very pale. Perhaps her skin was always as white as newly fallen snow, or perhaps she spent all her time indoors practicing, so she never got out into the sun. Except when there was a fair in the church garden.

Beside her sat an old, old woman with a face like a tired raisin, but she had dark skin and was dressed in a curious material that looked stiff, like frozen snow. This wasn't the woman who had been at the fair; he could see that. On the other hand, she couldn't very well be Joanna's mother either. Did Joanna actually have a mother?

He crept back to the door of the house and rang the bell. It went *ding ding dong ding . . . dong.*

Then about four years went by, and finally he heard footsteps, and all of a sudden there was the sour old bag from the church garden, staring at him.

Buster jumped. "Er . . . good afternoon," he stammered in confusion. "Here's the things from the church . . . er . . . I mean the eggs from the hens. . . ." For some reason or other, his tongue had turned to spaghetti, and when the woman went on staring down at him, the tremors reached his legs, which began to wobble in an alarming manner.

128

"Where's the crate of soft drinks?" snapped the sour old bag.

"Outside on the bike," said Buster. Carrying the heavy basket had turned his upper arms to jelly.

"Then I suggest you fetch it."

Buster nodded, wondering what on earth the woman thought he was supposed to do with the wretched basket. However, he dared not put it down, so he dragged it back to the delivery bike and put it on the pavement. Then he picked up the crate of soft drinks and staggered back to the door. The sour old bag had decided to cross her arms.

Buster's face was quite purple with effort.

"And where's the basket of goods?" snapped the woman.

"I couldn't carry the basket and the crate both at once," panted Buster, feeling the crate pull his arms further and further down.

She finally took it from him and sent him back for the basket. On his way he noticed that the music had stopped.

The sour old bag came back with a purse about the size of a school satchel. "Haven't I seen you somewhere before?" she asked, narrowing her eyes.

"Could be," said Buster. "I sometimes get into the papers."

He didn't know why he had said that, but he disliked this woman so much that he had no scruples at all about lying to her.

"In the papers?" She took the basket and went through the items on the bill.

"Yes, I do conjuring tricks and play music and so on. . . ."

She fished out a 100-kroner note. "Conjuring tricks and music? What sort of instrument do you play?"

Buster gave her the change. "A concertina."

The woman's eyes seemed to get bigger, and Buster had to admit, unwillingly, that they were beautiful.

"Yes, it's got kind of six sides. . . ."

"Oh, I know what a concertina is. What do you play on it?"

Buster made a face. He didn't particularly want to mention the fact that all he could play was half a sea shanty.

"Well . . . mostly andante and so on," he muttered.

She stared at him. At that moment, Joanna appeared in the background. She had not seen Buster, who started breathing heavily and jingling the wallet. He had to jingle it quite a bit before she spotted him. But then she came over.

"Hi!" she said, looking deep into his eyes.

Buster contented himself with making a sound like a car that won't start.

The woman looked from one of them to the other.

"His name's Buster," said Joanna, smiling, and she kept on looking at him.

"Buster Oregon Mortensen," he introduced himself.

There was the hint of a smile in the woman's eyes. As for Joanna, she was beaming like the sun. After a bit, however, Buster felt the silence was getting rather awkward, so he said, "My grandfather was the Cannon King of Husum."

As soon as he had made this remark, he realized that he had said exactly the right thing. Joanna hopped up and down and clapped her hands delightedly, and at the same time the woman switched on a 100-watt bulb somewhere in the back of her head, so that her whole face changed and was almost as pretty as Buster's mother's when she was going to go out with Buster's father.

"Oh, can't he come this evening?"

Joanna snuggled up coaxingly to the woman,

and at the same time fluttered eyelids as big as garage doors in Buster's direction.

"Well, I don't know," muttered the woman, stroking her chin as she inspected Buster from his brown sneakers to the cap with the visor. "I suppose if you play the concertina . . . Do you have anything else to wear?" she asked.

"You bet!" cried Buster, thinking of his bright red conjuror's shirt and his new black trousers with the Chinese alphabet down the sides. Not to mention all his medals.

"Good . . . er . . . Buster. We're having a little party this evening, starting with a meal at six, so if you'd like to come along about eight, how would that be?"

Buster nodded, feeling quite intoxicated.

"Happy now, Joanna?" asked the woman.

"Oh, yes!" laughed Joanna. "Don't forget to bring your dragon. . . . Have you still got the dragon?"

"Yes," said Buster, who was already on his way to the garden gate. "I only have to paint it on again."

"Good-bye, Buster!" she called, blowing him a kiss.

He cycled along Frederikssund Road. His legs went up and down automatically, and he remembered to signal when he was turning left or right, but apart from that, all he saw was curly-haired Joanna. "Good-bye, Buster!" she had called.

He steered the bicycle into the yard and floated on air down to the room at the back of the shop, where Mr. Jensen was waiting for him, hands on hips.

"And where, if one may ask, have you been all this time?"

"On Brookwood Road," said Buster, his eyes half closed.

"So just how, for heaven's sake, can anyone take almost an hour cycling to Brookwood Road and back again? Tell me that!"

"Mr. Jensen," said Buster, trying to pull himself together, "it's like this—I've been invited to Joanna's this evening. There's a little party there. I guess that's why they wanted all those things. I'm supposed to take my concertina, and of course I have to paint my dragon on again too."

Buster looked dreamily at Mr. Jensen, who shouted for his wife. She came rushing down from their living quarters with rollers in her hair, looking like a hedgehog.

"Here, Mother, look at the lad, will you?" groaned Mr. Jensen. "He's got a screw loose, that's what it is—could it be the warm weather, or have they fired him out of a cannon too?"

Mrs. Jensen crouched down and examined Buster carefully. "Look right into my eyes," she said.

"I've been invited to Joanna's," he said.

"Is that the girl from Brookwood Road, Buster?" asked Mrs. Jensen.

Buster nodded and went weak at the knees for the second time that day.

At this Mrs. Jensen straightened up and smiled. "Goodness me, I do believe our Buster's in love," she said, glancing at Mr. Jensen with a mischievous smile.

"In love!" cried Mr. Jensen. "Well, that's about all we need, and right in the middle of working hours too. I've been waiting here over an hour, taking the temperature of the water and measuring the water level in those containers, and here he is at last with his thoughts somewhere else entirely! When I was a lad we had backbone where young people today have nothing but jelly!"

Only now did Mrs. Jensen and Buster see the three big containers of water that Mr. Jensen had put on the table. One of them was covered with a black velvet cloth.

"Whatever is that for, Arnold?" asked Mrs. Jensen.

"Nothing to do with you," growled Mr. Jensen, sounding hurt and turning his back to them.

But now Buster spoke up. "Are those the preparations for the trick with the connected containers, Mr. Jensen?"

Mr. Jensen glanced at him. He nodded, with some embarrassment, but proudly.

"That's a very difficult trick, Mr. Jensen. Can you really do it?"

Mr. Jensen nodded again, looking like a large child who has just shown his grandfather that he can draw figure eights.

"I learned it yesterday evening," he murmured.

"Can somebody tell me what's going on here?" asked Mrs. Jensen crossly.

Buster looked at her reproachfully. "Mrs. Jensen, your husband is going to do a very, very difficult trick, in which he will make water wander from one container to another. You should be proud to have a husband who is such a good conjuror," he added, sitting down on a crate of ale.

Mr. Jensen walked over to the containers, wringing his hands. As he did so, Buster whispered into Mrs. Jensen's ear. "It took me two weeks to learn that trick last year."

Mr. Jensen's neck turned redder and redder. And turning red in the neck was the only trick he pulled off that day.

13

The Party

Buster was ready on the stroke of seven o'-clock, when Ingeborg inspected him for the third time. He was wearing his bright red shirt and his new black trousers with the Chinese lettering on them, and of course he had the indispensable pointed hat on his head. He had opened his shirt at the neck so that you could see the dragon breathing fire. It had been re-painted with Ingeborg's watercolors in honor of the occasion.

"How do I smell?" he asked, turning this way and that in front of the mirror.

"Like a perfume shop that's had an accident," groaned Ingeborg, holding her nose.

"I put Dad's deodorant under my left arm and Mom's under my right arm," said Buster.

"You smell of more than just deodorants,"

objected Ingeborg, straightening his collar.

Buster cleared his throat. "Well," he muttered, "I did spray the dragon with some of that stuff Mom has in the blue bottle."

Ingeborg stared at him. "Are you crazy? So that's why you smell so strong. Mom just dabs a tiny bit behind her ears. The way you stink, you could explode four tons of granite."

Buster shrugged his shoulders, picked up his conjuring things, and rushed downstairs yodeling.

* * *

It took less than fifteen minutes to get there. Traffic was relatively light. He made himself a peephole in the hedge through which he could see the whole wonderful scene.

It was quite a big party. They were eating out in the garden under a yellow awning. All the gentlemen wore white shirts, but their ties—ordinary ties or bow ties—were all the colors of the rainbow. The women and girls mostly wore pale dresses, but they all had tan legs.

Buster enlarged the hole in the hedge a bit, and just then he saw Joanna. She was sitting on a funny little swing, sucking a mauve lollipop with green stripes. Her big straw hat was pushed far back on her head. She looked happy and was contentedly swinging her legs. Buster had never seen such dear little socks in his life.

But then he saw the sour old bag. She was going from guest to guest, nodding and smiling. However, he couldn't spot the old lady who looked like a gypsy and wore that stiff white dress.

Two ladies dressed exactly the same were sitting in a corner arm wrestling with each other. Buster felt sure they must be twins: They looked so like each other, and both of them had brown moustaches. But now the funny little piano (which Ingeborg had told him was called a harpsichord) was brought out into the garden, and while Joanna swung her arms like windmill sails, and a white-haired gentleman squinted at his wife to make her laugh, the sour old bag arranged two rows of folding chairs around the little instrument.

Joanna put her straw hat down on the harpsichord and wiped the remains of her lollipop off her mouth. The sour old bag turned around, folded her hands on her breast, and looked at the guests, who had seated themselves expectantly on the folding chairs. At that moment a figure appeared in the terrace doorway. A very small but nonetheless striking figure, wearing a tall pointed hat that drew all eyes to it.

"Buster!" cried Joanna, running to meet him.

The sour old bag tried to brush him aside with a few sweeping movements of her arm, but by now he had the entire company spellbound. They were all staring at the enormous egg he was conjuring out of his mouth.

Joanna clapped her hands with delight. But the sour old bag had pulled herself together.

"Thank you very much . . . er . . . Buster, but that will do," she stammered, trying to smile at the astonished guests, who had spilled half their coffee on the lawn.

The sour old bag turned her back to the guests in order to push Buster out again the same way as he had come, but to the horror of all present, it could now be seen that she had a dagger sticking into her between her shoulder blades. The quick-fingered Buster had managed to plant it in her back without her noticing at all. When a lady rolled sideways off her chair, however, he pulled the dagger out again and demonstrated its clever trick by mingling with the audience and stabbing several of his spectators in the stomach. This naturally caused a certain amount of uneasiness, but amidst the general agitation he pulled four meters twenty-nine centimeters of orange paper out of his mouth, and having successfully done that too, he asked the sour old bag for a strong hammer and a pair of good kitchen scissors so that he could perform his latest trick.

The sour old bag seemed rather nervous. However, she could see that despite everything, most of the guests were enjoying themselves, so she fetched Buster what he wanted.

"And that's no lie," said Buster, getting into his stride with his patter. "Yes, my dear old grandfather spent four years being shot from a cannon in Husum, and the last time they shot him so high it was three days before he came down to earth again. And then he landed in a strawberry patch in Lumske Bay, south of Great Heddinge. Luckily, and with great foresight, he had taken some sandwiches up with him. But, but, but, ladies and gentlemen, that's the way of the world and it's not for slackers, and you'll never get far if you don't know math, and my grandfather had a dog, his name was Quick, who could count up to seven, but all the same he died in Fredericia. However, as the ladies' legs are so nice and tan now, I'll show you a trick my own father, Osman the Great, used to perform. Oh, and he had a cat called Edgar too, and this cat could eat four plates of tapioca and waggle his ears at the same time. But, but, but, ladies and gentlemen, joking aside, I'm not here for my own pleasure, you know. I'm here just for fun, and now, would that gentleman—yes, sir, the gentleman with the handsome blue tie on—would you be kind enough to step up here?"

Joanna clapped, the audience clapped, even the sour old bag patted her hands cautiously together, and an elderly man in a blue tie came up to Buster, who welcomed him with open arms.

"So what's your name, sir?" he asked.

"Millard Dinst," said the man, pronouncing it piously and looking embarrassed.

"And what's your job?" shouted Buster, so loud that the tops of the flagpoles wobbled.

"I'm first violin in the City Orchestra—all of us here are musicians and music lovers, and we really came along to hear the young prodigy Joanna play. . . ."

"Take your tie off, Millard!" Buster told him.

The man took off his tie and handed it to Buster. Next moment it had been cut into little pieces and put into a bag.

There was great excitement in the audience. Millard was bemoaning the loss of his tie, which he said he had won in a gift lottery in the Austrian Tyrol and which was irreplaceable.

"Listen to Mr. Max's magic words!" cried Buster, murmuring something or other, and then pulling the tie out of the bag. It was all in one piece again.

For a moment everything was so quiet you could have heard a sparrow in Bellahøj cleaning its nails. Then thunderous applause shook the garden. Some of the spectators even rose to their feet, and Buster took this opportunity to display his dragon, whereupon the sour old bag asked Joanna if she had been spraying insect repellent in the garden.

"Ladies and gentlemen," shouted Buster, now well into his stride, "who'd like to step up here and be my next guest? Maybe the gentleman in the second row, yes, you, sir, with your arm in your mouth, right behind the two ladies with their moustaches tied together; would you mind coming a little closer?"

The blushing gentleman clambered up on the terrace. He was knock-kneed. Buster asked him to take his watch off. The gentleman obediently handed it over. Buster held it up. People were already beginning to clap.

"Here's a hammer," cried Buster, "and here's a watch. Now, we put the watch in this bag— like this . . . and now we need a volunteer. How about the lady in the third row? Would you come a little closer, madam? That's it." A nice-looking little old lady climbed up to Buster, chuckling. He kissed her hand in a very elegant way and asked her name.

"Viola Elgard Lischenstein, but you can just call me Stella," she chirruped, enraptured, waving coyly to her friends, two other elderly ladies who were sitting at the back.

"Now, take this hammer, Stella," said Buster, "and be kind enough to hit this bag containing the gentleman's watch with it three times."

Stella giggled, picked up the hammer with both hands, and brought it down on the bag with such force that there was a mighty crash and bang. The audience clapped. Stella curtsied, but Buster said very little as he shook a few crushed bits of metal out on the table. It was very quiet. Even Stella's giggling stopped.

The man stared at the bits of ruined watch.

"That's funny," muttered Buster, looking around him in confusion. All of a sudden the cheerful faces turned serious. Several elbows removed themselves from coffee cups.

"Oh, well," said Buster, "I see I shall just have to say my most secret magic spell of all." The company held its breath. The sour old bag wrung her hands. But Buster recited:

> Thirty tons of cod's roe,
> rusty nails and screws,
> bogeymen in boxes,
> bruises in the news.

Then he took off his pointed hat, and there was the gentleman's watch underneath it, safe and sound and ticking away.

At this the audience leaped up, knocking over their chairs in their enthusiasm, and in the middle of all the cheerful noise, Joanna sat down at the harpsichord and sent sweet notes floating out into the warm summer night, notes that shone like the sparks of a Midsummer Eve bonfire over Brønshøj.

And when all the grown-ups had finally gone indoors, Joanna took Buster's hand and showed him a white bench at the back of the garden. They sat down there and looked at one another's hands.

They sat for a long time. It was not until someone called her that Joanna finally went into the house, but first she gave Buster a little kiss on the mouth.

* * *

He turned his back to the hedge and looked dreamily up at the clustering stars. Then he looked through the peephole one last time and walked away down the road.

14

Buster Gets By

It was the week before summer vacation. The luxuriant freshness of early summer turned to a dry heat wave that withered all the lilacs.

One evening, Buster's father brought home a pile of travel brochures and spread them out on the dining room table. They cut out some of the best pictures and played cards with them. Buster won, his "Ceylon Holiday" card beating "Five Days' Full Board in the Black Forest," which was his mother's last card. After that they took out the cardboard box containing his father's old safari outfit. He'd gotten it when he was assisting with a very famous act in which, among other things, you had to do conjuring tricks with four very life-like rubber snakes, as well as a genuine Central American grass snake, said to be extremely dangerous—one drop of its venom on a chocolate mint being enough to kill four grown men, or at least give them a nasty cold in the head.

The safari outfit consisted of a pith helmet, a khaki jacket, and knee-length shorts. And although all the family could do this year was go camping by a Danish lake, the outfit stirred their imaginations and put them in a cheerful mood.

That day, Buster had been down at the Jensens' and given notice because summer vacation was coming.

"Oh, my word," Mr. Jensen had groaned, wiping the sweat from his brow. "Kids are so spoiled these days they won't do a thing during vacation except lie around sipping fizzy green drinks. They don't want to work, of course, oh, no! But they can waste time and money; they can do that all right. What the country's coming to I can't think, all these young people without any backbone. Soft as jelly, like I said, soft as jelly. Here, there's your week's money, and I suppose you'd like ten kroner extra too, so you can buy one of those cheap magic tricks, not that it'll be good for anything. But heaven help you if you say anything about ten kroner to my wife. We're not millionaires, you know, swimming in money. Might as well give away our last few kroner and be done with it!"

Jensen sighed, and Buster, who thought there probably really would be a few coins extra, held out his hand, smiling. But Mr. Jensen just looked crossly at him and stumped upstairs to his living quarters for his midday nap.

However, when Buster came back from his last delivery, Mrs. Jensen drew him aside and gave him two shiny coins.

"Not a word to Jensen," she whispered, rolling her eyes. "You know what he's like about money."

"My lips are sealed," said Buster.

Mrs. Jensen smiled. "My husband's all right," she added. "Better a man like that than a man who throws his money out the window."

Buster nodded understandingly. "Folk who have both feet on the ground don't grow on trees," he said, very reasonably.

On the way home that day, he rehearsed the egg trick. The one where you conjure four jumbo-size eggs out of your mouth. But just as he was practicing the mouth movements inside a telephone booth, someone knocked very loudly on the glass.

Two familiar faces were gaping at him.

Lars and Ivor.

Lars flung the door open. Buster's chance to grab the phone and tell the fire brigade the school had burned to the ground was gone.

Ivor was behind Lars, grinning away. Both boys rolled their sleeves up.

"What are you doing in this phone booth, idiot?" asked Lars.

Buster cleared his throat. "Spitting out eggs," he said.

Ivor stuck his long red head into the booth. "What's the dimwit's problem?" he asked blankly.

Lars now lost his temper in earnest. "Trying to pull my leg, Buster?" he growled. "Spitting out eggs! What are you? Solid bone between the ears?"

"Honest, I'm telling the truth, Big Lars!" said Buster guilelessly. "I've got a job as delivery boy for the dairy, and so the eggs won't break I swallow them and keep them safe inside me on the way to the customers. Then they don't even get cracked."

"Know what you are, Buster?" said Big Lars. "You're so incredibly stupid, we could laugh ourselves sick if you weren't so incredibly crazy. Are you ready to be clobbered on the head with the phone book? Because Ivor and I can't stand to listen to you blabber anymore. Our nerves can't take it."

Buster turned around. "There's only the local directory in here," he pointed out.

"That'll do!" shouted Lars, practically turning purple.

"Um," said Buster. "Can I bring the eggs up first? Mr. Jensen will hit the roof if anything happens to them."

Lars and Ivor stared at one another. Then Ivor nodded, slowly.

Buster pulled himself together and spat out the first egg. The other three followed at regular intervals.

"There we are," he said.

"I think," said Big Lars, "I'll have to go home and lie down. I don't feel too well."

Ivor clutched his head and backed away from the telephone booth. Soon afterward the big boys disappeared.

Buster himself went to the butcher. He knew the butcher had cheap bones for sale. Now that he had the money, he thought Nero deserved a treat, not that it would do much for his occasional cross-eyed squint.

"Just a bone," he told the butcher. "I mustn't go throwing money out the window."

* * *

These were the last few minutes of the last gym period before summer vacation. Water was pouring down on the shrieking boys in the shower. Buster was drying himself when Eric snatched his towel.

"Hey, look, he's growing hair round his weenie," cackled Jens from the corner.

"Come on, you've got to do the horrible great ape!" shouted Eric. "Last performance before vacation! Do the ape act if you want your towel back."

All the others straightened up to watch, screaming and shouting. Buster, however, was watching a film inside his head. He smiled to himself.

"Take his things away!" shouted Jens, trembling with excitement as Gunnar rolled Buster's clothes into a bundle and jumped up on a bench.

Buster looked out the window. It was beautiful weather. He had found a place on Crabholme Road where you sometimes heard the strangest music.

He bent down and picked up his pencil case.

Meanwhile, the other boys had rolled up their towels and dampened them so that they could be used as clubs.

"Come on, Buster, do the gorilla act!" they called.

But Buster was listening to the sounds from the girls' locker room. He took a lot of time getting his erasers into place. Slowly, he pushed his hair up and bared his fangs menacingly.

Now the sounds were outside in the corridor. The girls had begun to leave. At that exact moment, the gorilla sprang into the middle of the yelling boys, and before anyone knew it, he had gotten Jens by the scruff of the neck and flung him out into the corridor, stark naked, where he turned around eight times, whimpering, while the snickering girls put their heads together.

Furiously, Jens burst back into the boys' locker room, threatening Buster with the worst fate he could think of.

"Ladies and gentlemen," shouted Buster, draping his towel in front of him, "you are about to see the finest trick with a weenie ever to . . ." But right then the gym teacher appeared. He looked wearily at Buster and the red-faced crowd of boys.

"Doing a gorilla act again?" he muttered. "Get some clothes on, all of you."

The other boys hurried to do as he said.

Summer vacation was ahead of them. Buster, however, had to find his things, and after that, as he was the last, he had to mop the floor.

The school was completely empty when he finally trudged out into the corridor. On the steps leading to the playground, he stopped and raised his arms. Then he took a deep breath and looked up at the sky.

"Hello, Mrs. Larsen, it's summer vacation," he called, "so don't send too many clouds down, will you? And we'd like it to rain only at night, if possible."

At this moment Mr. Martinsen came along, pushing his bike. He was wearing his Boy Scout shorts, with badges on them that told you he could tie eighty-seven different knots and imitate the hoot of a long-eared owl.

"Shouldn't you be going home?" he asked Buster.

"Yes, Mr. Martinsen," laughed Buster. "I just had to make sure we'd have good weather for vacation first."

He grinned as he passed the math teacher.

"What in the world is going to become of you, Buster Mortensen?" Mr. Martinsen sighed, looking at his watch.

"Oh, I'll get by," said Buster, smiling.

154